D1327706

French Politics and Public Policy

French Politics and Public Policy

edited by Philip G. Cerny and Martin A. Schain

St Martin's Press
New York

© Philip G. Cerny and Martin A. Schain 1980
except 'Power and its Possessors' from *Class and Status in France: Economic Change and Social Immobility 1945–1975* by Jane Marceau, © Oxford University Press 1977. Reprinted with permission of Oxford University Press

All rights reserved. For information, write:
St. Martin's Press, Inc., 175 Fifth Avenue, New York, NY 10010
Printed in Great Britain
First published in the United States of America in 1980

ISBN 0–312–30509–5

Library of Congress Cataloging in Publication Data
Main entry under title:
   French politics and public policy.
   Includes bibliographical references.
   1. France – Politics and government – Addresses, essays, lectures.
   2. France – Economic policy – Addresses, essays, lectures.
   I. Cerny Philip G., 1946–   II. Schain, Martin A., 1940–
JN 2738.F74   320.944   80–36877
ISBN 0–312–30509–5

Typeset by Anne Joshua Associates, Oxford
Printed in Great Britain by A. Wheaton & Co., Exeter

For Wendy, who was there at the beginning;
and for Alexander and Marcus, whose energy provides inspiration.

1922999

CONTENTS

Preface   *Stanley Hoffmann*   vii

Introduction   xv

PART I: POLITICS AND THE POLICY PROCESS

1   The Political Balance   *Philip Cerny*   1
2   The New Rules of the Game in France   *Philip Cerny*   26
✓ 3   Power and its Possessors   *Jane Marceau*   48
4   The Higher Civil Service and Economic Policy-Making
    Anne Stevens   79
5   The Budget and the Plan   *Diana Green*   101
6   Centre and Periphery in the Policy Process   *Howard Machin*   125

PART II: ECONOMIC POLICY: THE CHOICES

7   A French Political Business Cycle?   *Kristen R. Monroe*   142
8   Economic Policy and the Governing Coalition
    Diana Green with Philip Cerny   159
9   The Economic Analysis and Programme of the French
    Communist Party: Consistency Underlying Change
    Mark Kesselman   177
10 Corporatism and Industrial Relations in France
    Martin Schain   191
11 Rural Change and Farming Politics: A Terminal Peasantry
    Sally Sokoloff   218
12 Communist Control of Municipal Councils and Urban
    Political Change   *Martin Schain*   243
13 Independence and Economic Interest: The Ambiguities
    of Foreign Policy   *William Wallace*   267

Preface

FRANCE'S CONDITION, 1980

This fine collection of essays will give the readers an overview of France as it has become after twenty-two years of the Fifth Republic, and particularly in the period of economic slowdown of the late 1970s. The views offered in this volume are always informed, often incisive, and remarkably balanced. Not all realms of public policy are covered; the emphasis is on domestic and foreign economic policy; but this has been both the area of greatest difficulty, and the one for which the regime has taken the greatest pride.

This preface has no other ambition than attempting to present one person's sketchy view of the whole picture — of the condition of France at the beginning of the 1980s. Foreign observers who visit France are likely to hear two radically different opinions. The optimists (who often happen to be supporters of President Giscard d'Estaing) describe a well-functioning Constitution, an effective Executive backed by a parliamentary majority, and an economic policy that is the only sound one under the circumstances, since it aims at preserving France's international economic independence by keeping the franc strong, and at making her industry strongly competitive. They find a general consensus under superficial divisions. They praise a foreign policy that safeguards France's autonomy in diplomacy and defense while promoting West European co-operation and enhancing France's role in Africa. They describe French intellectual life as vigorous and productive. Opponents of Giscard, and pessimists, deplore a creeping Presidential authoritarianism, a cracked and squabbling majority, an economic policy that has failed to curb inflation and seems resigned to mass unemployment. They find deep divisions in society along a variety of lines: ideological ones, the line that separates the young from the old, the one that segregates immigrant workers from the French, regional divisions, etc. . . . They describe the pretense of official foreign policy as a sham, a vain attempt at disguising the crass pursuit of material interests. As for the intelligentsia, it is sterile and has allowed its standards to be lowered by the insatiable media.

Which of these views is correct? Obviously, there can be no clear-cut answer. An attempt to judge can only be made piece by piece. Let us begin with the political system. France has become again what (according to some) it had never ceased being: a bureaucratic monarchy. A Rip van Winkle asleep since the eighteenth century would soon recognize the landscape. The institutions of the Fifth Republic have enormous advantages — for the President. The dual Executive allows him to leave the details of policy, indeed the whole of *la conjoncture* in the hands of men and women he selects and can fire. He can (as does the present incumbent) concentrate on two essentials: the long range (Giscard's 'Third Millenium') and personnel (putting into positions of power people loyal to the President). All the differences between the American President and the French one are in favour of the latter. He is able, so to speak, to shift unpopularity to the Premier, and to leave the handling of the parliamentary majority to him; cabinet members do not risk becoming barons whom the presidential staff cannot easily manage and whose dismissal may create turmoil; he does not have to improvise the recruitment of his top personnel, for he can rely both on the parliamentary fishpond and above all on the permanent bureaucracy, especially on the *Grands Corps*. Whereas Congress can destroy a President's legislative programme, the French cabinet can practically impose its own as long as there is no majority in the National Assembly willing to overthrow the Premier; nor do investigative commissions have any real powers. There is no Supreme Court (even if the Constitutional Council can at times be mildly bothersome), and the French judiciary is less independent of the state than the American one. Pressure groups, on the whole, prefer negotiating with the Executive to bullying a rather powerless legislature. And the media are remarkably respectful; television is the instrument of the state, and the press shows little enthusiasm for investigative reporting — the pro-majority press respects sacred cows, the opposition press prefers principled denunciation to empirical scrutiny. Thus, the President continues — as de Gaulle had intended — to enjoy the combined advantages of presidential and cabinet government.

Are there no disadvantages? The remarkably bad relations that have developed between the two elements of the Majority: Giscardians and neo-Gaullists — leading to a mini-Constitutional crisis in the late Fall of

1979 during the discussion and vote of the budget by the Assembly —
point to the main focus of trouble: the party system. The 'gang of four'
is not in good shape. The union of the Left has disintegrated, and each
of its two ex-partners has its problems. Georges Marchais has succeeded
in reversing the line he himself had imposed, toward a kind of Franco-
(not Euro-) Communism, but he meets resistance from party members
whose admiration for the Soviet model or for Soviet behavior is limited.
And the Socialist party has no simple clear line; but it has a battle of
succession. In the Majority, the neo-Gaullists foster their own factional
disputes, which reflect a constant tension between two views of the best
way to survive the Giscardian grinder and to make Giscard pay attention
to the RPR — the view of those who preach resistance, and the opinion
of those who plead for some accommodation. And the UDF has succeeded
in being neither much more than a party of notables, nor a party of ideas.

Another source of trouble is the continuing overdose of centralization.
Nowhere is the gap between what the President had advocated in his book
on French democracy, and what has actually happened, more evident.
Some areas of (limited) decentralization established earlier have been
almost emptied of substance, as in higher education, and the reform of
territorial government is still on the drawing boards. To be sure, the
economic policies of Raymond Barre have removed controls from industry and (partly) from commerce. But the grip of the state on industrial
policy remains heavy — only the modes of intervention, and the targets,
have changed.

How successful has been the so-called Barre plan? The Prime Minister's
priority has been national, and enterprise, competitiveness. The so-called
Albert theorem (named after the current Commissioner of Planning),
which expresses Barre's policy, states that employment depends on growth,
growth on external equilibrium, and equilibrium on industrial adaptation.
The latter was to be promoted by price decontrol, aimed at allowing
firms to restore high margins of profit, thereby making more resources
available for investment, and in the long run providing for more jobs;
and also by 'redeployment', a euphemism for letting non-competitive
enterprises die. In order to cushion the social effects of a policy that,
in the short run, allows unemployment to rise, and tries to protect competitiveness by slowing down wage increases, the government has taken
a variety of measures aimed at freezing or even improving the standard
of living of the worst paid workers, at keeping an increasingly costly social
security system afloat, and at funding at least partial and temporary com-
pensation for workers out of a job. The government has thus attempted
to find a compromise between the risks for social stability which a too

strictly deflationary policy — one that accepts a reduction in the average standard of living — would have entailed, and the risks for competitiveness of the kind of inflation both which decontrol and a big budget deficit engender — not to mention OPEC's oil price increases.

The results, after several years, are mixed. They have been, so far, reasonably good in so far as investments and growth are concerned. But whether this will continue depends on foreign and domestic demand, and the American recession, the low rates of growth of France's main European partners, and the need to accept some cuts in the standard of living in order to slow down inflation justify gloom. The rate of inflation has increased, threatening French competitiveness. Trade imbalances have been piling up despite good performances of French exports — but the cost of energy imports keeps rising, and France still has a trade deficit with its EEC partners. There is no end in sight for high unemployment. The Prime Minister assures the French that any other policy would be disastrous; but it is not merely critical political parties that offer alternatives consisting of public stimulation of the economy (accompanied either by some protectionism, or by measures aimed at alleviating the burden of taxes and social security payments on enterprises), in the belief that only a return to high rates of growth can eliminate unemployment (but with what effects on inflation?). Now experts too offer scenarios that give central importance to the problem of employment, suggest some reduction in the length of work, and accept a temporary external disequilibrium.

In any case, after the Presidential elections of 1981, the government will have to face a series of serious, long-term economic problems. Will 'redeployment' have been successful in making French industry competitive, or will not France be squeezed between the performances of some of its EEC partners — above all West Germany — and of Japan, and the increasing competition of the new industrial countries, whose products do not have much access to French markets, but to which France sells very little? And hasn't French agriculture been allowed to grow slack under the protective umbrella of a common agricultural policy with which France's partners are fed up, but whose reform would provoke painful and perhaps violent 'redeployment' in France's rural population and activities?

If we turn from politics (and public policies) to French society, we find many signs of progress. One, undoubtedly, is the indifference of the public to the squabbles within the party system: the scandals and agitations of a political class deprived of real power as well as of any hope for an early *alternance* — after twenty-two years of rule by the Right and

Center — simply do not stir up a sceptical and prudent electorate. Also, authority relations have loosened up in many domains. Mores are far more open and free — this is the one area in which Giscard has been a reformer, allowing state legislation to keep up with the changes in sexual attitudes and in family relations. Associational life is far more varied and vigorous than before. In the business community the need for modernization, better management, a more aggressive export policy is widely understood. And the labor unions, despite their own divisions and the ideological thrust of the still dominant CGT, have behaved with far more pragmatism than foreign observers often credit them for.

However, there have also been regressions and repressions. I have already mentioned French Universities, which are in some ways less autonomous now than the pre-1968 *Facultés*. The government's measures to fight rising criminality and to make the exclusion or expulsion of immigrant workers easier have been very badly received by jurists and concerned citizens, but they have been adopted anyhow. The system of collective bargaining remains creaky, with too much happening (or failing to happen) at the centre and not enough taking place at the plant level; also, a segment of the *patronat*, noting that both the dismal employment picture and the rivalries among unions weaken the authority of the *syndicats*, prefers what one journal has called 'scientific paternalism' to bargaining with union representatives

Thus, French society remains paradoxical. On the surface, the visitor find opulence and ease, a prosperous 'consumer society' despite the hard knocks of the late 70s (and the attempt by the President to tell the French that he and they never liked the headlong rush to consumerism). People's lives are, it seems, ruled by the rhythm of holidays, by the seasonal tides that carry them to and from their secondary residences. But behind the façade, there is uncertainty about the economic future, a persistence of multiple inequalities, and the survival of the Communist party as a 'counter society' amidst the rest of society. As before, there is great homogeneity on top — the real governing class (in the Executive) and the business leadership emanate from the same *grandes écoles* and the same social *milieux* — and great fragmentation below.

Foreign policy is, perhaps, the area of best results (I say perhaps, because many of my colleagues — especially in France — would not agree, and many Americans continue to find the diplomacy of the Fifth Republic obnoxious). To be sure, some of the acrobatics are distracting: French officials are still willing to go to great lengths to dissociate themselves publicly from American and NATO moves, while applauding them privately and taking 'independent' but parallel decisions of their own (for instance with respect to nuclear force modernization in Europe, or to non-proliferation); and their reaction to Afghanistan has not always been very coherent or very candid (partly because of disagreements within the top bureaucracy). But if one accepts the view that the purpose of a nation's foreign policy is to protect and promote its interests in ways compatible with the concerns of others, it becomes hard to object to French diplomacy. To be sure, it looks — sometimes rather avidly — after French material interests: in Francophone Africa (including Zaïre), in the Middle East (especially Iraq); French policy toward its Central African protégé has not been a model of idealism. But one can argue that French efforts against 'destabilization' in Africa, and France's concern with a settlement of the Palestinian issue, are serving more than just France's interests. In the West European arena, Giscard's policy has been a blend of Gaullist preservation of independence from supranational or majority rule, intergovernmental co-operation *à la* Fouchet plan, in direct continuation of de Gaulle's own efforts of 1958–63 (the summit meetings, the Franco–German 'axis', the beginning of a common foreign policy), and — a very unGaullist move — acceptance of a popularly elected Parliament. In East–West relations, the French have remained on speaking terms with Moscow (at a time when Soviet-American communications have broken down) while increasing their own military might in Europe and inching their strategy closer to NATO's.

This does not mean that a diplomacy which is one of distinctive presence (rather than grandeur) does not encounter any problems. Giscard's multiple attempts at fueling a North-South bargain have yielded very little. West European cohesion remains problematic — the strains created by Britain's recurrent demands and by the prospects of a further enlargement are serious, and, as indicated before, the future of the agricultural policy is likely to be stormy. Above all, the return to a Cold War between the superpowers risks making France's attempts at being both Washington's ally and Moscow's interlocutor, both a pillar of the EEC and a friend and supporter of such Eastern European regimes as Poland's, or Romania's, or Finland's, exceedingly difficult. Nevertheless, there is a coherent and purposeful diplomacy — this had not been the case in the interwar period or under the Fourth Republic.

What, finally, about French culture? French scholarship is strong in many areas: history (where the *Annales* and its descendants have exported their ideas and influence to the US), sociology, certain fields of science and technology. But much else is bankrupt. With the exception of Foucault, the traditional gurus of the intelligentsia — Sartre, Lacan, Levi-Strauss — are dead or declining. And the vacuum has been filled, not by intellectuals respected for their expertise in their respective fields, but by fleeting fashions, coquettish coteries, and media mediocrity. Book reviewing is dominated by 'copinage'; writers, social scientists, even some scientists tend to become temporary and limited cult figures, or television oracles, and seem all too willing to tailor their message to the medium or to subordinate their craft to the appeals of spectacle. Hence a disturbing loss of quality control — almost anyone seems able to say almost anything and to be taken seriously, as in the recent debate on monotheism v. polytheism as the source of modern totalitarianism. Hence also the stifling, hothouse and hermetic character of controversies: Paris intellectuals, often still convinced of speaking for all mankind, speak mainly to (or at, or past) one another, in a language only the *initiés* can fully grasp. The sound and the fury, the type of arguments artificially stimulated by a television system that uses the high brows to produce low brow (or middlebrow) programmes flattering to the self-esteem of the viewers or by an increasingly concentrated press that finds speculations signed by big names more cozy than grubby investigations or reportage of journalists, the posturings and the frenzy for novelty led one commentator, some years ago, to compare the *prêt-à-porter* of the fashion designers with the *prêt-à-penser* of the intellectual world. What is remarkable, in the middle of all this, is the survival, solidity, and *sérieux* of a handful of journals (not the weeklies), and the creativity of some scholars, despite the identity crisis of the Universities and the ponderously bureaucratic centralized system of research.

Thus France offers the spectacle of a series of delicate balances: between a society that strives to emancipate itself in part from the grip of the state, and a state framework that won't let go (and to which many still cling for support); between an obstinate desire for a distinctive role on the world stage, and a world that does not make it easy to play for a country of France's weight and location; between an elite tradition of intellectual life, and the many pressures that tend to cheapen it and to debauch that elite; between an institutional system that has provided stability, continuity, and a great deal of efficiency in the functioning of the state, and a certain sense of sterility that results from the narrowness of the government class, the length of its power, a lack of imagination in shaping reforms that would match the considerable economic and social changes of the past thirty-five years, and the absence of a realist prospect of *alternance*. These are the tensions and uncertainties that are reflected in — and in no small measure produced by — the political and economic processes which the authors of this book examine.

Stanley Hoffmann
C. Douglas Dillon, Professor of the Civilization of France
Chairman, Centre for European Studies
July 1980   Harvard University, Cambridge, Massachusetts

Introduction

This book was undertaken with the aim of making some connections and filling some gaps in the study of French politics. It has developed into a more ambitious attempt to describe and analyse the workings of the French state. Most general surveys of politics and government in France have tended to focus either on the structures and processes through which, according to liberal democratic theory, the 'popular will' is expressed and political decisions are reached, or on those which are charged, according to classical notions of public administration, with the execution and implementation of decisions. In France, this division of scholarly focus has been reinforced by the historical confrontation between the administrative *étatiste* tradition, rooted in the role of the state in the *ancien régime* and often regarded as profoundly anti-democratic, and the representative revolutionary tradition, descended from the popular movements of the nineteenth century and profoundly anti-authoritarian in both its individualistic and socialistic manifestations.

This analytical division has tended to obscure the complexities of the political process in France, particularly the links between inputs and outputs. The state is neither a Janus-figure, standing at the threshold of two fundamentally different sets of structures and processes and providing some sort of channel between them, nor is it a monolithic instrument of enforcement. Rather it is a complex phenomenon in itself, characterised by cross-cutting and overlapping processes at various inter-acting levels, where social relationships as well as ideological and material objectives and resources are regularly at stake in the determination of priorities and the allocation of values. Thus, the identification of the broad patterns of the exercise of power and influence within this intricate environment gives form to political reality and helps to explain certain paradoxes which democratic and administrative theories generally obscure.

The articles in this study focus on relationships and linkages. Of particular significance are those relationships which cut across the representative and administrative structures and processes — relationships among public and private elites, between elites and masses, and between the formal and informal processes of political decision-making on the one hand, and the skewed distribution of socio-economic power on the other. Some of these articles focus on linkages between the social environment and the process of decision-making, while others consider the link between the political process and substantive policy outputs — which, in turn, act upon the social environment. The analyses raise important questions both about the meaning and significance of popular demands and mass input into politics, and about the related issues of the control of the state and the ability of elites to define the limits of conflict and to exert social control.

Part I deals with the decision-making processes themselves, and the ways in which these processes are controlled by the various actors who participate in them. Chapters 1 and 2 examine the role of political parties in policy-making. Chapter 1 argues that parties, seen as the democratic expression of the popular will, historically have had only a limited impact on actual policy decisions, and that individual relations among politicians, local and national interests and the bureaucracy have played a far more important role than either party organizations or party programmes in the allocation of resources by the state. Since 1958, despite the re-organisation of the party system, political parties have been further removed from policy decisions to the benefit of the administrative apparatus. This is explained by the dominance of the presidency in organisational and electoral terms, the passivity of the center-right party coalition which has been in power for twenty-two years, and the majority consensus around the values of industrial expansion and technocratic efficiency which has been assimilated into the *colbertiste* tradition of the French state bureaucracy. The last two of these elements may be under strain, however, because of the rivalry within the coalition, the frustration of supporters of the opposition Left, and the impact of the world economic crisis of the late 1970s and early 1980s.

Chapter 2 suggests that the institutional rules of the game, far from imposing a gradual process of 'bipolarisation' on the parties, actually reward certain forms of intra-coalition conflict behaviour which reflect both French political traditions and the new conflicts inherent in advanced capitalist society. While institutional rules have apparently increased the range of alternatives available to the mass public, a more important consequence has been to highlight the dominance of the executive over the parties in the making of the key decisions concerning public policy.

Chapter 3 then examines the people who actually hold public and private power, analysing in particular their backgrounds and the social linkages among them. Their narrowly-based social origins — mainly from the Parisian bourgeoisie — and the well-established educational, personal and institutional contacts which characterise their interaction across various fields of power, reinforced by tacit or explicit social norms, give them the potential to act in a strategically coherent fashion in the pursuit of goals which are rooted in their class experience. However, Chapter 4 argues that these goals and behaviour are not monolithic, but related to the institutional positions held by members of the dominant elites — in this case, in the higher civil service.

The importance of the public and semi-public sectors, the tradition of state intervention in the economy, the special role played by the higher civil service in the policy-making process and the relationship between the higher civil service and big business, all reinforce the closure of the decision-making process. However, intra-elite social rivalries, the compartmentalisation of the French administration, conflicts between the Finance Ministry and the spending ministries as well as between different groups within each ministry, and different political ideologies and policy priorities among civil servants demonstrate the limits of elite cohesion. The mechanisms necessary for arbitration and conflict resolution emphasise the political, rather than the technical nature of the administrative process.

Chapters 5 and 6 further demonstrate the limits of cohesion and coherence, by focusing on two features of public policy-making and implementation: the budgetary and planning process, and the relations between the central administration and local and regional politics and government. In Chapter 5 it is demonstrated how the planning process, one of the most innovative features of postwar French state capitalism, has evolved over the past three decades. The lack of government commitment to economic planning, plus the lack of co-ordination between the Plan and the budgetary process, have marginalised planning in the over-all policy process, especially over the past few years when economic crisis has undermined the long-range forecasts of the Plan and the President and Prime Minister have demonstrated a deep-seated scepticism of the exercise. In fact, the all-embracing character of 'democratic' national planning has been replaced by medium-term budgeting of specific programmes which are more easily controlled in a 'technocratic' manner.

Chapter 6 examines the way in which the more diffuse bargaining process which characterised centre-periphery relations in an era when France was primarily a rural society — a period in which the services provided by the state were essentially local, and in which local officials and interests were far more important than traditional theories of the Jacobin state would admit — is changing as France becomes an urbanised industrial society. Here, direct relationships between city authorities and the central administration in the allocation of state resources have become crucial; thus, the bargaining process has itself become more centralised, and the circle of decision-makers more limited. The development of regional policy has reinforced this trend.

Part I, therefore, highlights several features of the French state which, though at first glance contradictory, in fact dovetail with each other in a pattern which is characteristic of democratic capitalist societies: the growing importance of the state in the economy and society, reflected in both the bureaucratisation of politics and the economy and the emergence of stable, interdependent elites in the public and private sectors; and the increasing salience of intra-elite conflict and bargaining relations within the state itself, as well as between public and private elites, reflected in the politicisation of the bureaucracy and the difficulty in developing coherent policy. These essays also emphasise the weakness of mass input into the policy-making process, as well as the absence of any influence of the political alternatives posed by the Left opposition. However, the isolation of the Left from any policy-making role is only one aspect of the more general lack of influence of party organisations in the Fifth Republic.

Part II focuses more directly upon the substantive areas of policy output and implementation which are related to the process described above. Chapter 7 demonstrates the inadequacy of any one, oversimplified model of mass-elite relationships, in this case the concept of a political-business cycle, in describing the linkages between electoral strategy and policy outputs. Thus, democratic theory, which is based on the relevance of voting and voter preferences to policy-making, falls down on two counts. First, as we have seen in Part I, it is inadequate to describe the initiation of policy measures; and second, even the idea that policy-makers *anticipate* (and attempt to manipulate) voter *reaction* may be less pertinent to an understanding of economic policy (and therefore the allocation of resources) than to that of other aspects of political strategy such as the presentation of personalities and the manipulation of symbols. Considerations about the policy preferences of mass publics, then, appear to be remarkably unimportant in the making of policy decisions.

On the other hand, these preferences are certainly given consideration in the development of party programmes. Chapters 8 and 9 explore this question by examining the policy proposals of the governing right-wing coalition and of the opposition left-wing coalition. Both of these chapters emphasise the dual nature of the economic programmes of political parties: as part of electoral strategy; and as more or less coherent responses to the economic problems with which the state must deal. One of the main differences between the chapters is the focus on the question of power. The governing coalition has inherited a continuous twenty-two year period in office, but, as Chapter 8 shows, the year 1974 marked a crucial turning point. Power within the coalition changed hands, passing − in a system in which economic policy-making is dominated by the executive − from the Gaullist UDR (now the RPR), the inheritors of the state capitalist tradition and of post-war Keynesianism, to the followers of President Giscard d'Estaing (loosely confederated in 1978 into the UDF), supporters of a classic liberal and monetarist approach to economic policy.

The world economic crisis has undermined the consensus policies of economic expansionism, upon which the majority had been built, but in seeking to deal with the crisis, the President and Prime Minister have been gradually forced to use many of the traditional instruments of state power associated with the Gaullists in order to tackle such problems as the restructuring of the steel industry. At the same time, the Gaullists have stressed more and more the need for greater macro-economic planning and full employment policies as part of a strategy to regain their lost dominance within the coalition. However, they have succeeded mainly in demonstrating their impotence in the face of a united executive, aggravating tensions within the RPR itself and seeing their own electoral support diminish. For the *majorité*, the upcoming 1981 presidential election dominates the scene more and more.

The economic crisis has aggravated tensions within the Left, too. Chapter 9 argues that the differences in policy orientation between the Socialist Party and the Communist Party have made the Common Programme alliance (1972–77) untenable. The Socialist Party, seeing itself as more pragmatic and realistic, and concerned lest it lose its new-found credibility with more centre-oriented floating voters, has moved steadily towards a social democratic approach to economic policy. Meanwhile, the PCF, seeing the only solution in a more radical reorientation of economic policy towards a dynamic public sector, has concentrated on limiting PS predominance within the Left and on strengthening its own organisational base.

Chapters 10, 11 and 12 look in more detail at the relationships between the state and certain specific issue-areas of domestic politics − labour, agriculture and local politics. Chapter 10 argues that the traditional weakness of trade union organisation in France, as evidenced by both low membership and the political divisions between different trade union confederations, has led to a situation where spontaneous industrial action has usually preceded the bargaining process, and where the unions continually must attempt to prove their links with, and control over, the workers in order to be treated as credible bargaining agents. This is a process which is most effective in a climate of crisis. At the same time, the state — and industry — have regularly attempted to bypass the unions and to create direct links with the workers, such as through works committees and profit-sharing schemes. Consequently there has not developed in France the corporatist bargaining structure which has characterised some other developed capitalist societies. While the failure to establish such a structure has restricted the ability of the working class to act as an effective participant in the policy-making process, and has probably reinforced class divisions, it has also restricted the ability of the state to exert social and economic control. Certainly, one real limit on the effectiveness of government policy and state control is the difficulty in keeping control over the 'social climate'.

In the case of the farmers, one of the most salient features of change in France has been their reduction as a proportion of the work-force. Chapter 11 shows how capitalist development, aided by government policies, has virtually eliminated the traditional peasant sector. It has been replaced by a dual agricultural economy consisting, on one hand, of large farmers, well-represented in established pressure groups, and able, through a corporatist bargaining process, to gain financial support from both the French government and the EEC, and, on the other, a marginalised, uneconomic, isolated subsector of small farmers, with little political influence, but also maintained by the state. In this process, agricultural politics have become far more conservative (the Left having lost much of its traditional peasant base in some areas), and the protests of the marginal farmers more bitter. The influx of proletarianised farmers and farmworkers into the industrial labour force has further diluted trade union and political influence within the working class.

In contrast to its isolation at the national level, the Communist-Socialist alliance, which made such sweeping gains in the 1977 municipal elections, has been demonstrating just how far alternative policies can be pursued at the local level. Chapter 12 argues that Left-controlled communes with a Communist mayor organise their expenditure in ways that are quite different from most non-Communist communes. Instead of road repairs and parking lots, Communist municipalities have concentrated on developing educational and other public facilities, and on expanding social services. Furthermore, they have gained support among their constituents and within the bureaucracy by presenting coherent and well-reached planning proposals, rather than special pleading on behalf of local interests. Thus, although they are outside the elite network for the most part, they have succeeded in obtaining effective outputs from the administrative system.

Chapter 13 examines the relationship between the broader ideological and symbolic themes of French foreign policy and the foreign economic policies followed by Fifth Republic governments. In fact, the two elements of prestige abroad and the attempt to achieve economic goals have been closely intertwined under both General de Gaulle and his successors. The pursuit of economic growth involved the expansion of both agricultural and industrial exports. French policy in the Middle East has reflected her dependence upon imported energy supplies. Finally, the development of a high technology base for industrial restructuring has been closely intertwined with the French nuclear programme and armaments development — including aggressive arms sales drives abroad. Although, under Giscard d'Estaing, the orientation of French foreign policy towards international co-operation has increased, this reflects the realities of the world economic system. The dilemma of France's policy continues to be one of high objectives with limited means, but this approach is now well-entrenched in the administration as well as in the political culture with its presidentialist orientation. It is likely that an active foreign policy would be pursued by any political group to gain power in France in the 1980s.

Thus Part II is complementary to Part I. Both the processes of decision-making and the policy choices which are seen to be available to the decision-makers, whether at macro-economic level or within more circumscribed issue-areas, demonstrate the interaction of French social structures, traditional and contemporary, with the imperatives of advanced industrial capitalism within a liberal-democratic institutional framework.

The phenomenon of the state, building upon its *colbertiste* tradition, dominated by a narrow elite, yet divided by the conflicts among sections of that elite, appears to be strong and stable. Policy choices are defined within these narrow confines, conflict is limited and circumscribed, and the issues raised by the major forces of the opposition are effectively excluded from consideration, except at the local level. However, it is the very narrowness and cohesiveness of the policy-making system that is the source of its vulnerability. The frustration of the Left opposition, isolated from national participation, but well-entrenched in the larger towns and cities, of the workers, whose action is not easily contained by the trade unions, and of the marginalised farmers and small shop-keepers, is an important source of potential instability at a time when such frustration is being nurtured by a world economic crisis. It remains to be seen whether the strains will develop to a point where the revolutionary tradition will regain its relevance, or whether the state will survive in its present form for the foreseeable future.

Exeter, England   Philip G. Cerny
April, 1980   Martin A. Schain

PART 1

POLITICS AND THE POLICY PROCESS

1 The Political Balance

Philip Cerny

France's turbulent political history and powerful democratic tradition, both of which are condensed into the imagery and symbolism of the Revolution of 1789, have thrust the conflict and competition of political parties to the forefront of the French developmental myth. And indeed, changes in the French party system have been closely examined as a key element in the modernization which the political system as a whole has been undergoing since the middle of the twentieth century. However, French parties themselves have never achieved the functional symmetry and structural autonomy which some contemporary theories of representative democracy demand. As organizations, they have tended to reflect change rather than direct it; in the struggle for power — and, in particular, for control over public policy and the state's allocation of resources — they have been the pawns, not the players. Therefore, to understand the political environment of public policy outputs in France, it is necessary to go beyond the competition of parties themselves and the formal relationship of forces which their electoral achievements denote, to a view of the party system as a screen which filters and mediates a complex socio-political reality. Only then can we assess the significance of the changes in the parties themselves and in the ways in which the system of party competition and coalition has affected how government works and what it produces in terms of policy output.[1]

I. THE PARTY SYSTEM, SOCIETY AND THE STATE: AN OVERVIEW

Although the broad *familles politiques* which historians frequently perceive as underpinning the structure of social and political cleavage in France can be traced back much further, the first steps which led to the development of more enduring party structures were taken in the first years of the Third Republic, in the last three decades of the nineteenth century. These structures, however, reflected a broad distribution of social, economic and political power which has undergone far-reaching changes in the twentieth century as France has been pushed and pulled into advanced industrial capitalism. And the party system, far from controlling and channelling this process of change, has tended to lag behind. Indeed, change in the party system itself has been characterized by a belated and often traumatized response on the part of the political class — a class which developed in the conditions of the nineteenth century and which possessed a particular set of traditions and norms which still permeate its self-perception — to changes in 'other' sectors of French society such as the industrial structure or the bureaucratic sphere. Thus the 'modernization' of French politics has been imposed upon the parties, whose response has been, to say the least, uneven.

The complex developmental process which has led to the present configuration of parties had its origins in a time of contrast between the conflict and fluidity of elites and regimes, on the one hand, and the underlying continuity of the socio-economic structure on the other. Had French elites been reconciled and united in a search for wealth and power, as were the landowners and the rising capitalist class in post-Civil War Britain, or the Junkers and the industrialists in post-unification Germany,[2] then the underlying social 'stalemate' would most likely have been broken, capital and industry expanded, regional markets integrated, and the peasant base of much of the society undermined, early in the nineteenth century, when the population and wealth inherited from the mercantilism of the *ancien régime* provided France with the most powerful 'base' for economic 'take-off' in all of continental Europe. Her central geographical position, her access to both land and sea trade, her resources as a food producer and her military power — evidenced by the extent of Napoleon's conquests so soon after the *déchirement* of 1789 — might have created the conditions for advanced capitalism at a relatively early date.

But it was not to be. The conflict between elites within France — between the aristocracy partially dispossessed in 1789 (and repossessing after 1814) and the bourgeoisie whose power had depended heavily upon the concurrence of much of the peasantry in that very Revolution, between the anticlerical revolutionary forces and the immense social power of the Catholic Church, between the military imperialists and those who gave primacy to domestic politics, or between the *petite bourgeoisie* much of which was still linked to the peasant economy and the *haute bourgeoisie* of Paris and the tight family circles of high finance — created a form of politics in which regimes, each linked to a particular but unstable coalition of forces, rose and fell, and every challenge to a disliked status quo was both pursued and opposed with ideological fervour. Democracy, monarchy, religion and revolution were the symbolic themes of a cutthroat politics played on a distant stage, while the peasant economy continued to dominate regional society, and politics was a process of negotiation between the *notables*: the deputy who (whatever his ideological affiliation) was concerned on a day-to-day basis primarily with constituency politics, even if he was a national figure; the prefect who was meant to be implementing centralized, national policy but who spent much time pleading with national government on behalf of local interests; and other local politicians, businessmen, landowners, etc. — and even the priest and the state schoolteacher who were forever locking horns on the highest moral and ideological grounds for control of the hearts and minds of the village children.

It is not surprising, then, that a gap developed between national politics — and national public policy — and the underlying social formation. And neither is it surprising that a *modus vivendi* was eventually reached which papered over the cracks between the fall of the Second Empire in 1870 and that of the Third Republic in 1940 — an accommodation which exhausted and resigned elites reluctantly accepted as necessary to prevent France from being torn apart by centrifugal forces or humiliated by a foreign enemy. The years 1848 and 1870, respectively, were crisis points which brought home the lesson that the internecine conflict of elites endangered the very survival of the French state and therefore of those elites themselves. But without a dominant 'modernizing elite',[3] and without an internal or external 'frontier' to alter the pattern of the peasant economy — the French Empire was never the successful capitalist outlet of the British Empire[4] or of the American 'informal empire' of the Open Door[5] — the French arrangement was less a 'consociational democracy'[6] or 'historic compromise' than (in Stanley Hoffmann's felicitous phrase) a 'stalemate society'.[7]

The institutional mechanics of this stalemate rested upon two elements: firstly, an historic tradition of *colbertisme* in the bureaucratic sphere (a tradition which could so easily have become the efficient tool of a dynamic capitalist class) which managed the state and even came to perceive itself as the only guardian of the true interests of that state; and secondly, a political class, made up of deputies, mayors, ministers, even journalists, who engaged in largely ritual party political battles while at the same time attempting, in an *ad hoc* manner, to negotiate and compromise pragmatic solutions to the most pressing challenges to the authority and legitimacy of the state. The political compromise which made this 'Republican synthesis' (Hoffmann's phrase again) possible involved, in effect, a return to the formula of the bourgeois monarchy of Louis-Philippe — an alliance between the more moderate Orleanist monarchists and the conservative republican right, at the expense of the legitimist monarchists. But it also included a new element — the rise and eventual integration into this mechanism of the Radical family, an anticlerical movement of the left which none the less opposed the extension of the state into redistributive public policy, and whose ideologist, Alain, exhorted Radicals to build their own small barriers against the encroachment of the Jacobin state into their daily lives.

Thus two crucial developments linked with the Third Republic eventually led to that republic proving insufficient for and ill-adapted to the development of advanced capitalism. In the first place, the alliance of the *haute bourgeoisie* and the *petite bourgeoisie* presaged the later development of a genuine alliance of the various elements of a capitalist class in favour of a kind of economic growth which would overturn the 'stalemate' and undermine the peasant economy. In the short run, the period of growth and prosperity in the years between the turn of the century and the advent of the First World War involved primarily the expansion of existing bourgeois-capitalist family firms, shielded by a protectionist wall (the most concrete economic policy to emerge from the stalemate), into domestic markets newly tapped, concentrating on quality rather than mass production, and based on self-financing rather than the raising of capital on the market.[8] But in the long run it created changes which, in different economic circumstances, demanded new responses. On the one hand, it created demands upon the state — for tariff protection, for subsidies, for assistance with foreign investment and with domestic infrastructure (a major legacy of the *colbertiste* tradition), for state education, for market regulation and labour legislation, for military protection against German expansionism and for domestic economic and political stabilization to counteract the revolutionary and reactionary groups which were such a fundamental part of the French political tradition. The economic chaos of the First World War multiplied this pressure, although the decimation of the working population in the trenches and the destruction of fixed capital made an expansionist state capitalism impossible.[9] On the other hand, the period around the turn of the century saw the beginnings of the long process of undermining the peasant economy through urbanization and proletarianization. A working class was created which retained and further developed the revolutionary tradition because in the wake of the Paris Commune it had been excluded from the 'Republican synthesis' and was not reintegrated into the pluralist left except through a number of painful experiences followed by setbacks: the Popular Front of 1936, the Provisional Government of 1944–46, and the Common Programme of 1972–77.

In the second place, the symbiosis between the political class and the administrative class, so important for the attainment of the synthesis, became increasingly unbalanced. The symbolic issues of constitution, monarchy and religion continued to define the cleavages around which party conflict revolved, with the Radical party becoming the dominant axis. It was defined as being on the left because of its anticlericalism and republicanism, but its tendency to desert the left in the middle of a parliament and to join coalitions of the right in government – only to revert to the left coalition at the next election – became one of the clichés of interwar politics. At the same time, the stagnation of the economy in the interwar period, combined with the financial orthodoxy of both financial and political circles, prevented the state from developing any response at the political level to the economic challenges of that period.

The large agricultural sector managed to absorb much of the unemployment of the Depression, and the isolation of capital from international market forces meant that the state was shielded from the sort of demands for a corporatist response to the crisis which characterized the Roosevelt years in the United States or Nazi armaments policy in Germany. French fascism, too, had a narrow base and was closely linked with the revival of traditional monarchism. Large sections of the bourgeoisie, especially the *rentier* elements (always important in French capitalism), actually became better off during the Depression, as deflationary policies led to falling prices. Only the emergence of the French Communist Party from its political ghetto following the Franco-Soviet Friendship Treaty of 1935 (itself a response to the disarray of the left in Germany in the face of the Nazi takeover) forced, through the Popular Front government of 1936, a partial realignment of political forces along the lines of greater state intervention, welfare provision and Keynesian economic management. The administrative class thrived on these developments, but the political class shrank back from their wider implications, with the Radicals once again changing horses in 1938 and supporting conservative financial policies. The right, which might have been rallied into a modern state capitalist movement under the *Parti Social Français* (a coalition of former members of the quasi-fascist Leagues with various industrial and administrative elements) in 1937, fell back into a fragmented state when no election took place (although some have seen the PSF as a foreshadowing of the Gaullist movement after the Second World War). The Popular Front dissolved in the face of numerous political and economic pressures. And the German invasion of 1940 provided the occasion for the establishment of the reactionary Vichy regime.

Throughout the Third Republic, the political balance represented a relationship of forces which had as its *raison d'être* the prevention of further outbreaks of political conflict of the intensity of those characterizing the period 1789–1870, with its many regimes. Its stability in the years 1870–1940 rested on a paradox: the maintenance of the forms and rituals of ideological conflict, on the one hand (it had not the emptiness of *trasformismo*; indeed, political and moral principles were exalted); and yet, at the same time, a complex pattern of power brokerage, at work primarily behind the scenes in the triangular relationships between individual parliamentarians, local and national interests, and the various levels of the administration. Thus the state, historically the greatest 'motor force' in French economy and society, could react only in an *ad hoc* fashion to the major challenges of social change in the twentieth century. It could not lead, and in not leading, it reinforced the forces of stagnation. And its lack of leadership was nowhere more obviously displayed than in the coalition manoeuvres of the political parties.[10]

It was ultimately the Second World War which became the crucial crisis point for the political modernization revolution in France. This modernization revolution was not, however, the production of industrial capitalism. Industrial capitalism in France retained its bourgeois structures: it had insufficient risk capital, a relatively static ideology which suspected expansionism, and insufficient social and political resources to lead the modernization process. If anything, the war exposed its weaknesses: the 'Maginot Line' mentality; to resort to Marshal Pétain and his traditional form of corporatism based on *travail, famille, patrie*; the rapid and demoralizing defeat, occupation and collaboration; and the structural deficiencies which it exhibited in the face of the economic and military power of Germany. In contrast, the modernization process had its source in a new coalition of forces in a new set of conditions arising out of the war and the Liberation. This new situation was characterized by changes both in the political economy of France, which moved rapidly towards advanced capitalism in a process in which the state was at the forefront, and in its institutional and party systems, which after 1958 seemed to achieve a new form of stabilization but which are still in flux and not fully tested.

The conditions which permitted these changes can be seen at several levels. At the social base, the lines of cleavage which had characterized the stalemate society had been irrevocably altered by the developments of half a century, and the experience of the war itself gave shape and substance to new demands. The modest equilibrium of the protected economy had been undermined by the pre-war economic crisis, and the swift collapse of the country in 1940 convinced many that recovery would involve massive economic modernization and industrialization. This was both defensive, as the war seemed to prove that only the most advanced industrial economies could protect themselves in the modern world, and internal, as many social groups wanted to create a world which would break once and for all with the cycles of poverty and war. Fascist solutions were discredited, and throughout Europe a spirit of social collaboration was the immediate result of the Allied victory. Religious divisions were blurred as the various European Christian Democratic parties sought to reconcile Church and State; the *Mouvement Républicain Populaire* supported social welfare and greater state intervention in the economy, and was at first regarded as a party of the left. The Communist Party collaborated in the governments which initiated the task of economic reconstruction, at first with the Socialists and later with the MRP as well. The national spirit engendered by the Resistance movement and by de Gaulle's Free France permeated the mood of the country. And though the mood quickly dissipated, the fragile balance of the stalemate society was submerged in new forms of division and cohesion.

The political elites also changed considerably. Many individuals were discredited by their role either in the pre-war period or in the Vichy regime, and the new, younger leaders thrown up in the Resistance and in Free France had less of a vested interest in maintaining the old Republican synthesis. Although the traditional parties, like the Radicals, soon reasserted themselves, they no longer played as important a role as they had done and had to contend with new parties which had emerged in the post-war period — including the Gaullist *Reassemblement du Peuple Français*. But it was not simply the parties which changed; their demands changed, too. The nationalization of basic industries, the legislation of new welfare provisions, the application of Keynesian measures in economic policy, and the establishment of the Plan, were evidence that the stakes of the political game had changed.

These changes were perhaps most important for the administration, which enthusiastically adopted the new *colbertisme*. The training of higher civil servants was streamlined with the establishment of the *École Nationale d'Administration*. Their tasks grew proportionately with the scope of government economic policy, and the traditional formal centralization of the bureaucracy was reinforced by the nature of those very tasks. In the new political and economic climate, the bureaucrats saw themselves as the key actors in the co-ordination of national and private interests — the guardians of the liberal democratic corporatist state. Through their old boy networks and the practice of *pantouflage* (movement between the civil service and private sector management) they, rather than the private corporations, could lay claim to be the new technocratic elite. Their scope was not limited to France, either; through the various forms of European and international co-operation and integration they developed a transnational base. And, particularly after 1958, they began to lay claim to the political sphere as well, as service in ministerial *cabinets* became a major route to a parliamentary seat and, ultimately, to a post in the executive.

A final set of conditions can be observed in the changing international environment. This can be seen at three levels. In the first place, the Allied victory also represented the victory of American economic war aims, which broke down the old protectionism through the Bretton Woods agreement, the General Agreement on Tariffs and Trade, and the undermining of the economic spheres of influence represented primarily by the British and French Empires.[11] At a second level, and closely linked with the first, was the move towards European economic integration, given its real impetus by the American conditions attached to Marshall Plan aid and the consequent establishment of the Organization for European Economic Co-operation (later to be widened to become the OECD). Thirdly, the tense political framework of the Cold War not only created new economic and political links both within Europe and in the Atlantic area, but also legitimated the more interdependent world capitalist system under the ideological umbrella of the 'free world'. In this sense, the political economy of France resembled less and less the traditional stalemate society, and more and more the other nations of the Western capitalist world.

In these changing conditions, the most spectacular characteristic of the post-war period in France was not its economic miracle, which was created more from above than from below;[12] rather, it was the re-establishment, with a few cosmetic changes, of essentially the same parliamentary system in the Fourth Republic as had characterized the Third. This was the result of two main developments. The first was the refusal of the Socialists and Communists, who had a majority between them in the first Constituent Assembly, to consider the establishment of a regime with the kind of strong executive which de Gaulle wanted. This clash led to de Gaulle's resignation in 1946, and to the marginalization of the

Gaullists as an 'anti-system' party throughout the Fourth Republic, despite the surge in strength of the newly-established RPF in 1947–48. The second was the Cold War, which resulted in the marginalization of the Communists. Thus the spectrum of prospective government coalitions was limited to the Socialists, the Radicals, the MRP (which declined after 1946) and the various conservative groups joined by breakaway Gaullists after 1952. In this context, while the economy grew and the apparatus of state capitalism functioned efficiently in promoting that growth, the instability of governments, faced with a very limited field of manoeuvre in the National Assembly, by the electoral challenge of 'surge' parties,[13] and by the problematic international challenges of the Cold War and of decolonization,[14] restricted the capacity of those governments to initiate and maintain coherent economic policy programmes over time.

Thus when the Fourth Republic collapsed in 1958 under the weight of accumulated burdens, the most critical of which was the Algerian independence struggle,[15] the Fifth Republic, under the strong influence of de Gaulle, its first President, was set up with the specific intention of rectifying the problem of political lag.[16] The significance of the Fifth Republic can be viewed in two ways in the context of the time. In the first place, the Gaullist perspective on French history and society, the institutions of the Fifth Republic were seen as an attempted cure for the traditional divisions in the French body politic, as an antidote to the evils of the 'stalemate society'. With a strong but democratic executive to bang the heads of the narrow and selfish political parties together, it was thought, a synthesis of democracy and efficiency could be achieved.[17] At the same time, the Fifth Republic, under the rhetorical surface, can be seen as an attempt to extend to the political sphere the kinds of changes which we have already seen to have been occurring in the various components of the social and economic environment. Thus the period since 1958 appears as the political victory of a new middle class,[18] the transformation of the civil service into a technocratic ruling class,[19] the consolidation of state monopoly capitalism,[20] the search for a 'third way' between cutthroat capitalism and totalitarian communism,[21] progress towards a bipolar party system based on 'catch-all' parties,[22] the achievement of 'consensus',[23] or the foundation for an 'advanced liberal society'.[24]

The party system of the Fifth Republic has been at the heart of the process of political change. And its major characteristic since 1962 has been the conservation of an absolute majority in the National Assembly by the coalition of the Gaullists with a growing and diverse group of coalition partners with roots in various right and centre parties. The centre has eroded, and the left, too, has undergone considerable structural change in order to compete with what has come to be called the 'majority' – implying not merely a relationship of forces but also an ascribed status. It will be traumatic indeed for the right-wing coalition when it eventually loses that status; therefore all generalizations must be tentative. But what has become clear, especially in the late 1970s, is that the party system has not settled into a pattern of stable competition, despite the realignments of the first decade and a half of the Fifth Republic. Old conflicts have re-emerged. But, even more importantly, new conflicts, conflicts of great significance for public policy, have arisen. These new conflicts blend the traditional ideological fervour of French politics with the characteristics of an advanced capitalist society in a period of world economic recession. In recent months only the most constraining constitutional mechanisms have prevented the re-emergence of a multiparty system. The strength of those mechanisms will be sorely tested in the months to come.

II. THE EMERGING PATTERN OF CONFLICT IN THE 1980s

The stabilization of the French party system in the 1960s was due to several factors. Broad agreement on the need to end the Algerian War was perhaps the most immediate issue which affected party politics, and its resolution by de Gaulle against intense opposition (some of which came from within the ranks of his own supporters) both weakened the non-Gaullist parties and strengthened his own position and that of the Gaullist *Union pour la Nouvelle République*; a series of referendums on the Algerian issue in 1960–62 conferred popular legitimacy upon the President, his party, and, most of all, upon the regime which could solve this most profound and divisive of issues. Other international issues similarly legitimized the new institutional arrangements under de Gaulle's tutelage: the widespread desire to see France play a more independent role in the Cold War, a desire which crossed class and party boundaries; the ability of the Government to assert French interests within the European Economic Community, while at the same time benefiting from the economic dynamism of EEC membership; and the swift process of decolonization, which at the same time preserved a closely-knit French sphere of influence among her former colonies.[25] The new mercantilism was both efficient and highly popular, and contrasted well with the international weakness of the Third and Four Republics – symbolized for all time in the Gaullist liturgy by the collapse of 1940.

Domestic issues, too, played a large role. In a period of economic expansion, rising standards of living and low inflation, the government took the credit for creating the atmosphere of political stability which made this possible. A kind of centre-right Saint-Simonianism was the order of the day, with a benevolent government relying more and more on technicians — both politicians with civil service experience, such as Giscard d'Estaing, or civil servants directly appointed to ministerial posts, such as François-Xavier Ortoli — for economic policy decisions at the highest level. Georges Pompidou, de Gaulle's Prime Minister from 1962–68 and his successor as President from 1969–74, had previously been a member of the Council of State and a high-level banking executive with Rothschild's as well as a long-time adviser to de Gaulle and his *chef de cabinet*; he did not hold elective office until he won the presidency in 1969. Party debate on economic policy, then, was submerged in what was seen at the time as a new expansionist, technocratic 'consensus', and those parties with clear alternative economic strategies, such as the PCF, were regarded as anachronistic hangovers from the pre-Keynesian era. In this context, the outburst of protest during the Events of May 1968 created a strong popular backlash. Widely depicted as the spoiled children of the consumer society allied with the displaced rump of the old political class, and as menacing the achievement of political and economic stability of the post-war period with a return to the old cycle of revolution and reaction, the protesters were disavowed by the voters in the June elections, which produced a crushing victory for the renamed Gaullist *Union pour la Défense de la République* and the hegemony of the *État UDR*.[26] Thus issues of economic policy were intertwined with the very potent issue of institutional stability, and both, in this period, reinforced the dominance of the Gaullist party in the political spectrum.

The reaction of the party system to these developments was not homogeneous, and manifested the primary characteristic of French party politics which we have identified throughout French political history — structural lag. Change was, in fact, led from the Right, and the Right was itself led from the top. Developments which were embryonic in the PSF in the late thirties and the RPF in the late forties required more than potential electoral support to come to fruition; they needed power. And it was the assumption by the UNR of the mantle of the *party of government* which gave it a platform from which to expand in the mid-sixties.[27] But the mantle of the party of government did not stem from the Gaullists' position in the National Assembly; rather, it was located in their control of the presidency, which controlled the composition of the Government and thus the broad lines of public policy-making as well as controlling the extremely hierarchical UNR from the top down from within. And it was the gamble of 1962 which paid off for the UNR. Opposition from much of the very conservative and extreme right was undermined by the granting of independence to Algeria — the one issue which united the anti-Gaullist Right against the regime. Opposition from the centre-Right, especially from the pro-European MRP, was undermined by de Gaulle's European and Atlantic policies, and this group was eroded from both sides during its long period in the wilderness from 1962 to 1974. Opposition from much of the moderate Right was integrated into the dominant coalition by putting conservatives — firstly the former Fourth Republic Prime Minister Antoine Pinay and later his protégé Valéry Giscard d'Estaing — in charge of the key Ministry of Finance. Thus the rise of what Charlot has called 'legislative Gaullism' depended for its very structure on presidential policies and initiatives.[28] But when control of the presidency itself became dependent upon the organizational strength and unity of the Gaullist party — as happened in 1974 — then 'legislative Gaullism' rapidly declined to become, once again, a faction (albeit a very large faction) within a much broader right-wing coalition. And the spillover upon which legislative Gaullism had been based — symbolized in de Gaulle's appeal to the voters in the elections of November 1962 to 'confirm your *Oui*', to transfer their support for the election of the President by universal suffrage which had been passed in a referendum the previous month into votes for the UNR and their Independent Republican allies — dissipated into history.

Changes on the Left reflect partly factors which are peculiar to the Left, and to the French Left in particular, and partly reactions to the structure of competition imposed by the Right and by the institutional constraints of the Fifth Republic itself. Like its counterparts in Western Europe and parts of Latin America, French social democracy has been faced since 1920 with a war on two fronts. Outflanked on the left by the PCF, with its deep roots in the urban working class and in some marginal farming sectors, the French Socialist Party, the SFIO (the 'French Section of the Workers' International', i.e. the Second International), deeply anticommunist since 1920 and reinforced in this stance by the Cold War, wavered between a gut socialist desire to recreate the Popular Front and a cautious welfare statism which had drawn it to ally with the Radicals and the MRP both in Fourth Republic governments and in local politics. Following the heavy defeat of the '*cartel des Non*' in the referendum of October 1962, limited second-ballot agreements between the SFIO and the PFC were experimented with in the general elections of November. But in the years 1963–64, the main strategic thrust of the SFIO was to back the presidential candidacy of the right-wing socialist, Gaston Defferre, in an alliance with the MRP and the Radicals. The collapse of the Defferre experiment in early 1965 led to a swing the other way — the presidential candidacy of François Mitterrand, backed by Socialists, Communists and most Radicals. With the exception of the 1969 presidential elections, when in the wake of the 1968 upheavals the right-wing Socialists presented Defferre as a candidate on his own (competing with both a Communist and a centrist, he received only 5 per cent of the vote), the history of French socialism since 1965 has been that of the vicissitudes of the union of the left and of the transformation of the renamed *Parti Socialiste* under the leadership of Mitterrand since 1971. The PCF emerged from its Cold War ghetto after the death of Maurice Thorez in 1964, signing the Common Programme of the Left with the Socialists and the Left-Radicals in 1972 (it lasted until 1977), flirting with Italian-style Eurocommunism in the mid-seventies and even renouncing its commitment to proletarian internationalism (thus denying Soviet leadership of the world Communist movement) in 1976 and reaffirming its pluralist vocation and democratic obligations. Since 1977, however, the PS and the PCF have moved apart.

In 1968, Pompidou predicted that the only real political forces in France in the future would be Gaullism and Communism, and that their opposition would be the focus of bipolarization in the party system. However, this has not been the case. And the reason for this is that bipolar competition tends to strengthen not the extremes, but the centre-oriented elements within each of the rival blocs.[29] It was indeed the bipolarization of the presidential election between coalitions of the right (originally dominated by the Gaullists) and left (in which the Communists were originally the larger, if not the dominant, grouping) which obliged both coalitions to compete for the centre ground, especially in 1974 when the second ballot between Giscard d'Estaing and Mitterrand was decided by less than 2 per cent of the votes. The 1970s have, if anything, been characterized by the rise to dominance within each coalition of its more centrist faction: the dominance on the right of the non-Gaullist alliance engineered by Giscard d'Estaing since 1974; and the rapid rise of the PS under Mitterrand to a substantial electoral advantage over the PCF, which has stagnated in terms of votes. And the fact that these factions have been built around presidential politics (as was the UNR in the 1960s) is no accident. But this has not meant the eclipse of the Gaullists and the Communists; far from it. Rather it has led to the emergence of what has been called a 'quadripolar' party system, with the four main groups eliminating the smaller parties, strengthening their internal organization, and competing on two quite distinct but interconnected levels: that of the two umbrella coalitions of Right and Left; and that of the separate parties, each competing with its nearest neighbour(s) for votes, an operation which has tended to focus less on its opponents in the rival coalition and more on its supposed partner. In this context, the anticipation of future elections plays a more important role than the ties created by a previous election. This is particularly true for presidential elections, partly because it is the President and his ministers who make public policy. And the French party system since the presidential election of 1974 has been overshadowed by the forthcoming presidential election of 1981.

In the 1970s, furthermore, both the stakes of party competition and the underlying divisions of French society have shifted significantly. In the 1960s, it could be asserted that the President's sphere of policy control was essentially limited to foreign affairs, defence, colonial and ex-colonial relations, and the like. However, after the Events of May 1968, de Gaulle began to take a greater role in the overseeing of domestic policy, too. When Pompidou succeeded to the office, he personally developed a much larger say in economic policy, financial policy and the like. It was his vision to further entrench the new *colbertisme* by stimulating a further process of industrialization and economic modernization in order for France to overtake West Germany as the leading economic power in Europe. With the destabilization of the Western economies which followed upon the boom in commodity prices in 1972–73, the most important of which was of course the quadrupling of the price of crude oil in 1973–74, the ability of the French state to pursue consensus politics in the economic sphere was severely curtailed. Economic policy came once again to the forefront of political debate, but it was no longer a debate about the distribution of the fruits of continued growth but one about restraining inflation, dealing with the slump and restructuring the French economy to make it more competitive in an economically Malthusian world. However, it was not only the revival of ideology in economic debates which was significant for the party system; it was also that the underlying power constraints of policy-making itself came to be more sharply defined. Differences between coalition partners (on both sides) over economic policy shifted to the centre of the debate. And the day-to-day resolution of that debate through the dominance of the executive branch over the legislature has come to be an ever more decisive feature of the balance of forces in the French party system.

The divisions within each coalition have blossomed over the past five years. They now resemble less the traditional cleavages of the stalemate society and more the divergences characteristic of all of the developed capitalist political economies. For various reasons, however, the conflicts run deeper in France. The symptoms are common enough. The peasant economy has been reduced severely since the 1940s. Its autonomous political traditions, in terms of both organization and ideology, have atrophied; the political behaviour of the farming sectors has become more solidly conservative, as is the case in most industrial societies. And it has been squeezed between the large, efficient farms with strong pressure-group influence in Paris and the growing marginal sector, increasingly uneconomic and with an ageing and isolated workforce. The industrial working class, with its fragmented, numerically circumscribed and political-party-dominated trade-union structure, has been divided both socially, with the insulation of different levels of skill and the growth of the marginal and immigrant sectors, and geographically, with the development of badly-planned and alienating dormitory suburbs. The white-collar sectors have grown, the artisanal and commercial sectors have been badly squeezed by concentration, and much of the middle and upper-middle classes, which had come to expect the continuing high rewards of the boom of the fifties and sixties, felt menaced by the slump. And all of these sectors looked to the political system for a lead. In this context, the division within the right-wing coalition between the conservative Keynesianism of the Gaullists and the liberal monetarism of the Giscardians (or at least of Giscard himself and of his closest supporters), and that within the left-wing coaliton between the social democratic Keynesianism of the PS and the mixture of radical Keynesianism and traditional socialism of the PCF, have dominated party and parliamentary politics. The new divisions have taken on an old fervour, and this fervour has been reinforced and extended by 'quadripolarization'. Here again, both the formal powers of the constitution and the informal power bestowed by the 'national constituency' have given the President the key resources in the decision-making process.

The changes which would take place in the party system in the 1970s were heralded by a shift in the balance of power within the right-wing coalition between 1969 and 1973. Two converging trends can be discerned. Firstly, the Gaullist UDR (now renamed the *Union des Démocrates pour la République*) declined from its position of hegemony within the right because of a recrudescence of centrist and conservative discontent over the regional and Senate reforms proposed by de Gaulle in the referendum of April 1969; centrist opposition, and the personal opposition of Giscard d'Estaing, reduced the Yes vote to 47 per cent, and de Gaulle resigned. The large support for Alain Poher in the June 1969 presidential election was evidence that centrism was alive and well, and at one stage early in the campaign it seemed not unlikely to be living in the Élysée for rather longer than Poher's short term as acting President. But several factors, including Giscard's return to the Pompidolian fold, shored up the Gaullist-led alliance. Secondly, however, it became evident that, given the bipolarizing tendencies of the second ballot at both presidential and parliamentary level, centrism could no longer survive in the centre; Pohr's defeat, and the failure in the early 1970s of the *Mouvement Réformateur* linking centrists and right-wing Radicals, provided clear lessons. In the parliamentary elections of 1973, the *réformateurs* owed most of their second-ballot successes to *majorité* support, and only formed a viable parliamentary group with the loan of some pro-government independents.

The culmination of an alternative centrist strategy was the victory of Giscard d'Estaing in the 1974 presidential election. This strategy was, firstly, to wrest control of the presidency from the Gaullists, and secondly, to challenge their legislative supremacy by federating all of the various non-Gaullist right-wing and centrist groupings. Although such a strategy could not be pursued too openly when Pompidou was President, his death in April 1974 revealed the process to be well advanced. Paradoxically, its success was only assured when a group of forty-three Gaullist deputies, led by Jacques Chirac, indicated their dissatisfaction with the official Gaullist candidate, Jacques Chaban-Delmas — and this move was taken as tacit support for Giscard. Although coming from behind, Giscard defeated Chaban by a 2–1 margin on the first ballot, before going on to defeat Mitterrand narrowly on the second.

The years 1974–76 saw a hardening of the battle lines within the right-wing coalition on two interconnected levels: party strategy and economic policy. Chirac, rewarded for his defection with the post of Prime Minister, soon revealed that his true aim was to develop an alternative presidential strategy of his own based on the renewal of the Gaullist party and the reduction of the movement's dependence upon the traditional 'barons' of the Gaullism of the 1940s and 1950s along with a more aggressive populist style. As Prime Minister he was able to assert his authority within the movement and prevent defections to a potential Giscardian federation, but he came more and more into conflict with Giscard himself. Determined to pursue a reflationary economic strategy in the wake of the oil price rises, Chirac alienated the more financially conservative President, who in turn attempted to control the Government's economic decisions more and more closely. At the same time, Chirac pressed for an early parliamentary election to head off the growing momentum of the left-wing coalition and especially of the Socialist party, which was growing in popularity and which made spectacular gains in the cantonal (county council) elections of March 1976. He was also concerned to prevent the President from effectively federating the non-Gaullist Right, and believed that an early election would show the Gaullist party (completely restructured by Chirac in 1976 and renamed the *Rassemblement pour la République*) still to be the dominant force on the Right and thus to provide the strongest base for the preparation of a right-wing coalition victory in the 1981 presidential election. The conflict came to a head in August 1976, when Giscard replaced Chirac as Prime Minister with the liberal economist Raymond Barre, who dug in his heels with an economic austerity programme designed to last beyond the normal date for the forthcoming parliamentary elections in March 1978.

The changes within the left-wing coalition took place on a rather different time scale, reflecting the fact that divisions within the Left, which had been much more profound in the 1950s, did not give way to a clear-cut national alliance until 1972. The elimination of both of the major left-wing parties from the second ballot in the 1969 presidential election forced a drastic internal reform of the Socialist party and convinced the PCF leadership that to fight a presidential election alone was a recipe for disaster. Following the signing of the Common Programme in 1972, the Left did creditably in the 1973 parliamentary elections, but did not achieve the levels of electoral support which had been predicted in opinion polls taken during late 1972 (which had suggested that the left might win a majority). The Communist party loyally supported Mitterrand in 1974, but the Socialist leader, in disputing the middle ground with Giscard on the second ballot in particular, ran an independent campaign and paid little heed to Communist fears that he was swinging to the right. During 1974–77, then, two trends can be discerned. Firstly, the PCF, while unhappy with Mitterrand, moved closer to Italian-style Eurocommunism and attempted to establish its democratic credentials. At the same time, the rapid growth of the PS (both in opinion polls and in the cantonal elections) tended to make Socialist leaders hope that in the long run they could marginalize the PCF and become — by themselves — a 'catch-all' party along the lines of the British Labour party. Although the 'unitary momentum' of the left-wing alliance scored notable victories in the 1977 municipal elections, the rot had already set in, and when the five-year Common Programme came up for renegotiation in the summer of 1977, a number of issues of economic policy — the scope and extent of nationalization, the level of the minimum wage, the reduction of income differentials between the worst-paid and the best-paid, and worker participation in public sector management — came to the fore, and the talks broke down in September. Each side blamed the other for destroying the momentum of the left and endangering the grassroots unity which had grown up over the previous five years and which was especially salient at municipal level following the March 1977 elections. The Communists feared not only the growth of the PS but also its shift towards what the PCF leader Georges Marchais called a *'social-démocratie à la Callaghan et Schmidt'*. and the Socialists feared losing the middle ground as well as being pushed into economic measures which could not be afforded and which might deepen the recession. In both cases, considerations of party *within* the coalition took precedence over those of bipolar second-ballot competition. On the right, 1977 was an indecisive year. Chirac defeated Giscard's hand-picked candidate for the mayoralty of Paris, and attempted to dominate the negotiations over a joint right-wing manifesto in July. The group closest to Giscard, formerly merely a 'federation', turned itself into the Republican party. In the autumn, secret negotiations began between the Republicans, the reunited centrists (mainly ex-MRP, now called the *Centre des Démocrates Sociaux*) and the right-wing Radicals under Jean-Jacques Servan-Schreiber. Chirac fulminated against his allies, but the dominant position of the RPR had been effectively undermined; in February 1978, the three non-Gaullist parties were to formalize their relations in a confederal structure to be called the *Union pour la Démocratie Française*, a presidential party mirroring both de Gaulle's early UNR and Giscard's book published in 1976 under the title of *Démocratie française*.

Thus the first ballot of the legislative elections of March 1978 showed the four groups taking a near-equal share of the votes. Between them, the four major parties took over 87 per cent of the vote; if one adds in their immediate satellites — the left Radicals and the independent right-wing candidates lumped under the heading *'majorité présidentielle'* — the figure rises to just under 92 per cent. The combined Left share was thus 45.24 per cent, the 'majority' 46.46 (although most observers added the various Trotskyist, Maoist and other 'extreme Left' parties' results — 3.33 per cent — to the combined left-wing figure, making it 48.57). The best result was that of the RPR, with 22.62 per cent, followed by the Socialists with 22.58; the UDF finished strongly with 21.45 per cent, and the Communists held on to their position with 20.55.[30] If the extreme Left is included (both times), then the overall swing from the majority to the opposition between 1973 and 1978 was 3.8 per cent.[31] But it was not enough to break the twenty-year dominance of the Right.

The paradox of French electoral politics was clearly demonstrated on the second ballot. On the morning after the first ballot, the PS and the PCF cobbled together an agreement which continued the practice begun in 1967 whereby the worse-placed candidate of the left in each coalition withdrew (if, indeed, he had not been eliminated by the 12.5 per cent rule),[32] and the same was done without fanfare on the right; indeed, there was a bipolar Left–Right contest in 404 of the 418 metropolitan constituencies still to be decided on the second ballot.[33] For this reason, exact percentages of the second-ballot vote are less important as a measure of party support than those of the first; on the other hand, the second ballot is, if anything, a better measure of the relative strength of the two coalitions. And the Right was in the majority for yet another parliament, having gained 50.5 per cent of the votes to 49.5 for the Left.[34] After the marginal label-changing which always takes place between a French parliamentary election and the formation of official parliamentary groups for the opening of the new session (in early April), the parliamentary parties looked like this.[35] The Communists had eighty-six seats, a gain of twelve over their strength at the end of the previous parliament. The Socialists (including the left-Radicals) had 113, a net gain of five; however, the PS had gained nine seats, while the MRG had lost three (there was one defection). The RPR had 154 seats, a net loss of nineteen; however, this figure includes a net gain of four from label-changing, and the original loss was twenty-three. At first, the UDF seemed to be the big gainers from the election; indeed, Jacques Fauvet, the editor-in-chief of the prestigious *Le Monde* regarded them as the only real winners.[36] Immediately after the election, they were credited with a total of 138 seats, a gain of nineteen (mainly PR and CDS); however, after defections to the RPR and the '*non-inscrits*' (not affiliated to a parliamentary group), the UDF total was 123, a net gain of four.[37] The overrepresentation common to systems with single-member constituencies and bipolar competition is confirmed in the French case, the majority having 56.4 per cent of the seats (277) and the Left opposition 40.5 per cent (199).[38] Thus in a system with fierce four-party competition, a clear majority emerged from a close election.[39] (See Map, p. 00).

It would be wrong, however, to think that the 1978 elections were the outcome of a process of change which would stamp a balanced quadripolarity upon the French party system over time. The fierce competition within the coalitions is not simply a battle for equality, but a struggle for hegemony. The strong stands, especially on economic policy, which have come to symbolize intra-coalition cleavages have spilled over into other areas. Recrimination with one's partners is today more bitter than debates with one's opponents. The European Assembly elections, which took place in June 1979, were a clear indicator of the divisive possibilities. Carried out under a system of proportional representation, they provided evidence of a clear victory for the UDF list headed by the then Health Minister, Mme. Simone Veil, which took 27.87 per cent of the votes, while the RPR list headed by Chirac slumped to 16.24 per cent.[40] At the same time the results for the Left were not so different from those of the first ballot of the 1978 elections: 20.42 per cent for the PCF and 23.42 for the PS. More important than the results, however, was the campaign. Chirac, closely seconded by the ultra-nationalist former Prime Minister Michel Debré, virtually accused the UDF of selling out the French nation. Although it seemed as if he would be forced to moderate his stand after the election because of opposition from within the RPR, the autumn and winter of 1979–80 have been marked by the RPR's refusal to vote for the Barre Government's budget proposals and the utilization by the Prime Minister of the drastic 'vote of confidence' procedure to force the budget through.[41]

Thus as the parties begin the run-up to the 1981 presidential elections, the divisions are being accentuated. As the Western capitalist economies seem set to enter a prolonged period of further recession, the different remedies proposed by the Barre Government[42] and by the Gaullists — who stress a return to comprehensive indicative planning and full employment policies and who reject the free-market monetarism of Barre and Giscard — will become ever more pertinent. But their pertinence will not be reflected in policy; here, Barre has all of the weapons in the immediate struggle. Rather, they will be reflected in electoral strategy. For Chirac wants to stand for President, and will accentuate his differences with Giscard in the hope that a deeper slump will rebound unfavourably upon the incumbent. Although this strategy has not worked so far (and was turned to advantage by Giscard himself in 1978 and 1979), Chirac has at least been consistent and may gain credibility if economic difficulties increase. This seems unlikely, however.

At the same time, the Communist Party has moved closer once again to Moscow and farther from Eurocommunism, even supporting the Soviet invasion of Afghanistan. The Socialists, preoccupied by the infighting between groups which will eventually contest Mitterrand's succession (will he run for President in 1981?), are in no position to enter negotiations for a renewal of the left-wing alliance. Indeed, the PCF seems set to present its own presidential candidate in 1981. The dangers inherent in this confrontation, as evidenced by the lessons of 1969, may, however, not provide a sufficiently strong constraint to prevent four major-party candidacies. Two countervailing possibilities exist: that given the present balance of forces, the progress of Giscard and Mitterrand to the second ballot is virtually certain in any case, and that separate candidacies are merely a membership strategy,[43] and will in fact ensure a high turnout and maximize second-ballot votes for each remaining candidate after the elimination of his partner-rival; and/or that each coalition will agree on a withdrawal procedure for its less favourably placed candidate. The first seems likely, the second much less so. But the three past presidential elections (1965, 1969 and 1974) were all characterized by late developments (as were two of the five Fifth Republic parliamentary elections, in 1968 and 1978), and there is no reason to think that 1981 will be an exception.

It must be remembered, in conclusion, that political debate and party competition in France have changed much with, firstly, the advent of advanced capitalism, and, secondly, the world economic crisis of the past few years. New cleavages have emerged, and an institutionally powerful Fifth Republic has channelled the political and social forces of the late twentieth century into a distinct pattern of conflict. At the same time, the late 1970s and 1980 have been marked by a growing bitterness in the public debate over economic policy in all of the Western capitalist democracies — Britain and the United States being no exception. But the cultural style of French politics, inherited from an earlier era, has reinforced and deepened the lines of conflict. And the strategic considerations of parties acting within the Fifth Republic system manifest a clear premium for intra-coalition confrontation. Thus, for example, the divergences which in Britain would be contained, however problematically, within the 'catch-all' Conservative and Labour parties (with the conflicts being fought out in the Cabinet or between the parliamentary party and the national executive), are represented in separate, proud, ideologically sophisticated parties in France. Given the clear hegemony of the presidency in the policy-making process, all else is rehearsal. The 1981 campaign has been in full swing since 1974. And with rising inflation and unemployment, with the problem of restructuring French industry in an increasingly complex world economy, and with the ever-present frustration of the left and its supporters — half of the French electorate, including those most affected by the economic situation — after being in the political wilderness for nearly a quarter of a century, the volatility of the French party system, and the fragility of the political balance, are bound to increase.

22   *Philip Cerny*

THE DISTRIBUTION OF METROPOLITAN SEATS IN THE FRENCH
PARLIAMENTARY ELECTIONS OF MARCH 1978 (Excluding Paris and
region. Source: *Les elections legislatives de mars 1978, Le Monde, dossiers
et documents*, p. 92)

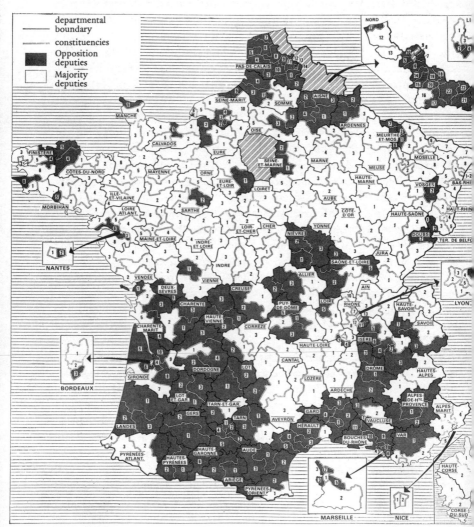

Notes

1 A more detailed analysis of the structural effects of the system of competition and coalition will be provided in Chapter 2.
2 See Barrington Moore Jr., *Social Origins of Dictatorship and Democracy: Landlord and Peasant in the Making of the Modern World* (Harmondsworth, Middx.: Penguin, 1967).
3 David Apter, *The Politics of Modernization* (Chicago: Chicago University Press, 1965).
4 See E. J. Hobsbawn, *Industry and Empire* (Harmondsworth, Middx.: Penguin, 1968).
5 William Appleman Williams, *The Tragedy of American Diplomacy* (New York: Dell, 2nd edn. 1972).
6 Arend Lijphart, ed., *Politics in Europe: Comparisons and Interpenetrations* (Englewood Cliffs, N.J.: Prentice-Hall, 1969); Martin O. Heisler, ed., *Politics in Europe: Structures and Processes in Some Post-Industrial Democracies* (New York: McKay, 1974).
7 Stanley Hoffmann, 'Paradoxes of the French Political Community', in Hoffmann, *et al.*, *In Search of France* (Cambridge, Mass.: Harvard University Press, 1963), pp. 1–117.
8 Cf. Charles P. Kindleberger, *Economic Growth in France and Britain 1851–1950* (Cambridge, Mass.: Harvard University Press, 1964), and Tom Kemp, *Economic Forces in French History* (London: Dobson, 1971).
9 See Tom Kemp, *The French Economy 1913–1939: The History of a Decline* (London: Longman, 1972).
10 See François Goguel, *La Politique des partis sous la IIIe République* (Paris: Seuil, 3rd edn. 1958).
11 See Gabriel Kolko, *The Politics of War: The World and United States Foreign Policy, 1943–1945* (New York: Random House, 1968).
12 See Jacques Guyard, *Le Miracle français* (Paris: Seuil, 1965).
13 Duncan MacRae Jr., *Parliament, Parties and Society in France 1946–1968* (New York: St Martin's Press, 1968).
14 Alfred Grosser, *La IVe République et sa politique extérieure* (Paris: Colin, 1961).
15 See Alastair Horne, *A Savage War for Peace: Algeria 1954–1962* (London: Macmillan, 1977).
16 For a summary of the Gaullist critique for the Fourth Republic, see Vincent Wright, *The Government and Politics of France* (London: Hutchinson, 1978), pp. 11–17.
17 Many interpretations of American politics attribute just this role to the President as a result of his unique 'national constituency'. See, e.g., Robert A. Dahl, *Democracy in the United States: Promise and Performance* (Chicago: Rand McNally, 2nd edn. 1972), pp. 131–8.
18 Jean Charlot, 'Les élites politiques en France de la IIIe à la Ve République', *Archives Européennes de Sociologie*, Vol. XIV, No. 1 (1973), pp. 78–92. See also François Goguel, *Modernisation économique et comportement politique* (Paris: Colin, 1969).
19 See Ezra Suleiman, *Politics, Power and Bureaucracy in France: The Administrative Elite* (Princeton, N.J.: Princeton University Press, 1974), and *Elites in French Society: The Politics of Survival* (Princeton, N.J.: Princeton University Press, 1978).
20 See the collective volume, *Le Capitalisme monopoliste de l'État* (Paris: Éditions Sociales, n.d.).
21 Charles de Gaulle, *Mémoires d'espoir*, Vol. I, 'Le renouveau' (Paris: Plon, 1970), pp. 144–5.

22   Cf. Otto Kirchheimer, 'The Transformation of the Western European Party Systems', in Joseph LaPalombara and Myron Weiner, eds., *Political Parties and Political Development* (Princeton, N.J.: Princeton University Press, 1966), pp. 177–200, and Jean Charlot, *The Gaullist Phenomenon: The Gaullist Movement in the Fifth Republic* (London: Allen and Unwin, 1971).

23   Harvey Waterman, *Political Change in Contemporary France: The Politics of an Industrial Democracy* (Columbus, Ohio: Merrill, 1969).

24   Valéry Giscard d'Estaing, *Towards a New Democracy* (London: Collins, 1977). This is the translation of his book *Démocratie française*.

25   See P. G. Cerny, *The Politics of Grandeur: Ideological Aspects of de Gaulle's Foreign Policy* (Cambridge: Cambridge University Press, 1980), Chapter 10.

26   Cerny, 'The Fall of Two Presidents and Extraparliamentary Opposition: France and the United States in 1968', *Government and Opposition*, Vol. 5, No. 3 (Summer 1970), pp. 287–306.

27   Jean Charlot, *L'U.N.R.: Etude du pouvoir au sein d'un parti politique* (Paris: Colin, 1967).

28   Charlot, *The Gaullist Phenomenon* (Paris: Colin, 1967), p. 38.

29   Although eroding any centre tendency independent of the rival blocs. See Anthony Downs, *An Economic Theory of Democracy* (New York: Harper and Row, 1957).

30   These are Ministry of the Interior statistics, from André Laurens, ed., 'Les élections législatives de mars 1978: La défaite de la gauche — partis, programmes, resultats', *Le Monde, dossiers et documents* (Paris: March 1978), p. 76. For a consideration of the problems presented by the reporting and analysis of French election statistics, see Nicolas Denis, 'Les élections législatives de mars 1978 en métropole', *Revue Française de Science Politique*, Vol. 28, No. 6 (December 1978), pp. 977–1005.

31   The figures used here, which vary marginally from those used above, are taken from John Frears and Jean-Luc Parodi, *War Will Not Take Place: The French Parliamentary Elections, March 1978* (London: C. Hurst, 1979), p. 63.

32   See Chapter 2.

33   Frears and Parodi, *War Will Not Take Place*, p. 84. Of the remaining twenty-two second-ballot elections, only one was a three-cornered contest (PS–RPR–UDF); the rest included five 'duels' within the majority and eight unopposed candidates.

34   Ibid., p. 88.

35   Figures relevant to the party labels adopted during the election itself are taken from *Le Monde, dossiers et documents*, p. 89; figures for parliamentary groups are taken from Frears and Parodi, *War Will Not Take Place*, p. 98.

36   *Le Monde, dossiers et documents*, p. 88.

37   A formal parliamentary group must include at least thirty deputies.

38   The *non-inscrits*, almost all right-wingers, had 3.1 per cent of the seats (fifteen).

39   There were certain 'equilibrating' effects noted in French elections, similar to those noted in bipolar elections in Britain and the United States. For example, there was a tendency for races to be closer on the second ballot than on the first in the same constituencies: Frédéric Bon and Jérôme Jaffré, 'Les règles d'élection au scrutin majoritaire: analyse des duels gauche/droite aux élections de 1967, 1968 et 1973', *Revue Française de Science Politique*, Vol. 28, No. 1 (February 1978), pp. 5–20; cf. Jean-Luc Parodi, 'Note sur une règle peu conne due deuxième tour en régime majoritaire bipolaire', in ibid., pp. 21–6. Furthermore, the major gains for the PS came in areas where it had previously been weakest: Jérôme Jaffré and Jean-Luc Parodi, 'La poussée et le reflux de la gauche (1973–1978); importance du niveau d'origine et effet de domination', *Revue Française de Science Politique*, Vol. 28, No. 6 (December 1978), pp. 1006–17.

40 These are the official figures released by the Commission de Recensement des Votes. The election reflected changes in the social bases of the parties' electoral support: see *Le Monde*, 25 July 1979, p. 6.

41 See Chapter 8.

42 See Diana Green, 'The Economic Policies of the Barre Government', paper presented to the panel on 'Economic Issues in French Politics' at the annual conference of the Political Studies Association of the United Kingdom, University of Exeter, April 1980.

43 See David Robertson, *A Theory of Party Competition* (London: Wiley, 1976).

2 The New Rules of the Game in France

Philip Cerny

Parties and party systems link environmental 'givens' (the distribution of resources among groups and individuals in society; cultural factors such as rituals and images; and the multifarious objectives of political actors) with the constraints — and opportunities — embodied in the formal structure of political institutions. A third, intermediate level of constraint lies in the party system, the structured action field within which political parties operate,[1] in two somewhat contrasting but closely linked ways. In the first place, political parties, as formal organizations, develop the characteristics of organizations — in particular, a vested interest in organizational persistence, and an internal division of labour or hierarchy which leads to the development of various internal vested interests. In the second place, party systems, in a much less formal (but no less rigorous) fashion, develop patterns of competition and coalition, seen here as two sides of the same coin, which may also persist over time by controlling uncertainty. Within the parameters of these various 'natural' and 'artificial' sets of constraints — which we call the 'rules of the game' — parties-in-party-systems act to transform the raw material of environmental resources into the finished product of collective decision-making and control within a given institutional structure. This transformation process is crucial.

In the first place, the formal structure of the political institutions provides an important set of constraints and opportunities. Of course, not all institutional rules are equally significant in shaping the transformation process. Certain activities are by their very nature reductionist, and act to *condense* inputs into relevant forms; the rules governing these activities are of an importance disproportionate to their place in the formal-legal corpus. Two of these activities are especially important to the party system: voting; and the decision-making process. Both of these activities can be more or less complex. On the one hand, not only do electoral systems differ, but the number of different types of office-holders who are elected (often at different times) may vary greatly from system to system. Thus the structures of *access* to elective office will vary greatly, and this variety will be directly related to the formal rules governing elections. On the other hand, decision-making processes involve a number of concrete stages (initiation, debate, voting, possibly the repetition of these stages in another house of the legislature, approval and implementation by the executive, possibly later legitimation, e.g. by a Supreme Court, and even renegotiation) within the legislative process alone, not to mention the broader question of legislative–executive relations, bureaucracy–clientele relations, centre-periphery relations, and the like. Thus the formal rules governing the *control* of the decision-making process will vary widely and will directly constrain the way that that control is gained and exercised in practice.

Access and control, then, are the necessary means to the achieving of goals within the system, and the patterns which characterize them (the structured action field) will fix one crucial set of parameters for strategic action. In the second place, of course, these patterns are constructed within an environment which includes actors with various kinds of objectives and capable of mobilizing a range of resources. The purpose of the actors' strategies will be to mobilize the *relevant* resources to attain the objectives which they might reasonably anticipate to be potentially obtainable within the structure of the 'game' as a whole.[2] But resources held *a priori* do not automatically convert into game-winning trump cards. The possession of capital, or of mass support, or of charismatic leadership, and so on, are crucial resources; however, their effective utilization depends upon their mobilization and upon the actors' capacity to manoeuvre these resources in competition with other actors possessing, possibly, different resources (or even the same sorts of resources in differing amounts or with different qualitative characteristics).[3] Thus the raw material of resource distribution and value preference in society must be *transformed* into goals and mobilizable resources which are relevant to the range of anticipated outcomes permitted by the various constraints built into the structured action field. In competitive party systems, where access to formal office within the decision-making process is in theory open, and where control of that process is dominated by those office-holders, the privileged vehicles for the transformation process will be the political parties.[4]

The lowest common denominator of the concept of party is, indeed, operation at the level of access.[5] The American party system is organized almost entirely in terms of controlling access.[6] However, in many party systems, party organization is also intended to control the day-to-day working of the decision-making process as well.[7] But parties, as more or less formal organizations, interact strategically with each other in structured ways. They compete with each other and form coalitions with each other. This process, while much less formal than intra-party organization, may be even *more* constraining. For example, the heterogeneity of American parties internally is legendary; but the many obstacles in the path of a third party attempting to join or replace the Republican or Democratic party at national level over time are equally so. Indeed, the two characteristics are often seen as complementary. And the structure of competition/coalition which constitutes a party system will be strategically dominated (*a*) by the normal requirements of access and control, and (*b*) by the capacity of parties as actors to adapt to and to manipulate these formal requirements in the pursuit of their goals through the mobilization of relevant resources.

Thus the morphology of a party system begins with two sets of independent variables. The first, deriving from history, economy, society and culture, is the *environment* — the raw material of social structure, goals and demands, and the possession of potentially mobilizable resources. The second is an *institutional topography* which isolates relevant rules of the game which shape the parameters of strategic action by increasing the possible payoffs for certain forms of strategic behaviour and by penalizing other forms. This approach can be particularly insightful when attempting to explain change in a party system. We have already seen, in Chapter 1, the importance of the institutional structures in France in leading the process of change in the party system. In effect, if the consequences of a particular configuration of environmental conditions are not massive and self-evident (for example, if party conflict does not simply mirror class, ethnic, religious or other conflict), then the control of uncertainty will depend more and more upon the intermediary constructs which we have been describing. And to the extent that actors (parties) within the structured action field act in a strategic fashion, then they will be constrained to engage in a process of *institutional learning*.

This process may be more or less lengthy; sometimes it is not completed before the system itself collapses because of environmental constraints (e.g. Weimar). It may be more or less even; sometimes particular parties, unable or unwilling to adjust, will block development or look outside the system for support (e.g. right-wing parties seeking military support, or Stalinist Communist parties). The frustration of a party or coalition excluded from power over a lengthy period can lead to the adoption of other strategies (including membership strategies); the French Left, as we have seen, is in this position today. And the process may be more or less successful;[8] sometimes parties with strong organizational resilience and resources can resist integration into an institutional system and even force pragmatic modifications of the rules of the game.[9] Indeed, all institutional learning is characterized by accommodation, pragmatic adjustment and the establishment of conventions or practices. Only in this way do the formal rules, which are more or less precise, become transformed into the real rules of the game.

This happens in three ways. First of all, the formal rules are crucial in that they define the very meaning of *winning* and therefore permit or constrain the range of coalition strategies open to actors. For example, zero-sum games constrain players in a way that positive-sum games do not.[10] This is the implicit core of Sartori's argument, for example, that proportional representation is analytically a 'weak' electoral system, while the single-member, simple majority single-ballot system is analytically a 'strong' electoral system; the first merely mirrors certain of the environmental resources of the actors (votes) while the second penalizes certain actors and rewards others systematically in a zero-sum fashion.[11] The same is true, analogically, in terms of the decision-making process (as distinct from access to formal office), for a parliamentary system where a simple majority controls both legislation and access to the executive.

Secondly, with regard to the internal organizational structure of the parties themselves, organizational theory suggests that strategic considerations frequently predominate over both goals and resources as the source of hierarchy and behaviour.[12] Joseph Schlesinger claims that the crucial determinant of party organizational structure is what he calls the 'structure of opportunities' presented by the system of formal office-holding characteristic of a particular set of political institutions. This structure of opportunities comprises a set of constituencies with particular features (size and composition of each constituency; number of constituencies; coexistence of different types of constituencies and the relative importance of each type; frequency of elections; etc.) and a hierarchy of offices (not so much in terms of formal powers as in terms of career ladders — the structure of ambitions among politicians as reflected in the wider political culture). The basic unit of party organization, then, is the 'nucleus' — the organizational structure necessary for the capture of one office — and the party organization as a whole can be seen as the articulation of a network of relations among the nuclei.[13]

Schlesinger, writing about American parties, describes a fairly loose form of articulation, though different political systems might require tighter hierarchies; indeed, most systems do.

The third way in which the institutional topography constrains the party system is the structure of *coalition arenas*. These are the different fields in which the different 'plays' of the overall game take place. Coalition arenas are identifiable because they possess *distinct* structures of access and control. Each is composed of individual offices (and their holders) chosen at elections which differ from elections to other coalition arenas in one or more of the following ways: rules of candidate eligibility, number and size of constituencies, timing of elections, length of tenure of office, institutional nomenclature (National Assembly, Senate, presidency, etc.), and, frequently, electoral system. Each arena embodies a set of formal powers and has a distinct role, *de jure* or *de facto*, in the decision-making process, a role which, at the very minimum, permits that body collectively to block or delay decisions. In military terms, each is a distinct 'theatre' in which battles are fought, and which together comprise the war.

The point about coalition arenas is that *each* arena contains the necessary elements for the formation of a distinct system of coalition and competition. Any party system, then, is a congeries of such coalition structures. But a number of factors, both endogenous and exogenous to the party system, intervene to structure and constrain the articulation of relations between such compartments: the *sequence* of elections to different arenas (a factor which we have already seen at work in France); the existence of *issues which cut across* arenas; the *perception* of politics on the part of the mass public in relatively *holistic* terms (ideology and/or power), frequently heightened by the mass communications media; the ongoing demands of organizational coherence (parties are themselves organizations with their own internal structures); specific powers and procedures which link arenas (veto, dissolution, the stages of the legislative process and of parliamentary coalition-building, specific linkage mechanisms such as joint committees, etc.); and the personal and social networks which develop around faction leaders or around common ideological, class, educational, cultural or other ties.

Institutional systems can be classified according to the systems of coalition arenas which characterize them. A familiar criterion for such classification is the *number* of such arenas, which can be seen, for example, in the traditional classification of parliaments into unicameral and bicameral. But a further, and crucial, criterion is that of the *relative equality or inequality* of arenas in terms of the collective influence of the members of each arena upon the political system as a whole (outputs, inputs, withinputs). And a third criterion is the *polarity* between arenas. Insofar as their impact upon the party system is concerned, a limited hypothesis would suggest that the greater the number of arenas, the more equal their weight in the decision-making process, and the greater the polarity between them, the less coherent and unified will be the role of *party* in terms of influence upon access and control; consequently, the more will coalition-building be an *ad hoc* process dependent upon the simultaneous maintenance of a variety of different strategies for use in more or less widely differing circumstances. Such a situation limits the influence of party organization upon political decision-making and privileges alternative channels of political communication and pressure — personal networks, pressure groups, organized interests, veto groups, and the like — in the generation of decisions and outputs.[14]

Thus, in the interaction of parties in a structured field (the party system), political institutions possess certain crucially relevant characteristics which shape the parameters of strategic action. An institutional topography would attempt to integrate three dimensions: the zero-sum/positive-sum nature of the competition; the unimodal/fractionalized configuration of coalition arenas; and the loose/tight articulations of relations between nuclei within party organizations in the face of the 'structure of opportunities' as perceived by party activists and career politicians.

I. A BRIEF INSTITUTIONAL TOPOGRAPHY OF THE FIFTH REPUBLIC

In the light of the Gaullist critique of the French political tradition, the rationale of the Fifth Republic was to create new and effective linkage structures firmly subordinated to a legitimated political authority, with the explicit aim of bridging the gap between the *pays légal* and the *pays réel* and of taming the 'perpetual political effervescence' of the French.[15] The stakes were thus set high. But the means were ambiguous. The enabling legislation which paved the way for the new constitution required that the government be responsible to parliament. Indeed, de Gaulle himself had never called for a fully presidential regime, although the strengthening of the presidency was at the heart of his institutional strategy. This new level of authority did not, however, simply replace traditional forms of authority; rather, it was overlaid on top of them, and given certain formal and informal powers — the latter deriving from de Gaulle's own position as a charismatic leader, but later partly routinized in several ways. The result was a separation of coalition arenas between the National Assembly and the presidency (the Senate, although a separate arena in the formal sense, had much less weight because of its indirect election and because it was easily bypassed in decision-making), but with the institutionalization of strong linkage structures between the arenas which prevented the kind of institutionalized conflict which had destroyed the Second Republic following stalemate between the President and the legislature. We shall now focus on certain characteristics of this structure which have particular consequences for the party system.

The main source of the legitimacy and autonomy of each of the relevant coalition arenas in the Fifth Republic, the National Assembly and the presidency, derives from the fact that they are both elected by universal suffrage. This has long been seen as the only true source of legitimacy in French politics, a factor which was reinforced by the plebiscites of the Bonapartist dictatorships as well as the general elections of the liberal democratic regimes. But, more importantly, separate channels of access to office already require political parties to follow at least two separate electoral strategies and to link and co-ordinate two distinct career structures in the recruitment and advancement of political leaders. These requirements are not, of course, isolated; the promotion of leaders must be tailored to the demands of electoral strategies. But while it has become a commonplace that a French political party, in order to have credibility, must possess a credible potential presidential candidate,[16] two qualifications are necessary: firstly, a credible candidate need not necessarily be a credible *winner*, but just one whose presence in the lists would alter the balance of forces and impel the modification of coalition strategy in the presidential arena; and secondly, the possession of a credible presidential candidate does not absolve a party of the requirement to have a credible parliamentary leadership and strategy – something which it took Jean Lecanuet, in the flush of his only relative success in the 1965 presidential elections, till 1974 to put into practice.

The structure of the decision-making process is, I would suggest, less important for the party system than the separation of the mechanisms of access, but it does have several significant features. In the first place, the formal powers which can be exercised by each arena independently of the other are limited. Presidential power derives not from the formal prerogatives of the office (the only independent power which he could wield against the wishes of a coherent and stable parliamentary majority opposed to the President – as distinct from powers of persuasion – would be that of dissolution, a power which was also formally possessed by the

President in the Third Republic but not used after 1877)[17] but from his direct electoral link with the public which legitimizes his authority. Parliamentary power derives from its role in the legislative process, but this role is formally limited by the restriction of the legislative domain[18] and the special procedures which the government can invoke in the course of debate or on votes of censure and confidence;[19] the latter, of course, have been highly salient in the budgetary disputes of the winter of 1979–80.

But the decision-making structure is important in a different way. Rather than reinforcing the compartmentalization of the two coalition arenas, it provides a set of linkage mechanisms which require the President and the Assembly to deal with each other directly, almost face-to-face, in the nomination and maintenance of the Government.[20] Thus the control of the decision-making process requires continual negotiation and accommodation between the two coalition arenas, leading in turn to a strategy in which party leaders will seek to air their differences and emphasize their *symbolic distance* (reinforced, as we shall see, by the imperatives of electoral systems) while at the same time maintaining minimal overarching coalitions which come into play for motions of censure and votes of confidence (the only situations in which the Government can actually be brought down).[21] In turn, the President, independently elected for seven years, will attempt to maintain control over the Government through his powers of nomination of the Prime Minister (and, ultimately, of dissolution of the Assembly), but in order to do so he will be forced continually to navigate between coalition partners who are always tempted to underline their divergences (whether over 'issues' or over 'territory'),[22] in public.

The strategy which the President chooses to use may be selected from a range of options, depending upon the balance of power in each coalition arena. Obviously, a President elected by a large majority will be able to offer a significant 'coattail' effect to members of his coalition, and thus be able to control the Government more closely, whereas a quasi-'lame duck' President, approaching the end of his term and unsure of re-election, will have to deal with threats of defection. Furthermore, a President whose main electoral base is not the dominant partner (i.e. is either weaker than or relatively equal to the other coalition partners) will have to deal with attempts to create alternative presidential majorities.[23] He may do this by naming a Prime Minister from his own party but acceptable to the coalition partners, or by appointing a leader of another party acceptable to his own supporters, or by appointing a non-party 'technician'. The success of any such strategy depends upon the

balance of forces within the coalition, the divisions and animosities between coalition partners, and the extent of the sphere which the President
is attempting to control.

As in the United States, the main bargaining weapon of parliamentary
party leaders is a negative one — the power to block decisions. Only the
executive (President and Prime Minister, depending on the balance of
power between them) is in a *position to initiate* innovatory decisions
as a coalition-building strategy within the majority; if its intra-majority
rivals seek to do so, the executive can choose either to block the decision
or to support it, and in the latter case credit would go to the executive
and not to the coalition partners! This position is perceived by the electorate as part of the basis of the legitimacy of presidential authority, and
a President who is in a strong electoral position either in his own right
or because he is the leader of the dominant party in the majority will
have maximum freedom of action in choosing his strategy. But even if
the President is in a position of relative weakness, he will retain something of this advantage. Of course, if the parliamentary majority is in the
hands of a coherent and stable coalition opposed to the President, then
his role will be reduced to that of a figurehead with a kind of watchdog
role (the threat of dissolution), but the innovatory power will pass to
the Prime Minister.

The consequence of the existence of these linkage mechanisms within
the broad framework of the separation of coalition arenas is to give an
important bonus to congruent majorities which control both the National
Assembly and the presidency, and in which the President's own party is
dominant. This is the configuration which Duverger called the 'republican
monarchy'.[24] At the other end of the scale, we find the presidency severely
penalized by the clear incongruence of majorities — when one coalition
controls the assembly and the other the presidency. This situation has
been the subject of much comment in France over the years, especially
during the run-up to the 1978 parliamentary elections, when it looked
possible for the left to win a parliamentary majority. However, these
polar types obviously do not exhaust the value of the scale. Indeed, I
shall argue that the normal consequences of the 'rules of the game' are to
prevent the first polar type and to mitigate the consequences of the second.

This effect is achieved in two ways. As we have just seen, controlling
the decision-making process can often reward behaviour on the part of
parliamentary leaders which makes intra-majority divergences more
salient rather than less so, although the President retains an important
degree of freedom of manoeuvre. Therefore the significance for the party
system of the balance of forces *within* each coalition can, at key times,

be even greater than the balance of forces between the two coalitions. These key times are less likely to consist of confidence or censure votes within the National Assembly, as these provide the lowest common denominator of majority cohesion (their zero-sum character is most pronounced). They are more likely to affect votes on certain policy issues (economic policy and foreign policy have both recently been focal points for policy disagreements within both coalitions!), but the damage of these to the Government can be limited by the judicious use of votes of confidence. They are most likely, however, to affect electoral strategy, where our first category of institutional topography — the means of access to formal office — contains a number of relevant structural features which reinforce this pattern of party interaction and shape it in important ways.

It is a popular fallacy to think that the effect of the electoral systems used to choose the French President and the members of the National Assembly is to 'bipolarize' the patterns of competition and coalition which constitute the French party system. Undoubtedly there are certain bipolarizing effects built into the system, but these are counteracted by other effects which both limit bipolarization and reinforce other tendencies. In this process, the electoral system used for presidential elections has marginally but significantly different effects from the system used for parliamentary elections. In seeking to explain change in the French party system, we must focus on the sequence of electoral events and see how party organizations and coalition structures have developed strategic orientations which may be more or less appropriate to the constraints imposed by the rules of access. But first let us turn to the rules themselves.

Both systems use a two-ballot procedure, with a barrier imposed on qualification for the second ballot. Qualification for the first ballot is relatively simple, and the rewards can be attractive to quite small as well as large political parties; these rewards include the allocation of free television time (with the proviso that in parliamentary elections parties must be fielding candidates in a minimum number of constituencies) and a contribution towards the cost of printing electoral propaganda. But these distributive rewards play a fairly small part in party strategy. For the party which participates on the first ballot, whether or not it has a credible chance of winning, frequently does have sufficient mobilizable resources to affect the balance of power among the leading candidates who do have a credible chance. This encouragement to the participation of small parties, in turn, reduces the chance that any one candidate of the leading parties will win the absolute majority necessary for outright victory on the first ballot, except in a few cases. Thus first-ballot strategic goals can be classed into two categories: firstly, those parties or candidates which are not perceived as having a credible chance of getting over the barrier into the second ballot will concentrate on either *preventing* other candidates from getting over the barrier or on putting pressure on other candidates to adopt certain issue positions compatible with the aims of the smaller parties; secondly, those parties or candidates which *are* perceived as having a credible chance of proceeding to the second ballot will concentrate either on coming ahead of its nearest rival (because of the constraints imposed by second-ballot rules) or simply on ensuring that it gets itself over the barrier, which it can do either by gaining or keeping votes from its rivals or by gaining or keeping votes from the non-credible parties.

The extent to which particular strategies are pursued therefore depends on (*a*) the size and strength of the other parties within a particular constituency and (*b*) the height of the barrier to the second ballot. The former criterion may depend upon environmental conditions (money, public sympathy, leadership, etc.), but it may also depend on *images of optimum size*. This is analogous to Riker's minimum winning coalition principle,[25] except we are here referring to strategic perceptions (taking account of the impact of imperfect information, ideological closure, positional power, and the like)[26] rather than to deductive principles. For example, winning too many votes on the first ballot may reduce the value of additional votes which would otherwise have come from a party which has been eliminated and cause the leaders of the small party to relax their support on the second ballot (or to seek deals elsewhere); similarly, too much first-ballot strength might frighten off second-ballot coalition partners who wish to maintain a position of relative equality, but who do not want to reinforce the growing dominance of another group in the coalition over themselves. Thus winning strategies are not necessarily the same as short-term maximizing strategies, and a variety of options exists on the first ballot.

The latter criterion will in fact impose more far-reaching constraints on first-ballot strategy. And here the difference between the presidential election and the parliamentary election is crucial. The important factor here is credibility. In a first-past-the-post system, only a party which has a chance of taking first place (i.e. winning outright) or second place (thus being in contention) will normally have the image of a credible party in terms of having the potential to be elected to office (a zero-sum game); votes for third parties tend to be thought of as wasted votes, although there are always reasons, often strategic as well as ideological or ethnic, for some voters to vote for third parties, and in times of upheaval they may be crucial. In a two-ballot system, credibility is directly related to the height of the second-ballot threshold. Obviously, where parties are of vastly unequal social weight, then this threshold will decline in importance. However, the more equal the weight of the main contenders, and the higher the barrier, the more the crossing of the barrier takes on the character of a zero-sum game, in which strategic considerations vastly increase in significance.

With regard to presidential elections, the barrier is relatively high. Only the candidates who are placed first and second on the first ballot are permitted to proceed to the second.[27] Extrapolating the principle of credibility, the conclusion would seem to be that only a candidate who has a credible chance of being placed first, second *or third* on the first ballot would be regarded as serious contenders. The third-placed candidate would be the only one who could supplant the second-placed candidate and 'win' by proceeding to the second ballot.[28] Thus it is the battle for second place on the first ballot which is the focal point of the build-up to a presidential election and of the first-ballot campaign; candidates who are not perceived as having a chance of running third can, of course, modify the balance of forces among the leading contenders, but they are not in contention themselves. Of course, on the second ballot, first-past-the-post rules apply — but they do not constrain the pattern of competition and coalition in the same way that they do in a single-ballot system; they merely force second-ballot *coalitions*, not a two-party system. Most of the time, party strategy is as much concerned with the balance of power within a coalition as with the balance between coalitions. In this sense, the presidential electoral system enforces a kind of uneven *tripolarization*, in which the division of one camp on the first ballot is strategically permissible (it may even lead to the potential formation of a wider coalition on the second). However, a division within *both* camps on the first ballot can be very hazardous; it opens up the possibility of one coalition being eliminated from the second ballot *entirely*, skewing the party system and reducing its overall credibility as a mechanism for electoral choice (as in 1969).

With regard to parliamentary elections, the barrier is much lower, although it has been raised considerably. In 1958, it was set at 5 per cent of *registered voters*, but this was raised first to 10 per cent and then to 12.5 per cent of registered voters in time for the 1978 elections. Thus, at present, on an 80 per cent turnout, a party would have to receive 15.6 per cent of *votes cast* to proceed to the second ballot; on a 70 per cent turnout, the barrier goes up to 17.9 per cent; and on a 62.5 per cent turnout, up to 20 per cent. If all the contending parties were of exactly equal weight, and turnout were 80 per cent, then a maximum of six could cross the threshold; however, the greater the weight of individual parties, the fewer can cross the threshold, and if two parties receive about a third of the first-ballot votes each (or two-thirds between them), then a maximum of one further party could join them on the second ballot. The figures can be elaborated at length, but the inference is clear. *Unless* the two biggest parties in a constituency (on an 80 per cent turnout) receive 84.5 per cent or more of the votes between them, at least one other party and perhaps a third or fourth would be entitled to join them on the second ballot. Thus a party can be seen as a credible party in a particular constituency if it is in a position to *challenge* for third (and occasionally fourth, depending on the size of the larger parties) place — i.e. to come *at least fourth* (or fifth!). Again, the first-past-the-post rules of the second ballot constrain parties to form bipolar second-ballot coalitions. However, most of the time, party strategy will concentrate on 'winning' by being in a position to proceed to the second ballot. In this sense, the electoral system used for parliamentary elections, while favouring second-ballot coalitions and eliminating all but middle-sized parties, still permits the competition of up to (usually) four credible parties, leading to a kind of loose quadripolarization. It thus permits division within both camps — both second-ballot coalitions — on the first ballot; it might even be said to *encourage* such divisions, as relative size within each camp will be the key to success in negotiating second-ballot agreements. And all this without fear that one or the other *coalition* will be eliminated from the second ballot except in highly skewed safe seats (a total in 1978 of sixty-nine metropolitan constituencies — fifty-six won the first ballot, five second-ballot duels within the majority, and eight unopposed second-ballot candidacies; twelve of the seventeen overseas seats, however, were won on the first ballot, and only five had second-ballot two-coalition duels.[29]

The Fifth Republic, then, imposes certain uneven and conflicting constraints upon the strategic interaction of political parties in the party system. There is no unimodal tendency towards bipolarization; indeed the mechanisms of both access and control would seem potentially to reinforce certain forms of conflict within each coalition. But parties are ongoing organizations, and coalitions, too, develop structural continuities and habits. The reconciliation of these conflicting constraints is a process which can only take place over time, depending on the strategic behaviour of leaders and the sequence of critical events which compress action into configurations which feed back into the structured action field and constrain future events. By looking at the structural consequences of events we can trace the development of the party system itself.

II. INSTITUTIONAL LEARNING IN THE FRENCH PARTY SYSTEM

The party system of Fifth Republic France has not been constructed upon a *tabula rasa*. Previously learned behaviour patterns as well as environmental factors (goals and resources) continue to constrain strategic interaction in ways both old and new. A Gaullist party does not rapidly shed the sense of mission which it developed in Free France, the Resistance, the years in the wilderness and the crucial role it played in the period of charismatic exemption under de Gaulle's presidency. A Communist party does not easily loosen its centralized organization, shed its revolutionary image or question the 'socialist' character of the USSR without calling into question its very identity as a Communist party. Socialist, centrist and conservative groupings do not readily give up their freedom of action and their conviction that they are the natural, centripetal governing forces of France, to tie themselves to a coalition representing one side of the Left–Right dimension only and limiting their access to ministerial responsibility. But in a period of changing environmental conditions, the ability of a party to resist decay is best demonstrated by retaining its credibility in competing for office. Although the temptation to opt out of the game may be great, the benefits of accepting the constraints of the competition may be even more valuable, even if only to prevent organizational decline and possible atrophy. Although any description here must be skeletal, certain key events stand out in the development of the party system of the Fifth Republic.

The analysis of the party system which was developed in the 1960s was clear and coherent.[30] The transformation of the parties, which began with the routinization and institutionalization of presidential supremacy on the foundations laid by General de Gaulle during his handling of the constitutional settlement, the Algerian crisis and foreign and defence policy, was completed by the development of a coherent and stable parliamentary majority based around the organizationally innovative Gaullist party and bringing the various smaller groupings of the Right and Right-centre into a broad, 'catch-all' party of the Right on the model of the British Conservative party. These developments would constrain the various opposition groups similarly to aggregate their forces behind a credible presidential candidate and with a view to strengthening coalition ties in parliament, thereby forming a 'catch-all' grouping on the Left. The presumed bipolarizing effects of second-ballot coalition-building would reinforce this pattern in both the presidential and parliamentary arenas. Yet persuasive as this analysis seemed, it later showed three significant sorts of weaknesses when viewed with hindsight. The first weakness was a predictable one. Although the UDR had effectively federated the right into a catch-all party, this was partially due to the fragmentation of the traditional right-wing groupings. The Left would not follow so easily; the strength of the organization of the PCF would prevent its full integration, and the Socialists would be continually tempted by alternative alliances with the centre. This proved to be the case during the 1969 presidential election. However, the renascence of the Socialist party under the presidentialist leadership of Mitterrand, and the signing of the Common Programme, did fit the prescription. Bipolarization arose again from the ashes, at least until 1977.

The second was the fact that presidential elections, unlike the referendums of 1958–62 in which the only possible response was 'Yes', or 'No', and which were said to be presidential elections by proxy, were clearly not having the bipolarizing effect they were supposed to be having. The most spectacular aspect of the 1965 election was the intervention of Lecanuet, who prevented de Gaulle from achieving his first-ballot absolute majority; coming a respectable third, he represented to the right-wing Socialists the possibility that an alternative Defferre-style alliance, excluding the PCF, might still be viable. When this option reappeared in the person of Alain Poher in the 1969 campaign (despite Defferre's candidacy), however, the lesson became rather more complicated. The centrist option was relatively successful, with Poher coming second and thus going on to the second ballot, however, the level of his support, and the opposition of the Communists (who had run him a close third) to supporting him on the second ballot, meant that his credibility against Pompidou was negligible. In other words, the centre-Left option gave the Gaullists a clear run. However, the combination of de Gaulle's defeat in the referendum of the previous April and the strength of Poher opened up the strategic possibility of developing a centre-*Right* alternative to Gaullism — a card played by Giscard as early as 1962. At the same time the parties of the Left did not just agonize over their exclusion from the second ballot, but set about correcting the situation — a process which led to the Common Programme. Thus, when the third presidential election suddenly approached, following Pompidou's death, it was the Left that was united, and the Right that was again divided, on the first ballot, leading to Giscard's victory over the traditional Gaullist Chaban-Delmas — an event more important for the party system, as we have seen, than his subsequent victory over Mitterrand on the second ballot. And so while the bipolarizing effect of the second ballot continued to operate, the first ballot's impact was no less clear: any attempt to build a majority coalition at the presidential level was ultimately valid for the second ballot only, and the first ballot could be used by parties within a coalition strategically to *alter* the balance of power within that coalition; furthermore, provided that the opposition was united on the first ballot, such confrontation would not harm, and might even help, the broader coalition's chances on the second ballot. Even a party as well organized as the UDR was vulnerable.

The third weakness was the fact that parliamentary elections proved to be even more permissive as regards intra-coalition conflict. The organized majority dominated by the Gaullists proved to have been the result of conjunctural factors — firstly the weakness and dependence of the Independent Republicans in 1962 (single candidates were nominated by the majority in all but a handful of constituencies in 1962 and again in 1967), and secondly the fact that the UDR, in the backlash to the 1968 May Events, was able to win an absolute majority on their own despite freedom of candidature (single candidacies were again imposed by Pompidou in 1973). However, the lessons of 1969 were extended by the relative success of non-Gaullist majority candidates in those few constituencies which did have 'primaries' (first-ballot competition among majority candidates) in 1973 and by the fact that Lecanuet's opposition centrists were, in the end, constrained to co-operate with the majority on the second ballot. This laid the groundwork for a two-tier party system to emerge, in which the opportunities for intra-coalition competition were to be exploited in a number of salient ways.

The two most important of these developments since 1974, as we have seen, have been the alteration of the balance within each coalition and the subsequent modification of the broad pattern of electoral strategy, on the one hand, and the change in the balance of power in the relations between the President, the Prime Minister and parliament, on the other. The façade of bipolarism cracked wide open, and the latent internecine competition which had been suppressed by the conditions of the 1960s — but which were latent not only in the political environment but also in the structure of the rules of the game — began to emerge more clearly in day-to-day events. The victory of Giscard d'Estaing threatened to undermine the position of the UDR, although the Gaullists still controlled two-thirds of the majority's seats in the National Assembly. Giscard hoped that by choosing Chirac as Prime Minister he might compensate the Gaullists for its loss of the presidency (at least for the time being); 1974 was the first time in the Fifth Republic that the Gaullists had lost control of the presidency, a post from which, in Gaullist ideology, flowed the legitimate authority of the regime. As we have seen, however, Chirac used the premiership not to keep the Gaullists within a Giscardian majority, but as a base to keep the UDR from splitting into factions and thus falling prey to poaching from the other elements of the majority. Chirac thus challenged the very concept of a 'presidential majority' and constituted an alternative pole of aggregation which would prove to be far more of a challenge to presidential supremacy than had been Giscard's famous 'oui, mais . . .' of 1967. The growing split within the majority, especially since 1976, has finally laid the notion of bipolarization to rest. And the 1978 election clearly demonstrated that the parameters of the institutional topography actually reinforced, rather than constrained, the development of structured intra-coalition competition along quadripolar lines.

This set of developments also affected the balance of institutional power. Faced with a Chirac freed from the constraints of his position as Prime Minister, and with his own supporters (in 1976) still relatively weak and divided in the Assembly, Giscard's strategy was to appoint a non-party 'technician', Raymond Barre, as Prime Minister with the brief of imposing an austerity programme. The President then relaxed his day-to-day oversight over the Government; he did not have to keep a wary eye on Barre as he had had to do with Chirac. Thus the hierarchical authority of the President, though predominant still in the last analysis, was faced, on a day-to-day basis, with two potential sources of challenge — from a relatively autonomous leader of the largest faction of the majority, and from a more directly accountable Prime Minister. On one level, Giscard has deflected much of Chirac's challenge away from himself and onto Barre, leaving himself the opportunity, in March 1978, to intervene in the election campaign in favour of the majority as a whole — an intervention which was well-timed and effective in electoral terms. And the extent to which Chirac's challenge to Barre's budgetary proposals during the past winter has been perceived as a confrontation from which the President has been able to maintain an aloof distance has reinforced an embattled Prime Minister at a time when widely reported rumours suggested that the President was considering seeking an electorally more popular replacement and has rebounded favourably upon the election prospects of Giscard himself, enabling him virtually to ignore potential scandal (Bokassa's diamonds) and to remain apparently calm and unperturbed in the face of the man whom in April 1979 he dismissed as an '*agité*'. But on another level, it is clear that presidential supremacy is no longer an adequate description of the Fifth Republic. The continual jockeying for power among President, Prime Minister and 'internal opposition' confirms, as Maurice Duverger has extensively argued,[31] that the regime is now a 'dyarchy' or even a 'triarchy', and no longer a 'republican monarchy'. Furthermore, developments on the Left seem to indicate that this sort of situation might be even more characteristic of a left-wing coalition government, even with a left President.

At the same time, certain aspects of bipolarization remain. In the first place, second-ballot coalitions are unlikely to disappear, as evidenced by the level of discipline characteristic of the 1978 elections (although Communist candidates suffered from a differentially high rate of abstention and defection among Socialist voters). In the second place, despite ever-increasing disagreement within the majority over economic policy and other issues, the Gaullists do not intend to vote against the Government on censure motions. Giscard has made it quite clear — especially in a radio interview in April 1979 — that the defeat of the Government would provoke an immediate dissolution of the National Assembly and fresh elections. And given the poor performance of the Gaullists in the cantonal elections in March 1979 and the European elections of June 1979, Chirac is unlikely to risk another parliamentary election before the presidential election of 1981; indeed his strategy only makes sense as a presidentialist strategy, in which the recapture of the presidency by the Gaullists might lead to a revival of the RPR at other levels. These constraints were at their least effective in the European elections, when a proportional representation system removed any bipolarizing pressure, and when a certain *rapprochement* between the Giscardians and the Socialists, and between the RPR and the Communists, over issues of foreign policy and European integration in particular, made the picture far more complicated in terms of institutional topography. But the 1981 presidential campaign, which is now virtually under way, is likely to reimpose a minimum of constraint. In addition, for the first time since 1965 there will be a significant presidential incumbency factor; indeed, 1981 will mark the first time that a President regularly elected by universal suffrage has faced reelection (de Gaulle was elected by an electoral college in 1958) and the first time since 1965 that an incumbent will have completed his full seven-year term.

The past six years, therefore, have seen the appearance of a new pattern in the French party system. The constraints latent in the rules of the game, constraints which had been partially suppressed in the years of Gaullist hegemony, began to play a more direct role in structuring the strategic interaction of parties in terms of both access (electoral strategy and party organization) and control (decision-making concerning economic policy and the configuration of power between the President, Prime Minister and majority parties). In an almost caricatured fashion, the four leading parties shared nearly 90 per cent of the first-ballot votes in 1978 (and, what is more important, shared it almost equally) and between them took all of the seats in the European Parliament in 1979.[32] Given the rules of the game, a two-tier party system is now the characteristic feature of French politics. Obviously, such a system is built on internal contradictions and tensions, and its maintenance in its present form will depend upon whether existing constraints will be sufficient to prevent internal tensions from leading to a crisis of legitimacy. The Fifth Republic has thus seen two realigning parliamentary elections. In 1962 the constraints on second-ballot competition were manifested in the winning of an absolute parliamentary majority by the Gaullist-dominated coalition. In 1978, the permissive conditions relating to first-ballot competition came into play and intra-coalition competition came to the fore. And each of these elections was preceded by significant changes in terms of competition for the presidency: de Gaulle's proxy election in the various referendums of 1958–62; and Giscard's defeat of Chaban-Delmas in 1974. Furthermore, each was preceded by significant changes in legislative-executive relations and in the relations between the President and the Prime Minister within the executive: Debré's replacement by Pompidou and Chirac's replacement by Barre. In both cases the party system — the structured action field of party politics — was changed by the adoption of new strategies of access and control, strategies which involved the adaptation to and the manipulation of the constraints embodied in the rules of the game.

This is not, of course, an inevitable process of increasing conformity to the logical imperatives of certain formal rules. However, the reduction and management of exogenous constraints on party competition — the development of supportive conditions for strategic interaction because of the decline of traditional forms of political conflict, the appearance of new forms in the global environment of the 1970s and 1980s, and the homogenization of certain characteristics of the actors themselves (the development of party organization, the end of charismatic exemption, executive/bureaucratic dominance of the policy process, etc.) — have made the mechanical constraints on competition and coalition more salient for party strategy. There are still important tests to come — not only economic crisis, but also the day when the presidency and the National Assembly are controlled by different majorities, are the most obvious. But the broad balance of power, and the constraints within which shifts *within* the parameters of that balance of power occur, have taken on a pattern which is consistent with the rules of the game and which will be reinforced by those rules in the future.

Notes

1   For the concept of a 'structured action field', see Michel Crozier and Erhard
    Friedberg, *L'acteur et le système: les contraintes de l'action collective* (Paris:
    Seuil, 1977).

2   Of course, the game structure dictated by a particular structured action field
    can, in making for predictable outcomes, 'select out' many possible goals which
    actors may wish to pursue. The resulting strategic decision may be to try to
    restructure the action field itself (change the nature of the game), to ignore
    the structured action field altogether either temporarily or permanently with a
    view to strengthening one's resource base by other means (play a waiting game),
    or to opt out of the game entirely (play a different game). Furthermore, ignor-
    ance of the rules of the game (i.e. of the consequences of adopting particular
    strategies), and/or tergiversation, are both common behaviour patterns. See
    also J. P. Nettl, *Political Mobilisation* (London: Faber, 1967).

3   For a study of the manner in which the possessors of capital in France are
    said to employ reproduction and reconversion strategies to perpetuate their
    social hegemony, see Jane Marceau, *Class and Status in France: Economic
    Change and Social Immobility 1945-1975* (Oxford: Oxford University Press,
    1977); for the impact of charismatic leadership, see P. G. Cerny, *The Politics
    of Grandeur: Ideological Aspects of de Gaulle's Foreign Policy* (Cambridge:
    Cambridge University Press, 1980).

4   Of course, analogous processes can be discerned in political systems to which
    access is closed, but where organized factions, elites, apparats, etc., compete
    for control. Cf. Ghita Ionescu, *The Politics of the European Communist States*
    (London: Weidenfeld and Nicolson, 1967).

5   Indeed, minimal *definitions* of what constitutes a political party focus on their
    role of nominating candidates. Giovanni Sartori, *Parties and Party Systems:
    A Framework for Analysis*, Vol. I (Cambridge: Cambridge University Press,
    1976), pp. 58-64.

6   See Frank J. Sorauf, *Party Politics in America* (Boston, Mass.: Little, Brown,
    2nd edn. 1972).

7   With more or less success. With regard to Britain, see A. H. Birch, *Representa-
    tive and Responsible Government* (London: Allen and Unwin, 1964).

8   It is the success — or lack of success — of this process which underpins Eckstein's
    notion of the 'congruence' of authority structures; cf. Harry Eckstein, 'A
    Theory of Stable Democracy'; in *Division and Cohesion in Democracy: A
    Study of Norway* (Princeton, N.J.: Princeton University Press, 1966), apprendix.

9   See Annie Kriegel, *The French Communists* (Chicago: University of Chicago
    Press, 1972); that vital contributions can come from outside the 'normal'
    game structure is argued by Jack Hayward in 'Dissentient France: The Counter
    Political Culture'. *West European Politics*, Vol. I, No. 3 (October 1978),
    pp. 53-67.

10 This theoretical proposition is explored in more detail in the conference paper
    upon which this chapter is based and which was presented to the annual con-
    ference of the Political Studies Association of the United Kingdom, University
    of Sheffield, April 1979.

11 Giovanni Sartori, 'European Political Parties: The Case of Polarized Pluralism',
    in Joseph laPalombara and Myron Weiner, eds., *Political Parties and Political
    Development* (Princeton, N.J.: Princeton University Press, 1966), pp. 137-76.

12 See Robert Michels, *Political Parties: A Sociological Study of the Oligarchical
    Tendencies of Modern Democracy* (New York: Free Press, 1962, originally
    published 1911).

13   Joseph A. Schlesinger, 'Political Party Organization', in James G. March, ed., *Handbook of Organizations* (Chicago: Rnad McNally, 1965), pp. 764–801.

14   A further consequence of the differentiation of coalition arenas can be the privileging of certain types of *decision* in each different arena; consider Theodore J. Lowi's contention that in the United States, Congress seems to be the source of distributive decisions, whereas the presidency is the source of regulatory and redistributive decisions, in 'American Business, Public Policy, Case Studies, and Political Theory', *World Politics*, Vol. 16, No. 4 (July 1964), pp. 677–15.

15   Speech at Bayeux, 16 June 1946.

16   John Frears, 'Moderates and Others: Some Recent Books on the Centre and the Right in France', *West European Politics*, Vol. 1, No. 3 (October 1978), p. 156.

17   Although in a period of revolution or war he could use the emergency powers of Article 16. On the problem of autonomous presidential power cf. Maurice Duverger, *Échec au roi* (Paris: Albin Michel, 1978), Part II; Léo Hamon, *Une République présidentielle? Institutions et vie politique dans la France actuelle*, 2 vols. (Paris: Bordas, 1975 and 1977); Georges Burdeau, *Cours d'institutions politiques: la recherche de l'efficacité du pouvoir* (Paris: Cours de Droit, 1974); and Jean Gicquel, *Essai sur la pratique de la Ve République* (Paris: Librairie Générale de Droit et de Jurisprudence, 1968); etc.

18   Articles 34 and 38.

19   See Philip Williams, *The French Parliament 1958–1967* (London: Allen and Unwin, 1968).

20   See the debate between François Goguel and Georges Vedel: Goguel, 'Quelques remarques sur le problème des institutions politiques de la France', *Revue Française de Science Politique*, Vol. XIV, No. 1 (February 1964), pp. 7–19; and Vedel, 'Vers le régime présidentielle?', in ibid., pp. 20ff. Cf. Jean-Luc Parodi, *Les rapports entre le législatif et l'executif sous la Ve République* (Paris: Colin, 1972); Francis de Baecque, *Qui gouverne la France? Essai sur la repartition du pouvoir entre le chef de l'État et le chef du Gouvernement* (Paris: Presses Universitaires de France, 1976); and Alain Claisse, *Le Premier Ministre de la Ve République* (Paris: Librairie Générale de Droit et de Jurisprudence, 1972).

21   Duverger, *Échec au roi*, pp. 103–4.

22   See J. R. Frears and Jean-Luc Parodi, *War Will Not Take Place: The French Parliamentary Elections, March 1978* (London: C. Hurst, 1979), pp. 23–5.

23   Duverger, *Échec au roi*, pp. 120ff.

24   Maurice Duverger, *La Monarchie républicaine* (Paris: Laffont, 1974).

25   William H. Riker, *The Theory of Political Coalitions* (New Haven, Conn.: Yale University Press, 1962).

26   Cf. Sven Groennings, E. W. Kelly and Michael Leiserson, eds., *The Study of Coalition Behaviour: Theoretical Perspectives and Cases from Four Continents* (New York: Holt, Rinehart and Winston, 1970); and Abram de Swaan, *Coalition Theories and Cabinet Formations: A Study of Formal Theories of Coalition Formation Applied to Nine European Parliaments after 1918* (Amsterdam: Elsevier, 1973).

27   There is a provision which states that if one of the first two candidates withdraws, his place is taken by the next in line, and so on.

28   Jean-Luc Parodi, *La Ve République et le système majoritaire* (unpublished doctoral thesis, Fondation Nationale des Sciences Politiques, Paris 1973).

29   Frears and Parodi, *War Will Not Take Place*, pp. 67, 74 and 84.

30   Especially Jean Charlot, *The Gaullist Phenomenon: The Gaullist Movement in the Fifth Republic* (London: Allen and Unwin, 1971), and Duverger, *La Monarchie républicaine*.

31 Duverger, *Échec au roi*, part II.

32 However, the 'rules of the game' did have a marginally reductionist effect here too: a party list had to receive a minimum of 5 per cent of the votes cast in order to be eligible for a share of the seats.

3 Power and Its Possessors*

Jane Marceau

Power in a society is an attribute both of persons and of positions. If Poulantzas[1] is right, political power is not a special case of economic power and vice versa, but both are aspects of a total structure and of active class relationships. This, however, remains an abstract formulation. On the empirical level, it is difficult to assess access to 'power' by a thorough-going analysis of decisions made and imposed by those in positions (institutionalized or not) of power, and indeed this is not necessarily the best approach.[2] However, by examining the social composition of, and recruitment to, institutionalized power positions, one may deduce at a secondary level, if not necessarily in whose interests the system works over time and overall, who at least has the greatest probability of access to positions which seem to carry most weight in the making of public decisions in the widest sense of the word. This is the approach taken here.

Recruitment to institutionalized political power positions, namely to power as Members of Parliament and to positions in the high civil service, and to economic power positions in business, particularly manufacturing industry, necessarily involves some consideration of the linkages between the different aspects of the institutions of power, whether personal or positional; an essential aspect of power is that it is cumulative, while also being apparently refractive.

BUSINESS

Cadres supérieurs

Positions of power in the everyday affairs of modern French enterprises, at least the larger ones, were dispersed and held by numbers of delegates, senior executives, *cadres supérieurs*.

It is not always easy to distinguish possibilities of access to high-level positions, for many studies look simply at *cadres* and do not divide them into *cadres supérieurs* and *cadres moyens*. However, in some ways this emphasizes the limitations on access, for taking all the *cadres* together shows patterns which other evidence suggests were accentuated when only the *cadres supérieurs* are considered. Moreover, although their numbers grew fast with the economic growth of the post-1945 years and the increase in size of enterprise, they remained a small part of the √ total active population (1–2 per cent in 1968), and possibilities of access to such positions necessarily remained limited. Most important perhaps, the social origins of *cadres* remained limited. Writing early in the period, 1955, Jacquin suggested that then *cadres* were from families rising socially over (at least) one generation. However, he adds:

> the dispersion of the origins of the cadres should not create too many illusions . . . but means of access do exist. Of the two major ones, the first comes via the group of white-collar workers, technicians, and lower civil servants while the second via that of artisans and shop-keepers. The first group is most numerous in the fathers' generation where it outnumbers those of peasants and workers. The second, a very large group among the grandfathers, is a more important source of supply for recruitment to *cadre* positions and to members of the liberal and industrial professions.[3]

More recent work by Maurice and his colleagues[4] found that the fathers of 397 *ingénieurs* and *cadres* studied were distributed roughly by thirds; 31 per cent were from the *classes populaires*, 37 per cent from the *classes moyennes*, and 35 per cent from the *class supérieures*. There was, therefore, room for social mobility even in these very modern enterprises. On the other hand, two qualifications are necessary. First, precisely because a modern industry was 'modern', there were fewer fully trained people available, and the school system had not operated upon recruitment to the industry to its full extent. Secondly, *cadres* of all levels were put together, and examining only *cadres supérieurs* in the metallurgical industry, on the whole, the familiar differences reappear; the higher the level of the post, the higher were the educational diplomas required to fill it. The social recruitment of the schools conferring such diplomas, indicates the higher social origin of the *cadres*. Table 3.1, referring to the metallurgical industry and carried out by that industry's own leaders, shows the pattern clearly. It illustrates the preference for high-level diplomas in recruitment to high-level posts in an industry whose leaders claim that it is 'still today and indeed more than yesterday

an open profession'.[5] The concentration of certain diploma-holders
in certain positions is striking.   Thus, Polytechnique ('X') graduates constitute only 2 per cent of the *cadre* and *ingénieur* labour force in the
industry, but 36 per cent hold director (chief executive) posts, and a
further 11 per cent the highest administrative posts. There is a clear
hierarchy of diplomas for the top posts. Thus, while 36 per cent of *polytechnicien* graduates in the industry hold director jobs, only 22 per cent
of *centraliens* and 18 per cent of *mines* graduates do so. Nearly half the
polytechniciens are in the top two sets of posts but only 32 per cent
centraliens and 28 per cent *mines*. Below these top schools the situation
is even clearer, with only 11 per cent of alumni of the various Arts et
Métiers Institutes being Directors, 3 per cent of those from the Faculties
and 3 per cent of those promoted from the ranks, and respectively 5.5
per cent, 13 per cent, and 8 per cent for the top adminstrative positions.
The contrast is evident.

Table 3.1   Recruitment to cadre posts by diploma, 1970

Functions	Polytech. (2)	École des Mines (1)	Centrale Paris (3)	Arts et Metiers (7)	Faculties (3)	PST
Direction	36	18	22	11	3	3
Administration	11	10.5	10	5.5	13	8
Commercial	8	7	10	4	7	4.5
Technico-Commercial	7	6	10	5	9	4.5
Labs. – R & D	26	23	26	24	52	38
Production/ Maintenance	3	22	13	34	5.5	22.5
Means/Control/ Tests	6.5	10	6	13	7	15.5
Diverse	2	3	3	3	2.5	1
Total	100	100	100	100	100	100

Source: Table constructed from data given in Union des Industries Métallurgiques
et Minières, *Ingénieurs et Cadres*, 1970: 40–7. Figures in brackets are the percentages from these schools in *cadre* and *ingénieur* positions in the industry. PST =
Promotion sociale du travail.

Referring to *cadre* recruitment as well as success in other fields, Girard
concluded:

Birth into a favourable milieu is a very useful trampolin if not a completely indispensable one for high-level success. If privilege is abolished
in law, French society has substituted for it a certain number of selective

tests, examinations, and *concours* which presuppose study up to the highest level. The great majority of the 'personalities' observed, 85 per cent, have followed such study and have been able to do it because they belong to a milieu where that is the rule.[6]

Ten years later, Benguigui and Monjardet writing about French *cadres* in the 1960s, could only come to the same conclusions, summarized in the following sentence: 'Those ruling business, the *cadres dirigeants*, are recruited from *ingénieurs* trained in the *Grandes Écoles*; the pupils of the *Grandes Écoles* spring from the ruling class'.[7]

Business leaders: owners and 'assimilated'[8]

The most important power-holders, because they control the crucial elements of the economic system, are the owners of businesses themselves. To them may be added those who in joint-stock companies frequently hold effective power, the chief executives, PDG (*Présidents Directeurs Généraux*), and other top managers, *cadres dirigeants*, 'assimilated' to ownership positions.[9]

An early study, carried out in the late 1950s, by Delefortrie-Soubeyroux gives a picture which may be used for comparative purposes. The study, based on a sample of 5,000 *cadres dirigeants* (of whom 2,947 returned usable questionnaires) mentioned in yearbooks such as *Who's Who in France 1953–54*, showed that men who were themselves sons of leaders of industry (*dirigeants*) constituted 27 per cent of the sample and 41 per cent of all the known professions, (not all the respondents answered that question). Of all the professions attached to industry they formed 35 per cent of the sample and 52 per cent of the known professions. The other social origins were concentrated in the upper echelons of the society, for the industrial leaders were the sons of high civil servants, parliamentarians, diplomats, and members of the liberal professions. In short, the majority of the *dirigeants* studied in the mid-fifties came from the bourgeoisie.

A study of 2,000 'personalities' in the *Dictionnaire biographique français contemporain* (1954–56), supplemented by a sub-sample from four of the major *Grandes Écoles* and another from among Paris University professors, showed that (the origins of) the personalities observed were very limited. Their recruitment was by no means left to chance. Accession to (high) posts and even more to fame or 'success' as generally only possible for men born in the highest groups on the social scale. Five per cent of the sample had fathers who were *cadres supérieurs*, 17 per cent *chefs d'entreprises*, 22 per cent in the liberal professions, and 23 per cent high civil servants. 'Such a distribution appears diametrically opposed to the professional distribution within the population as a whole' and 'more than 68 per cent of contemporary personalities are recruited from 5 per cent of the population, or 81 per cent from 15 per cent'. Because success there depends more on special 'gifts' than on success in the institutions of education, widest recruitment was found among personalities in sports, politics, religion, arts, and letters. On the contrary, recruitment to the civil service, industry, and business, those for which family and education were important, was narrowest.[11]

That the situation changed little in the 1960s was confirmed by a much later study. In the mid-1960s three teachers at the Institut Européen d'Administration des Affaires (INSEAD), carried out a study of the PDG of the 500 bigger French companies in 1966–7.

Table 3.2   Social origins of the leaders of French industry, 1966–67: percentages

Professional Origins	Fathers	Grandfathers	Fathers-in-law
Head of Enterprises*	42	25.5	31
Liberal Professions	20	21	27
Executives**	15	7	13.5
Shopkeepers***	7.5	9	7
Civil Servants****	6	6	10
Working Classes†††	11	31	9

   * *Chefs d'entreprise*.
  ** *Cadres*, including civil servants in senior and middle-level posts.
 *** *Commerçants*, including both large and small.
**** *Fonctionnaires*, civil servants other than those above.
††† White-collar and manual workers, farmers and artisans.
Source: Hall and de Bettignies, 1968. 2–5.

As the authors themselves admit, nearly three out of four PDGs were sons of the 'upper- and upper-middle classes'.[12] Only 10 per cent were born in the 'working-classes', including therein artisans and farmers, half of the total. Over 40 per cent of the PDG has fathers who were themselves business leaders and 50 per cent had grandfathers who belong to the upper classes; indeed one-quarter of the grandfathers were also chief executives, so that one in four came from at least two generations of men at the top in the business world. The tendency to social closure was reinforced by marriage within similar social circles.

Comparing these findings with the situation in other European countries — Germany, Italy, Britain, Belgium, and the Netherlands — Hall and de Bettignies conclude that 'France appears to have the most rigid society of all the countries in our study. Over 85 per cent of [French] chief executives come from the upper social class and less than 3 per cent from the lower.' Interestingly, French PDG were also the oldest and the most highly educated in terms of diplomas held.[13]

Other, later, studies confirmed the major conclusions of Hall and de Bettignies. Studying the PDG of the 300 and 100 biggest French firms in 1972, Bourdieu and his colleagues found the expected link between social origins and education, but also suggested the link between changes in recruitment of business élite to changes in the economic structure and the mode of ownership and control of enterprises.[14]

THE CENTRAL ADMINISTRATION OF THE STATE

Senior Civil Servants

Senior civil servants are both instruments and sources of power. In France, this duality is assured, not only by the particularities of recruitment to senior posts in the civil service, but also the personal, as opposed to positional, links between them and business through *pantouflage* – movement from a high civil service post to a similar one in industry and commerce.

Governmental instability under the Fourth Republic led many French observers to consider whether the country was really ruled by senior civil servants, rather than its elected representatives, and a good deal of the early work on the *hauts fonctionnaires* concentrated on that question. It seems highly likely that at least during that period the higher civil servants formed an important part of the policy-making area of government, a position probably strengthened under the Fifth Republic because of the presidential nature of the regime and the deliberate bypassing, at least under de Gaulle, of deputies and senators. Indeed, since ministers did not have to be elected, some civil servants became ministers. In 1974, for instance, Giscard d'Estaing chose Simone Weil, then a highly competent magistrate in the Ministry of Justice, to be Minister of Public Health. Moreover, an accepted part of the promotion ladder for young and gifted civil servants was a period in the *cabinets ministériels*, the small groups of advisors around each minister. But such opportunities were not open to all.

The Grands Fonctionnaires

The Civil Service contained many levels, with personnel recruited in different ways. Gournay estimated *hauts fonctionnaires* to number between 3,000 and 10,000 persons, depending on definition. The *grands fonctionnaires*, however, were numbered in hundreds rather than thousands, and occupied the top posts in the *grands corps*, the dominant sections in the different ministries, arranged in a hierarchy of power and prestige, and culminating in the controlling body within the Finance Ministry, the *Inspecteurs des Finances*.[15]

After 1945 recruitment to the senior parts of the civil service was via a special school, the École Nationale d'Administration (ENA), created at the Liberation to try to ensure a wider social representation among members of the *grands corps*, to 'democratize access' to state administration.[16] Entry to ENA was through two different competitive examinations (*concours*), one for students and a minor one for members of the junior grades of the civil service.

Theoretically the *concours* were open to all students holding a higher diploma, but in practice to succeed it was virtually necessary to have studied the Section Administration Publique for the Institut d'Études Politiques (IEP) in Paris, the ex-'Sciences Po', which was a major training ground for high public servants before 1939.

ENA

First, then, recruitment to ENA. In 1951–52 Bottomore carried out a study on the social origins of students at ENA between 1945 and 1951, and compared them with those of candidates to the school. He found that candidates from the higher social origins had greater success rates than those of lower social origins – a phenomenon common to all the Grandes Écoles in the 1960s. Of the accepted students, 65 per cent came from the upper classes (23 per cent were sons of industrialists and members of the liberal professions, 42 per cent sons of senior civil servants and *cadres*), 28 per cent from the *classes moyennes* (11 per cent artisans and shop-keepers, 17 per cent lower civil servants and white-collar workers) and only 3 per cent from the working classes all of whom were the sons of skilled workers, and 4 per cent from the farming community.[17]

Democratization of public service through ENA was totally ineffective. Fifteen years later Bourdieu and his colleagues found almost identical proportions – 8 per cent from the *classe populaire*, nearly 30 per cent from the middle classes, and over 60 per cent from the upper classes.[18]

There is even some evidence that recruitment from ENA to the *grands corps* increased the proportion from high social origins from 55.5 per cent to over 60 per cent,[19] although it decreased professional heredity in the more limited sense, in that there were fewer sons of senior civil servants. The social origins of ENA students necessarily formed the social origins of an increasing ˙part of those of members of the *grands corps* and the central administrations as the students moved on to fill these places.

The ministries and the different functions within them themselves formed a hierarchy and each ministry offered places according to the *rang de sortie*, the over-all position in the final examinations of the students. Thus, the Inspection des Finances offered places to the top few and so on down the list, while the diplomatic corps, the 'career', had sometimes − to its shame − 'to go down almost to the middle'.[20] The technical ministries were nearer the lower end. The top students, thus, had a wide choice of career offers, the choice becoming progessively more and more limited as the *rang de sortie* went down. There is, moreover, reason to suppose that those who did best while at ENA and who, therefore, went into the most prestigious ministries, were those from the higher social origins.

The order of prestige in the 1970s was the same as that before the war; by descending order, Inspection des Finances, Conseil d'État, Cour des Comptes, the Civil Administration Ministries, and, indeed, it may have been becoming more rigid. Once inside, chances of moving 'up' to another *corps* remained virtually non-existent and the hierarchy of prestige was reflected even in salaries.[21] In their earlier book, Darbel and Schnapper pointed out that

> civil servants whose fathers belonged to the 'popular' classes, constitute 9.5 per cent of the 'external' services [i.e. not the central administration] 10 per cent of the central administration, and only 5.5 per cent of the *grands corps*, the *corps de contrôle*, and the technical *corps* . . . Civil servants from middle-class origins are mainly to be found in the central administration (39.5 per cent), external services (39.5 per cent), and 30 per cent in technical *corps*, 26 per cent in the *corps de contrôle*, and 18 per cent in the *grands corps*. [On the other hand] civil servants from the upper classes constitute 76.5 per cent of the *grands corps*, 67.5 per cent of the *corps de contrôle*, 63.5 per cent of the technical *corps*, and only 50 per cent of the external services and 47.5 per cent of the Central Administration corps.[22]

As the same authors said earlier:

> It is in the Social Ministries (14 per cent) and Education (13.5 per cent) that the fraction of higher officials from working-class origins is highest; then in the technical (7 per cent) and controlling (*régaliens*) (6 per cent) . . . it is in the Ministry of Finance (5.5 per cent) and the services of the Prime Minister's office (2 per cent) that they are lowest.[23]

Working-class representation in all ministries remained extemely feeble, and that of the middle class only slightly less so. When they were present at all, these classes were mostly to be found in the less powerful ministries and almost never in the services of the Prime Minister's offices. The same was true of opportunities to be even advisers to other ministers.[24]

L'Inspection des Finances

The first choice of the best graduates from ENA (and often from Polytechnique) was the Inspection des Finances, that small body of men who controlled the working of major sectors of the French economy, particularly the nationalized industries, and oversaw the working of ministries and other official organisms. They were *par excellence grands fonctionnaires* in all senses of the phrase. Constituting the most powerful body within the high civil service, they formed the major links between government and administration and the world of business. Because of their key position it is essential to examine membership of the Inspection.

Writing in 1953 Charles Brindillac remarked that of the forty crucial economic direction positions in the administration, thirty-five were occupied by members of the Inspection, and they were the most important in the State. In 1952 there were seventeen attached to the Pinay government and at the same time they controlled fifteen financial organisms, including the big banks. A further forty-five could be found running other public enterprises. Brindillac concludes:

> Thus, it is that above 3,000 or 4,000 senior administrators who form the high *cadres* of the public service but who rarely rise to control the 'command levers', there emerges an oligarchy composed of men who have passed similar *concours*, after receiving the same training, and who are linked by the solidarity of the *corps*.[25]

What were the social origins of this group? Basing himself on the work of the American Jesse Pitts, Brindillac shows the pre-war preponderance of the aristocracy and *haute bourgeoisie*, followed by the *bonne bourgeoisie*

and, far behind, the *moyenne* and *petite bourgeoisie*; the first two categories provided sixty out of the 112 Inspecteurs recruited between 1919
and 1939, while the last two groups only produced twenty. During the
post-war period the predominance of the higher levels of the upper classes
dropped in favour of an equalization of representation of all categories
of the bourgeoisie.[26] This, however, appears to have been the limit of
'democratization'.

In a study later in the 1950s Lalumière, confirming the narrow recruitment of the *Inspecteurs*, added that over the previous eighty-five
years nearly half, approximately 40 per cent of the *Inspecteurs* had been
Parisians, of whom two-thirds came from the 6th, 7th, 8th, and 16th
arrondissements alone. Thirty-five per cent of the most powerful body
in the Central Administration was recruited from 1 per cent of the French
population. Important family traditions were involved in entry to the
Inspection; the biggest contingent of fathers was that of *haut fonctionnaires*. Between 1919 and 1954, thirty-five of the 260 *Inspecteurs* (13
per cent) joined their fathers there.[27]

After 1947, two-thirds of the sixty-eight *Inspecteurs* recruited through
ENA came from the highest social strata — the aristocracy, the *haute
bourgeoisie* of industry and banking, and the liberal professions, senior
civil servants, and *cadres*. There were no representatives of the working
class (including farmers in that term), although there were 27 per cent
from artisan and commercial families. The major beneficiaries of the
creation of ENA were the children of the *petite bourgeoisie* — a reflection
of the educational expansion throughout the 1950s and 1960s. Nevertheless, high-level business and administration family names frequently
recurred, although this was less the case in the 1950s than it was before
1939. Members of the Inspection des Finances retained considerable
links via their families of origin with major sectors of the economy and
it was they who most often left public service to go into private or
nationalized business.

POLITICS

Political Leaders and Quasi-leaders

The third 'Pillar of Power' is the most directly political. Who is it who
makes, or at least has formal responsibility for, the central policy decisions,
those embodied in laws? Whether the under-developed state of research
in France on deputies and senators, their professional and social origins,

and attachments to different sectors of the community, reflects the low level of importance accorded to Parliament by the Government is not clear, but there exist few major studies of the legislators as a group over the years of the post-war period.

On the other hand, much has been written on electors and on the electoral geography of the nation at each time of voting, showing, for instance, that voting alignments changed very little in France between the early 1900s and the late 1960s (except in exceptional times such as 1936, 1945 and 1968). Although the names and the number of the parties changed, political tendencies and the positions of electors on the political spectrum remained stable, only sliding occasionally slightly to the right or to the left and perhaps accepting for the time new alliances, as in the short-lived Rassemblement du Peuple Français started by de Gaulle in the late 1940s. Occasionally, threatened groups expressed anger in times of rapid economic change, creating movements such as Poujadism in the early 1950s. Links between social position, religious convictions, and voting behaviour remained important, and the left-wing parties were well entrenched in Paris, other industrial cities, and industrial regions and the south-west, while the right gathered most votes in the predominantly rural areas of Brittany and the east, with the centre having basic support in the Centre and prosperous rural areas and smaller towns and cities.

Deputies and senators 'represent' these interests in Parliament. Major studies of deputies were carried out by Mattei Dogan in the 1950s and early 1960s. Examining first the social and professional origins of deputies elected during the Third and Fourth Republics, and later extending his studies to include persons who stood as candidates but who were not elected, Dogan covered more than 4,000 deputies in the Third Republic. Some of these studies are available in English, and the data are presented here in greatly abridged form.

Changes of parliamentary personnel were extremely slow, and would have been even slower if, during the period, 650 deputies had not died, 938 moved to the Senate, and 100 resigned. Although half the 4,300 deputies elected during the Third Republic ended their careers in electoral defeat (voting alignments were stable, but many were elected on margins of less than 10 per cent), many were elected for very long periods. Indeed, just under 500 deputies (one-ninth) had between them around 12,000 years of parliamentary time and sat in between five and twelve parliaments, each holding their seats twenty years at least, and often a quarter or a third of a century or more. Excluding the extraordinary circumstances of the first and last two legislatures of the Third Republic, two-fifths of the deputies were elected between three and ten times.[28] There were thus considerable opportunities for certain voices to be heard. Under the Fourth Republic (1945–58), itself a much shorter period, the duration of mandates was also very much shorter. However, nearly half of the deputies were elected between three and five times. Unfortunately, Dogan's study does not examine tenure of office under the Third Republic by party affiliation.

Representatives and Represented

While deputies may have represented the different sections of the nation in terms of defending their interests, their socio-professional origins show the different strata unequally represented; indeed, the greater the proportion of a group in the total population, the smaller was its representation in the Chamber of Deputies, and vice versa.

Table 3.3 reveals two important phenomena. First is the numerical importance of what Dogan calls the 'intellectual professions', teachers, journalists, doctors, and lawyers principally, with a few engineers, architects, and senior government officials. The teachers were concentrated in the Communist and Socialist parties, while the lawyers were concentrated in the radicals and moderates, although there were also a number on the socialist Left. The reasons for the predominance of intellectuals included local importance (especially for teachers and doctors) and a less clear association with particular interests, enabling them to present themselves as representing either a wide variety of interests or no particular interests but those of the French 'people' and public well-being.

Only one-fifth of the deputies were from the working class, including in that the lowest levels of the civil service, and only 12 per cent were, before election, manual workers. Moreover, the latter were mainly constituted of union officials, often from the major unions, and had long since ceased to exercise manual professions. *Cadres*, shop-keepers, and industrialists together formed 10 per cent of the deputies, although their numerical importance in the total population was much smaller, but the striking fact, Dogan suggests, is that the Fourth Republic was the reign of the middle and lower-middle class. 'After the Republic of the Dukes came the Republic of notables, after the Republic of the upper-middle class there came . . . the reign of the middle and lower middle class'.[29] The 'reigning' personnel became separated from the 'ruling' groups. There is some evidence that under the Fifth Republic there was no further enlargement of the social base, and with the decline of the Communist party until elections in the 1970s there may even

Table 3.3   Original occupation of deputies in metropolitan France 1945–58

Professions	CP	Socialists	MRP	Radicals	Mods. Indeps.	RPF and 'Gaullists'	Extreme Right and Poujad.	Unclassifiable	Total	%
Cadres	4	9	14	4	7	2	1	3	43	
Merchants & shopkeeprs	1	2	15	5	6	6	29	–	64	16
Industrialists etc.	–	2	9	14	16	18	6	3	68	
Engineers and architects	4	5	11	8	9	8	–	9	54	
High public officials	3	4	9	8	6	7	1	4	42	
Lawyers	2	28	25	28	38	11	2	8	142	
Doctors/Pharms.	3	13	15	13	8	10	3	–	65	48
Journalists	5	19	17	12	6	2	1	2	64	
Professors, 2e and higher	12	35	21	13	7	7	–	4	99	
Primary school teachers	29	32	1	3	–	–	1	1	66	
Farmers	29	10	29	11	40	12	–	5	136	12
Subordinate pub. officials	7	15	5	3	1	–	–	–	31	
White-collar workers	37	16	19	2	–	–	–	1	71	21
Manual workers	99	11	21	–	1	1	–	–	133	
Army and eccles.	1	–	3	1	6	6	–	1	18	
Women, no profes.	11	1	2	–	1	1	–	–	16	3
Total	246	198	216	124	152	91	44	41	1112	100
% distribution	22	18	20	11	14	8	4	3	100%	

Source: Slightly adapted from Dogan, 1961:67.

CP = Communist Party   MRP = Mouvement Républicain Populaire   RPF = Rassemblement du Peuple Français

The Socialists were composed of the Section Française de l'Internationale Ouvrière (SFIO) and the Independent Socialists.

have been some narrowing. It would also be useful to know how length of parliamentary service varied according to the social origins of deputies as well as according to their party affiliation.

More detailed information on candidates shows that chances of election as well as final representation were highly dependent on social origins: 'The most numerous social categories, which are also the least privileged of the nation, provide fewest candidates'.[30] There were almost no women. The average of one elected for seven candidates hid important differential chances of election by socio-professional origins. 'List dosing' by many parties — that is, presenting candidates from different social groups to 'balance its image' — enlarged the apparent social base: right-wing parties put up workers, and all parties put up farmers (included on nine-tenths of all lists except in the Seine *département*), but placed them so low down on the lists as to have virtually no chance of election. Only the Communist party ensured some worker representation.

No workers were first or second on RPF lists, and only one worker was elected for the RPF, which gives some indications of the nature of the 'people' de Gaulle assembled in his party. Even within the working class, as was suggested above, not all sections were equally represented. 'The political potential of workers working in the very concentrated [i.e. very important] industries is greater than that of those belonging to medium-sized industries'.[31] Of the forty-nine worker MPs, thirty-four came from big industries which only occupied one-third of all French workers, principally from four *départements*. For other categories the reverse was true: not only were they 'over-represented' among the candidates, but a far greater proportion were elected. For instance, one lawyer in thirty-nine was a candidate (one in fourteen if one considers only male lawyers), and constituted the proportion of one in eight deputies against one in seventeen candidates, although lawyers only formed half of one per cent of the electoral body.

Deputies and Ministers

Although during the Fourth Republic Parliament carried considerable weight, cabinet ministers represented government power and at least initiated policy. Unexpectedly, in comparison with the Fifth Republic, there was considerable ministerial stability, even though the Governments nominally were unseated. Who had the greatest chances of becoming ministers and thus of having most influence on policy is an important question.

Some deputies accumulated power; twenty-seven deputies had previously been in the top levels of the civil service, and at least sixteen of these had, before becoming deputies, spent long periods in ministerial cabinets, and so were well experienced in political decision-making and had a number of high-level contacts within the civil service, where they had held posts in the most important sections. Of these six had been in the Conseil d'État, two in the Cour des Comptes, five had been diplomats, three were *Inspecteurs des Finances*, three *Inspecteurs Généraux* in the Central Administration, three *Préfets*, and so on. A third of all senior civil servant candidates were elected and of these thirteen held ministerial posts. Similarly, one-third of the doctors and one-half of all the lawyers became ministers (before or after 1951). Thirty-eight barristers became ministers or secretaries of State. Amongst them, six became *Présidents du Conseil*, including such well-known figures as Paul Reynaud, Robert Schumann, Edgar Faure, and Pierre Mendès-France. Other lawyers became important party leaders, president of parliamentary groups, and indeed President of the Republic (Auriol and Coty). By contrast, only four shop-keepers and deputies and only six worker deputies, all communists, acquired ministerial functions. University teachers stood a better chance of becoming ministers — and they were from higher social origins — than did the lower-grade teachers.

It is evident, therefore, that access to the higher levels of political power remained open very unevenly to different social groups, at least in terms of direct representation. Possibilities of access to power remained as systematically patterned as did those within other parts of the opportunity structure.

Dogan's studies of the social and professional backgrounds of deputies and of the paths leading to the holding of political office were carried out in the 1950s. Later studies showed the situation to have remained virtually unchanged.

A major study was carried out by the Centre d'Étude de la Vie Politique Française Contemporaine of the Fondation Nationale des Sciences Politiques in 1969–70 on the social and professional origins of the deputies, and examined how and at what age they had first become interested in politics and the political paths (*filières*) which led them to stand for office and be elected. It showed systematic variations by party on almost all the dimensions in question, with parties on the left and right being most homogeneous and those in the middle, and particularly the composite Gaullist UDR, being most heterogeneous.

Many deputies came from families with strong political interests. More than half (56 per cent), had a father who carried out political functions, a quarter had a grandfather in politics. A fifth had another near relative, such as mother or uncle and 13 per cent had both a father and a grand-father who were active politically. Politicians thus tended to be drawn from political families, were political 'specialists'.

In the late 1960s, therefore, 79 per cent of the previous professions of the deputies placed them in the well-off sections of the population, with 11 per cent being industrialists, 28 per cent members of the liberal professions, 21 per cent *cadres supérieurs*, and 5 per cent shop-keepers (3 per cent large-scale merchants), while only 13 per cent came from lower on the social scale and had previously been manual or white-collar workers and technicians (5 per cent in all), or primary-school teachers, artisans, or *cadres moyens* (8 per cent).

A similar situation was shown by family origins: thus, 25 per cent of the Républicains Indépendants (RI) were from the dominant classes, while 13 per cent of the PDM,[32] 20 per cent of the Radicals, and only 4 per cent of the Socialists were so (and no Communists).

It is clear, then, that under the Fifth Republic there occurred little widening of the socio-professional basis for recruitment to elected political office; indeed there was some narrowing.

> The proportion of persons in the Palais Bourbon belonging to the *catégories dirigeantes* has been growing; the increase is particularly clear when one compares the deputies of the present majority party (UDR and Républicains Indépendants) who were first elected under the Third and Fourth Republics, and those who have been elected since the beginning of the Fifth Republic. The progression can further be seen in comparison between those elected in the elections of 1967 and 1968.[33]

The party which subsequently produced the current President, Valéry Giscard d'Estaing, the Républicains Indépendants, in terms of the back-grounds of the deputies, represented the most traditional, Catholic (practising), Parisian fractions of the bourgeoisie and had close links with the highest levels of industry, banking, and commerce.[34] Only in the left-wing parties, especially the Communist party, were worker deputies in the majority, and only there was there a majority of members with considerable numbers of men from humble social origins.

The social patterning of access to the upper levels of power also re-mained strong under the Fifth Republic. Ministers tended to be of higher social origins than the ensemble of parliamentary personnel. An American observer, E. Lewis, analysing the occupational and educational back-grounds of ministers between 1944 and 1967 shows that ministers through-out the period were a cross-section of the upper bourgeoisie; most were lawyers (58), civil servants (41), industrialists and directors of corporations (40), and teachers (34) (1970: 566). These four categories accounted for 63 per cent of all ministers after 1944 and 76 per cent of all ministers under de Gaulle. Adding doctors, engineers, and career officers to the above professions accounts for 86 per cent of all Gaullist ministers; industrial workers only accounted for 3 per cent and farm workers 4 per cent. Of ministers over the period, only 14 per cent (out of the 87 per cent known) had less than university education, and the ministers included twelve *polytechniciens*, twelve *normaliens*, and forty-three graduates of Sciences Politiques, graduates of the most prestigious and bourgeois Grandes Écoles.[35]

Further information on the composition of the other elected body, the Senate (indirect election by electoral colleges), and the departmental administration (*conseils généraux*) would be useful; the Senate had the reputation of being more conservative than the Chamber of Deputies and of holding up legislation it disapproved. Unfortunately, such studies are few, as are those of local government, elections to *conseils municipaux*, and of mayors.

One short study on the Senate, however, does make the important point that

> the stability of the electoral regime of the Senate has as a direct result the stability of its political colouring and its personal composition . . . The High Assembly is renewed by one-third every three years . . . and therefore, is not subject to radical changes. Except in 1879, 1885, and 1909 the [electoral] colleges have always re-elected two-thirds of the previous members.[36]

As Le Reclus points out, senators must be more than forty years old and tend to be the 'enemies of abstract deductions and "adventures" in all domains, especially the financial and social.'

Under the Fifth Republic, the Senate was composed of men from the professions listed in Table 3.4. The majority of senators were also the mayors of small *communes*, showing the representation of the people at that level as well. In both these political spheres, Senate and *communes*, there was an important 'over-representation' of members from the liberal professions and, particularly in the Senate, from rural areas.

Tremendous social inertia could be seen in the stability of election of the *conseillers généraux* (who formed the electoral colleges of the Senate). Between 1945 and 1964 the number of *conseillers généraux* re-elected each time was never less than 65 per cent, and in 1964 more than one-third of them had been in power constantly since the Liberation,

Table 3.4   Social origins of Senators

Profession	*Percentage*	
Liberal professions	27 (of which 11 per cent are lawyers)	
Farmers	23.5	
Industrial/commercial professions	16	
Cadres supérieurs (including senior civil servants)	13	
Teachers	9	(4 per cent high-level)
White-collar workers/cadres moyens	8	
Workers	3	

Source: Le Reclus, 1969: 56.

showing not only the entrenchment (*enracinement*) of the political class but also, through the apathy of the electors seen in massive abstentionism, the total incapacity of the system to select new élites[37] Many *conseillers généraux* were also mayors, and as such the lowest level in the administrative hierarchy, spending at least as much time implementing government decisions as passing upwards the wishes of their electors.

THE POWERS AROUND THE THRONE

Analysis of recruitment to positions of power in two of the major institutions of the State, the high civil service and the legislature, and to the major areas of the private economic sector, shows the limited origins of personnel, mainly from the Parisian bourgeoisie, either major or minor.

It is therefore important to assess the extent to which the personnel emanating from these major groups were linked together, thus joining groups within these power institutions, whether or not they were linked outside them. It has been argued that it is not sufficient to demonstrate similarity of social origins in order to prove that a 'ruling class' exists; some demonstration of common purpose is also required.[38] Such demonstration would involve an analysis of major decisions, and some attempts have been made at this by French political scientists, although these have not been conclusive. Regardless of common purpose, certain sections of the population manifestly had and continued to have greater or lesser access to important decision-making posts. The most important of the mechanisms behind such limitation was the education system which selected young people at an early age but after that ceased to operate directly as other forces, in part caused and in part justified by and justifying it, entered the arena.

Overlapping Personnel

Powerful persons may be linked together through the overlapping of personnel, through their social contacts (reinforced through marriage in particular), and through the symbolic (cultural) factors encouraging the cohesion of the group. The separation is an artificial one — in reality all are aspects of the same phenomenon. Whether in politics, administration, or business personal linkages tend towards the closure of the ruling groups.

Civil Service and Business

In the late 1950s *pantouflage* from positions in the high civil service to top posts in industry and commerce became more and more common. By the use of the *mise en disponibilité* and detachment, as many as 50 per cent, over the previous eighty years, of the *Inspecteurs* left the central administration after ten to twelve years' service, the rate varying somewhat with economic circumstances. It was especially those who had family links with the upper echelons of the private sector who moved, and the latest resignations seemed to confirm that trend, for twenty-nine of the thirty-four leaving in the late 1950s were cited in the Bottin Mondain, the French equivalent of the Social Register. Family links meant rapid introduction to important posts in business life, and constituted the best of recommendations. Indeed, it is possible that certain *Inspecteurs* already had a place reserved for them in big firms before even going into the civil service, and their experience in the administration was simply their 'apprenticeship' for their private business career.[39]

Such movements were into the most important and dynamic sectors of the economy and to the crucial nationalized industries, above all important merchant banks, metallurgy, chemicals, and cars. Directing the nation's most important financial organs, the *Inspecteurs* formed part of the 'capitalist oligarchy'. In great majority they joined boards of directors, and, although sometimes beginning as *cadres supérieurs* (especially those with no family connections), this was usually brief.

The internal coherence of the *Inspecteurs* as a group was assured by a number of factors. In the early days of a career similar backgrounds and similar education, if not the same graduation class (*promotion*) in the same school of *préparation*, were paramount factors of solidarity. At work, the group of *Inspecteurs* was fairly small, facilitating close contacts and identification, and within it even smaller groups and closer links were formed in the *tournées* (rounds) of the early career, where everal inspectors toured the provinces to carry out financial controls on the different administrative organs and spent much time exclusively n each other's company.[40] The central administration's link with politics springs from its very unction, but certain members were more closely involved than others. Many men from the highest social origins served in ministerial cabinets and became deputies or ministers themselves.[41] Useful to business because hey knew intimately both the central organization's rules and methods and, no less important, how to get around them, ex-civil servants also held an important amount of social capital (*relations*) as they retained many contacts with persons still in office, in their own branch of central government and in many others. Further their previous education in one of the *écoles du pouvoir* (Polytechnique, HEC, ENA, etc.) forced links of camaraderie, both potential and actual, with members of the *promotion* who followed different career paths.

Business and Politics

mportant sections of business were well represented in terms of families of deputies under the Third Republic and the reign of the *grand bourgeoisie*. In the nineteenth and twentieth centuries, under the Third Republic, State and business were inextricably interlinked. Studies of the origin of the French *patronat* show the closeness of the business, banking, and political careers of the major figures of the nineteenth century — for example the Périer brothers, the Méquillet-Noblot family, and the de Wendel family, as well, of course, as such international families as the Rothschilds (in whose bank Georges Pompidou held high office before going into politics under General de Gaulle). Members of the de Wendel family, owners and managers of a giant metallurgical firm, have always been attentive to their relations with the government, and were to be found in Parliament, as deputies and senators, throughout the nineteenth century and in the twentieth until the Second World War.[42] According to Priouret, the family controlled the elections in their *département*, and Robert Schumann was 'their' deputy in Meurthe-et-Moselle from 1919 to 1936 inclusive. They were the counsellors of political leaders of the time and one de Wendel, a friend of Poincaré, was also *régent* of the Banque of France, whence he precipitated the financial crisis in 1926 that brought Poincaré back to power.

After the Liberation the French *patronat* reorganized. The American political sociologist Henry Ehrmann wrote that, after 1947, the CNPF (equivalent of the Confederation of British Industry) moved close to open support for de Gaulle's right-wing movement, the Rassemblement du Peuple Français. Because of the low electoral pull of big business, influence over the *rapporteurs* of the powerful standing committees seems to have been especially cultivated. The *rapporteurs*, suggests Ehrmann, seem to have had more faith in private sources of information than the Government ones,[43] and he quotes Williams's conclusion that such committees soon became the 'institutional façade for the operation of pressure groups'. Business interests, however, were still directly represented. In a rather polemical work, *Les Français qui mènent le monde*,[44] Coston lists some of the business interests of the Fourth Republic's ministers. From one cabinet alone fourteen ministers are listed with extensive business interests in almost all sectors of the French economy, banking, metallurgy, the electrical industry, agricultural implements, and oil, to which should be added many overseas interests, especially in the French colonies, such as mining and transport. Even under the socialist government of Pierre Mendès-France business interests were important, although not usually so open. Although there is little direct evidence, there is indirect evidence that under the Fifth Republic links between business and politics seen in direct representation increased.

Business and Business

Business is the most dispersed and in some sense heterogeneous of all powerful groups. Recruitment studies showed the similar social origins of major business leaders and their passage through élite schools, creating strong relationships of camaraderie.[45] Apparently distinct businesses were linked by holding companies and organized into 'groups'. The number of these concentrations from the mid-1950s onwards grew fast, with a consequent diminution in the number of leaders.

A study by J. Houssiaux on the 100 biggest French firms in 1952 showed 998 known financial links between them, of which 27 link firms within the group of 100 . . . Certain sectors are the field of an intense control activity: 150 financial links for one firm in the group in the glass industry, 45 links within the group of 100 for the 352 metal transformation companies, and financial links are further reinforced through the merchant banks. The accounts of the twelve big merchant banks show 677 links, of which 75 are between firms within the hundred . . . If to the financial links one adds the personal links, which permit a more or less direct control of the boards of directors (*Conseils d'Administration*), one discovers that the internal consistency of the group is greater by far . . . 975 Directors belonging to the firms in the group between them formed 3120 personal links between different companies, and there are 473 interlinkages within the group of 100. The average number of links per firm is therefore 31.2 and per director 4.73. As for the financial links, there are important differences between the sectors; mining and the glass industries are in the lead, with paper and the press last. With 1124 personal links, the 348 directors of the 35 firms in the metal transformation industry contribute greatly to the consistency and density of the network along whose channels circulate information, suggestions (*injonctions*), and commands.[46]

Examining *La Structure financière du capitalisme français*, François Morin shows the powerful groupings which grew up throughout the 1960s, in particular alongside the traditional control of even many big businesses by single families. Half of the two hundred biggest French companies were still family controlled in the early 1970s and of the biggest twenty, six were family controlled. The remainder, and many others of slightly lesser stature, were increasingly linked into groups of companies, often dominated by banking and finance houses. For example, 103 firms were linked together in Pechiney-Ugine-Kuhlman, 113 in CGE and, through the group, to banks such as Paribas (Banque de Paris et des Pays-Bas) in the CGE case. Within these groups, and between many of the groups, there existed important links in the form of overlapping directorates and especially links between the *grands fonctionnaires* and the major banking groups. For instance, examining the composition of the Conseils d'Administration of the companies Paribas and Suez (Compagnie Financière de Suez), Morin says,

> one cannot avoid noticing the dominant share held by ex-senior civil servants (*grands commis de l'État*). By *grands commis de l'État* we mean persons who, by virtue of their past (or present) duties, occupied for many years (or still occupy) posts of responsibility at the highest level in the state's administrative apparatus. This is particularly the case of the Inspecteurs des Finances, who by their training have access to the highest economic and financial responsibilities.

He adds: 'in June 1974 there were five Inspecteurs des Finances in the Conseil d'Administration of Suez and six in Paribas; where they held all the major *direction* posts.[47]

Further, amongst a wider range of the major financial-industrial groups, personal links between members of the banking 'technocracy' were particularly strong, and there were links with the 'traditional' capital held by families such as de Wendel, Peugeot, de Dietrich, etc.[48]

LINKS, UNIONS, AND SOCIAL SURFACES

Marriage and Family

Many of the studies on recruitment to power positions emphasized the role of links of family and affinal relationships through marriage in maintaining the social homogeneity of the important recruiting grounds of the nation's political, administrative, and economic élites. In a large-scale sociological study on the choice of a marriage partner,[49] Girard, using a sample of 14,000 people drawn from the census of 1954 and, from them, a sub-sample of 1,646 couples who were interviewed, revealed overwhelming social and geographical homogamy (marriage within the same group). Nearly six-tenths of spouses lived in the same *commune*, seven-tenths in the same *canton*, eight-tenths in the same *arrondissement*, nine-tenths in the same *département* or region at the time of their marriage. Over time a slight drop in numbers in the same *commune* appeared, which represents the increasing mobility of the French, but the drop was still relatively small. The top social categories married geographically 'furthest away', but even there fully one-half of all marriages took place between persons from the same region — and some of those who lived in 'separate' administrative regions may in fact have lived virtually next door.

Social homogamy is similarly pronounced: Girard calculates it as being twice as high as if the spouses were chosen independently of social origins, for over two-thirds of households were formed of spouses both from the same milieu or two adjacent milieux, whether measured by professions of spouses or those of fathers of spouses (and women did not raise themselves by marriage more than men). In all milieux the spouses always had more chances of having the same social origins than of having different ones. The highest social groups especially married into their own group, effectively limiting access to the group through marriage. At the lowest levels, too, there was little movement.

Social mixing (*brassages sociaux*) through marriage was greatest in the milieux of the petty bourgeoisie, *cadres moyens*, shop-keepers, and other small independent businessmen and craftsmen. Thus, all three factors in the analysis — education, socio-professional mobility, and marriage — appeared to be linked, and it is clear that they all formed part of the same system and all both reflected and acted on each other, social origins affecting access to education, which in turn was basic to profession exercised, and both of these acted to limit the choice of marriage partner.

Marriage had an extremely important role as a means of concentrating, maintaining, and expanding capital of all kinds — economic, cultural, and social. Dowries remained important to the transmission of economic capital; nearly half of the couples, studied by Girard, belonging to the liberal professions and the *cadres supérieurs* had dowries, either from both parents or the parents of the wife (especially), and of these 30 per cent had money or shares. Similarly, 43 per cent in these same categories had a marriage contract serving to maintain the patrimony of the spouses intact. Delphy found similar results for shop-keepers and my own research on a small sample of French upper-middle-class families has confirmed both the importance of social homogamy and the continuation of the practice of dowries.[50] The latter research has also suggested the importance of the wives for their husband's social and economic position in terms of social as well economic capital. The wives came from families usually well-established in the liberal professions, especially law and medicine, the Army and business, thus providing through their families important social contacts and relationships. Larger than average families continued to be the rule at the higher end of the French social scale, so that these relationships were numerous both at the level of the parents' generation — a large number of uncles — but also at the level of spouses' generation, where there were many brothers and many sisters to marry into similar milieux.

Marriage acts to limit access to the higher positions of power in French society. Numbers of power positions may, however, seem large, and there arises the problem of means of control of these posts by the milieux concerned. Perhaps the most important is the overlapping of personnel, the multitude of posts covered by the same persons, the number covered rising systematically with place in the social scale.

The 'Fields of Power'; Multiple Position-holding and Social Capital

Multiple post-holding was the centre of an important study by Luc Boltanski, of the Centre de Sociologie de l'Education. Taking as his point of reference the professors, all part-time, of the prestigious Institut d'Études Politiques (formerly École Libre des Sciences Politiques) in Paris, which principally recruits students from the Parisian bourgeoisie and prepares many of them for ENA and the higher ranks of the Civil Service as well as of business, Boltanski examines what he calls their positions in the different 'fields of power' (*champs de pouvoir*).

Taking a continuum from the 'intellectual pole' to the 'power pole', Boltanski analyses five fields of power: the academic field, the field of cultural diffusion (mass media, etc.), the administrative field, the economic field, and the political field. Each teacher at IEP possessed on average three positions, or nearly five if we include those held in the past, and many held six, seven, or eight, spreading across all the fields of power. This positional analysis allows one to describe the 'social surface' (*surface sociale*) held by powerful individuals; the 'social surface' being

> that portion of social space which an individual is able to pass through (*parcourir*) and dominate by occupying *successively* the different social positions that he has the right to occupy *simultaneously*, the only condition being that he physically possess the gift of ubiquity which is socially conferred on him.[51]

The size of the individual's 'social surface' depends as much on the dispersion as on the number of positions held.

Using this concept, Boltanski finds that the professors of IEP had very unequally distributed social surfaces. While some held only a small number of positions situated close together in the same field of power, others held a large number of very dispersed positions. The number of positions held regularly increased with the social origin of the holder — those with fathers who were manual or white-collar workers occupied on average 1.7 positions as against 2.8 for those whose fathers were shop-keepers, 3.6 for middle-level state administrator fathers, 4 for teacher or other intellectual professions, 4.4 for the liberal professions and *cadres supérieurs* (private sector), 5 for senior civil servants, magistrates, or officers, and 6.7 for fathers who were *patrons* of industry.[52]

These differences are important, for they reveal not only the systematic and significant role played by social origins in access to power positions, even when small groups among the élite are considered, but also, and as a reflection of this, the importance of 'extra-professional' factors in the extension and holding of power positions. Thus Boltanski says:

> To understand the social advantages which are the correlates of the possession of an extended social surface, one should remember that among the *ensemble* of the privileges which are the instrument and the product of power, there is none more important than the capital of social contacts (*relations*); by the intermediary of the network of contacts, familial or of friendship, are carried out an important number of transactions, which are objectively political or economic but which, not being carried out with money, are not perceived as such . . . for example, recommendations, exchanges of information, etc. Moreover, the occupation of a given position implies itself the possession of a certain capital of social relations, of prestige, of symbolic credit,

legitimacy, and power. It follows that the social capital that an individual can mobilize depends not only on his family origins but also on the social surface that he can himself dominate (which is itself at least in most cases social capital accumulated by the family), which depends in its turn on the breadth of one's network of contacts, multiplied by the social surface controlled by each member of one's extended family, and, to a lesser extent, that of each of the members of the network of contacts. One could not explain the omnipresence of certain names, certain lineages, of certain individuals, able to control indirectly, at a distance, a far greater number of positions than that which they are able to occupy directly, nor the breadth of their power, without bringing into [the analysis] a multiplier of this kind.[53]

Further, Boltanski's analysis shows the five fields of power to be of unequal weight in the total power system and as giving unequal possibilities for a broad network of contracts and the holding of a multiplicity of power positions. The intellectual pole had fewest possibilities — academics remained within the academic field, especially those who taught letters rather than law. Maximum power was given to those belonging to the major state administrative bodies, once again, the *Inspecteurs des Finances*, who tended to hold positions in the administrative, political, and economic fields, sometimes even in the academic field.

The sample, drawn from professors at the Institut d'Études Politiques who were selected by the criteria of the school is a rather special one. However, the image that the school presented, and wished to present, of itself was one closely linked to the most important sectors of the society since it was preparing students to occupy élite positions in that society. Hence, it seems likely that the sample reflects the reality to a considerable extent in terms of the differential numbers and breadth of positions held by persons principally involved in one field of power rather than another, in other words that the hierarchy revealed was the 'real' or relevant one.

Such an analysis shows both the differential power of different factions of the élites and overlapping and interaction in terms of possible roles and positions, and how a small number of persons can hold a large number of posts. This in effect limits access to such positions. Further, the fundamental interests of the system for the dominant class are summed up by Boltanski as follows:

[multi-positionality] permits, in conformity with the logic of magic by which the whole of a personality, individual or collective, resides in each of its parts, the division of the dominant class while at the same time maintaining its unity, as the existence of automomous fields of power is counterbalanced by the freedom of individuals . . . to circulate between positions and fields.

This is important for ideological reasons because

by favouring the import and export of persons between fields and thus the circulation of ways of speech (*langages*), manners, themes, and questions, [such circulation] leads to the production of *problématiques* common to the whole of the dominant class. Thereby, too, it contributes to the production of the class consciousness of the ruling class as a sentiment of familiarity and solidarity, which does not need to be raised to a verbal and explicit level to maintain the unity of the class, by containing within tolerance limits the different factional quarrels born of the objective diversity of material and symbolic interests.[54]

The symbolic representation of the interests of the class serves not only to permit group cohesion but also to 'recognize' and recruit the relevant personnel. In their analysis of the 'symbolic goods market' and its relationship to accepted 'culture' and cultural capital and the appropriate attitude towards it and use in interpersonal contacts, Bourdieu and his colleagues emphasize the expectation of social ease and cultural and intellectual 'excellence' and a 'cultivated' approach which must in all cases seem natural and in no way 'learned'.

At different levels of the educational system, the importance of symbolic means of differentiating almost 'identical' products becomes more and more important, perhaps being seen to culminate in the major written and oral examinations taken by candidates to ENA, which explicitly judged the general culture of a person but did so less by *what* he expressed, those sentiments being common to many, than by the *way* he expressed it and the ease and sophistication of his approach. As the ENA examiners themselves said, the 'first-day examination', the most general dissertation, is that which 'should be the expression of the personality of a young man or young woman'.[55] This can be seen to favour students from upper-class Parisian backgrounds, as does to an even greater extent the oral test, which is designed to appreciate the 'moral and intellectual quality of a candidate' and to check that the future élite of the administration 'will not lack humour and be reduced to the *forts en thème*' (good essay writers), as expressed by the president of the ENA admission jury in 1969. Such qualities do not explicitly form part of school curricula at any level, and must be developed in homes where discussion and repartee are the norm and which are developed by contacts with those already in place, as essentially was the case with the students of IEP in Paris, who constituted more than two-thirds of the accepted students at ENA.

Such privileged relationships with, and access to, the most legitimate and general and yet at the same time most exclusive aspects of 'culture' continued to play their part throughout the career of many, and in particular of those in the senior levels of the civil service. Promotion juries were composed only of civil servants who chose to promote those most like themselves.[56]

It is clear, then, that the dominant social groups in France throughout the period after 1945 remained linked together in a multiplicity of ways. Marriage, multiple position-holding, family links and the capital of relations, camaraderie based on common education and the values imparted by a bourgeois (and aristocratic)[57] upbringing, constant contacts made in and reinforced by everyday professional activity, linked together men powerful in the major institutions of the society. Business was linked to politics, administration to both. In all a network, more or less dense as one approaches the centre (geographical concentration in Paris was important here too), becoming sparser around the periphery, joined together men and women active in the most important spheres of life in the public and private sectors. These linkages, allied to the major mechanisms of educational selection and professional 'choice', continued to act to limit severely the possibilities of access to powerful positions by members born into any groups but those already in dominant positions.

Notes

* From Jane Marceau, *Class and Status in France: Economic Change and Social Immobility, 1945–1975* (© Oxford: Oxford University Press, 1977), pp. 129–56. Reprinted by permission of Oxford University Press.

1 Nicos Poulantzas, *Pouvoir politique et classes sociales* (Paris: Maspéro, 1968), Vol. I.

2 Steven Lukes, *Power: A Radical View* (London: Macmillan, 1974).

3 F. Jacquin, *Les Cadres de l'industrie et du commerce* (Paris: Colin, 1955), p. 139.

4 M. Maurice *et al.*, *Les Cadres et l'entreprise* (Paris: Université de Paris, Institut des Sciences Sociales du Travail, 1967).

5 Union des Industries Métallurgiques et Minières, *Ingénieurs et cadres* (Paris: UIMM, 1970), p. 36.

6 A. Girard, *La Réussite sociale en France*, Cahiers de L'INED no. 38 (Paris: Presses Universitaires de France, 1961), p. 103.

7 G. Benguigui and D. Monjardet, *Etre un cadre en France . . .?* (Paris: Dunod, 1970), p. 101.

8 Although the social significance of the petty bourgeoisie is undeniable and small *patrons* in industry and commerce exercised power over their workmen, the area of their power tended to be greatly restricted. Moreover, while they

did in some instances carry some influence in local politics (although even here it seems that members of the liberal professions were more likely to hold official positions such as mayor or *conseiller général*: see M. Longepierre, 'Permanence des conseillers généraux et renouveau des traditions administratives départementales', in *Aménagement du territoire et développement régional*, Vol. 3 (Grenoble: Institut d'Études Politiques, 1970), pp. 3–32, it seems reasonable to treat them as important parts of the local, but only minor parts of the national, power structure of principal concern here. Indeed, the very number of small businesses in France, in every sector and in every region, precluded their *patrons* from forming a coherent group, except for defence when their interests were directly threatened, as in the Poujadist movement. Although in the last Government of President Pompidou, they had their own minister, M. Royer, and the industrialists had their voice in the PME, while the small shopkeepers had theirs in CID-UNATI, their national-level political effectiveness was largely limited to that of prevention rather than positive action. Primarily, therefore, access to senior positions, in large-scale or otherwise nationally significant, industry, is discussed here.

9 See Nicos Poulantzas, *Classes in Contemporary Capitalism* (London: New Left Books, 1975).

10 N. Delefortrie-Soubeyroux, *Les Dirigeants de l'industrie française* (Paris: Colin, 1961).

11 Girard, *La Réussite sociale en France*, pp. 91–3.

12 D. Hall and H.-C. de Bettignies, 'The French Business Elite', *European Business*, No. 19 (1968), p. 4.

13 D. Hall, H.-C. de Bettignies and G. Amado-Fischgrund, 'The European Business Elite', *European Business*, No. 23 (1969), pp. 52–3.

14 P. Bourdieu, *Esquisse d'une théorie de la pratique* (Geneva: Librairie Droz, 1972).

15 B. Gournay, 'Un groupe dirigeant de la société française: les grands fonctionnaires', *Revue Française de Science Politique*, Vol. 14 (1964), pp. 214–42.

16 *Polytechnique* graduates were also entitled to enter the senior ranks of the civil service but decreasing numbers did so. Suleiman has suggested that ENA reinforced previous recruitment patterns and by formalizing promotion through one school actually cut down possibilities for civil servants of lower social origins: Ezra Suleiman, *Politics, Power and Bureaucracy in France: The Administrative Elite* (Princeton, N.J.: Princeton University Press, 1974).

17 Tom Bottomore, 'La mobilité sociale dans la haute administration française', *Cahiers Internationaux de Sociologie*, Vol. 13 (1952), p. 169.

18 P. Bourdieu, Y. Delsaut and M. de Saint-Martin, 'Les fonctions du système d'enseignement: classes préparatoires et facultés' (unpublished paper, Centre de Sociologie Européenne, 1970). The civil service *concours* was more 'democratic' in social origins than the student one — if only ENA entrants from the latter were considered the social origins would appear higher — but it was very minor.

19 A. Darbel and D. Schnapper, *Les Agents du système administratif: Morphologie de la haute administration française*, Vol. 2 (Paris: Mouton, 1972), p. 105.

20 J. Chazelle, *La Diplomatie* (Paris: Presses Universitaires de France, 2nd edn. 1968), p. 5.

21 Darbel and Schnapper, *Les Agents du système administratif*, Vol. 2, pp. 142–4.

22 Darbel and Schnapper, *Les Agents du système administratif*, Vol. 1 (Paris: Mouton, 1969), p. 102.

23 Ibid., p. 95.

24 Ibid., p. 103

25 C. Brindillac, 'Les Hauts Fonctionnaires', *Esprit*, Vol. 12 (1953), pp. 864–5.

26 Id.
27 P. Lalumière, L'Inspection des finances (Paris: Presses Universitaires de France, 1959), p. 45.
28 Mattei Dogan, 'Political Ascent in a Class Society: French Deputies 1870–1958', in D. Marvick, ed., Political Decision Makers (Chicago: Free Press, 1961), p. 58.
29 Ibid., p. 74
30 Ibid., p. 292.
31 Ibid., p. 303.
32 Progrès et Démocratie Moderne, a centrist party.
33 Roland Cayrol, Jean-Luc Parodi and Colette Ysmal, Les Députés français (Paris: Colin and Fondation Nationale des Sciences Politiques, 1973), p. 43.
34 Ibid., p. 27.
35 Ibid., p. 565.
36 F. le Reclus, 'Le Sénat républicain', Politique, Vol. 12 (1969), p. 45.
37 Longepierre, 'Permanence des conseillers généraux', p. 9.
38 Raymond Aron, 'Catégories dirigeantes ou classe dirigeante?, Revue Française de Science Politique, Vol. 15 (1965), pp. 7–27.
39 Lalumière, L'Inspection des finances, pp. 68–76.
40 Ibid., pp. 125–6.
41 Dogan, Political Ascent in a Class Society, and Cayrol, et al., Les Députés français.
42 Roger Priouret, Origines du patronat français (Paris: Grasset, 1963), p. 24.
43 Henry Ehrmann, Organized Business in France (Princeton, N.J.: Princeton University Press, 1957), p. 233.
44 H. Coston, Les Financiers qui mènent le monde (Paris: La Librairie Française, 1955).
45 Cf. J. Kosciusko-Morizet, La Mafia polytechnicienne (Paris: Seuil, 1973).
46 Cuisenier, in Darras (collective pseudonym), Le Partage des bénéfices (Paris: Editions de Minuit, 1966), pp. 377–8.
47 F. Morin, La Structure financière du capitalisme française (Paris: Calmann-Levy, 1974), pp. 94–5.
48 Ibid., p. 92.
49 A. Girard, Le Choix du conjoint (Paris: Presses Universitaires de France, 2nd edn., 1974).
50 C. Delphy, 'Le patrimoine et la double circulation des biens dans l'espace économique et le temps familial', Revue Française de Sociologie, Vol. 10, numéro spécial (1969), pp. 664–86; and Marceau, 'Education and Social Mobility in France', in F. Parkin, ed., The Social Analysis of Class Structure (London: Tavistock, 1974) and The Social Origins, Educational Experience and Career Paths of a Young Business Elite, final report for the Social Science Research Council (INSEAD Monograph 1/76, June 1975).
51 L. Boltanski, L'espace positionnel: les professeurs des écoles du pouvoir et le pouvoir (Paris: Centre de Sociologie Européenne, 1972; a shorter version of this paper was subsequently published in the Revue Française de Sociologie, Vol. 14, No. 1 (1973), pp. 3–26), p. 9.
52 Ibid., p. 11.
53 Ibid., pp. 10–11.
54 Ibid., p. 33.
55 Quoted in Darbel and Schnapper, Les Agents du système administratif, Vol. 2, p. 99.
56 Gournay, 'Un groupe dirigeant de la société française', p. 224.
57 De Negroni has shown the customs by which members of the grande bourgeoisie and aristocracy maintained contact from early childhood to old age. At goûters (teas), school (private and Catholic), dances, weddings, and, for men, in

business, political and leisure activities (sports clubs), members of the most important Parisian factions of these groups, constantly met the same 'suitable' people. F. de Negroni, *La France noble* (Paris: Seuil, 1974).

4 The Higher Civil Service and Economic Policy-Making*

Anne Stevens

The higher civil service in France plays a major part in the economic life of the country. The process of economic policy-making within the administration is particularly important, because of the size of the public sector, because of the French tradition of intervention by the state (still widely accepted), because of the persistence of the belief that the civil service is well-qualified to intervene in economic matters and that it is important and right that it should do so, and, finally, because of the close relationship which exists between the upper levels of the administration and of French industry and commerce. This chapter explores these factors, which might be expected to lead to a rational, even monolithic, process of economic policy-making within the French administration and goes on to argue that the process is subject to pressures and conflicts of various kinds, from both inside and outside the administration, which may influence the formation of policy, and may impede its execution.

I. THE STATE AND THE ECONOMY

The Size of the Public Sector

That the higher civil service is able to play an important role in the economic life of France, is due in part to the size of the French public sector. The main outlines of this sector were set during 1944–46, under the combined pressures of the Resistance for a fresh start and an end to the influence of the industrial and commercial élites which were thought to have acted against the true interests of the nation in the 1930s and contributed to the *débâcle* of 1940, of Socialist and Communist influence in the Government in which they took part, and of the old jacobin *dirigiste* tradition which saw the state as the source from which reconstruction must flow. The public sector is difficult to define rigorously. Types of state intervention and control vary, and many of the public enterprises have subsidiaries and secondary shareholdings.[1] In 1976 it was estimated that public corporations employed nearly 1.6 million people, which amounted to 11.5 per cent of French non-agricultural employment.[2] In 1975 they produced over 9 per cent of France's Gross Domestic Product and accounted for over 26 per cent of national investment.[3]

The public sector includes the old state manufactures and monopolies — munitions, tobacco and matches, posts and telecommunications — and the public service enterprises — gas and electricity for example. It also includes, as wholly-owned undertakings, the Renault car company, three major banks and three major insurance companies (formed by the merger of the larger numbers initially nationalized). The state controls the railways, the ports, the two main airlines (Air France and the domestic airline, Air Inter) and two merchant shipping lines. Its stake in the aerospace industry, of which it already controlled about half, was greatly strengthened by the 1978 intervention in Dassault. Both the Elf and Total petrol companies are state-controlled.

The public and semi-public sector gives the state scope for the exercise of considerable economic influence, a scope which the economic crisis has tended to increase. Over the period 1973–79, it

> has resulted in the stepping up of state assistance and, one suspects, control, for public and private industry alike. Thus, under what has been labelled 'Operation Red-Cross', 431 firms received financial assistance through the CIASI (Comité Interministériel d'Aménagement des Structures Industrielles) in under three years and the Industrial Development Institute intervened in 82 firms in just over five years, to mention two of the mechanisms used by professed liberal Governments. And, as a source close to the President of the Republic remarked, the *formal* nationalization of the steel industry . . . would involve little more than the formal transfer of the industry's indebtedness to the taxpayer and the replacement of one *grands corps* élite by another.[4]

The Tradition of State Intervention

The size of the public sector is one of the factors which explain the importance of the role of officials in economic policy-making. This role is supported by a long-standing and important tradition of state intervention and interest in all the branches of economic life. In 1815 a nobleman with a distinguished official career, writing a memorandum for submission to the King on the training required by officials of a restored and parliamentary monarchy, could take it for granted that such officials would have to deal with manufactures, agriculture and transport, and recommend that they should learn enough about these subjects to be able to communicate readily with specialists.[5] The habit of state control and regulation, but equally state encouragement and protection, in economic fields, is commonly traced back even further, at least to the seventeenth century and to Colbert. Peyrefitte characterized Colbert's ideals thus: 'to make the kingdom prosper by turning each individual into the submissive executant of rational economic decisions taken at the top . . . Colbert decided everything . . . he had no intention of *supporting* but of *creating* industrial and commercial activity . . . private initiative was *a priori* suspect and could be tolerated only if subordinate or limited.[6] Peyrefitte is making a polemical point and adds that Colbert should be regarded rather as the symbol of a system than as the sole creator of it. The mentality survived, however, despite the arguments of the eighteenth century physiocrats and the nineteenth century proponents of *laissez faire*. During the nineteenth century 'it was essential to secure state as well as para-state centralized intervention to cope with the difficult conditions of French industrialization'.[7] The tradition of state intervention survived the years of 'liberal' economic doctrine, for free-trade and competition were always placed under the state's sheltering umbrella. Jean Monnet and the founders of French economic planning were anxious to reconstruct the economy so that it would withstand a more international economy and to involve industrialists as partners within the process but they did so within an essentially *dirigiste* framework. Over the past twenty years, the *colbertiste* tradition has come under some pressure from the opening up of the French economy, but in the early 1970s it could still be said that:

> French governments had for centuries oscillated between policies of passive protection and active promotion — state-sponsored capitalism and state capitalism — based upon close collusion between the private sector and its public senior partner . . . Despite the dramatic industrial revolution . . . which France . . . is still undergoing, the weight of this long-standing *dirigiste* tradition still makes itself felt in the sense of dependence upon government, which French businessmen more or less explicitly acknowledge.[8]

The debate about the consequences of this *dirigiste* tradition is immaterial to the argument that its existence even today supports the activities of the administration within the economy.

The Legitimacy of Higher Civil Service Intervention

The state's activity in the economic field both supports, and is supported by, a tradition which claims, by implication at least, that higher civil servants are especially suitable for the management of the economy. The claim of the higher civil servants to a pre-eminent place in the management of the French economy is not only supported by their manifest educational prowess, but also by a tradition that associates public servants with a rational and dynamic approach to the economy. It was amongst the former students of the École Polytechnique that Saint-Simonian ideas about the importance of the rational guidance of the State by experts in the economic and industrial fields, spread particularly rapidly in the 1840s. Something of the same current of ideas was to be found in the movements which, prompted by the experience of the First World War, the economic crisis of the interwar years and the failure of the governments of the 1930s to cope with economic problems, began to study the possibilities of economic forecasting and planning. These 'technocratic' groups, one of the most important of which centred round the *polytechnicien* Jean Coutrot, and which included a number of officials (the liberal Jacques Rueff as well as the future planning commissioner Pierre Massé), saw themselves as providing a dynamic progressive element in national economic life. As Kuisel points out, the 'technocratic' groups emerged from the war unscathed, into an atmosphere of widespread support for economic renovation and state action: 'armed with new governmental organs, granted autonomy by de Gaulle and backed by the public's desire for structural reforms, the technocrats had come to stay'.[9]

The attitude that had been found in these groups was also to be found after 1945 amongst the students of the newly created École Nationale d'Administration (ENA). The founders of the ENA and its staff (a great many of whom were serving civil servants) emphasized the contribution which the higher civil servant could and should make to the reconstruction and growth of the post-war French economy. The School was, in the eyes of its creators, to produce an active and dynamic civil service which would be prepared to take responsibility for the economic development of France. The training which was provided at the ENA in Keynesian economic ideas — lecture courses given in the early 1950s by Jean Marchal on Keynesian theories and by Pierre Mendès France on the problems of the reconstruction of France were particularly influential — possibly helped to instill confidence in an interventionist approach. A study of the topics chosen for the report which students were, until 1971, required to produce at the end of their year of practical attachments within the administration (*mémoire de stage*) shows a clear preference for themes with some economic aspects. Throughout the 1950s and 1960s, most former students aver, the ENA's training had as one of its central guiding themes the idea that the reconstruction and growth of the economy could not be left to individuals or enterprises. It depended upon the state, and thus, essentially, upon the state's most senior servants.

> We were clear that the renewal and growth of the country depended upon us.[10]

> The training at the ENA . . . presented the top administration as the 'active force' in French society.[11]

It would be wrong to convey the impression that it is the former students of the ENA alone who are responsible for the attitude of the higher civil service towards economic policy-making. The ENA experience is merely illustrative of a wider phenomenon. The technical *grands corps* have played their part, and it is notable that while the men whom Carré, Dubois and Malinvaud list as being particularly involved in a dynamic economic policy were not students at the ENA, several of them were involved in the 'technocratic' groups of the 1930s.[12] The ENA students have prolonged and intensified a previous trend.

Ezra Suleiman, examining the nature of the higher civil servant's role, quotes one *grands corps* member:

> It is that members of the *grands corps* are something of an aristocracy in French society. But why? Simply because they are superior to others. They are the most brilliant. They are the top graduates of their schools and they have been very carefully selected. Put in a nutshell: they are the ones who have performed the best.[13]

The system of recruitment is the second factor which reinforces the higher civil service's claim to a pre-eminent role in economic policy-making.

Most senior officials are recruited through one of two main channels: the École Polytechnique, through which members of the Corps des Ponts et Chaussées and the Corps des Mines are recruited; and the École Nationale d'Administration, which provides members of the non-technical *grand corps* and also senior general administrators. Selection takes place at several levels. The École Polytechnique takes in about 300 students a year, who prepare for the highly competitive entry examination in special classes attached to certain *lycées*, after having passed the *baccalauréat*. Entry into these classes is in itself highly competitive. At the end of the students' period at the École Polytechnique they are ranked in order of merit on the basis of examinations, and choose their careers on the basis of their rank. Those ranked highest invariably choose the *grands corps*.

The École Nationale d'Administration does not recruit directly from the *lycées*, but is open to university graduates and to officials who have spent at least five years in the public service. In practice success in its fiercely competitive examinations requires a period of specialized preparation. Most of the successful graduate candidates undertake this at the Institut d'Etudes Politiques in Paris. A measure of selection operates within the IEP. Bodiguel's figures suggest that only just over 20 per cent of those who are candidates for entry into the first year of the IEP diploma course emerge after three years with the diploma.[14] And finally, as at the École Polytechnique, a second stage selection operates at the ENA, in that those who achieve the highest rank in the final assessment examinations have the widest choice of jobs and invariably choose the *grands corps*.[15] Membership of the *grands corps* thus reflects repeated success in negotiating a series of intellectual hurdles and it is hardly surprising if this produces cases like those cited by *Le Point* in 1974: that of the forty-year-old head of a department in a large electronics firm in the Paris area with a brilliant career behind him who knows he will go no higher, and explains 'to go higher you have to come from X [the École Polytechnique]. It's the unwritten rule';[16] and that of the executive of the semi-public petrol company who knows that 'I shall always have an *énarque* (a former student of the ENA) above me. It is inconceivable that I, with only my IEP diploma, should be in charge of a former student of the ENA.'[17]

The part played by the higher civil service in economic policy-making is thus important, at least in part, because it is expected to be important, and this expectation has had practical consequences. Civil servants themselves have taken an exalted view of their role, and this view has been widely accepted, both outside the administration, and even abroad, as the admiring glances cast from Britain at French recruitment and training demonstrate. Certainly, the success of the strategies of the *corps* as they have adapted themselves to new situations, giving priority to their own survival and the furtherance of their *corps* interest has had its part to play in the acceptance by society of the *grands corps'* own image of themselves. The place occupied by present and former higher civil servants and especially by members of the *grands corps* in the direction of public, semi-public and private enterprises clearly illustrates the extent to which membership of the higher civil service, and particularly of a *grand corps*, is regarded as proof of an individual's capacity for the exercise of important responsibilities in the economic sphere, a capacity based both on his abilities and on the nature of his professional activities. It is to the close relationship which this engenders between the highest levels of the administration and industrial and commercial life that the next section of this chapter turns.

The Relationship between the Higher Civil Service and Big Business

The relationship between the upper levels of the administration and of industry and commerce is important because it provides the environment within which economic policy is made and facilitates its execution. 'The apparent degree of cohesion that characterizes the French business and administrative élites has allowed for a relatively smooth formulation and implementation of economic and industrial policies.[18] As Ezra Suleiman points out, two distinct attitudes can be taken to the close relationship between the upper levels of the administration and the business world, which he sees as being partly founded upon the commitment of both sides to the goal of industrial growth. It is possible to see it as reflecting 'a commonality of class interests', with the link between political and financial power indicating the cohesion of the capitalist class in France. Equally, it can be argued that the links are a symptom of a technocratic society, and arise because administration and business share goals of rationality and growth. Suleiman does not see these two approaches as necessarily incompatible; rather they reflect two related and simultaneous phenomena — 'the predominance [sic] of directorial posts in the public and private sectors by an elite sharing a common training and background, and the sharing of goals concerning industrial growth.'[19] Jean-Claude Thoenig identified one of the consequences, when he spoke of the upper levels of the administration as being able to act effectively in relation to business 'not only because of their capacity to manage the administrative pyramid, but also because they have an extraordinary ability to create . . . a sufficiently coherent climate of personal relationships within which negotiations can take place'.[20]

This capacity stems from the extent to which industrial leaders and higher civil servants have a common background and training. Pierre Birnbaum and his collaborators, studying the social origins of members of the higher civil service and top industrialists on the basis of samples drawn from *Who's Who* concluded that both categories were, in the main, recruited from the same *espace sociale*. Observing, in samples taken at a twenty-year interval (1954–74) an increase in the proportion of higher civil servants who were sons of businessmen (from 17 to 28 per cent) and of businessmen who were the sons of higher civil servants (from 5 to 10 per cent) he concluded: 'if the members of the *catégories dirigeantes* usually follow a profession different from that of their father this is not because they have risen up the social ladder. They almost all originate from the governing class'.[21]

A common educational and training experience also assists the development of relationships between the administration and business. This training may be either the mathematically based training of the École Polytechnique or the studies of law, economics and politics undertaken at the Instituts d'Études Politiques and extended, for some students, at the École Nationale d'Administration. Suleiman asserts 'that the *grandes écoles* now have the major responsibility for training the presidents of the largest industrial enterprises has been clearly established',[22] and adds that a study of the directors of the 500 largest industrial corporations in France showed that about one-third of them were former students of the École Polytechnique. Birnbaum is concerned to stress the increasing competition which *polytechniciens* are facing, within business, from those who have undertaken the *études juridico-politiques* which traditionally led to administrative posts. Thirty per cent of those considered in his 1974 sample who had undertaken such studies held posts in the private sector, compared with only 10 per cent in 1954.

The fact that higher civil servants and business leaders have a common experience of education and training is not only due to some students from the École Polytechnique and the École Nationale d'Administration choosing to enter business immediately upon graduation, although this does occur. About one-third of the graduating *polytechniciens* go directly into industry each year — up to 100 out of 300. Graduates of the École Nationale d'Administration, however, tend to start their careers within the administration. Bodiguel found that between 1947 and 1962 only forty-four out of just over 1,800 ENA graduates had resigned on completing their course, and the proportion has never been higher than in 1969, when nine of the ninety-four graduating students resigned. Far more important than this early choice is the movement that occurs out of the administration at a later stage, known as *pantouflage*. This movement, it should be noted, is essentially one way. No mechanism exists for the late entry into most of the *corps* of the higher civil service of people with industrial experience. The government does, however, have, in theory, complete discretion in the filling of posts at the highest levels (*directeur* and equivalent) and in ministerial private offices (*cabinets*), and a small proportion of posts at the upper levels of the Council of State, the Finance Inspectorate and the Court of Accounts are open to people who have distinguished themselves in other fields. In practice although this discretion is used occasionally to recall senior officials who have taken up posts outside the central administration — the Planning Commissioner appointed in 1978 (Michel Albert), a Finance Inspector, came from a post in the financial sector — it is seldom used to appoint people who are strangers to the administration. Over 80 per cent of the 'outsiders' appointed to the Council of State and over 95 per cent of those so appointed to the Court of Accounts since 1958 have been either higher civil servants from other *corps* or magistrates.

Movement out of the civil service is, in contrast, easy. A graduate of the École Nationale d'Administration or the École Polytechnique who resigns from the public service within ten years is required to reimburse to the state a proportion of the costs of his training. This does not constitute a major deterrent, particularly since the regulations provide for civil servants who move outside their *corps* of origin to be either *détaché*, a position which enables the official to retain rights to seniority and a pension, and gives him a right to re-incorporation within his *corps* on request, or *en disponibilité*, retaining, for up to six years, a right to re-employment. These rights are not often exercised, and in general officials who have moved into public or private industry or commerce return only exceptionally, and usually to fill very senior posts.

At the end of 1977 about 10 per cent of all ENA graduates were employed in public or private enterprises. The proportion of *polytechniciens* so employed was certainly very high. Birnbaum found that only 22 per cent of the individuals listed in the 1974 *Who's Who* whom he chose to study who had begun their careers in the administration were still employed there. Given that those who appear in *Who's Who* are those who have reached the highest posts, this startling figure reflects the fact that *pantouflage* has a disproportionate effect at the top. It is the members of the *grands corps*, and especially the Corps des Mines and the Finance Inspectorate who are most likely to move to posts in the public and private sectors, and there they often occupy the most senior posts.

> In 1972 thirty out of the forty-four key posts in the twenty largest public enterprises were in the hands of civil servants . . . In 1976 . . . there were only 560 French firms employing more than 1000 workers, but they completely dominated the French market, and a majority of them were headed by ex-students of the prestigious École Polytechnique . . . Almost all of those firms had ex-civil servants on their boards of directors.[23]

The role of the higher civil service in economic policy-making is important because it is expected to be so. The legitimacy of higher civil service interest and activity within the economic sphere is recognized. The relationship between the higher civil service and top business circles facilitates administrative action. The cohesion of the elite enhances the role of the higher civil service. It eases communication. But it does not result in a monolithic system of policy-making. Indeed policy is made in an environment that is fashioned by extraneous pressures and by internal blockages and conflicts. It is to these aspects of economic policy-making that this chapter now turns.

II.   THE PROCESS OF ECONOMIC POLICY-MAKING

Administrative Cross-currents

The environment within which the higher civil servants, whose role was considered in the previous section, operate, is not, despite appearances, a simple one. It is easy to construct a picture of an economic policy-making machine dominated by ENA trained Finance Inspectors and *administrateurs civils* in the Finance Ministry. A widely-held view of the higher civil servants who do so much to shape economic policy depicts them as linked by their common training, shaped in a common mould, sharing a common ethos with an emphasis upon dynamism and progress and a Keynesian basis, occasionally swayed by common enthusiasms – for Mendèsiste ideas in the 1950s, for the Club Jean Moulin in the 1960s – but essentially staunch supporters of the political ideas of the Governing Coalition, which occasionally lures them into active political careers. There is, in this as in many caricatures, a grain of truth. But reality is more complex.

Firstly, the old barriers and divisions within the administration persist. In the late 1920s Walter Rice Sharp described the rigidly hierarchical structure of most ministries, and stressed the lack of horizontal communication which resulted. In 1945 this excessive 'compartmentalization' *(cloissonement)* was one of the failures of the French administration which Debré hoped a common recruitment and training would remedy. Nevertheless, the concept of authority as strictly located within an area marked out by the texts which define a ministry's or a division's jurisdiction persists. A division which has been in existence over a long period can trace its evolution through a series of legislative texts. The influence of a division may depend upon its standing and longevity, and some – the Budget and Treasury divisions are the most outstanding examples –

are regarded as *nobles*. The result of this compartmentalization is the *batailles des compétences* vividly described by Suleiman. He reports:

> I once heard two Directors in the Ministry engage in a heated dis-
> cussion over a sentence that threatened to shift an element of control
> over a minor domain from one *direction* to another . . . Power, for
> them, is strictly definable: it does not emerge from complex relation-
> ships. It is to be located, as the quarrel between the two Directors
> suggested, in the list of jurisdictions. That there is no necessary con-
> nection between the legally defined jurisdiction of a *direction* and
> the influence that a Director actually exerts is not evident to most
> of the Directors.[24]

This mentality — 'when I go to a meeting my task is to defend the interests of my division'[25] — tends to lead on to the adoption of the ideas and approach of that particular division or ministry.

> Each division has its own patterns of thought and is used to arguing
> within its own intellectual framework which is often based on a view
> confined to the management of its own services. 'In the light of the
> matters with which I am concerned. . .' thus a *directeur* of the Treasury
> division often prefaced his remarks . . . The divisions of the Ministry
> [of Finance] are often reluctant to pass on the information required
> to carry out their respective tasks. Each branch prefers to work within
> a closed circuit.[26]

Kessler pointed out that where ENA graduates were faced with 'the choice between their legitimate hopes of a normal career, or giving up the ideas and methods in which they had been trained, they usually took the easy way out.'[27] An official of the Ministry of Finance spoke of 'The golden rules of the *rue de Rivoli* [the Ministry of Finance], domin-ance of the Ministry of Finance, financial orthodoxy, cult of the balanced budget . . . anyone who breaks them is shunted out of the way. Not because of their opinions, but because they are incapable'.[28]

The policy-making process is further complicated by the relationships between the different *corps* of which the higher civil service is composed. The *corps* system has effects which go beyond merely structural problems and seem to extend into policy-making areas.

A higher civil servant's *corps* membership results from his performance in the assessment examinations of the ENA or the École Polytechnique. A choice of posts is open to graduating students who make their choice in the order of merit in which the assessment has placed them. Those who choose first choose the *grands corps*. Membership of one of the *grands corps* provides the sense of belonging to a small and exclusive club; it conveys a certain social status; it offers opportunities for interesting and remunerative occupation both within the administration and outside it; it allows a certain freedom in the organization of one's time and activities. However, the maintenance of this status requires that each *corps* should retain its claim to expertise in certain areas and should if possible seek to extend the area which it dominates.

The desire of the corps to maintain their positions may have policy consequences. Jean-Claude Thoenig, for the Corps des Ponts et Chaussées, and Ezra Suleiman, for the Corps des Mines have shown how the *corps* tend to approach policy in terms of the opportunity which it offers for the maintenance of the power and position of the *corps*. Suleiman says

> It would be difficult to pinpoint a coherent set of policies that the Inspection des Finances or the Corps des Mines are committed to within the areas of the economy or energy. It is not difficult to find examples where policies have been embraced, sometimes smoothly, sometimes after a difficult adjustment period. But the important point is that it is not the policies per se that matter, for policies are judged according to their impact on the power and position of the elite.[29]

and adds

> The commitment of the elite is to the health and well-being of its corporate organization, rather than to a set of policies. Policies are looked upon as a means of enlarging a *corps'* domain, of leaving it unchanged or of reducing it.[30]

Jean-Claude Thoenig cites the motorway building programme as an example of such a policy. The Corps des Ponts et Chaussées opposed the extension of the motorway network largely on the grounds that the projects were too large to be handled by their traditional autonomous basic local units.[31]

Thirdly, the attitudes of higher civil servants within the policy-making process may also vary according to their role. The conflicts which arise between the members of a minister's private office — themselves usually higher civil servants — and the divisions of the ministry are a particularly clear example of this type. Membership of the staff of a private office (*cabinet*) does not necessarily imply a close political identification with the minister; rather it is for many a necessary step in a successful career. The division does not only represent a separation between 'political' and 'technical' spheres. It is characterized by what Jean-Luc Bodiguel describes as *un climat de défiance*. There is a division between those who seek to co-ordinate and resolve conflicts — and this is in part the *cabinet's* role — and those who seek to maintain their own point of view. There is equally a division between the *cabinet* that seeks to ensure the implementation of the minister's policy against what may seem to be the hidebound reaction of the divisions, and the heads of the divisions who feel that the *cabinet* does not take sufficient account of 'reality'.

> If the ministers and their entourage concern themselves with the implementation of policy and check the details, it is because they are wary of the *directeurs*.[32]

> It is not in fact unusual for the *cabinet* to devise the principles of a new policy virtually without consultation, and even for it to take on almost unaided the drafting of the texts which embody this policy.[33]

Examining relationships between the budget division of the Ministry of Finance and the Minister's *cabinet* Diana Green concluded they were in part a question of personalities.[34] During the preparation of the budget the appropriate member of the *cabinet* staff was closely involved at every stage, and there was an awareness that conflicts could arise, although this was partly mitigated by a shared reaction of defence of a general interest against the partial arguments of the spending ministries.

Changes have, however, come to the administration since 1945. While the common background of the higher civil servants has probably not had a major effect upon their behaviour, it has certainly affected the ease and speed of communication between them. 'I remember the old days, how slow and rigid everything was, all on paper. Now I telephone a fellow former student of the ENA'.[35] Diana Green found that great use was made within the budget division of informal contacts, often on the basis of membership of the same graduating class at the ENA. While most ENA students seem to retain a close working relationship with only a handful of contemporaries, the relative ease they feel in any dealing with a fellow former student is important.

Secondly, higher civil servants can no longer be confined for their entire working career within one division. If they are to be eligible for appointment to the most senior posts they must have spent at least two years outside their ministry of first posting. The institution of this obligation was seen as a means of breaking down some of the barriers between ministries, and of making the *corps* of *administrateurs civils* a more genuinely inter-ministerial *corps*.

The effects of the ENA training should not, however, be exaggerated. Competition exists at the top between *énarques* and *polytechniciens*. It also exists between *énarques* whose *corps* membership may have been determined by a very small margin in the final assessment examination. The desire to achieve the necessary marks led, in the early years of the School, to intense rivalry. If such fierce competition now affects only about a third of the students each year, a certain bitterness can still sour those who see prospects blocked and interesting posts permanently occupied by members of the *grands corps*.

The conformity and similarity which the ENA training induces is essentially a conformity in style, but not necessarily in content. There is no doubt that style plays a vital part in success both in the entrance examinations to the ENA and in the assessment examinations. In their advice to candidates the examining boards stress the importance of structure and clarity of expression. Much of the training, especially in the two core subjects of administrative texts and documents and fiscal and budgetary problems, has the effect of teaching the student to express himself and present his work in an acceptable, and fairly uniform way. Stress upon style is not, of course, unique to the ENA — the student only reaches the ENA after an educational process in which he has consistently been more successful than most of his colleagues in presenting his work in an articulate and acceptable way. Uniformity of style, however, does not imply uniformity of ideas. As Professor Ridley pointed out in 1966, 'The technocrats as a group have no common policy on specific issues. It is not simply that they may differ on what is the "scientific" answer to any particular problem. More fundamental is the fact that the technocratic outlook gives little guidance, except in broad terms, where there is a choice between different ends'.[36]

Not only is there no one policy or set of policies that result from a common background, there is also no one political orientation. Certainly former students of the ENA have moved from the administration to politics, and many of those who have been successful within the governing coalition have been conspicuously so. Before the 1978 election twenty-three former ENA students had been elected to the National Assembly, and twenty of them had held ministerial office. Four other former ENA students had served as ministers without having held a parliamentary seat. However, leading members of the opposition are also to be found in the higher civil service. Michel Rocard for example is a Finance Inspector, Christian Pierret came to his seat as a Socialist Member of Parliament in 1978 from the Forecasting Division of the Ministry of Finance, and his colleague in that Division, Philippe Herzog, is a *polytechnicien* and a Communist.[37]

The policy-making process within the administration is, thus, subject to both conforming and contradictory pressures. One of the effects of the training provided by the ENA since 1945 has been to provide officials with some economic competence and understanding for a number of ministers and administration. This may, at least in recent years, have had the effect of enlarging the scope for conflict over economic questions, and of making more acute the need for political direction. The administrative environment is not divorced from the political structure — indeed the two overlap closely, both in institutions such as the *cabinets*, and in personnel. As Saint-Geours points out, 'Some years ago, a continuous and homogeneous politico-administrative line, based on the Finance Inspectorate, linked the Prime Minister to the young desk officer in the Treasury Division, through the Minister of Finance, his *directeur du cabinet*, the *directeur* of the Treasury division, and the appropriate *sous-directeur*.'[38] Paradoxically, however, the effects of link may have been to increase the scope for political action and direction. Another Finance Inspector recognized this:

> Twenty years ago it was relatively easy for a *directeur* to impose his wishes, disguised as technical necessities, upon a well-meaning veterinary surgeon. Nowadays, even if he says 'tu' to his boss, who may have been a member of the same *promotion*, his relationship is actually one of strict subordination.[39]

> The French State . . . has the structural potential for autonomous action, but structure does not determine how or whether that potential is used. A political explanation will always be required to explain the direction of State activity.[40]

Thus John Zysman insists upon the necessity of political direction for economic policy-making. However, the nature of the decision-making structures at political level in France also gives scope for ambiguity and conflict. The concluding section of this chapter attempts to examine the location of economic policy-making at political levels.

Economic Policy-making at Political Levels

Under the Fifth French Republic three actors have had a major influence upon economic policy-making at the political level. However

> 'apportioning influence of economic policy-decisions among the triumvirate of president, prime-minister and finance minister in general terms can only be done in a very crude way'.[41]

None the less, from the beginning of the Fifth Republic, the President has clearly been concerned with the main lines of economic development. For

President de Gaulle, the economic achievement and competitiveness of France were closely linked to her international standing. From time to time he played an active role: his desire to stop inflation lay behind the introduction of the deflationary stabilization plan in 1963, and he was responsible for the decision not to devalue the franc in 1968; the decision to do so in 1969 was taken by President Pompidou.

Pompidou, as President, took a more active part than his predecessor in the details of economic decisions, and was especially concerned with industrial policy and the encouragement of large-scale enterprises. His experience in banking, and as Prime Minister, had accustomed him to intervention in economic matters. President Giscard's training and experience as an official (he is a Finance Inspector) concentrated upon economic and financial matters, and all his ministerial experience was within the Ministry of Finance. In the first government formed after his election he ensured the appointment to the Ministry of Finance of a close personal friend and colleague. He appointed Raymond Barre as Prime Minister in 1976 largely on the strength of his standing as an economist, and it is Barre's name that has been attached to economic policy since then, but observers agree that it is a policy 'conduite par le Président de la République et appliquée par le Premier Ministre.'[42] In the international economic field President Giscard has been particularly active; he took the decision that the franc should enter the European monetary snake in 1975 and leave it again in 1976, and his personal efforts and collaboration with the West German Chancellor Helmut Schmidt were largely responsible for the setting up of the European Monetary System in 1979.

If the scope and nature of presidential intervention in economic policy have varied, so too have the roles played by the Prime Minister and, until 1976, the Finance Minister. The variation in roles may depend upon the personalities involved; for example, when in appropriate office Michel Debré was always firmly in control of economic policy, regardless of whether his office was that of Prime Minister or Minister of Finance. Certainly the Prime Minister has formal mechanisms under his control which may enable him to exert his influence on economic matters. There is a network of interministerial committees of which the most important is the Interministerial Economic Committee of which he is the chairman, with the Finance Minister as a permanent member, and which, Guy Lord concluded, works in the Prime Minister's favour.[43] Secondly, when conflicts arise between the Ministry of Finance and a spending ministry the Prime Minister's view is usually decisive. Thirdly, the Prime Minister is largely responsible for the strategy to be adopted in steering the measures required for the implementation of any economic policy through Parliament. Fourthly, the Planning Commission is attached to the Prime Minister's office.

The strength of the Ministry of Finance for most of the post-war period should, however, not be underestimated.[44] The functions of the Ministry before its division in 1978 included the establishment of the budget, and the oversight of all public expenditure — all regulations involving the spending of public funds required the countersignature of the Minister of Finance. The treasury division was responsible for monetary policy, for public sector borrowing, and the management of public receipts and payments. Working with the Banque de France and the Caisse des Dépôts et Consignations it had a determinant role in the control of the financing of public and private investment. The Ministry also had an interest in commerce, through its competition and prices division, and in export policy, since the corps of commercial attachés in French embassies is attached to its external commercial relations division.

In addition to this range of functions, the Ministry of Finance had sources of information available to it which provided the Minister with substantial technical backing for his policies. In particular, the forecasting division and the statistical service (INSEE) provide large amounts of essential statistical and macro-economic material. In addition, some of the Ministry's functions, and especially the budgetary process, combined with the presence in each spending ministry of a financial controller appointed by the budget division, gave the Ministry an extensive overview over the evolution of policy throughout the central administration.

The possibilities which arise, within this structure, for difficulties and ambiguities, are considerable. A delicate relationship between Prime Minister and Minister of Finance frequently ensues. This was certainly true when Chaban-Delmas was Prime Minister and Giscard Finance Minister; the situation was complicated by the fact that Giscard was the leader of the minority party of the Governing Coalition. When he himself became President it was his close colleague Fourcade who was appointed to the Ministry of Finance. Alain Vernholes, writing in Le Monde, said that relations between Fourcade and Chirac, the Prime Minister, became so bad that the two were scarcely on speaking terms, and what amounted to contradictory policies were being pursued.[45] When Raymond Barre was appointed Prime Minister in 1976, with a clear brief to take the economic situation in hand, he combined the posts of Prime Minister and Finance Minister, with the assistance of a junior minister.

The Ministry of Finance, before 1978, operated within, and usually dominated, an environment in which, nevertheless, other actors claimed an influence on economic policy-making. The most important of these actors is the Planning Commission. Founded in 1945 the Planning Commission which in its early years was able to use the resources of Marshall Aid to assist it to play a vital role in the reconstruction of the French economy, and to secure a good deal of co-operation for both the Ministry of Finance and the private sector, found itself, from the early 1960s, increasingly faced with difficulties. Saint-Geours alleges that successive Ministers of Finance never really accepted the procedures or disciplines of the Plan, and from about 1960 fought to decrease the role of the Plan — for example by the creation of the forecasting division within the Ministry, and through the production of alternative strategies to deal with economic crises.[46] Diana Green has shown how the nature of French planning has changed.[47] Although the scope and influence of the Plan has varied, and planning has proved particularly vulnerable in the face of sudden changes in the economic situation and external crises, the process remains a fairly large-scale one, with a good deal of political importance, indeed it has come increasingly to be seen as a political activity — the fact that the main guidelines of the Seventh Plan were decided upon before the consultative processes which should have produced them were complete clearly indicates this.

In addition to the Plan, other bodies also have claims to a place in the formulation of economic policy. For instance, the regional development and planning body DATAR attempts to influence the deployment of public investment so that it will be consistent with regional planning objectives. The Ministry of Industry has a particularly close relationship with private industry and has been a source of proposals and policies in the industrial field. Again, the strength of the Ministry has varied; both the political weight and attitudes of the Ministers involved and the economic circumstances have affected the Ministry. While the effects of the economic recession seem to have led to some strengthening of the Ministry of Industry, in that industrial policy decisions assume greater importance, the general trend of economic policy has been a neo-liberal, and not an interventionist one.

The Division of the Ministry of Finance

Into this already complex situation a further factor was introduced immediately after the general election of 1978, with the division of the Ministry of Finance into two separate ministries, one for the budget and one for economic affairs, both under the control of a cabinet minister. The idea of a distinct ministry concerned with economic affairs was not new. In some respects it can be traced in the Second Empire, when, at a period of rapid development, for example of the railway network, Agriculture and Commerce were attached to the Ministry of Public Works which became for a while effectively a Ministry of the Economy.[48] A Ministry of the National Economy, with the task of co-ordinating the economic activity of the government was set up by Leon Blum's Popular Front Government in 1936. Lacking, as tends to be the fate of co-ordinating ministries, the resources to act, it did not survive the fall of Blum's Government. In 1944 a Ministry of the National Economy again appeared, under Pierre Mendès France. After the resignation of Mendès France in 1945 the Ministry maintained, for most of Fourth Republic, an independent existence, but it was not usually headed by a minister of cabinet rank, and it never had the strength to impose itself against either the Ministry of Finance, or the Planning Commission. By 1962 it had been completely absorbed by the Ministry of Finance.

The reform undertaken by President Giscard and Prime Minister Barre was thus not a completely new departure. Nevertheless, it differed from previous attempts in that the functions of the Ministry of Finance were actually divided between two ministries. Vernholes alleged that Giscard especially had wanted to see the handling of economic problems separated from the largely financial concerns of the old Ministry of Finance. Other commentators regarded the division as a 'divide and rule' tactic, Barre having found that, although he kept the control of the Ministry in his own hands, its weight in the administration meant that it nevertheless tended to dominate. It was clear that the Prime Minister intended to keep the direction of economic policy firmly under his control. Saint-Geours takes the view that this division is a device without fundamental consequences. It is equally possible to suggest that the creation of a cabinet minister with powerful administrative backing has opened the way for increased diffusion and conflict in the field of economic policy-making, and has introduced an important new actor who may alter the balance of relationships in this sphere. Suggestions of conflict between M. Barre, the Prime Minister, and M. Monory, the Economics Minister, seem to support this latter view.[49]

CONCLUSION

The role of the higher civil service in economic policy-making is both crucial and complex. The traditions which uphold the legitimacy of action by civil servants and the importance of intervention by the State reinforce this role. The environment within which higher civil servants operate is subject to pressures and conflicts which arise from within the administration. It is also fashioned by complex relationships between higher civil servants and the world of big business, and between higher civil servants and the political world. The process of economic policy-making is certainly influenced by the general economic orientation of the President and Prime Minister — at present neo-liberal. It is affected by political, even electoral pressures — how else is the *Loi Royer* in favour of small shopkeepers to be explained? The process of economic policy-making is never monolithic; but it is highly political. The very diverse and diffuse nature of the process at both the administrative and the political levels ensures this: despite the powerful positions of the bureaucrats and 'technocrats' important strands of policy — whether they be the choice of the major options to be highlighted in the Plan, or Barre's 1976 anti-inflation plan, or the abandoning of price controls in 1978 — develop as a result of political decisions.

Notes

*   I am grateful to Dr Diana Green, Handley Stevens, and Dr Vincent Wright, who read an earlier draft of this chapter.

1   A list of public corporations and their subsidiaries is given in François Chevallier, *Les Entreprises publiques en France*, Notes et Etudes Documentaires Nos 4,507-8 (Paris: La Documentation Française, 1979), pp. 223-48.

2   Ibid., p. 34.

3   *France* (Paris: La Documentation Française, 1975), p. 194.

4   Diana Green, 'Individualism versus Collectivism: Economic Choices in France', in Vincent Wright, ed., *Conflict and Consensus in France* (London: Frank Cass, 1979), p. 91.

5   Guy Thuillier, 'Un project d'école d'administration en 1815: Le Comte d'Herbouville', *Revue Administrative*, No. 166 (juillet-aôut 1975), p. 354.

6   Alain Peyrefitte, *Le Mal français* (Paris: Plon, 1976), pp. 106-7. All translations from French sources are by the author.

7   John A. Armstrong, *The European Administrative Elite* (Princeton: Princeton University Press, 1973), p. 59. This was especially true of the development of the railways. See Louis Girard, *La Politique des travaux publiques du Second Empire* (Paris: Armand Colin, 1952).

8   Jack Hayward, *The One and Indivisible French Republic* (London: Weidenfeld and Nicolson, 1973), p. 152.

9   R. F. Kuisel, 'Technocrats and Public Economic Policy: From the Third to the Fourth Republic; *Journal of European Economic History*, Vol 2, No. 1 (Spring 1973), p. 83.

10   Interview with former ENA student, graduated 1954, October 1977.

11   Personal communication from former ENA student, graduated 1954, October 1977. See also Jean Saint-Geours, *Pouvoir et finance* (Paris: Fayard, 1979), p. 33-4.

12   J.-J. Carré, P. Dubois and E. Malinvaud, *French Economic Growth* (Stanford, Calif.: Stanford University Press, 1975), p. 504.

13   Ezra N. Suleiman, *Elites in French Society* (Princeton, N.J.: Princeton University Press, 1978), p. 136.
14   Jean-Luc Bodiguel, *L'École Nationale d'Administration: Les Anciens Elèves de l'ENA* (Paris: Presses de la Fondation Nationale des Sciences Politiques, 1978), p. 207.
15   With the sole and isolated exception of the students of *promotion* 'Charles de Gaulle' in 1972.
16   *Le Point*, No. 87 (21 mai 1974).
17   Id.
18   Suleiman, *Elites in French Society*, p. 113.
19   Ibid., p. 269.
20   Jean-Claude Thoenig, 'Administration et pouvoir economique', *Esprit* (janvier 1973), p. 61.
21   Pierre Birnbaum *et al.*, *La Classe dirigeante française* (Paris: Presses Universitaires de France, 1978), p. 112.
22   Suleiman, *Elites in French Society*, p. 113.
23   Vincent Wright, *The Government and Politics of France* (London: Hutchinson, 1978), p. 90.
24   Ezra N. Suleiman, *Politics, Power and Bureaucracy in France: The Administrative Elite* (Princeton, N.J.: Princeton University Press, 1974) p. 263.
25   Interview with official of the Budget Division, Ministry of Finance, October 1977.
26   Saint-Geours, *Pouvoir et finance*, pp. 55–6.
27   Jean-François Kesler, 'L'Influence de L'École Nationale d'Administration sur la rénovation de l'administration et ses limites' in Société Française de Sociologie, *Tendances et volontés de la société française* (Paris: SEDEIS, 1966), p. 257.
28   *Le Nouvel Observateur*, 7 juin 1976, p. 42.
29   Suleiman, *Elites in French Society*, p. 242.
30   Ibid., p. 247.
31   Jean-Claude Thoenig, L'Ère des technocrates: le cas des Ponts et Chaussées (Paris: Les Editions d'organisation, 1973), p. 61. For a similar reaction on the part of the prefectoral corps to proposals for regional reform see Howard Machin, *The Prefect in French Public Administration* (London: Croom Helm, 1977), pp. 52–8.
32   Jean-Luc Bodiguel and Marie-Christine Kessler, 'La Haute Fonction Publique en France', note prepared for the Groupe D'Etudes Comparatives sur la Fonction Publique (February 1979), p. 88.
33   Francis de Baecque, *L'Administration centrale de la France* (Paris: Armand Colin, Collection 'U', 1973), p. 189.
34   Diana Green, *Economic and Financial Decision Making in the Fifth French Republic: The Budgetary Process* (Unpublished doctoral thesis, London School of Economics and Political Science, 1976), p. 237.
35   Interview with former ENA student, internal entrant with previous experience in the administration, graduated 1954, October 1977.
36   F. F. Ridley, 'French Technocracy and Comparative Government', *Political Studies*, Vol. XIV, No. 1 (1966), p. 44.
37   He stood in the 1978 general election as the Communist party candidate in the fourteenth Paris constituency (XIIIe arrondissement: Maison Blanche-Croulebarbe).
38   Saint-Geours, *Pouvoir et finance*, p. 206.
39   Jean-René Bernard in *Le Monde* (29 décembre 1976).
40   John Zysman, *Political Strategies for Industrial Order: State, Market and Industry in France* (Berkeley, Calif.: University of California Press, 1977), p. 195.

41 Hayward, *The One and Indivisible French Republic*, p. 155.
42 René Maury, 'L'Inflation: politiques: les racines politiques', *Cahiers Français*, No. 186 (mai–juin 1978), p. 62.
43 Guy Lord, *The French Budgetary Process* (Berkeley, Calif.: University of California Press, 1973), p. 77.
44 For a description of the Ministry of Finance from an official who served in Giscard's *cabinet* when he was Minister of Finance, see Xavier Beauchamps, *Un Etat dans l'etat? Le Ministère de l'Economie et des Finances* (Paris: Bordas, 1976).
45 *Le Monde* (1 février 1977 and 7 avril 1978).
46 Saint-Geours, *Pouvoir et finance*, pp. 72–3.
47 Diana Green, 'The Seventh Plan — The Demise of French Planning?', *West European Politics*, Vol. 1, No. 1 (February 1978), pp. 60–76.
48 Girard, *La Politique des travaux publiques du Second Empire*, p. 122
49 *Le Nouvel Observateur* (8 octobre 1979), p. 59, described a member of Barre's *cabinet* as 'unable to hide his dislike of Monory's demagogy'.

5 The Budget and the Plan

Diana Green

The publication of the Government's *Report on the main options of the 8th Plan*[1] in April 1979 seems to indicate that, despite predictions of its imminent demise,[2] French national planning has managed to survive the Giscardian axe. Introducing the Report, the Prime Minister, Raymond Barre asserted that the new Plan will be inspired by 'a new conception of planning'.[3] This reflects a more realistic assessment of the feasibility of attempting to construct a national economic and social development Plan in an increasingly unpredictable international environment and against the backcloth of the 'changing economic geography of the world'.[4] At the same time, it highlights and is a response to 'les déceptions du 7e Plan'.[5] This most recent Plan was virtually rendered redundant by the Barre 'Stabilization Plan', introduced in September 1976 at the time at which the National Plan should have come into force. Although the Seventh Plan was simply suffering the fate of some of its predecessors,[6] it does offer a particularly pertinent illustration of the failure of the French to find an effective means of harmonizing short-term and longer-term economic policy objectives, i.e. to resolve the inherent conflict between the Budget and the Plan.

This chapter will focus on these two policy processes, looking at changes introduced in a bid to resolve this problem, notably the attempt to 'rationalize' budgetary decisions through the introduction of RCB (Rationalization of Budgetary Choices) and the designation of 'priority action programmes' (PAP) in the process of plan preparation.

WHAT IS FRENCH NATIONAL PLANNING?

French plans are five-year economic and social development plans. They are said to be 'indicative' or 'guideline' plans, to distinguish them from the command plans of the Soviet system. Conceptually, they are depicted as providing a 'middle way' between the anarchy of the free market system and central direction. Their function is to *supplement* market forces (rather than replace them), by providing information to reduce uncertainty and generate a climate of expansion. For this reason, planning has never been an ideological issue in France and has escaped the 'great debate on planning and democracy' which preceded the British planning experiment.[7] Indeed, French national planning is, according to the official line, 'democratic planning', i.e. it is not the artefact of faceless (and unaccountable) technocrats but the end product of a complex process of consultation between Government and its 'social partners'. In practice, however, although 'concertation' has served as a model for government – industry relations in other political systems (notably the tripartite British planning machinery), its effectiveness as a mode of joint decision-making is open to question. In other words, the ostensibly democratic nature of this democratic planning process is one of the many controversies which surround French planning.[8]

French national planning has changed considerably since the First (Monnet) Plan was introduced in 1947. This, which is arguably the only 'true' National Plan, was essentially a plan to reconstruct the economy in the wake of the devastation suffered in the Second World War, and was financed primarily through Marshall Aid.[9] The Second, Third and Fourth Plans were essentially development plans, although the Fourth also emphasized the *qualitative* aspects of an expansion which was, by now, taken for granted.[10] The Fifth Plan (sometimes called the Massé Plan, after the then Commissioner), marked a further evolution in the nature of French planning to the extent that 'generalized market research' resulted in a general framework for State economic policy in the medium term ('une fresque de l'évolution à moyen terme de l'économie et de la société française'). The Sixth Plan focused on industrialization, in response to the increase in international competition (especially from the Germans, whose economic and industrial performance is the benchmark for French success); while the main thrust of the Seventh, and most recent Plan, was the search for ways in which the economy could adapt to the post-oil crisis. Work has now started on the next, Eighth Plan, due to come into force in 1981 (see p. 115). What, then, has been the impact of planning on the conduct of economic policy in France?

French planning has managed to survive a series of crises, both economic (e.g. periods of runaway inflation followed by stabilization policies), and political (*inter alia*, the Algerian War, the Revolution *manqué* of 1968 and the accession of Giscard d'Estaing, a convinced anti-planner, to the presidency), to the extent that the machinery of planning still exists and produces a Plan every five years. The survival of the institution should not, however, be read as implying that it has a determinant role in the economic policy-making process. There are two main reasons. The first springs from the nature of French planning. Related to that is an organizational problem: the traditional division of economic policy functions between the Planning Commission and the Ministry of Finance, which both highlights and exacerbates the problem of co-ordinating short-term and medium-term policy objectives.

Firstly, French Plans have never constituted a firm commitment on the part of the Government (at least, not until the Seventh Plan, see p. 113). In other words, despite the fact that they are formally endorsed by Parliament, French Plans are not, *per se*, mandatory. Rather, they constitute a statement of the Government's expectations and/or intentions in the medium term.[11] French planning is therefore, at most, *provisional*, planning. The Plans contain not policy decisions, but 'pre-decisions' which have to be confirmed, both politically and financially, in the actual conduct of economic policy. This is underlined by the *de facto* division of labour between the Planning Commission and the Ministry of Finance.[12] Although the Commission formally has overall responsibility for planning, in practice, its influence is limited by its lack of executive powers (i.e. it has no means of enforcing the implementation of the Plan). The implementation of the Plan is, in fact, conditional on the decisions taken each year in the framework of the preparation of the Finance Bill (State Budget). The Finance Ministry (now the Budget Ministry, since the division of 'Les Finances' into two ministries in 1978) therefore effectively controls the implementation of the Plan, (insofar as it provides the funds needed to finance the public investment programmes), i.e. the implementation of the Plan depends critically on the way the Budget and the Plan are linked. Thus, for example, the Plan may serve as a point of reference for budgetary decisions[13] and may play a useful role in the delicate negotiations between the spending ministries and the Budget Ministry.[14] But if close co-ordination between the Budget and the Plan are a necessary condition of the implementation of the latter, in practice there has been a notable absence of such co-ordination. Indeed, there is a long history of conflict between the Budget and the Plan, visible in both the policy processes and the institutions responsible for them.

THE CONFLICT BETWEEN THE BUDGET AND THE PLAN

There are a number of reasons for this conflict. Firstly, the budgetary procedures concentrate attention on expenditure in the year ahead. This makes it difficult to harmonize the Budget with the multi-annual investment objectives of the Plan. Secondly, the inflexibility of the Budget, which accepts the greater part of current expenditure as given,[15] and concentrates on changes at the margin, makes it almost impossible to modify expenditure according to the priorities defined in the Plan. Thirdly, the budgetary format has traditionally been geared to *funding the administrative structure* (i.e. the activities carried out by the State machine) rather than the activities and/or objectives which ought to be pursued, according to the Plan. At the same time, changes in the nature and scale of planning have been accompanied by the development of increasingly sophisticated techniques. The methodology of planning, in other words, (sectoral programming frameworks, prospective economic budgets, national accounting, etc.) was developed under the direction of the Planning Commission in the absence of any formal links with the work of the traditional ministries, especially the development of budgetary techniques.[16] Indeed, at the institutional level, conflict has been sharpened by opposition between the macro-economists staffing the planning machinery, who tend to be expansionist in their outlook, and the budgetary specialists in the Finance Ministry who (at least until 1975) were constrained by the need to adhere to the sacred Giscardian tenet of budgetary balance. Translated into policy, this has meant that the Finance Ministry has been engaged in a permanent battle to contain the inflation which inevitably resulted from the growth oriented policies pursued by the Commission. Conversely, the Commission has fought valiantly to protect ministerial investment programmes from the Finance Ministry's swingeing cuts, especially in the various stabilization or counter-inflationary packages introduced throughout the post-war period (notably in 1963 and 1976).

To some extent, discontinuity between the Budget and the Plan springs from the *nature* of the two processes. Broadly speaking, they fulfill similar functions in a different time horizon, i.e. the Budget fulfills, in the short term, the function of securing the general consistency that planning attempts to exercise in the longer term. In this respect, both policy processes have suffered from the same basic fault: rigidity. Thus the National Plan, fixed for its five-year term, has been unable to take account of environmental uncertainty or adapt to unexpected crises.[17] Similarly, the state Budget is rather like an iceberg, with by far the largest part of expenditure committed.[18] This has made it virtually impossible to allocate resources in line with the changing priorities of subsequent National Plans. Consequently, there was increasing pressure, (especially during the late 1960s) to improve the co-ordination and harmonization of budgetary policy and medium-term economic planning.

The problem has been tackled in three main ways. At the institutional level, a series of attempts have been made to integrate the Plan more closely into the economic policy-making process. The most important of these was the setting up of the Central Planning Council which shifts the responsibility for co-ordinating short-term and longer-term policy decisions to the presidential level.[19] Meanwhile, changes have also been made within the two policy processes with the same end in view. The first of these experiments was in the budgetary policy area where RCB was introduced in a bid to rationalize budgetary decisions. This was followed, shortly after, by the definition, within the Seventh National Plan, of 'Priority Action Programmes' (PAPs) which implicitly take up some of the principles of RCB.

PLANNING BUDGETARY DECISIONS: THE RCB EXPERIMENT

RCB (*Rationalisation des Choix Budgétaires*) is the French approach to a movement which took place in a number of industrialized nations during the 1960s, focusing on the allocation of public expenditure. It owes much to the American experience of Planning, Programming and Budgetary Systems, although in many ways, it is a distinctively French approach.[20] Its introduction was in line with the general desire to managerialize administrative practice.[21] At the same time it reflected the belief that the introduction of the newest methods of computation and management would make good the relative backwardness of economic policy techniques (especially *vis-à-vis* planning techniques).[22] More specifically, the desire to 'rationalize' public expenditure decisions was essentially a response to three main problems: an excessive increase in public expenditure; the ineffective nature of the traditional budgetary process; and the absence of justification, in *quantitative* terms, of public expenditure proposals. Thus it was felt that the continuing increase in public spending (at a rate greater than that of the Gross National Product) was a real threat to economic stability. It was therefore essential to find a means of evaluating the consequences of proposed expenditure at the macro-economic level. At the same time, before asking the economy to support this ever-increasing expenditure, it was rational to examine its current size to determine whether the expenditure associated with 'existing policy' (*services votés*), which represents 90–95 per cent of the total Budget, was really justified and inevitable. (In this respect, the adoption of 'rational' budgetary techniques was clearly seen by the Ministry of Finance as a way of cutting ministerial budgets.) Moreover, in practice, ministers tended to justify their estimates in *qualitative* rather than quantitative terms. No attempt was made to measure the economic advantages which might result from the pursuit of the various ministerial activities.

The RCB Scheme was therefore very ambitious; right from the outset it attempted to revolutionize administrative practice, changing the nature of the role of the State, introducing methods of economic computation to guide ministerial decision. This was to be achieved by three means: firstly, the use of quantitative and analytical techniques in the examination of public investment projects; secondly, the transformation of the traditional budget into a 'programme budget'; thirdly, the introduction of modern management methods (e.g. management by objectives) into the field services of the ministerial departments.

Ten years after the start of the RCB experiment, results have fallen far short of expectations. For example, RCB studies have clearly 'improved' decision-making to the extent that they have introduced into public policy decisions the use of techniques such as cost benefit analysis (which takes into account not only quantative costs and benefits but also the non-quantifiable effects of policy decisions), economic accounting and multi-criteria analyses. But, despite the tightening up of the guidelines in 1975 and the introduction of 'priority studies' ('les études prioritaires') centered on the most urgent economic problems facing the government (e.g. the future of the motor car in France, immigration policy, etc.) they have had little impact on the policy-making process.[23] Similarly, progress in the modernization of management within the administration has been relatively slow, and limited to the introduction of certain techniques (e.g. management by objectives and the computerization of resource management) in a limited number of ministries (mainly those which have field services, *inter alia* the old Ministry of Public Building and Works and the PTT). It is the programme budgeting exercise, however, which is of more interest here. It is through this exercise that the French have attempted to make public policy-making, if not perfectly rational, at least more rational.

The main objective of a programme budget is to improve the efficiency of the allocation and management of resources. It differs from a conventional budget[24] in establishing (at all decision-making levels) the relationship between political objectives, the results of administrative activity and the resources needed to carry them out. The programme budget, focuses attention on administrative activities and on the final product of the administration (i.e. policy output). The administration is therefore seen as a *producing* rather than a consuming (spending) unit. The programme budget has four main features.[25] First, all ministerial activities are presented, as its name implies, in the form of a *programme* which specifies the objective to be attained, the financial resources required, the personnel to be allocated and the expected results. All ministerial programmes are then collected together and presented in a budgetary document. Thirdly, the discussion of each ministerial budget with the Finance Ministry in the annual budgetary cycle should be in programme terms. Finally, indicators should be specified which allow the costs and results of each programme to be measured.

All ministries have now produced programme budgets so that for the first time the estimates of 1980 are to be presented simultaneously in the traditional classical form (*les bleus*) and in the new programme form (*les blancs*).[26] In other words, although in principle programme budgets imply a radical change in the French budgetary process, in practice, this has not happened.[27] For most ministries, a programme budget is simply a new and more systematic means of presenting their annual estimates, *in addition* to (rather than instead of) the traditional presentation. Its chief value is as a source of information (both for the Government and Parliament); it clarifies public expenditure decisions, insofar as it relates a ministry's estimates to its activities. The impact of programme budgeting on decision-making has, however, been negligible. At most, it seems to have improved the *preparation* of decisions, by increasing the information available and clarifying the context in which decisions are made.

After ten years of operation, it is quite clear that the RCB experiment has fallen short of expectations. On the one hand, it is condemned (especially by the Ministry of the Budget) as an artifice which has had no impact on basic budgetary procedures, a gadget, even an administrative game. On the other hand, it is still seen by the 'converted' as a prodigious system which opens up the possibility of revolutionizing administrative practice.[28] Its actual impact lies somewhere between these two extremes. The introduction of RCB has, in fact, highlighted a number of problems. At the administrative level, it has introduced a new way of working. Based on the concept of *efficiency*, it has exposed some of the worst inefficiencies of administrative practice such as the excessive weight of precedents, the rigid compartmentalism of the French bureaucracy and the confusion which surrounds decisions which makes it impossible to determine responsibility. The concept of efficiency had not been used

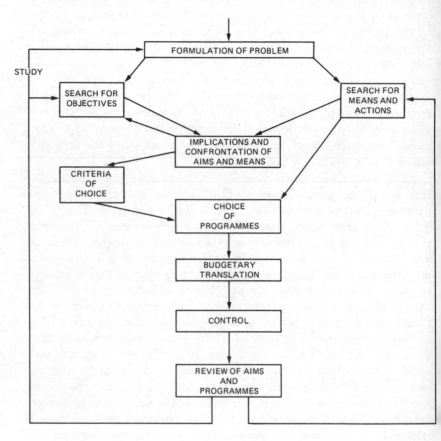

Source: 'RCB: vers une nouvelle raison d'Etat', Notes et Documents, No. 3815–6, 20 September 1971.

Fig. 5.1.   The RCB cycle

in the administrative context before the introduction of RCB. It was rarely — if ever — asked whether the money voted in the Budget to a specific Ministry for a specific purpose was spent efficiently (i.e. whether it brought the desired result — or even if it was actually used for the purpose claimed. The inability of the Ministry of Finance to check on this had led to the widespread habit of ministries increasing their manpower

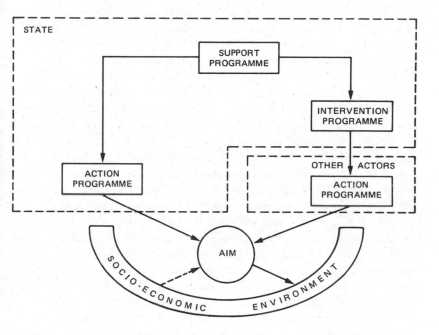

Source: J. Bravo and B. Walliser, 'Les Systèmes d'indicateurs de programmes', *Statistiques et Études Financières*, 1975/19.

Fig. 5.2. Typology of programmes

under the disguise of obsolete programmes). RCB therefore represents a shake-up of old procedures and methods of work by introducing the notion of efficiency into administrative practice.

The emphasis on concepts previously foreign to administrative practice (e.g. efficiency, quantification of the costs and benefits of government programmes, the measurement of government costs and output, etc.) generated a certain scepticism about the method which seemed to herald a take-over by the technocrats. It was feared that decisions would be pre-empted by 'technicians' — a fear expressed both by non-technical civil servants and decision-makers at the political level. It was only after the appearance of the first RCB studies and as a result of an extensive programme of courses and seminars mounted by the RCB 'Mission'[29] that some of the doubt was alleviated.

The RCB experiment has not, however, been a total failure. Although there is not yet an integrated system of studies/budget/control in the French administrative system, there has been some progress. Thus decision-making has benefited from the fact that the linkage between studies and decisions has been improved, and in some cases programmes have actually been implemented. Experience has shown, however, that RCB is most successful, and most useful *within* individual ministries, in the allocation of resources to different programmes, in line with ministerial policy objectives.[30] It has been less successful at the political level where choices *between* ministerial programmes are more dependent on social, economic and political judgements for their respective weighting. Indeed, for many of the disillusioned RCB has failed precisely because it has failed to provide some magic formula for ranking basic alternative policy options. Yet, clearly there are advantages to be gained from the introduction of programme budgeting, even in its present, limited form, to the extent that governmental activities are clearly and explicitly related to their costs. But if programme budgets are, in principle, the prerequisite of a 'rational' budgetary process, in practice, making them operational (i.e. changing the way economic and financial decisions are made) is a daunting — if not impossible — task. At the limit, one is forced to ask whether RCB can work in a *political* context. To predicate rational decision-making in the public policy area is to assume that the Government should be held accountable for producing results, i.e. it presupposes that objectives can be specified against which governmental efficiency can be measured in respect of achieving the desired results. But in a public expenditure situation, decisions have to be made which reflect what the electorate will accept (or can be persuaded to accept) and which also take account of relatively short-term *political* factors, such as the state of the economy and the proximity of the next elections.

At the same time, the specification of objectives has little to do with the reality of budgetary decisions (at the national level) which relate primarily to on-going activities. It is not so much the objectives of ministerial programmes which tend to be contentious, as the *priorities* attached to the respective programmes (i.e. what matters is not *why* a programme is proposed, but the order of precedence, in terms of funding). The use of rational techniques, then, in the public policy area is constrained by political and institutional factors which considerably limit the usefulness.

RCB AND THE NATIONAL PLAN

It was initially hoped that the introduction of RCB would eventually result in a greater co-ordination between the annual budgetary process and the preparation of the National Plan. The adoption of programme budgeting clearly implies the consideration of public expenditure programmes in the medium rather than the short-term.[31] But, as has been indicated, the introduction of RCB has had little real impact on the method of resource allocation. Has it had any impact on the process of Plan preparation? And to what extent has it contributed to the greater co-ordination of decisions made in the two policy processes?

The first three National Plans, centred initially on the problems of reconstructing the economy and subsequently its modernization in response to increasing international competition, paid little attention to the State Budget. It was not until the Fourth Plan that the notion of 'collective functions' emerged and that their evolution, as spelt out in the Plan, became a political issue (i.e. determined by the Government and formally endorsed by Parliament). The Fifth Plan, like its predecessor, dealt only with the overall ceiling of public expenditure (more precisely capital expenditure since current expenditure was excluded). By the Sixth Plan, however, it had become apparent that this conception was too narrow and that some means should be found of programming total public expenditure (capital and running costs). Investment credits were therefore grouped into a number of headings corresponding to the main 'collective functions', e.g. transport, and programmed over the five years' term of the Plan. There were a number of other important innovations, notably the definition of six experimental 'finalized programmes'. These spelt out objectives to be attained in certain priority sectors, as well as defining the corresponding financial resources required and performance indicators.[32] Although clearly drawing heavily on RCB principles, the links between these programmes and the RCB studies are very tenuous.[33] Indeed, the preparation and execution of the Plan and the launching of the RCB operation were completely separate exercises.

French planning emerged from the crisis of confidence it experienced at the end of the Sixth Plan in a radically modified form: changes were made in the Plan preparation process, and the planning machinery as well as the content of the Plan proper.[34] As has already been indicated, the creation of the Central Planning Council at the presidential level marked an important step in the attempt to harmonize planning more closely with short-term economic policy. Furthermore, the 'collective functions' of the Sixth Plan were abolished and replaced by twenty-five

'Priority Action Programmes' (PAPs) which spelt out the principal public investment projects (social or economic) to be programmed over the term of the Plan. These differ from the 'finalized programmes' to the extent that they are shielded from future cutbacks by the Government's formal pledge to carry them out (underpinned by voting a specific proportion of budgetary credits over the term of the Plan for their realization).[35] The PAPs are interesting for a number of reasons. Firstly, they underline the fact that although the Plan is less ambitious in scope than its predecessors, within this narrower framework, planning (= programming) is more important. Secondly, *prima facie*, the PAPs indicate a far greater degree of commitment, on the part of the Government (i.e. to the limited range of actions spelt out in these programmes) than in previous Plans (with the provision, of course, that they still have to be confirmed, annually, by the actual voting of funds in the Budget).[36] At the same time, they appear to represent the first serious attempt to harmonize short-term and medium-term expenditure decisions. A close examination of the PAPs reveals, however, that they do not correspond to the ministerial priorities which emerged through the RCB studies, suggesting that at the level of the definition of policy priorities there has been little improvement in co-ordination. Moreover, although in principle, the PAPs are supposed to have been chosen according to their relevance to the Plan's main objectives,[37] it is quite obvious that many were adopted simply because they were fashionable or because of pressure from powerful lobbies. Indeed relatively low rates of execution of some programmes have reinforced the suspicions of the Budget Ministry that ministers have used the PAPs simply to boost their overall budget rather than to rationalize (redeploy) expenditure.

Yet, interestingly, the PAPs were clearly drawn up according to the principles of RCB: they are sectoral or intersectoral; they specify their objectives as well as the resources needed to implement them (investment and operating credits); performance indicators are specified; and a simple, clearly identified person is made responsible for this implementation. Indeed, it has been argued that the PAPs suggest that the Plan has been more influenced by RCB than the Budget.[38]

But perhaps the most obvious indicator of the failure to co-ordinate the medium-term objectives spelt out in the Plan with the problems of day to day economic management was the introduction of the Barre Stabilization Plan in September 1976, at the time at which the Plan should have come into force.[39] *Prima facie*, the Barre Plan is another in a long line of counter-inflationary packages interrupting the development path predicted in the Plan and rendering its objectives redundant.

But is this the case? To what extent are the aims of the Barre Plan and the Seventh Plan incompatible? To what extent has the government departed from past practice and honoured its commitment to protect its stated priorities (i.e. the PAPs) from short-term fluctuations?

THE BARRE STABILIZATION PLAN AND THE SEVENTH NATIONAL PLAN

Apart from their nominal similarity, the Barre Plan and the National Plan are totally different animals. The former is not a plan at all, in the strict sense of the word. Arguably, it has been so designated primarily to suggest that the package of measures to which it is attached relates to some longer-term strategic purpose rather than constituting an *ad hoc* response to an unexpected crisis. The discussion of their compatibility therefore hinges directly on the sticky issue of the relationship between short-term crisis management and medium-term planning.

Did the introduction of the Barre Plan make the realization of the National Plan impossible? The question implies that the divergence between the Plan's forecasts/targets is not simply the result of the economy moving away from its predicted development path but reflects a *voluntary* decision, on the part of the Government, to depart from that path. If this were the case, the 'deceptions' of the Seventh Plan shown in Table 1 in fact disguise a deliberate change in policy priorities. In other words, the lower growth rate recorded would not simply imply bad planning (i.e. inaccurate forecasting). On the contrary, it would indicate that the Government consciously abandoned the Plan's forecasts/targets, opting for a lower growth rate as part of its counter-inflationary strategy. Although the balance of payments target has clearly been undermined by successive oil price rises which were beyond the Government's control, the argument would appear to have some foundation if we examine the National Plan's full employment objective. As is shown elsewhere (see below, Chapter 8), the Barre government's decision to give priority to industrial competitiveness and concomitant refusal to allow feather-bedding has meant that unemployment has increased rather than declined. It would be simplisitic to blame this increase wholly on the Government: clearly it reflects the general decline of economic activity at the international level. Yet, significantly, Barre does accept that the government's policies have exacerbated worsening trends. Similarly, the pledge to return to a balanced budget (symbol of good management since the days of Pinay, and a sacred Giscardian tenet) has been sacrificed in the interests of both

Table 5.1   The 'deceptions' of the VIIe Plan (annual rates)

	Forecasts (1976–80)	Results (1976–78)
Production	+ 5.2%	+ 3.8%
Imports	+11.9%	+ 8.5%
Consumer Spending	+ 4.7%	+ 3.7%
Corporate investment	+ 6.9%	+ 2.5%
Housing	+ 2.0%	− 0.9%
Public investment	+ 4.3%	+ 2.2%
Exports	+12.0%	+ 7.4%
Retail prices	+ 7.2%	+10.3%

Source: *L'Expansion*, April 1979

Table 5.2   Budgetary deficits 1969–1980 (in millions of francs)

Year	Forecasts Deficit	Surplus	Results
1969	6,354		− 1,369
1970		5	+ 528
1971		2	− 1,754
1972		1	+ 3,395
1973		3	+ 7,432
1974		346	+ 5,614
1975		27	−38,011
1976		7	−20,046
1977		5	−18,041
1978	8,900		−34,124
1979	15,000		−40,000†
1980	31,000		

Source: *Le Monde*, 7 September 1979.
* Excluding IMF operations and exchange adjustments.
† Approximation

economic and political expediency. Thus, with what has been described as a '*frisson Keynesien*',[40] Barre has drawn up the Budget for 1980 with a planned deficit of Fr. 31 billion, more than twice the planned deficit for the previous year, and predicted to rise, on past experience, to at least Fr. 50 billion. (See Table 2).

The official explanation of this apparently voluntary departure from the National Plan's predicted development path is that the Barre Plan corresponds to the first phase of this path, which was forecast by the planners in outlining the Plan's strategy for the five years ahead. Indeed, both are explicitly designed to restore order to the economy (*remise en ordre*) as a prerequisite of the renewal of expansion.[41] Unfortunately, the severity of the problem and the continuing crisis have necessitated the extension of this first phase so that the Seventh Plan has almost run its course without actually reaching the planned expansion path. In other words, the Barre Plan is officially held to be in line with, rather than incompatible with, the principal objectives of the National Plan. Indeed, this fact is explicitly recognized in the Report on the options for the Eighth National Plan which, in examining the main problems confronting the French economy over the next five years, re-states and defends current economic policies.

THE EIGHTH PLAN: UNPLANNING THE NATIONAL PLAN?

Introducing the Report on the main options of the Eighth Plan, the Prime Minister asserted that the new Plan will be inspired by a 'new conception of planning'. Close analysis of the text of the Report suggests, however, that the Eighth Plan will mark a further stage in the evolution of French planning rather than a complete break with the past. Like its predecessor, the Eighth Plan will not attempt to be a comprehensive plan for the French economy but will constitute a 'strategy for development'. Where it could be argued that the new Plan will depart from the past practice is in the decision to reinforce its strategic nature by paying greater attention to changes in the international environment in the longer term.[42] At the same time, the Eighth Plan will be more selective than earlier Plans. Further, it should 'no longer be articulated around the normative macro-economic objectives which experience has shown to be so illusory'.[43]

The decision to scrap the normative projections which have been a central feature of French Plans is officially explained by the uncertainty of the international environment which makes it 'pointless and even dangerous' to attempt to quantify France's economic prospects.[44] At the same time it is clearly a tactical decision: replacing them by a qualitative formula ('as high and regular a growth rate as possible') is a neat way of obtaining consensus and retaining credibility (i.e. it avoids any debate about whether growth should be 'fast' or 'moderate' while allowing the Government to escape committing itself to some arbitrarily chosen rate which turns out to be hopelessly over-optimistic). Yet it was also a political decision: given the nature of French planning, to include

Table 5.3   The Priority Action Programmes (PAPs) of the Seventh Plan and the rate of implementation over the term of the Plan (in millions of francs)

	1976 (MF 1976)	1977 (MF 1977)	1978 (MF 1978)	1979 (MF 1979)	1980 (MF 1980)	Total planned expenditure over the term of the Plan (MF 1975)	Rate of budgetary implementation (as %age)
1. Agricultural production	739	699	782	848	910	3,378	90.1
2. Construction	21	27	32	34	34	130	86.4
3. Small business	71	234	398	424	1,378	1,536†	114.0
4. Telecommunications (PTT)	(18,700)	(24,800)	(25,749)	(24,500)	(24,800)	(104,400)	(91.4)
5. Development of the West, Southwest and Massif Central	898	1,665	1,731	1,575	1,645	5,790	98.6
6. Rhine–Rhône link	157	179	165	141	140	780*	78.2
7. Economic development of the overseas territories (DOM)	244	305	389	358	383	1,339	95.1
8. Reduce dependency on imported energy and raw materials	163	361	446	489	510	1,530	95.8
9. Export promotion	663	814	907	990	1,116	3,780	89.9
10. Job creation	469	608	726	829	978	3,052	88.7
11. Training the young	164	1,245	3,656	2,184	2,151	5,918†	116.9
12. Improved working conditions for manual workers (figure for PTT in brackets)	406	483	564	704	739	2,861	76.2
	(627)	(850)	(873)	(987)	(1,030)	(3,330)	(99.4)
13. Equality of opportunity in education	4,409	4,987	5,745	6,671	7,356	20,551	107.2
14. Family policy	130	142	202	244	242	1,005	71.6
15. Policy for the aged	67	78	101	122	159	480	81.7

16. Preventative health care	805	956	1,167	1,370	1,512	4,000	109.2
17. Justice	159	186	292	305	352	837	115.2
18. Consumer protection	360	413	472	555	580	1,900	94.6
19. Hospital service	585	670	689	791	795	3,729	72.2
20. Road safety	166	194	199	230	300	899	91.3
21. Improve urban life	1,632	2,247	3,016	2,896	3,252	12,899	76.1
22. Architectural preservation	173	175	255	308	433	959	103.8
23. Rural zones	554	724	831	871	1,081	2,925	104.5
24. Environmental policy	294	332	413	595	698	2,208	78.4
25. Research promotion	1,819	2,168	2,512	2,888	3,290	10,489	91.1
Total excluding PTT	15,148	19,892	25,690	26,422	30,034	92,975†	94.8
PTT	19,327	25,650	26,622	25,487	25,830	107,730	91.6
Overall Total	34,475	45,542	52,312	51,909	55,864	200,705*†	93.1

* Taking into account the changes introduced under the terms of the Report on the Revision of the Seventh Plan.

† Including expenditure under the National Employment Pact schemes, i.e. Fr. 940m. in 1977, Fr. 3,115m. in 1978, Fr. 300m. in 1979 and Fr. 3191 in 1980 (that is, a total of Fr. 5,425m. at 1975 prices since the start of the 7th Plan and Fr. 2,029m. more than initially forecast).

‡ The price index used here for conversion into 1975 Francs is as follows: 1976/5–1097; 1977/6–1084; 1978/7–1101; 1979/8–1094; 1980/79–1089.

realistic forecasts would be politically suicidal, since, by definition, the Government would be committing itself to a policy of declining growth and rising unemployment.[45] This could be interpreted as an attempt to reduce any medium-term constraints on the Goverment's action and, by implication, constitutes a further emasculation of the national planning as traditionally conceived.

Yet, at the same time, the Government appears to be re-affirming the importance of planning as it evolved in the Seventh Plan, i.e. the programming of public investment projects. It has been decided to repeat the exercise of designating a limited number of ministerial programmes for which priority funding will be reserved over the term of the Plan (PAPs). Despite a number of problems, the exercise is regarded as having been successful. By the end of the financial year 1978–79, the average rate of execution for the PAPs is 95 per cent (see Table 3) suggesting that despite the sacrifice of other objectives, the Government has honoured its pledge to protect these programmes from arbitrary cutbacks. In this respect, the PAPs seem to have been a useful devise for harmonizing the Budget and the Plan, if only on a limited scale.[46]

It is not yet clear how many PAPs will be designated for the Eighth Plan[47] and the problem of how to tighten up the election procedure to ensure that they represent *genuine* priorities still has to be tackled.[48] It is quite evident, however, that the Government sees the exercise as a means of rationalizing public expenditure by encouraging ministers to carry out a voluntary redeployment each year, bringing their spending plans much more closely into line with the Government's objectives as spelt out in the National Plan.[49]

Does this suggest the progressive merger of the budgetary and planning processes? Clearly, the Plan is being 'budgetized' to the extent that a small proportion of public expenditure is guaranteed within a medium-term framework. Conversely, the Budget has to some extent stepped out of its annual framework in programming a limited number of public investment programmes over the medium term. The Planning Commission would like to go further and integrate the PAPs with ministerial Programme Budgets. The Budget Ministry is sceptical of such an integration, partly because it would lose part of its freedom of manoeuvre to respond to conjunctural crises. There are, of course, a number of practical difficulties. Firstly, the PAPs are interministerial while Programme Budgets are related to specific ministerial departments. Secondly, a ministry's contribution to a PAP is only part of its activities whereas the Programme Budget spells out, by definition, the complete range of its activities. These problems are not, however, insurmountable but could be overcome by the expedient of spelling out in any Programme Budget the ministry's contribution to one or more PAPs. A third and more difficult problem is the different *functions* of the PAP and the Programme Budget. While a PAP is essentially an instrument of execution (i.e. it provides the resources for implementing medium-term public expenditure decisions), a Programme Budget is, at present, only an information document, not a decision document. In other words, integration of the PAPs with ministerial Programme Budgets would necessitate the translation of the latter into decision-making instruments for the allocation of resources at the interministerial level, a condition which seems far from realization.

Should the PAPs be in the Plan? Is there not a contradiction between the macro-economic approach of national economic planning and the micro-economic approach used in the designation of the PAPs? At the institutional level, for example, RCB focuses on the machinery of government (i.e. attempts to improve the efficiency of decision-making at the ministerial or administrative levels) and has little bearing on the kind of 'decision' made by the tripartite planning commissions (significantly, the commissions were not consulted in the choice of the PAPs of the Seventh Plan). The designation of the PAPs, and their implementation over the term of the Plan, has, however, been accompanied by a lessening of the conflict which has traditionally existed between the Finance Ministry and the Planning Commission. More importantly, the PAP exercise has resulted in a *rapprochement* between the Budget and the Plan to the extent that a limited number of investment programmes have been shielded from the government's counter-inflationary axe. That there is some doubt about the importance of individual PAPs (i.e. to what extent they represented *true* priorities) matters little compared with the fact that the *principle* of harmonizing short-term and medium-term policy objectives has been established and made operational *via* this mechanism. Moreover, the impact of the PAPs on the Plan itself has clearly been beneficial to the extent that they have provided it with a 'rolling' element which has done much to ease the problem of rigidity affecting earlier Plans.[50]

But is this really planning? The global, macro-economic character of the traditional French Plan is gradually disappearing. The five-year rolling plan which is replacing it (and which has, in the past, been steadfastly resisted) is, of course, less constraining, but can it still be called national planning? In other words, is national planning, as traditionally conceived, being gradually replaced by multi-annual programming for a limited number of State actions (i.e. by medium-term budgeting)? The Government continues to pay lipservice to the need for planning, but qualifies this by urging that, in the light of uncertainty in the international environment, the traditional conception be revised. Yet the decision to scrap the central normative projections suggests that, despite the rhetoric, the Plan is being steadily emptied of content (over and above the budgeting of a limited number of medium-term actions); rather than a new conception of planning, in other words, the Eighth Plan threatens to be a further stage in the 'un-planning' of National Planning. Similarly, and at a different level despite the lipservice paid to the continuing importance of consensus-building in the process of Plan preparation, a further and radical pruning of the consultative machinery (chopped back to seven commissions and seven committees)[51] seems to suggest a further emasculation of the planning process. In other words, 'democratic planning' (in the shape of consensus building) is gradually and explicitly being replaced — if indeed it ever really existed — by 'technocratic planning' (in the shape of medium-term budgeting).

This suggests a rather pessimistic conclusion. On the one hand, national economic planning as traditionally conceived of in France, has, over time, demonstrated that it does not lead to efficient decision-making. And, conversely, the rationalization of planning decisions has inevitably meant that they have become less democratic. At the same time, the changes currently taking place in the planning process suggest that its prospects for survival in adverse economic and political circumstances (at the national and international level) are far from good. Although the preparation of the Eighth Plan has begun, this should not, in other words, be taken as an indication that the Plan will have a crucial role in the policy-making process. At most, it implies that the question of the feasibility and/or desirability of French planning has temporarily been shelved.

Notes

1   *Rapport sur les principales options du VIIIe Plan* (Paris, La Documentation Française, 1979).
2   See Diana Green, 'The Seventh Plan — the demise of French Planning?', *West European Politics*, Vol. 1, No. 1 (Feburary 1978), pp. 60–70.
3   Prime Minister's address to the Economic and Social Council, 2 May 1979.
4   *Rapport sur les principales options du VIIIe Plan*, p. 5.
5   See note 3.
6   For example: the Third Plan (1958–61) was interrupted by an 'Interim Plan'; the execution of the Fourth Plan (1962–65) was similarly interrupted, after 1963, by the Stabilization Plan which lost Giscard the Finance portfolio; the Fifth (1966–70) was more or less abandoned after the Events of May 1968; and the Sixth Plan (1971–75) was thrown completely off course by the 1973 energy crisis, to which the Government responded with a further series of counter-inflationary measures.
7   See Trevor Smith, *The Politics of the Corporate Economy* (Oxford: Martin Robertson, 1979).

8   See note 2 above, also Susan J. Koch, 'Non-democratic non-planning: the French Experience', *Policy Sciences*, Vol. 7 (1976), pp. 371–85.
9   For further details, see Y. Ullmo, 'France', in Jack Hayward and Michael Watson, eds., *Planning, Politics and Public Policy*, (Cambridge: Cambridge University Press, 1975); Jacques Leruez, 'Macro-economic Planning in Mixed Economies: The French and British Experience', in Jack Hayward and Olga A. Narkiewicz, eds., *Planning in Europe*, (London: Croom Helm, 1978); D. Liggins, 'What can we learn from French Planning?', *Lloyds Bank Review* (April 1976), No. 120.
10 The Fourth Plan, which signalled the high-water mark of French planning was the first to be specifically called a *Plan for Economic and Social Development*, reflecting both the change of emphasis and the greater comprehensiveness of future plans.
11 There has always been some ambiguity surrounding the status of the figures recorded in the earlier plans, i.e. to what extent they were specific objectives or forecasts of expected results.
12 The Planning Commission (Commissariat General du Plan, (CGP)) is a small, non-hierarchical body attached to the Prime Minister's office, staffed by about sixty senior officials (drawn mainly from the *grands corps*). It works in close collaboration with ministerial departments and research organizations (public and private), producing prospective studies based on analyses of the current economic situation. It is also responsible for setting up and servicing the commissions, sectoral study groups and working parties which provide the forum for 'concertation'. Despite its strategic position as an arm of the Prime Minister's office, its lack of executive powers and its 'foreignness' (*vis-à-vis* the machinery of government) means that it has a permanent propensity to isolation. Ministries tend to treat it with contempt – or ignore it – (on the grounds that it has little to do with the problems of day-to-day management), except when it is in their interest to use it, (e.g. defending their estimates in the annual budgetary battles with the Finance Ministry).
13 This is not always the case, but it is said to have done so during the 1960s, i.e. during the heyday of planning.
14 Interestingly research shows that the Plan tends to be used by both the spending ministries and the Finance Ministry for different ends. Thus, the former will use it to increase their estimates while the latter will use it to cut them back! Diana Green, *Economic and Financial Decision-making in the Fifth French Republic: The Budgetary Process 1968–74* (unpublished Ph.D thesis, London, 1976).
15 About 90 per cent of current expenditure: ibid.
16 The development of budgetary and management techniques lagged behind that of planning techniques. The 'functional budget' has been used since 1959, but is essentially a new way of presenting the complex budgetary documents (*bleus*) rather than a new way of budgeting. Similarly, Organization and Methods, introduced at the same time, hardly revolutionized administrative practices.
17 It has, in fact, never pretended to eliminate environmental uncertainties. At most, the Massé 'generalized market research' model attempted to reduce *market* uncertainties.
18 A Wildavsky, *The Politics of the Budgetary Process*, (Boston, Mass.: Little, Brown, 2nd edn, 1974), p. 13.
19 Chaired by the President of the Republic, the Council brings together the Prime Minister, the main economic policy ministers and the Planning Commissioner. Other ministers are invited to attend as appropriate. (See Diana Green, 'The Seventh Plan').
20 A number of senior officials in the Ministry of Armed Forces visited the United States to study PPBS (Planning, Programming and Budgetary Systems) as practised at the Pentagon under MacNamara.

21   At a meeting of the Council of Ministers in January 1968, it was decided that quantitative techniques should be progressively introduced to increase the efficiency of administrative practice.

22   Jacques Chirac, opening address of the RCB Seminar held at Tours, February 1969.

23   Whereas earlier studies had been carried out by *ad hoc* study groups, the new type of study would be carried out by senior officials with direct access to ministers. (J. P. Fourcade, Minister of Finance, opening address of the 6th International RCB Commission meeting, January 1975). It was hoped that the importance of the studies, (i.e. their inter-ministerial nature and the fact that they focused directly on current policy issues rather than the marginal subjects treated in the earlier studies) would induce the administration to take the exercise seriously.

24   A great deal of the literature distinguishes the conventional from the programme budget by describing the former as *resources*-oriented (*budget de moyens*), and the latter as *objective*-oriented (*budget d'objectifs*). This is inaccurate. In the conventional budget, expenditure has traditionally been classed by nature, destination *and* policy objective. The programme budget is more complex insofar as it is a *synthesis* indicating what, with what resources, financed how, and to satisfy which objectives.

25   See J. Bravo, 'l'Experience française des Budgets de Programmes', *Revue Economique*, No. 1 (1973), pp. 1–63; Ph. Kessler and F. Tixier, *Les Budgets de Programmes* (Paris: Berger-Levrault, 1973).

26   So called because of the colour of the paper on which they are printed.

27   *Lois de programme* were five year 'contracts of intention' between the Government and Parliament for public investment programmes.

28   The religious analogy is apt: one is asked if one 'believes' in RCB!

29   A public relations organization attached to the Ministry of Finance for the introduction of RCB.

30   In fact the programmatic approach has been criticized to the extent that it focuses attention on the individual programme of individual areas of the Ministry's policy at the cost of the Ministry's *global* policy. In practice, the programmatic approach has tended to underline the divisions between both activities and personnel, thus exacerbating one of the problems (administrative compartmentalism), it set out to resolve. (For example, roads are dealt with in separate programmes in separate ministries from the Ministry of Transport to the Ministries of Health and the Interior — in fact, it has been estimated they affect about eighteen different ministerial programmes (!), without any co-ordination between these programmes.) This raises the whole sticky issue of inter-ministerial activities which RCB has not yet managed to resolve.

31   This was not strictly speaking new: the 'programme laws' (*lois de programme*) introduced by Debré represented a similar attempt to move towards a more coherent and planned public investment policy. (These were five year 'contracts of intention' between Parliament and the Government which defined the ceiling for certain investment credits.)

32   'Finalized programmes' ('*programmes finalisés*') were created for the creation of new town, road safety, the prevention of perinatality, the improvement of the job market, the retention of old people in the family home, and the protection of forests in the Mediterranean area.

33   Only two programmes relate directly to issues examined in RCB studies, road safety and perinatal policy.

34   See Green: 'The Seventh Plan'.

35   Fr. 200 billion at constant (1975) prices was allocated to the programme, (national and regional), representing about 15 per cent of total public expenditure.

36 Since the Constitution insists on an annual Budget, the programmes are financed over the five year term of the Plan within the traditional budgetary procedure. The fact that each annual tranche is recorded separately in the given ministerial budget, together with a recapitulation of previous tranches in one of the annexes to the Budget, mean that, in principle, Parliament can check that programmes are, in fact, being implemented, as well as compelling the Minister to justify any changes introduced.

37 The twenty-five PAPs are, in principle, grouped around the six main objectives of the Seventh Plan, namely: reinforce the dynamism of the economy; guarantee national independence through the balance of foreign payments; guarantee full employment; reduce inequalities; improve the quality of life; promote research.

38 Jean Carassus, 'The Budget and the Plan in France', in Hayward and Narkiewicz, eds., *Planning in Europe*, p. 62.

39 Chronologically, the Seventh Plan was promulgated at the end of July 1976. Two months later, the incoming Barre government drew up the package of counter-inflationary measures which became known as the 'Barre Plan'.

40 *L'Expansion*, 7/20 September, 1979.

41 According to the planners the term of the 7th Plan would be divided into two distinct phases: a first phase (*remise en ordre*) during which wages would grow in line with prices; a second phase (phase de consolidation) during which expansion would begin again, leading eventually to full employment.

42 Where the Seventh Plan only gives a cursory glance to the international scene, a prominent feature of the Eighth Plan will be the analysis of structural changes in the international economy and longer-term problems such as the supply of energy and raw materials, the employment consequences of technological change, etc.

43 Letter from the Prime Minister to the Planning Commissioner, spelling out the guidelines for Plan preparation, 10 September 1979.

44 Interview with the Deputy Planning Commissioner, June 1979.

45 The National Statistical Institute (INSEE) will publish the forecasts, quite separately from the reports of the Planning Commission and the actual Plan.

46 The PAPs eventually constituted between 7 and 8 per cent of total public expenditure over the term of the Plan.

47 One or two may be carried over from the Seventh Plan. It is expected that the remainder will relate closely to the main options of the Plan as defined in the April 1979 Report.

48 The PAPs are a controversial issue, for a number of reasons. Firstly, doubt has been expressed about the logic of fixing priorities over a five-year period when, by definition, these are continually changing. At the same time, it is impossible to *prove* a close correlation between the designation of a PAP and an accelerated rate of funding. The Budget Ministry is highly suspicious of the whole exercise on the grounds that *genuine* priorities will be funded anyway, regardless of whether they are designated a PAP. This has resulted in *false* priorities being put forward; i.e. rather than redeploy funds, ministers have used PAPs to boost their overall budgets. The implication is that rather than ask Ministers to define their priorities after the budgetary ceilings are fixed, (as happened for the Seventh Plan), they will be defined by the *Prime Minister* before ministers are advised of the budgetary ceilings, to ensure that they reflect *governmental* priorities.

49 'Les programmes d'action prioritaires devront contribuer activement au re-deploiement des finances publiques. Vous étudierez . . . les voies et les moyens de dégager les marges de manouevre nécessaires pour l'exécution des PAP, compte tenu notamment des perspectives que vous dessinerez par ailleurs pour les finances publiques (Letter from the Prime Minister to the Planning Commissioner, 10 September 1979).

50   Each minister can undertake corrective action, at the time the annual Budget is prepared, in respect of the programme for which he is responsible. The co-ordination of these individual corrections is the responsibility of the Central Planning Council, which also carries out any 're-evaluation' of the overall Plan deemed necessary in the light of these changes. It is an ingenious way of getting round the problem of the rigidity of the fixed Plan. (Mid-term revision has not been conspicuously successful.)

51   There are six committees organized around the six main options (energy and raw materials, industry, agriculture, employment, social policy and the quality of life). The seventh commission, the Development Commission, will provide the synthesis of their reports. Five 'horizontal' committees are attached to the Development Commission (finance, regional policy, the international economy and trade, research and the overseas territories). A committee on wages and salaries is attached to the Employment Commission and a separate committee has been established to deal with transport. This represents a considerable cutback compared with previous Plans (e.g. twenty-six commissions for the Sixth Plan and thirteen for the Seventh Plan).

6 Centre and Periphery in the Policy Process

Howard Machin

'The One and Indivisible French Republic' has long been caricatured as the most centralized state in Western Europe. Observers have even compared servile 'local administration' in France with lively, independent 'local government' across the Channel. In practice, however, participation in, and influence over, the making and implementing of public policy has never been restricted to national politicians and the central government machine. The needs for local consultation over national policy choices, for local adaptations in the execution of national policies and for allocating some policy areas for local decision and implementation (albeit under national supervision) were recognized and respected even when France was a rural, backward, agricultural, divided and disunited society. In practice, power has always been dispersed within central government, between central and local political and administrative bodies, and at the 'periphery' between the various actors and forces involved.[1]

Since 1945, however, France has become an urban society, with exporting, industrial and commercial, economic roots, an increasing population (until the late 1970s), growing prosperity and high expectations of extensive public services to maintain and improve the quality of life. In consequence, 'local problems' are urban problems for most French citizens, and they concern town planning, the provision of services, and the defence of group interests. Growth and prosperity, however, have not been equally distributed across France, and in those geographical regions which have suffered relative decline (and especially when local cultures seemed doomed by depopulation) demands have been voiced for drastic economic intervention by central government. As national politicians and administrators have wished both to assist and to promote local self-assistance, local politics is now partly concerned with the regional implications of national economic policy-making. At the same time, for an ever-decreasing minority of the population (occupying nine-tenths of the actual land-mass of France) local government has continued to deal with rural life — with villages, small market towns, and agricultural society. In a televisual, telephonic age, however, rural citizens expect similar services to those provided for their urban cousins, so that, even in 'traditional' peripheral France, the extent of public policy making has greatly expanded. In short, socio-economic change has reduced the size of the rural periphery, but increased its problems, whilst urban and regional local politics are those which are today of most concern to four-fifths of all French citizens.[2]

It is not surprising that the recent changes have resulted in increased peripheral participation in policy-making. Most urban citizens now hope to get more, many of the ever-increasing number of interest groups seek to do more, and even suspicious ministers and hostile central civil servants have realized the necessity of encouraging local initiatives. What is, perhaps, unusual, is that there has been no comprehensive reform of local political and administrative institutions to cater for the new patterns of settlement and consumer demand. The last successful attempt at global reform of local government institutions was begun during the Revolution and completed by Napoleon. Since then, however, a multitude of minor modifications of the existing institutional arrangements has been enacted, with the result that co-operation and co-ordinated action between local actors and between local and national politicians, administrators, and interest group leaders is even more essential than in the past for the efficient intermeshing of local and national policy-making. Before analysing and assessing the practices and effects of this present complex system it is, however, valuable to consider the traditional pattern of local–national relations to appreciate the great inheritance from both the theory and the practice of the past.[3]

TRADITIONAL THEORIES AND PRACTICES OF
LOCAL–NATIONAL RELATIONS

1. The Jacobin Elements

Centralization was a natural policy for the kings of France. The kingdom was created by dynastic marriage and military conquest out of the independent feudal territories around the Île-de-France. Vast differences of laws, languages and customs, and strong local indentities and loyalties made effective royal control very difficult to achieve. Hence, the kings attempted to erect a strong centralized state and to use it to create an integrated nation. They sought to reduce the powers of feudal nobles and provincial assemblies (the *Parlements* and *États*) and to concentrate responsibility for the local administration of central government policies in the hands of royal officials (the *Intendants*).[4] The 1789 Revolution did not lead to the creation of a more decentralized system, as the Girondins proposed, but rather, under the dominant Jacobins (and later Napoleon) of a more efficient system of centralization: one tenet of the Jacobin belief was that popular sovereignty was indivisible, and from this arose the wish to concentrate all political power in a central national representative agency for the articulation of the general will (first the Assembly, but later, the Emperor). The Jacobins also held that all citizens should be equal before the state, and hence that there should be no local divergences from national norms but only central government policies executed in a uniform way throughout France. In short, at the time of the Revolution, centralization was hailed as highly democratic, egalitarian and republican.

During the Revolution, the Jacobins redrafted the administrative map of France. The 38,000 parishes, renamed as *communes* were retained as the lower tier units, whilst eighty-nine *départements*, equal geographical parts of a 'one and indivisible Republic', replaced the feudal counties and provinces. Napoleon (and all subsequent rulers) retained these 're-publican' local units but established a new hierarchy of central government officials to direct all administrative activities within them. The responsibility for implementing government policy in the *département* was given to a government official, the Prefect, the sole representative of the whole government. In his *département* he gave orders and instructions to his subordinates, the Sub-Prefects, and through them to the Mayors and the *communes*. In addition to his own administrative services in the prefecture (the building housing both his official residence and his offices), the Prefect also controlled the state employees in a number of specialist 'field services' located in his *département*.

The Napoleonic prefectoral system served not only for hierarchical central control of the provinces from Paris, but also as a channel of communication between the periphery and the centre. Mayors registered births, marriages, deaths and electoral rights. They informed their Sub-Prefects about all aspects of life in their communes, and the Sub-Prefects gave regular accounts about local politics, economics and even crimes to their Prefects, who, in turn, wrote detailed monthly reports to the Minister of the Interior.

In this system authority was highly personalized: the few decision-making powers delegated were given only to Prefects, Sub-Prefects and

Mayors who bore responsibility for all deeds performed by their services. Just as the Minister of the Interior had competence for all 'internal' policies, so the Prefects had responsibility for almost all administrative activities in their *départements*: hence, public works, conscription, law and order, education, charities, religion, elections and agriculture all formed part of the Napoleonic Prefects' responsibilities. Inevitably, Prefects, Sub-Prefects and Mayors were all appointed agents of the central government, paid by and answerable to the Minister of the Interior and subject to instant dismissal. Whilst obliged by their large and varied administrative tasks to be generalists the Napoleonic Prefects and their subordinates were not simply bureaucrats. All members of the prefectoral heirarchy performed highly political duties. They supplied the government with information, they repressed opposition and sought to create support for Napoleon and his policies by wooing the most influential and wealthy citizens (the *notables*) of every *commune*, and *département*; by means of propaganda, social flattery and simple clientelism.[5]

In addition to the prefectoral system the Napoleonic structures also included a number of specialist field services. In most cases these were subordinated to prefectoral supervision at the local level and answerable, through the Prefects, to specialist divisions of the Ministry of the Interior. There were also three areas of governmental action outside the scope of the Ministry of the Interior, and covered by separate independent ministries: these were war, justice and finance. These three ministries established their own field services which were exempted from prefectoral supervision: the armed forces, the courts and the taxation and payment services were all technical field services of national ministries, staffed by government appointees. The existence of such services established the precedent of the legitimacy of specialists to administer at the local level without 'generalist' prefectoral control.

Many features of the Napoleonic system survive to the present day. The boundaries and names of almost all the units at all levels have remained largely unchanged since 1800. There are now ninety-six *départements* (five new *departements* were created in the Paris area in 1966 and in 1975 Corsica was divided into two *départements*), and apart from the Haute-Loire and the Var, all are still administered from prefectures in the original 'capital' towns (*chefs-lieux*). The *communes*, despite the encouragement to amalgamate provided by the 1971 Local Government Act, still numbered over 36,300 in 1979 (only 2,000 fewer in number than in 1970). In short, in the 1970s the local government units remained very largely those chosen for the rural, backward, agricultural France of 1800, so that no single French *commune* includes the whole space or population of a built-up urban area.[6]

Other features of the system have also stayed unchanged. Mayors (electoral posts for over a century) still have responsibility for certain tasks as state agents. They still provide registration facilities and supervise elections. Prefects still provide reports to the Minister of the Interior, despite the apparent futility of this activity in an age of television, opinion polls and detailed economic statistics. The Prefects remain 'representatives of the whole government' and, as such, they attempt to supervise and co-ordinate the work of the specialist field services and still wield almost all the decision-making powers delegated from the ministries. In 1953, 1964 and 1970 governmental decrees were issued with the hope of restoring the 'unity of state action' in the *départements* by increasing the supervisory powers of the Prefects.

Many local government services in France are still, as in the past, provided by civil servants in the prefectures and the field services. The scope of the government action has expanded greatly during the twentieth century, and in consequence 'technical' ministries — and field services — have proliferated. The provision of administrative services by civil servants, rather than council employees, remains the pattern of organization. Hence almost all school teachers and policemen and most civil engineers and planners are civil servants in field services, directly answerable to ministries and not to committees of local councils (as in Britain).[7]

2. The Representative Elements

After the fall of Napoleon, France witnessed the gradual introduction of parliamentary government and elected local councils, and both these changes had profound effects on local and national politics. Governments wished to ensure their parliamentary supporters were re-elected and so encouraged the Prefects to use their control over local services to support pro-governmental Deputies. Members of Parliament, in theory representatives of the whole nation and joint articulators of the national interest, in practice became constituency delegates and protectors of local interests. Almost all Deputies, whether favourable or hostile to the Government of the day, attempted to influence all decisions affecting their constituencies, and hence increasingly intervened in Paris and in their local prefectures. Above all, Deputies sought to take credit for all popular policies, and to renounce responsibility for unpopular decisions. After the *coup d'état* by Louis-Napoleon in 1851, an attempt was made to wipe out this parliamentary influence over local administration: the Prefects were even empowered to choose the 'official candidates' for the parliamentary election. Once elected, however, these members of the *corps législatif* soon adopted old habits: by the time the Second Empire fell (1870) parliamentary interventions in Paris and the prefectures were again the rule rather than the exception.[8] Throughout the Third and Fourth Republic many Deputies and Senators still demanded, and obtained favours for their constituencies from ministers in Paris. As the life of every Government was short and fragile, ministers were constantly sensitive to individual Members of Parliament and their requests. In practice, the influence of individual Deputies or Senators extended over governmental policy choices, appointments to prefectures and even to local policy decisions and employment in field services and prefectures (formally powers of the Prefects). It does not appear that the advent of the Fifth Republic has totally destroyed the powers of Members of Parliament in questions concerning their constituencies; although it may be, as opposition parties have claimed, that only members of the governmental coalition now enjoy the privileges formerly shared by all.

Nor did the change of régime in 1958 radically affect the role of the locally elected councils. Since the local government laws of 1871 and 1884, the General Councils of the *départements* and the Municipal Councils of the *communes* have been freely elected bodies with independent powers for local policy making in those areas not dealt with at higher levels: prefectoral interference in *commune* affairs has been limited to a simple *'tutelage'* — a check on the legality of decisions by Mayors and Municipal Councils — and in 1970 this *'tutelage'* was reduced to a mere formality. The Prefect does not supervise the General Council of the *département*; rather he acts as its chief executive officer.

General Councillors are elected from single-member constituencies (*Cantons*) for six years with half the seats of each Council contested every three years. The General Council meets for two sessions each year when it elects its own officers (including its President and a Permanent Committee) and votes its own budget. The Permanent Committee meets once a month to supervise the Prefect's activities in the execution of its policies. General Councils have a large number of responsibilities, which include the building and maintenance of departmental roads, rural police centres (for the *gendarmerie*) teacher training colleges and prefectures, and the provision of many personal social services.[9]

Municipal Councils vary in membership according to the population of their *communes* which also determines the precise electoral system. All communes employ different types of list systems but all elections take place on the same day every six years. Each Council elects its Mayor and, in the larger *communes*, a number of Assistant Mayors. The Mayor and his Assistants are the real leaders of the Council and ordinary Councillors do little except attend the annual budget debates. In the past, Mayors did relatively little: almost all *communes* were small and rural and the main services required were local roads and the provision of a school building.[10]

If the fragmented nature of local authorities, their dependence on prefectoral and field services, and their lack of independent fiscal resources all appear to indicate an inevitable weakness of the local councils, this impression is inaccurate. In the first place, Prefects and directors of field services, if theoretically all-powerful and answerable only to their ministers in Paris, are in practice highly sensitive to local needs. On the one hand, discretion is shown in the execution of orders from Paris, whilst on the other hand, field services and especially Prefects spend a considerable amount of time and energy seeking assistance for local problems from the ministries in Paris. The field services are often manned by the same civil servants for long periods of time, with the result that these people themselves acquire local sympathies and interests. In contrast, the Prefect, who is very frequently shifted from one *département* to another, may be dependent for information and advice on the well-established personnel of his own prefecture, of the field services and of the local councils. In any case, as we have noted, the Prefect is obliged to establish good working relations with the local Deputies and Senators and with the General Council. If the Prefect is still, in formal legal theory, incredibly powerful, in practice he is subjected to pressure and advice which he cannot ignore.

The influential role of Mayors and Councillors, in practice much greater than the legal texts suggest, reflects a number of factors. In the first place, many Mayors and Councillors, especially in traditional rural *communes* and *cantons*, have well-established local roots. In 1964, 90 per cent of all General Councillors lived in the *cantons* they represented. This means they have very strong personal involvement and very detailed knowledge and experience of their constituencies. Hence, in dealings with prefectures and field services, Mayors and Councillors can claim not only the superior legitimacy of being elected by universal suffrage but also a considerable local expertise.[11]

A second traditional factor of even greater importance is the practice of accumulating elective offices. Traditionally election to a local council, or as a Mayor, was a first step in the path towards national office, but when subsequent steps were taken — election to a General Council and then to a seat as Deputy or Senator — these low-level offices were retained. In practice, of course all 36,300 Mayors cannot become General Councillors, but most General Councillors are also Mayors or Muncipal

Councillors and almost all national politicians have local roots as General Councillors or Mayors or both. In the 1971 elections to the Municipal Councils four-fifths of the Deputies and two-thirds of the Senators were candidates. This phenomenon of the accumulation of elective offices greatly affects the relations between local civil servants and local Councillors. No Prefect or state civil engineer is likely to offer anything less than full co-operation with the Mayor of even a tiny *commune* if that Mayor is also a Deputy or Senator, or even a minister in Paris. It should also be noted that senior civil servants in Parisian ministries are not excluded from active participation in local politics (there are certain obvious exceptions, including former Prefects), so that a local political–national administrative accumulation of offices is by no means rare. Whatever the nature of the accumulation of offices, the result is clear: the influence of some Mayors and Councillors greatly exceeds their theoretical powers,[12] and the whole notion of excessive centralization is considerably weakened.

3.   Rural Politics and Administration

The inherited pattern of local–national relations, described above now only affects a small section of the French population and even here changes have taken place. In 1979, under 10 per cent of the working population was involved in agriculture. In 1975, only 9 per cent of the population lived in *communes* of under 500 inhabitants, although there were no fewer than 22,700 of these *communes*. About two-thirds of the *départements* remained predominantly rural at the end of the 1970s.[13] Urbanization and rural depopulation have complicated the problems of the rural *communes* and *départements* in a number of ways.

Firstly, some old services are now more difficult to provide. This is most acute in the case of primary schools, for with a small number of inhabitants the upkeep of a school building becomes a large burden and, in any case, the Ministry of Education (in theory at least) will not provide a school-teacher if there are less than sixteen children, so that bussing, even for primary-school children, becomes inevitable. In the second place, there are some new demands. Even in the smallest, most obscure village, citizens expect electricity and water supplies, paved roads and street lighting, all of which are costly to provide. Furthermore, the empty countryside is now the area for holidays for the urban-dwellers. The emptied farm-houses, cottages and barns have been bought up (or inherited) to become second homes, giving France the largest number of second homes, relative to population, in Western Europe. The tourists not only expect the provision of normal urban services (water, electricity, sewage) but also expect well-surfaced roads and the provision of such facilities as swimming pools and tennis courts. Furthermore, the second home phenomenon creates new crime problems, as it is only too easy to burgle isolated houses during the long empty months of winter. A third feature of present rural politics reflects the resentment felt in many areas that the new economic prosperity is not being shared equally and that the result of depopulation is the disappearance of traditional local cultures. Local pressure groups have always played some role in rural politics, but the fact that the accumulation of elective offices often extended to Chambers of Agriculture and Commerce meant that these bodies rarely acted in competition with the formal political institutions. In the post-war period new groups have appeared and some old groups — notably the farmers unions — have gained renewed vigour. The new groups include the Young Christian Farmers (JAC), the Young Economic Chambers (JCE), the Poujadists (in the 1950s) and the CID-UNATI of Gérard Nicoud (in the 1960s and 1970s), these latter groups defending the interests of small shop-keepers and artisans. Furthermore, the resurgence of regionalist movements, in Britanny, in Corsica, the Basque countries and *Occitanie* is also, in part, a result of the rapid rural depopulation. Many of these groups have distinguished themselves by their willingness to resort to violent action, and wine producers, fruit growers, small-shopkeepers, the Bretons and the Corsicans have recently been most effective in this way.[14]

In contrast to this renewal of groups and group activities, the personnel of the local Councils has remained very traditional. In many respects the elites of the 'old France' — tradesmen, solicitors and landowners — predominate whilst young people, modern farmers, trade unionists and managers are conspicuously absent. This does not, however, imply that there has been no attempt at institutional adaptation to modern circumstances. Co-operation between *communes* for the purpose of providing a joint service has long been possible but the number of such Single-Purpose Syndicates of *communes* has grown in the post-war period, so that there are now over 10,000 groupings of this kind. Since 1959 it has been possible for *communes* to associate in a Multi-Purpose Syndicate to carry out any number of tasks at the decision of the member *communes*. By 1977 over 1,700 of such Syndicates existed including almost 17,000 member *communes*.[15] Each Syndicate is managed by a committee made up of two delegates for every member *commune*, so that it acts as a kind of local federation of Mayors. Furthermore, local co-operation between *communes*, Syndicates and the General Council is organized by the General Council itself, so that such services as school bussing and tourist development are also co-operative ventures. Inevitably, in all these joint ventures the central authorities are involved, if only as the major supplier of funds. Certainly, since 1958 successive Governments have so favoured such co-operative schemes that they have offered financial inducements in the form of larger grants and subsidies.[16]

In addition to these forms of association there has also been an attempt to reorganize rural local government by merging neighbouring *communes* together. Since 1958 central government has encouraged such mergers and in 1971 a law was passed to speed up this process. Local resistance to these plans has proved most effective: less than a thousand mergers have taken place and the total number of *communes* has been reduced by only two thousand. Since the death of President Pompidou there has been no new attempt to press reluctant *communes* into unwanted mergers and the main hope has been to encourage a more widespread use of co-operative Syndicates.[17] The ability of the apparently weak and fragmented *communes* of rural France to resist these attempts at institutional modernization is in itself a reflection of the reality of local power.

Rural politics today involves the Prefects, the General Councils, the Mayors and Municipal Councillors, the heads of field services, and the local pressure groups. Local decision-making is still subject to legal, technical and financial controls from central ministries, to audit by the Finance Inspectorate and the Court of Accounts and to the decisions of the Administrative Tribunals and Council of State. The fragmentation of the local authority units, the dependence on financial subsidies and loans from Paris and the archaic, socially unrepresentative nature of the local elected elites all undermine the influence of the local authorities. But it should be remembered that today, as in the past, centre–periphery relations are based on mutual co-operation and interdependence. Very often the centre, in issuing circulars determining minimum standards, is only responding to the wishes of local councils themselves. Frequently the centre hopes that local councils will take initiatives and find solutions to its own problems. Furthermore, as the size and scale of interventions of central ministries has increased, the effectiveness has decreased, and it is frequently possible for tacit conspiracies of local politicians and administrators to exploit differences between politicians or administrators in Paris to achieve their goals. Paris may often delay a project but it rarely arbitrarily blocks any reasonable plan. The system may appear arbitrary and confused, but it is neither ineffective nor profoundly undemocratic. There are still over 450,000 Municipal Councillors in France, the vast majority elected in the small provincial villages. Finally, it should be noted that as the size of the traditional sectors of the French economy have declined, their relative political importance has increased, as the electoral margins of the Presidents and their parliamentary coalitions have been reduced. As a result, recent Governments have shown increasing sympathy towards the interests of rural France, as the Royer Law of 1973 on supermarkets and the intransigent defence of agricultural prices at the EEC meetings demonstrate. Traditional, rural France may be smaller, but it is still politically significant.[18]

URBAN POLITICS

France is an urban society. Four-fifths of the population lives in conurbations of over 50,000 inhabitants. The Paris agglomeration, covering only 2 per cent of the land-mass, contains one quarter of the population (making Paris, in one sense, the largest single part of the periphery!), whilst a handful of other urban areas contain over a million inhabitants. All the stages of urbanization — rapid expansion, suburbanization, commuterization, immigrant ghetto formation and the reconquest of urban centres by the middle class — have taken place with amazing speed, placing huge demands on local authorities and local offices of national ministries. The expansion of existing services, such as housing, water supply, roads and schools, the provision of new services, such as public transport, parks and cultural facilities and above all, the planning of urban growth — both within individual urban areas, but also on a national level — have been major pressures on the urban authorities.

As in rural France, several attempts have been made to adopt local authority structures to present living patterns. Mergers of *communes* have been encouraged, and even enforced in the case of the nine New Towns created in the 1970s. The formation of Multi-Purpose Syndicates has also taken place, and for the bigger urban areas, two special forms of urban federal authorities, the District and the Urban Community, have been enacted. The Districts (148 in number in 1979) carry out certain defined common services for all their constituent *communes* (notably housing, structure planning and fire-fighting) and may take over any other services at the decision of their members.

The Urban Communities numbered nine in 1979: Strasbourg, Lille, Lyons, Bordeaux, Le Creusot, Brest, Cherbourg, Le Mans and Dunkirk. Each Community takes over several services from its member *communes* and becomes an important federal authority. Town-planning, public works, rubbish disposal and school buildings all become Community services as do those services normally run by Districts. By all these devices, it is possible for urban areas to evolve common policies in spite of the continued existence of the fragmented *commune* structure. Indeed it could well be argued that the traditional *commune* structures are a positive asset in that they encourage local participation and maintain a sub-structure of secondary commercial, administrative and cultural centres which humanize life in the massive urban sprawl. Furthermore, the Mayor of a small *commune* in a big urban area may often act as a useful guide for his citizens to the complex administrative structures affecting planning, education or housing.[19]

In many urban areas, one single *commune* is dominant and provides the effective leadership. Almost all these big-town *communes* have powerful and dynamic Mayors. In the majority of the towns, the Mayors are also Deputies or Senators, although this is not essential for the influence of the Mayor. Pradel, the Mayor of Lyons until 1976, held no national office but was none the less the virtual dictator of his city and the political boss of the Urban Community. Everywhere the Mayor of a big town is full-time, well-paid and a major force in all local questions. He does not need to bother with Prefects or other local civil servants but deals directly with Paris.

The Mayor is the leader of the party coalition which won the last elections. He is helped in local policy making by Assistant Mayors and although the Mayor may have to make concessions to his coalition partners he still has considerable freedom in choosing his own team. The Municipal Council meets infrequently and in all but the very biggest towns is entirely composed of the members of the Mayor's coalition list. When the Mayor leads a left-wing coalition (as in the majority of big towns since 1977) he can also rely on the party organizations for support, and can expect at least a sympathetic understanding from local trade unions. In short, between elections, most big town Mayors face little real local political opposition.

One other common feature of the big town authorities is that they are not dependent on the field services or the prefectures for services. Whilst they continue to work through the unified departmental Treasuries for all financial services and remain, like rural *communes*, largely dependent on central funding by grants, loans and subsidies, they do possess a certain degree of financial autonomy. The local tax rates may be small but the tax base is large, and this enables the municipal authorities to exert some choice over the type of taxation and the pattern of expenditure. Moreover, the big towns have large bureaucracies and growing technical services of their own. Hence, the employees of a town such as Rennes (population 250,000) number almost 3,000. The municipal services are managed, under the Mayor and his Assistants by a General

Secretary who is normally highly competent. In addition, the Mayor may employ the service of private consultants, especially in town planning.[20]

It is, of course, simply beyond the competence of the central ministries to fix all policies for all big towns even if a Government had a clear idea of what it wanted and was willing to accept the political results of over-riding the elected officials of a large town. In general central initiatives have been limited to projects to assist the towns in planning and controlling new developments and to give special encouragement to eight large conurbations to develop into regional economic capitals. More recently, governmental policy has included several attempts to give the town authorities more certainty about the nature and extent of central funding (by rationalizing the grant system) and to offer 'contracts' for several years funding to assist the development of the medium-sized towns.

Municipal leaders in town have considerable scope for taking initiatives. They can grant or refuse building permits and determine how and where land is expropriated. They are largely responsible for both the local structure plan (*Schéma Directeur d'Aménagement et d'Urbanisme*) and the land-use plan (*Plan d'Occupation des Sols*) which sets down rules for construction, lists precise public projects (the main highways and the location of public services) and fixes functional zoning of space. Obviously, these powers are limited by the interventions of local field services and appeals by individuals (notably over land-use) for ministerial intervention to over-rule local decisions. They are none the less very real sources of local influence.

A similar possibility of direct intervention from above, or complaints from below, also exists in other areas where the Mayor and his Assistants are the main local policy-makers. Housing and public transport, zoning industrial areas, school building, social, cultural and sporting facilities are all very largely locally determined in the big towns, but are subject to appeal. It is rare for a determined Mayor to lose an appeal, however, especially when he can demonstrate his local support. This desire for strong local consensus support for municipal policies (together with an ideological belief in participation amongst left-wing politicians) is a reason for the widespread development in big towns of consultative committees (where the Mayor and his Assistants meet interest group leaders), district committees (*comités de quartier*), and a more active role for Municipal Councillors.[21]

Urban policies vary not only between towns of different party-coalition Councils but also between Councils dominated by the same types of coalition. Strasbourg (Centre–Right coalition) and Grenoble (Left coalition) have both given special emphasis to the development of cultural facilities. Lyons (Centre–Right) and Lille (Left) have both built massive highway systems. In general, however, left-wing Councils do raise more taxes, in ways which disproportionately affect the middle classes, and spend a higher percentage of their budget on public housing, transport and education. The victories of left-wing coalitions in the big towns in the 1977 Municipal elections brought noticeable changes in local policies in many areas. In some places, financial assistance to Catholic schools stopped immediately. Elsewhere urban redevelopment projects have been halted, or reconsidered, and in many places the local tax structure has been modified. In short, urban elected authorities are influential in determining local policies, and party and coalition politics do matter.

REGIONAL POLICY

Although there have long been political demands for the establishment of regional local authorities (notably from 'ethnic' minorities in Brittany, Alsace and Corsica, and from opponents of the Government in power) the main preoccupations of those who created France's present regional structures were purely functional: they sought economic growth and administrative efficiency. In the 1960s a number of reforms were made to define regions and to organize a political, economic and administrative representation of these regions; and to establish in Paris an agency for co-ordinating central policy towards all aspects of regional development. This body, the Delegation for Regional Action (DATAR) linked to the Prime Minister's office, worked closely with the Planning Commissariat and the Finance, Industry and Infrastructure ministries in Paris and with the new regional representative bodies, the CODERs (politico-economic) and the CARs (administrative). In each of the twenty-one regions a Regional Prefect became the official centre–periphery administrative link man. It was hoped that these informal, consultative structures would be sufficient to permit the consideration of regional problems in national economic planning and annual budgeting, and the co-ordination within regions of field service and local authority spending and private investment for greater economic growth.[22] These hopes were unfulfilled, and, after the referendum rejection in 1969 of de Gaulle's fairly radical proposals for the creation of regional local authorities, new regional structures were introduced by law in 1972 under President Pompidou. This 1972 law did not change the boundaries of the existing twenty-one regions (although Corsica later became a separate region), but gave them a legal status as Public Establishments (corporate bodies empowered to transact legal and financial business in specific areas) although they did not become local authorities. In short, the federal–co-operative model for joint action by *communes* was again employed.

The specified task of the region is to contribute to the economic and social development of its area by carrying out detailed studies of possibilities for development, by proposing how public investments should be made in the region, by financial participation in public works projects of direct regional importance and by itself initiating and supervising such public works projects in association with central and local agencies.

Regional policy is determined by the Regional Council, which is advised by an Economic and Social Committee. The Regional Prefect, in addition to his duties of co-ordinating administrative action by prefectures and field services through the CAR, is now the chief executive officer of the region. The Regional Council (except in the Île-de-France) is composed of all the Deputies and Senators of the Region and an equal number of representatives of General, Municipal and Urban Community Councils. Seats are distributed in proportion to the populations of the constituent *départements*. The Economic and Social Committee comprises interest group representatives, chosen in a highly complex manner.[23]

The present regional structures have been widely criticized during their first six years of operations. It has been alleged that there is no longer any attempt at regionalized national planning, that regional boundaries are unnatural, that the Councils and Committees are unrepresentative, that the financial resources of the regions (in 1974 only 15 francs per head but later increased to 45 francs) are totally inadequate, and that the entire system does not allow the articulation of regional policies but merely provides a forum for negotiations between *départements* and big towns. All these criticisms contain some elements of truth, and certainly since national economic planning is, if not dead, at least in deep slumber, direct regional participation in national economic policy making has not been increased. In spite of all the attacks and the many practical problems, some regions do appear to have become influential in deciding local policies. The Nord-Pas-de-Calais and Midi-Pyrénées regions, for example, are frequently cited as success stories. There are also clear differences between the policies followed by the different regions and these seem to correlate to some extent with the politics of the majority coalition in the Regional Council. In all cases, the regions merely exacerbate the practice of office accumulation, for members of Councils and Committees alike are appointed precisely because they are already holders of elective office. Given that half the members of every Council are Deputies and

Senators, it is hardly surprising that, if there is local consensus in favour of certain policies, Paris can only delay their application.

CONCLUSIONS

In recent years one of the most widely quoted analyses of centre–peripheral relations in France has been the 'cross-regulation' model of Thoenig. This approach stresses the institutional interdependence of the administrative and public services of the state on one side and the local political and socio-economic leaders on the other. It emphasizes the impossibility of autonomous action and the importance of interventions from higher authorities to achieve co-ordinated decision-making. It also stresses the inefficiency and insensitivity, the undemocratic and deeply conservative nature of the system.

It is not the aim of this study to argue the efficiency of the present arrangements or to deny, for example, that long delays frequently occur. It has, however, been attempted to show that the 'cross regulation' analysis is now more relevant to the exceptional situation of rural areas than to the norms of urban and regional politics. The Mayor of a large town is generally also its Deputy, but even if not he has direct access to national politicians and administrators in his own right. He may have conflicts with local pressure groups, with the local newspaper and with local Deputies or Senators, of party loyalties different from his own, but he will not tolerate intervention from other local actors whether Prefects or General Councillors. In a similar way the Presidents of Regional Councils are almost all important national politicians who are unlikely to demand or even tolerate unwanted initiatives from regional civil servants. It is perhaps not surprising that centralization, so long under attack from all sides, is again becoming a respectable doctrine in France and that the present President, previously an advocate of decentralization and regionalization, seems to be changing his mind.[24]

Notes

1   J-M. Pontier, *L'Etat et les collectivités locales*, (Paris: Librairie générale de droit et de jursiprudence, 1978); G. Dawson, *L'Evolution des structures de l'administration locale en France* (Paris: Librairie générale de droit et de jursiprudence, 1968).

2   J-C. Thoenig, 'Local Government Institutions and the Contemporary Evolution of French Society', in J. Lagroye and V. Wright, eds., *Local Government in Britain and France* (London: Allen and Unwin, 1979), pp. 74–104.

3 J. Aubert *et al.*, *Les Préfets en France, 1800–1940* (Geneva: Droz, 1978); A. Tudesq, *Les Conseillers généraux en France au temps de Guizot* (Paris: A. Colin, 1967).

4 H. Machin, 'Traditional Patterns of French Local Government', in Lagroye and Wright, *Local Government in Britain and France*, pp. 28–41.

5 S. Kent, *Electoral Procedure under Louis-Phillipe* (New Haven: Yale University Press, 1937); J. Siwek-Pouydesseau, *Le Corps préfectoral sous la IIIème et al IVème République* (Paris: A. Colin, 1969).

6 J-C. Thoenig, 'Local Government Institutions'.

7 A total of over one million civil servants in 1976.

8 T. Zeldin, *The Political System of Napoleon III* (London: Macmillan, 1958); B. Le Clère and V. Wright, *Les Préfets du Second Empire* (Paris: Presse de La Fond, 1974).

9 M. Longepierre, *Less Conseillers généraux dans le systeme administratif français* (Paris: Cujas 1971); M-H. Marchand, *Les Conseillers généraux depuis 1945* (Paris: A. Colin, 1970).

10 M. Jollivet and H. Mendras, *Les Collectivités rurales françaises* (Paris: Librairie Armand Colin, 1972).

11 P. Birnbaum, 'Office-holders in the Local Politics of the French Fifth Republic' in Lagroye and Wright, *Local Government in Britain and France*, pp. 114–26.

12 A. Mabileau, ed., *Les Facteurs locaux de la vie politique nationale*, (Paris: Pedone, 1972).

13 *Annuaire statistique de la France*.

14 J. Hayward, 'Dissentient France', *West European Politics*, Vol. 1, No. 3 (October 1978).

15 J-C. Thoenig, 'Local Government Institutions'.

16 D. E. Ashford, 'French Pragmatism and British Idealism: Financial Aspects of Local Reorganization'. *Comparative Political Studies*, Vo. II, No. 2 (July, 1978).

17 H. Machin, 'All Jacobins Now', *West European Politics*, Vol. 1, No. 3, October 1978).

18 S. Tarrow, *Between Centre and Periphery*, (New Haven: Yale University Press, 1977; Institut Français des Sciences Administratifs, *Vers la Reforme des collectivités locales*, (Paris: Cujas, 1977); P. Gremion, *Le Pouvoir périphérique* (Paris: Éditions due seuil, 1976).

19 IFSA, *L'Administration des grandes villes* (Paris: Cujas, 1973).

20 J. Milch, 'Urban Government in France', *Administration and Society*, February 1974.

21 C. Sorbets, 'Control of Urban Development in France', in Lagroye and Wright, *Local Government in Britain and France*, pp. 150–64; B. Jobert and M. Sellier, 'Les Grandes Villes: autonomie local et innovation politique', *Revue française de science politique*, Vol. 27, No. 2 (April 1977); J. Milch, 'Influence as Power: French Local Government Reconsidered', *British Journal of Political Science*, Vol. 4, No. 2 (April 1974).

22 M. Mourjol, *Les Institutions régionales de 1789 à nos jours*, (Paris: Berger-Levrault, 1969).

23 IFSA, *La Région en question* (Paris: Cujas, 1979).

24 Introduction, in Lagroye and Wright, *Local Government in Britain and France*.

PART II

ECONOMIC POLICY: THE CHOICES

7 A French Political Business Cycle?*

Kristen R. Monroe

'. . . economic policy has to do with complex reality where economic phenomena are only one aspect. It is conducted amid political, psychological, demographic and social constraints that have to be taken into account.' (Prime Minister Raymond Barre)†

Is there a political business cycle in France? As originated by Kalecki, and developed further by Nordhaus, MacRae, Tufte, Frey, and Frey and Schneider, the theory of a political business cycle suggests the economy in many Western democracies fluctuates not just in rhythm with general economic changes but also in harmony with the timing of elections.[1] This cycle is manifested by pre-election economic growth and post-election contraction. These changes are stimulated by an incumbent government which recognizes the trade-offs in economic policy-making and deliberately follows policies designed to secure optimal pre-election economic conditions for the groups most critical politically for the incumbent party. Tufte and Frey argue further that this is a successful strategy for incumbents, resulting in actual electoral gain since most voters maximize short-term economic interests when they vote and do not realize or care that the political business cycle may have long-range negative economic consequences.

After a critical analysis of the theory of a political business cycle, I will consider whether such a cycle has existed in the French Fifth Republic. Consideration of a French political business cycle is long overdue since the only works on France are Nordhaus's important but cursory cross-national examination of pre-election and post-election changes in French unemployment from 1947 to 1967 and Tufte's even briefer examination of pre-electoral changes in income from 1961 to 1972. Given the tremendous political change during this historical period, the political importance accorded the smooth functioning of the economy by French politicians and public in the years since 1967, the French historical tradition of active government intervention in the economy, and the institutional tools available to French policy-makers should they wish to manipulate the economy for immediate political gain, the French case warrants a more systematic and detailed examination.[2]

Discovering and describing a French political business cycle would be important for several reasons. First, knowledge of pre-electoral economic growth and post-electoral economic contraction would help both policy-makers and the public make economic plans with more certainty. Second, the increasing scholarly interest in political business cycles makes it important for scholars to test this theory by making careful systematic examinations of the pattern in individual countries. Too often in political science, theoretical work is based on detailed empirical examination of only one or two countries; in this case, too much attention is paid to the United States experience, an experience which is interesting and instructive but may be atypical. A careful, detailed examination of the French experience will help correct this problem. And, finally, it is important for all economists and political scientists to consider further aspects of the interactions between the economic and political systems. Much important recent work in political economy has concentrated on explaining the linkages between the economy's effect on political popularity or voting, the government's response to changes in its popularity, and the translation of this governmental response back into specific economic policy-making. By adding to our knowledge of how the government considers political popularity in making key economic policies, the analysis presented below will add to our general knowledge of how the economic and political systems interact in Western industrial democracies.

Analysis proceeds in two main sections. The first section outlines the development of the theory of a political business cycle and points to several weaknesses in the theory. The second section is an empirical examination of the pattern of French government expenditures and the money supply from 1958 to 1979. These data will measure the government's attempt to manipulate the economy through the two main tools available to incumbents: fiscal and monetary policy. On the basis of this empirical examination, I conclude that the existence of a political business cycle in France is dubious and that the economic shifts around election time may be more the result of ordinary economic fluctuations than they are the reflection of the government's attempt or ability to control the economy.

THE POLITICAL BUSINESS CYCLE: THE THEORY
AND A CRITIQUE

Let me begin by outlining the most important aspects of the political business cycle and by suggesting certain points at which the theory seems overstated or logically flawed. The main idea of the theory is that incumbent politicians and administration policy-makers 'manipulate the short-run course of the national economy in order to improve the party's standing in upcoming elections and to repay its past political debts'.[3] This policy produces a business cycle of pre-electoral economic stimulation and growth followed by post-electoral economic contraction.

The theoretical impetus for the modern political business cycle orginated in Kalecki's Marxist-oriented analysis of business cycles.[4] Kalecki contends that lasting full employment is not desired by business leaders who fear the workers would then 'get out of hand'. Focusing on the interrelated nature of unemployment, inflation and income which Nordhaus later formalizes into his political business cycle theory, Kalecki argues that full employment will lead to price increases that hurt the rentier class. This class then applies political pressure which results in orthodox deflationary policies and an eventual economic slump. Thus, Kalecki fears, the disproportionate control of the political mechanism by the capitalist business class and the unrepresentative nature of the political system will 'sabotage the Keynesian revolution'.[5]

Nordhaus picks up Kalecki's basic concern and develops a well thought out and sophisticated theory of how democratic political systems make choices between present and future welfare.

> In the analysis presented above we have discussed the behavior of democratic political systems which face choices between present and future welfare. The specific case examined was the trade-off between inflation and unemployment. The general conclusion was that a perfect democracy with retrospective evaluation of parties will make decisions biased against future generations. Moreover, within an incumbent's term in office there is a predictable pattern of policy, starting with relative austerity in early years and ending with the potlatch right before elections.[6]

The optimal partisan policy, according to Nordhaus's theory, will produce a political business cycle manifested by unemployment and deflation in the period following elections and inflationary boom as elections approach.[7]

Nordhaus's work is the first systematic empirical work in this area and the first analysis to consider a French political business cycle.[8] Nordhaus looks at unemployment rates and the timing of national elections in ten countries selected because they have (1) periodic competitive elections to choose the government, (2) the government has sufficient control of the economy to be able to move it in the desired direction just before an election, and (3) the voters are somewhat 'myopic' and will not realize what the government is doing.[9] Nordhaus tests for the existence of a political business cycle by determining whether unemployment decreases in the period before national elections and declines after these elections. Nordhaus finds 'modest indications' of a French cycle, with six of the nine elections from 1947 to 1967 fitting the pattern of pre-electoral stimulus and post-electoral contraction. Nordhaus finds a marked cycle in Germany, New Zealand and the United States, a weak cycle in Sweden, and no evidence of a cycle in Australia, Canada, Japan and the United Kingdom.[10]

MacRae's work accepts the basic theory developed by Nordhaus, refining it into a sophisticated mathematical analysis using optimal control theory and turnpike behaviour. Focusing on the same trade-off between unemployment and inflation which concerns Nordhaus, MacRae assumes re-election is the main, although not the exclusive, goal of the incumbent party.[11] Governmental policies on unemployment and inflation will be dictated by this need for re-election.

> From the beginning to the end of the period between elections the time horizon of the party in power is only the forthcoming election. Economic policy, therefore, is devoted solely to minimizing the vote loss in this election. Once the election is over, however, the horizon shifts to the next election . . . The result is a repetition of the turnpike behavior of every election period. At the beginning of the period the economy moves toward the turnpike and at the end it moves away.[12]

The only solution to this, MacRae reasons, is strategic voting on the part of the public. To determine whether this occurs, MacRae examines unemployment rates in the United States between 1957 and 1972. He compares the actual unemployment rate with the rate which would have occurred (1) if the government had assumed myopic voters and therefore could maximize its election chances by policies resulting in a political business cycle or (2) if the government recognized that the public could see through such manipulation of the economy and would vote strategically on economic issues. A myopic voter hypothesis would be consistent with the existence of an American political business cycle. A strategic voter hypothesis would not. MacRae finds that 'the myopic hypothesis does a superior job of explaining aggregate demand policy, as reflected by the unemployment rate, during the Kennedy-Johnson and Johnson administrations, while the strategic hypothesis does a better job in the second Eisenhower and Nixon administrations.[13] MacRae concludes by pointing out the tentative nature of this test, however, given 'the fact that unemployment is not controlled directly but only indirectly through fiscal and monetary policy', a caution which underlines the need for the kind of examination presented here.[14]

Tufte's analysis of the *Political Control of the Economy* is the best known scholarly work in this area and the work which has attracted the most public attention to the existence of a political business cycle.[15] Tufte adopts Nordhaus's basic assumptions and logic, offering little theoretical innovation or refinement of his own. Tufte's major contribution comes from his comprehensive analysis of the political business cycle in the United States. His only test for a French cycle comes in an introductory cross-national comparison of annual growth in real disposable income and timing of elections in twenty-seven democracies from 1961 to 1972.[16] Tufte finds a French cycle, with increases in income in 60 per cent of election years as opposed to increases in only 33 per cent of the years without elections. Tufte does not present data on post-election contractions in France. His general conclusions strongly support the theory of political business cycles.

Frey's work, while still relevant, is less comparable with the systematic empirical examinations of Nordhaus and Tufte.[17] It is more theoretical in its consideration of a wide variety of economic phenomena and public goods. Frey does examine inflation, unemployment and growth rates of disposable nominal income in the United States from 1953 to 1976 and in the United Kingdom from 1952 to 1974. He considers American budget transfer payments (tax receipts) from 1953 to 1975. And he presents data on the growth rates of per capita consumption in six elections from 1952 to 1973 in Israel. Frey concludes that in general a government will 'use its instruments of economic policy not as is often suggested to further social welfare but rather to increase its re-election chances.'[18] Frey's conclusions on political business cycles are the most extreme and at times almost seem to suggest that the government's concern to create politically advantageous business cycles results in governments taking measures which are economically unsound but which help incumbents get re-elected.[19]

In later joint work, Frey and Schneider present a broader econometric model of the 1951 to 1974 German politico-economic interactions of which a political business cycle is a part.[20] They assume governmental manipulation of the economy can come about through (1) current government expenditures, (2) government transfers to wage earners, (3) the wage rate of government employees, and (4) employment in the public sector. According to Frey and Schneider, fluctuations in these variables should be explained by tax income, the government's current popularity, the time before the next election, the ideology of the incumbent government, and the lagged policy instrument for each of the four dependent variables. Inclusion of this last variable may be necessary to avoid certain statistical problems but it also distorts the findings and makes the R^2 so artificially high as to be unreliable. Frey and Schneider's important contribution thus lies in their more sophisticated analysis of the political business cycle and their recognition that variables more directly under the government's control (than income or unemployment) will be the ones to examine for politically motivated manipulation of the economy. They conclude their construction of a formal model of the political business cycle by advocating the introduction into future analyses of other governmental decision-makers, in particular the central bank, parliament and interest groups.[21] While the present volume is not the place to develop a comparable econometric model for France, the work by Frey and Schneider is important in underlining the necessity of shifting attention from the unemployment and income variables analyzed by Nordhaus and Tufte and to the kind of variables such as government expenditures and money supply analyzed below.

Both the logic and the empirical evidence used to test whether there are political business cycles seem problematic for several reasons. The most serious logical difficulty centers on the assumptions concerning the government's control of the economy and its ability to manipulate the economy so that economic expansion occurs just before the election and the economic contraction just after. No doubt incumbents do try to manipulate the economy for political gain. But their capability to do this is seriously limited by the constraints placed on them by external economic forces and by internal economic, legal and political factors.[22] Beyond this, the theory requires voters to be myopic both in their economic perceptions and economic maximization and to be remarkably obtuse in not recognizing the government's manipulation of the economy for political gain.[23]

Given these logical weaknesses, then, the convincing nature of the theory must rest heavily on the strength of the empirical evidence supporting it. Here, too, there are difficulties. What Nordhaus and Tufte actually examine in testing for the existence of political business cycles is not whether the government tries to or succeeds in manipulating the economy but whether economic conditions actually *do* improve right around election time. These are distinct issues, particularly when dealing with economic phenomena such as income and unemployment, both phenomena which are highly complex and strongly affected by factors beyond the control of any national government.

A more satisfactory test for a political business cycle would consider not whether economic conditions happen to improve before elections but whether the government utilizes the tools available to it to try first to improve the economy before elections and then to recover from these excesses by contracting the economy after the election. Rather than examining income, unemployment or even transfer payments, which have definite time trends and where most increases in expenditures are built into the original program by law, we should instead consider government activity in the two main areas of economic policy which are most amenable to sudden manipulation of the economy: fiscal and monetary policy. The following empirical analysis thus will examine the pre-election and post-election pattern of government fiscal expenditures and the money supply as the main measures of governmental attempts to manipulate the economy. If there is a political business cycle, then fluctuations in fiscal expenditures and in the money supply should conform to the pattern suggested by the political business cycle theorists: pre-election increases and post-election contraction.

THE PATTERN OF GOVERNMENT EXPENDITURES AND
THE MONEY SUPPLY, 1958–1979

Examining monthly data on French government expenditures and quarterly data on the money supply compiled by the International Monetary Fund, we find that this is not, in fact the case.[24] The evidence at best provides weak support for a theory of a political business cycle. These are interesting findings, particularly given the French historical tradition of state intervention in the economy and the fact that the French case has not previously been examined in detail.

Consider Table 1, presenting the pattern of government expenditures during the Fifth Republic. The table is divided into the three-month periods preceding and following elections since, according to the theory, the government will attempt to stimulate the economy just before an election and then correct the excesses by an economic contraction when the political costs are lower. This time period seems the proper unit of analysis for France rather than the annual or bi-annual periods examined by Nordhaus and Tufte since French elections are held too frequently to use annual changes and since the precise date of French elections were

Table 7.1 Pattern of Government expenditures, French Fifth Republic

Kind of election	Pre-election stimulus				Post-election contraction			
	All	Pres.	Legis.	Local	All	Pres.	Legis.	Local
Stimulus/contraction each of the three months preceding the election	0	0	0	0	0	0	0	0
Stimulus/contraction two of the three months preceding the election	3	0	3	0	0	0	0	0
Stimulus/contraction one of the three months preceding the election	4	2	1	1	8	2	5	1
No stimulus/no contraction in any of three months preceding the election	3	1	1	1	2	1	0	1
% supporting political business cycle:								
Strong support	0%	0%	0%	0%	0%	0%	0%	0%
Some support	30%	0%	60%	0%	0%	0%	0%	0%
Weak support	70%	66%	80%	50%	80%	66%	100%	50%
% at variance with theory of political business cycle	30%	33%	20%	50%	20%	33%	0%	50%

not always known in advance during this period, therefore minimizing the longer, fixed periods of potential manipulation by the incumbent government which Tufte finds in the United States. In addition to this, fiscal and monetary policy work more quickly than the kind of incomes policy Tufte examines, although Nordhaus's unemployment measure also would seem better suited for a monthly analysis by this same reasoning.

Strong support for the theory would be demonstrated by a consistent increase in government expenditures in the pre-electoral period and a consistent decrease in the post-election period. Weaker support for the theory would be found if we see stimulus in any two of the three months preceding the election. This would confirm the deliberate stimulation prescribed by the political business cycle theorists. Stimulus in only one of the three months would be consistent with an explanation of a politically induced business cycle but would not constitute strong support for the theory. Pre-election periods with no expansion in government expenditures are judged to be inconsistent with a theory of a political business cycle. Similar logic is followed for post-electoral contractions.

Examination of Table 1 provides only weak support for the theory of a French political business cycle. Looking first at pre-election economic stimulus for all the election years, we find none of them fit the pattern of strong support for a political business cycle and only 30 per cent provide mixed support. Seventy per cent fit the pattern of weak support, i.e., economic stimulation in only one of the three months preceding the election. And 30 per cent of the pre-election pattern in expenditures are totally at variance with the theory of a political business cycle.

Breaking the elections into presidential, legislative and local election years, we can test Tufte's theory that political manipulation of the economy will be most extreme in years when the most important political incumbents are up for re-election. In the American case, this meant presidential election years should have the most extreme political business cycle. In France, we would expect presidential election years to be the most extreme although the clear cut distinctions concerning economic decision-making break down for the Fifth Republic.[25] This test cannot be as conclusive as it was for Tufte's analysis of the American case. In fact, we find more pre-electoral stimulus in legislative election years. Given that none of the pre-election-year patterns shows strong support for the theory, however, and that the number of years is so small, one must be careful not to read too much into the data. Examining the pre-electoral economic stimulus according to the kind of election essentially reinforces the earlier conclusion of weak support for the theory, with the qualification that three of the five legislative elections were preceded by economic stimulus in two of the three months before the election. The pattern of post-electoral economic contraction shows no variation according to kind of election, however, and the over-all impression from Table 1 is that the pattern of government expenditures during the Fifth Republic offers weak evidence in support of a political business cycle. The pattern is equally consistent with a non-political business cycle reflecting the vagaries of the market place and the routine ups and downs of pre-legislated expenditures rather than any deliberate manipulation of the economy by the political incumbents.

Consideration of Tables 2 and 3, depicting the pattern in the expansion and the rate of growth of the money supply, offers even less evidence in support of a political business cycle. Examination of the pre-election and post-election pattern of money supply from 1958 to 1959 provides an important test of governmental success in manipulating the economy for immediate political gain. Table 2 presents data on the pattern in the growth of the money supply during the Fifth Republic. Again, according to the political business cycle theory, we should expect to find pre-election stimulus and post-election contraction, with the pattern slightly more accentuated in presidential election years than in years with only legislative or local elections. This is not, in fact, what we find.

Table 2, presenting the pattern of monetary policy from 1958 to 1972, reveals pre-electoral stimulus but no post-electoral contraction in the money supply. Looking first at the growth in the money supply the quarter in which the election occurred, we find seven elections with pre-election stimulus and four with post-election contraction.[26] This pattern is slightly higher for years with legislative (80 per cent) and local (66.7 per cent) elections than for years with presidential (33.3 per cent) elections. Since the money supply is traditionally a slower tool for economic stimulus than government expenditures, we also consider the pattern of election stimulus which might occur during the quarter preceding the quarter during which the election occurred. When we do this, we find that all (91 per cent) of the elections save one local election fit the pattern predicted by the political business cycle theorists. This is strong evidence supporting the existence of such a cycle.

When we consider the post-electoral pattern, however, we find equally strong evidence at variance with the theory. In only one of the quarters following an election since 1958 do we find a decrease in the growth of the money supply. This points out the trend problem involved in looking at the money supply: it nearly always expands. In only 10 of the

Table 7.2   Growth of money supply, French Fifth Republic

Kind of Election	Pre-election stimulus the quarter of the election				Pre-election stimulus the quarter preceding the election				Post-election contraction the quarter after the election			
	All	Pres.	Legis.	Local	All	Pres.	Legis.	Local	All	Pres.	Legis.	Local
Elections with increases in money supply	7	1	4	2	10	3	5	2	10	2	5	3
Elections with decreases in money supply	4	2	1	1	1	0	0	1	1	1	0	0
Total % in support of political business cycle	64%	33.3%	80%	66.7%	91%	100%	100%	66.7%	9%	33.3%	0%	0%
Total % at variance with theory of a political business cycle	36%	66.7%	20%	33.3%	9%	0%	0%	33.3%	91%	66.7%	100%	100%

eighty-four quarters since 1958 did the French money supply fail to grow. What we need to examine, then, is not the growth of the money supply but rather the rate of growth since if the amount of francs in circulation almost always increases, then to find pre-election growth neither supports nor confirms the theory. It is possible that a theory of a political business cycle exists because of this superficial evidence of pre-electoral growth and that on closer examination this pattern is the routine economic pattern having little to do with the timing of elections. We therefore need to consider whether the government stimulates the economy for electoral gain by increasing the *rate* of growth before an election and whether this is followed by post-electoral economic contraction, as measured by a growth rate which decreases after an election. Table 3 presents data on this.

The data in Table 3 do not support the existence of a political business cycle, although the evidence is mixed enough so that it is understandable why only an impressionistic consideration of events might have given the appearance of a political business cycle in the first place. Looking at the pattern for the quarters during which elections occurred, we find that five (45 per cent) of all the elections show a pre-election pattern of stimulation, with three of the four legislative elections falling into this pattern. But 55 per cent of all the elections are at variance with the theory.

Considering a longer period for stimulation, a test which we have argued earlier should be a more appropriate test of the theory given the length of time needed for monetary policy to take effect, we find only four (36 per cent) of the elections support the existence of a political business cycle while seven (64 per cent) are at variance with such a cycle. Only one of the three presidential and one of the four legislative elections fits into the pattern. Turning to the post-electoral period, we find the same pattern: five (45 per cent) of the post-election periods support the theory but six (55 per cent) are at variance with the theory of post-election contraction outlines by the political business cycle theorists and only one of the four legislative elections fits the predicted pattern.

For monetary policy as with fiscal policy, then, we must conclude that the existence of a French political business cycle remains in doubt, with an equally convincing explanation being simply that the pattern of rate of growth for the money supply is as much the result of non-political factors as it is the result of deliberate manipulation of the economy for immediate political gain.

Table 7.3   Rate of Growth of money supply, French Fifth Republic

Kind of election	Pre-election stimulus the quarter of the election				Pre-election stimulus the quarter preceding the election				Post-election contraction the quarter after the election			
	All	Pres.	Legis.	Local	All	Pres.	Legis.	Local	All	Pres.	Legis.	Local
Elections with increases in growth of money supply	5	1	3	1	4	1	1	2	6	2	1	3
Elections with decreases in growth of money supply	6	2	1	3	7	2	3	2	5	1	3	1
Total % in support of political business cycle	45%	33.3%	75%	25%	36%	33.3%	75%	50%	45%	33.3%	75%	25%
Total % at variance with theory of a political business cycle	55%	66.7%	25%	75%	64%	66.7%	25%	50%	55%	66.7%	25%	75%

CONCLUSIONS AND IMPLICATIONS OF THE STUDY

The analysis presented above considered the question of whether there is a political business cycle in France. The theory of a political business cycle assumes a myopic voter and a government which adopts economic policies designed to maximize the chances of electoral victory by the incumbent political party. The political business cycle takes the form of pre-electoral economic stimulation followed by a necessary period of economic contraction after the election. We tested this theory by examining French fiscal and monetary policy as measured by government expenditures and fluctuations in the money supply from 1958 to 1979. These data suggest only weak support for a political business cycle. The pattern for both government expenditures and the money supply is equally consistent with a nonpolitical business cycle reflecting the vagaries of the market and the routine fluctuations of previously legislated expenditures or changes in the money supply set by apolitical organs.

This somewhat negative conclusion on the existence of a French political business cycle is particularly important for the general theory since the French institutional and historical experience suggest we should find a stronger cycle in France than in the United States or Great Britain. Shonfield argues that the French have a longer historical tradition of state intervention in the economy than the British or Americans.[27] The traditional French attitude toward government intervention in the economy is characterized by both Shonfield and Lüthy as a 'synthetic capitalism . . . completely in the tradition of the French mercantilism which was inherited from the *ancien régime* and consists of protectionism and enlightened state intervention.'[28] The historical tradition crystallized in institutional form during the Fifth Republic by involving the Parliament in the planning process at earlier and more critical stages in the planning process than had ever been done before.[29] The acceptance of extensive state intervention in the economy and the institutionalization of this intervention in the bureaucracy, according to Shonfield, provides greater room for manipulation of the economy than in the United States or Britain, where the free-market forces remain strong among important segments of the politically significant population. If we accept Shonfield's argument that French planning 'officials automatically accept it as part of their task . . . to offer rewards to allies and to try to make life awkward for others' then we would expect to find a political business cycle demonstrated more easily in France than in the United States or Britain since both the institutional mechanisms for intervention and the political culture facilitate such state political control of the economy.[30]

The fact that we found only weak support for the theory of a political business cycle in France is not meant to suggest that governments do not consider political costs and benefits when making economic policy. No doubt incumbents do wish to manipulate the economy for their own political advantage. Desire should not be confused with capability, however, and the room for political manipulation of the economy would seem to be much less than that assumed by the political business cycle theorists. Future analysts in this area should allow for this fact and should concentrate on refining the theory of a political business cycle to allow for the limitations imposed on policy makers by institutional constraints, by domestic political factors, and by external economic forces.

Notes

* An earlier version of this chapter was presented at the Annual Meetings of the Public Choice Society, San Francisco, March 1980. I would like to thank the discussants for their comments and Laura J. Scalia for her assistance in preparing this paper.⁻

† 'The Theory of Economic Policy: The Lessons of One Person's Experience'. (address delivered at New York University, Institute of French Studies, 8 February 1980).

1 M. Kalecki, 'Political Aspects of Full Employment', *Political Quarterly*, Vol. 14 (1943), 322-31; William D. Nordhaus, 'The Political Business Cycle', *Review of Economic Studies*, Vol. 42, No. 2 (1975), 169-90; C. Duncan MacRae, 'A Political Model of the Business Cycle', *The Journal of Political Economy*, Vol. 85, No. 2 (1977), 239-63; Edward R. Tufte, *Political Control of the Economy* (Princeton, N.J.: Princeton University Press, 1978); Bruno S. Frey, *Modern Political Economy* (New York: Wiley, 1978); Bruno S. Frey and Friedrich Schneider, 'An Econometric Model with an Endogenous Government Sector', *Public Choice*, Vol. 34, No. 1 (1978), 29-43.

2 For an inside discussion of both the political pressures and the institutional mechanisms and policies available to French policy-makers in the last decade, see Raymond Barre, 'The Theory of Economic Policy: The Lessons of One Person's Experience'. Address delivered at New York University, Institute of French Studies, 8 February 1980. For a discussion of the historical tradition resulting in a political culture amenable to extensive government direction and control of the economy, see Andrew Shonfield, *Modern Capitalism* (London: Oxford University Press, 1969).

3 Tufte, *Political Control of the Economy*, p. 4.

4 Kalecki, 'Political Aspects of Full Employment'.

5 Nordhaus, 'The Political Business Cycle' p. 192.

6 Ibid., p. 187.

7 'The typical cycle will run as follows: immediately after an election the victor will raise unemployment to some relatively high level in order to combat inflation. As elections approach, the unemployment rate will be lowered until, on election eve, the unemployment rate will be lowered to the purely myopic point.' Nordhaus, 'The Political Business Cycle', p. 184.

8 Frey and Schneider, 'An Econometric Model with an Endogenous Government Sector', p. 30, classify the work by J. Akerman, 'Political Economic Cycles', *Kyklos*, Vol. 1 (1947), 107-17 as falling within the political business cycle

literature although its emphasis on the economy's impact on American presidential popularity seems to place it more accurately in those works which, in Frey's terminology, estimate popularity functions.

9 These last two criteria seem highly questionable. At the least, they should be treated as propositions to be tested rather than as assumptions underlying the work.

10 Nordhaus, 'The Political Business Cycle', p. 186.

11 MacRae, 'A Political Model of the Business Cycle', p. 240.

12 Ibid., p. 252.

13 Ibid., p. 262.

14 Ibid., p. 263.

15 Tufte, *Political Control of the Economy*.

16 Several of the 'democracies' analyzed, e.g., the Philippines and Uruguay, seem poor choices given the selection criteria set forth by Nordhaus and accepted by Tufte.

17 Frey, *Modern Political Economy*.

18 Ibid., p. 161.

19 Ibid., pp. 123–4.

20 Frey and Schneider, 'An Econometric Model with an Endogenous Government Sector'.

21 Ibid., p. 38.

22 One example of the limitations of the government's capability to control the economy comes from Nordhaus, who seems to acknowledge the unrealistic aspect of this assumption while still continuing to base his analysis on it. Nordhaus sets up unemployment as a 'control or policy variable of the economic system which the policy-makers can set at any level they wish'. Yet, he continues, 'the assumption that unemployment is a control variable is unrealistic in a decentralized, capitalist economy. It is generally agreed, however, that through judicious choice of fiscal and monetary policy the government can (within a margin of error) set unemployment rates at any desired level.' Nordhaus, 'The Political Business Cycle', p. 170.

23 Nordhaus is most explicit about the assumption of ignorance on the part of voters. 'It should be stressed that ignorance of the structure of the economy is extremely important for the behavior we are about to describe.' Nordhaus, 'The Political Business Cycle', 1972. The role played by political parties varies among the different analysts. The general view of parties is that they follow whatever economic policies will best help them get re-elected and that voters do *not* affiliate with parties for noneconomic reasons. Nordhaus, 'The Political Business Cycle', p. 174. Frey and Schneider, however, allow for parties to follow economic policies in line with their ideological views when doing so will not jeopardize their re-election. Frey and Schneider, 'An Econometric Model with an Endogenous Government Sector'.

24 Although the International Monetary Fund statistics are uniformly considered the most reliable in this area, their consistency leaves much to be desired. In instances where there was a revision of an earlier reported amount of expenditure, the later revision was selected as being more reliable.

25 Prior to 1962 the president was not elected by mass popular vote, and, therefore, the Fifth Republic would not initially conform to Tufte's theory of presidential elections being the ones when we should find the most extreme political manipulation of the economy. After 1962, however, the Fifth Republic should conform to the pattern proposed by Tufte if in fact a political business cycle exists.

26 Monthly data are not available.

27 'The state as entrepreneur is taken very seriously [in France] . . . No doubt the

158 *Kristen Monroe*

French state is more adept at these things partly because it has been in active business, one way or another, two or three centuries longer than the British or American.' Shonfield, *Modern Capitalism*, p. 86.

28 Shonfield, *Modern Capitalism*, p. 87 quoting H. Lüthy, *The State of France: a Study of Contemporary France* (London: Secker and Warburg, 1955), p. 455.

29 See Shonfield, *Modern Capitalism*, Chaps. 7 and 8, especially pp. 142–3, for details on the institutional mechanisms for government intervention in the economy.

30 Ibid, p. 150.

8 Economic Policy and the Governing Coalition

Diana Green with Philip Cerny

In competitive political systems, a government's economic policy stands at the crossroads of political decision-making. It involves, on the one hand, questions of the substance of policy — long-range ideological goals and the short-term management of the economic conjuncture. On the other hand, the strategic and tactical exigencies of gaining and maintaining governmental power, whether for a governing coalition as a whole, or for the separate parties composing the coalition, are often determined by economic promise and performance. A government is, by its very nature and by its position in the wider political spectrum, in the unremitting position of having to mediate and to navigate between these two sets of constraints. The juxtaposition of these dimensions forms the basis of any political analysis of public policy.

Since 1974, two things have happened. The world has moved into a period of stagnation, inflation and rising unemployment, from which France has not been immune; the relative ease with which Fifth Republic governments had made economic policy gave way to strong disagreements between its constituent groups. And the slow but progressive development of the dominance of the non-Gaullist Right within not only the presidency, but also the Government and the coalition of right-wing parties, has provoked an ever-sharper competition for power between the Gaullists and the Giscardians; this competition has focused on economic policy. Style and substance, manoeuvres and genuine alternatives, have now crystallized into a clear pattern.

The 1973 Energy Crisis severely dislocated the French economy. Faced with a four-fold increase in oil prices (all the more critical since France imports 75 per cent of her energy needs) and a paralysis of political leadership (since President Pompidou was dying, although the fact was not publicly admitted), the country drifted along without any sense of direction until after the accession of Giscard d'Estaing to the presidency in May 1974. Between 1974 and 1975, the Chirac government's economic policy was characterized by a series of 'stop–go' cycles which merely added to the country's economic difficulties. At the same time, France was much slower than other industrialized nations to realize the nature and the scale of the problem it was confronting. These economic difficulties were compounded by a political crisis — a clash between Giscard and his Gaullist Prime Minister — which was only resolved when Chirac 'resigned' in August 1976. In the subsequent reshuffle, an economist, Raymond Barre, was appointed Prime Minister with a remit to put the ailing economy back on its feet again.

This chapter will attempt to draw up a balance-sheet of the Barre government's economic and industrial policy since 1976. It will also look at the 'alternative economic strategy' offered by Chirac and the Gaullists, asking if and how their proposals differ from the policies currently being pursued by their coalition partners.

ECONOMIC POLICY SINCE 1976: THE BARRE PLAN

According to Barre, there were three main objectives: to bring foreign trade into balance, to strengthen the franc and to control inflation. Following in the footsteps of some of his more eminent predecessors, he therefore introduced a counter-inflationary 'Stabilization Plan' in September 1976.[1] This was extended for a further year, at the end of 1977, despite the approaching legislative elections (due to be held in March 1978), and despite pressures from both the Opposition Left and the Gaullists on the Right, to modify the austerity of his policies in the light of steadily mounting unemployment. Barre justified his decision to stand firm on the grounds that his first duty was to 'cure' the economy (*assainissement*). Economic health required the establishment of a number of 'basic balances' (the balance of payments, moderate growth in the money supply, a stable currency, wage moderation and a balanced budget) as a first step to renewed economic stability and inflation-free economic growth.

Over the term of the Stabilization Plan (which has nothing to do with National Planning, which is examined elsewhere),[2] the control of inflation has emerged as the most important of the Government's economic objectives and the prerequisite of all other policy objectives. This was underlined by Barre's announcement in July 1979 that rather than relax his austerity programme in September when it was technically due to end, the previous month's oil price rises would mean further retrenchment. Perhaps more importantly, it has become increasingly apparent that wage increases are deemed to be a critical factor in determining the rate of inflation in France. Consequently, although a formal incomes policy is both politically and tactically out of the question, retrenchment means another year of wage restraint. Now, the French have learned to live with inflation (which has been a fact of life for most of the post-war period) largely because economic growth has ensured that wages have kept pace with prices.[3] The post-oil recession and the emergence of the 'new' economic growth (a euphemism designed to suggest that the dramatic decline is the result of a deliberate policy choice – i.e. planned) have forced the Government progressively to abandon this unwritten law. Thus, while purchasing power was growing by about 5 per cent per annum in 1974, this had fallen to 2 per cent per annum by 1976 and 0.6 per cent by the end of the first quarter of 1979. The storm of protest which followed the announcement that, in the future, the Government could guarantee, at most, the *maintenance* of purchasing power which 'should determine the ceiling rather than the floor of wage increases',[4] was predictable. The decision is interesting to the extent that it indicates both a more realistic assessment of the country's ability to award itself wage increases in a situation of oil-induced inflation and declining growth, and a change in Government thinking as to who should foot the bill. For the last two years, the burden has fallen primarily on industry. Since increasing industrial competitiveness is now seen as the key to coming to grips with the 'oil challenge', this burden will now be shifted to the taxpayer. Moreover, the Government is pledged (as part of the Barre Plan) to attacking the problem of social inequalities. Companies are therefore expected to make a special effort to improve the position of the lower paid, suggesting that the cost of wage awards is to be borne by the higher income earner and the professional classes.

Confronted with a third year of austerity, the French became openly critical of the Prime Minister and his policies during the summer of 1979. An opinion poll in *Le Nouvel Observateur* at the end of August showed that 63 per cent of those interviewed considered that the Government 'agit au jour le jour sans bien savoir où il va'. Furthermore, despite the Prime Minister's painstaking attempts to educate them in the facts of economic life, the French apparently believe that price rises are inevitable. Perhaps more importantly, the poll showed that they consider that *Government policies* have a greater responsibility for pushing up prices than the oil-producing countries. Another poll, published in *L'Express* at the beginning of September, confirmed this. It showed that 82 per cent of those interviewed considered that the Government was not doing enough to control inflation and unemployment, and 62 per cent of them considered that Barre has quite simply failed in the three years he has been at Matignon.

Has the Barre Plan really been such a complete failure? One way of answering this question is by comparing what has actually been achieved over the three years that Barre has been in office with his initially stated aims.

Measured by crude statistics, the record is not particularly impressive. Perhaps the most obvious failure is in respect of the Government's main policy plank: the control of inflation. In the three years since the launching of the Barre Plan, prices have increased by 32.4 per cent, an annual rate of 9.8 per cent, and in the last six months have increased, by the most conservative estimate, at a rate of 11.4 per cent. The price of bread alone has risen by 22 per cent in the last year while the abolition of rent controls has resulted in rent increases of between 30 per cent and 90 per cent.[5] By contrast, prices rose by 9.5 per cent per annum during the Chirac government's last year in office. Thus, measured both absolutely and relatively, Barre's policies have not been particularly successful in this area.

Similarly, during the three years spanned by the Stabilization Plan, the money supply has increased by 44 per cent, at an annual rate of 14 per cent compared with a target of 11 per cent; hourly wages, which were to rise no faster than prices, have risen by 48.2 per cent (an annual rate of 14 per cent); and, despite the commitment to return to a balanced Budget, the deficit has continued to grow and looks set to reach Fr. 40 billion by the end of 1979 (1.9 per cent of GDP), more than double the deficit recorded in 1976 (Fr. 17.9 billion, or 1.1 per cent of GDP). The persistence of a high inflation rate (and a short spell of speculation before the 1978 elections) has strained the franc. During the last three years, it has fallen 15 per cent against the Deutschmark, 13 per cent against the Belgian franc and 7.4 per cent against sterling. If it has increased against the dollar (+17 per cent) and the Italian lira (+14 per cent), this is arguably attributable to the weaknesses of these currencies rather than the strength of the franc. On the balance of payments front, however, the record has been more respectable. During the first two years of the Barre Plan, a Fr. 22.3 billion deficit was turned into a Fr. 6 billion surplus, largely as a result of a major export drive in which sales of French goods overseas increased by 50 per cent in value and 25 per cent in volume. This improvement came to an abrupt halt, however, with the OPEC decision to increase oil prices again in June 1979 and the Iranian crisis, and the year is expected to end with a deficit of at least Fr. 10 billion.

Barre takes exception to the Government's policies being judged simply on the basis of crude statistics. Pointing to 'la myopie des indices mensuels',[6] he argues that the balance-sheet of his three years at Matignon is, in the end, positive. Whatever the statistics say, the French economy is in a healthier condition than it was in 1976 and is therefore better equipped to face the difficult times ahead. As evidence, Barre points to French industry. In what ways is French industry 'healthier' than it was under the Gaullists? And to what extent is this as a result of policies which differ significantly from those of the previous regime? If the 'liberal' approach of the Giscardians and their commitment to reduce State intervention is, in principle, the antithesis of Gaullist *dirigisme*, has this distinction been translated into political practice? Before looking at the Barre government's 'new' approach to industrial problems, we must first examine that of its predecessor, notably its responses in the difficult period immediately after the 1973 Energy Crisis.

A.   INDUSTRIAL POLICY UNDER THE GAULLISTS

The Chirac government's initial response to the crisis was defensive: an instruction to companies to postpone redundancies for as long as possible, the creation of an agency to bail out 'lame ducks' (the CIASI),[7] and the launching of a plethora of 'plans' covering almost all industrial sectors.

This was the period of the so-called 'Industrial Redeployment' strategy. In theory, this was a new approach to industrial problems in so far as it marked an attempt to go beyond the 'fire-fighting' approach of the past and formulate a coherent policy for industrial development. Conceptually, 'Industrial Redeployment' was quite useful. It neatly managed to convey the notion that the process of rationalization which was imperative for French industry if it was to adjust to the 'new international economic order' was related to a coherent and overall economic strategy. In short, it suggested that future industrial policy decisions would be *planned*, rather than reactive. Hence the launching of sectoral 'plans' which, strictly speaking, were not plans at all (and had nothing to do with French National Planning). On the contrary, many of them were basically an attempt to control (i.e. slow down or, in the case of the most sensitive declining industries, postpone indefinitely) the rate of structural adjustment. Nor was there anything really *new* about this new strategy. To the extent that this 'defensive' approach was matched by a more 'offensive' posture in the promotion of advanced technology industries and the continuing creation of 'National Champions', Gaullist policy evinced the same mixture of protectionism and selective entrepreneurship which has traditionally characterized the French approach to industrial problems.[8]

B.   INDUSTRIAL POLICY UNDER BARRE: A LIBERAL ALTERNATIVE

A change of government in the autumn of 1976 brought a change of both economic and industrial policy. This was not simply a change of strategy but was — at least in principle — dictated by the ideological differences between the two regimes.

The foundation-stone of the new liberal approach was a commitment to eradicate all symbols of irreversible state intervention (from budgetary deficits to National Planning) and a determination to rely progressively on market forces to carry out essential industrial restructuring. In line with these principles, the Barre government set about dismantling the apparatus of state intervention immediately after the 1978 elections. The first victim was price controls — which had been in force for most of the post-war period, resulting in widespread distortions. Controls have now been removed from almost all industrial prices and are to be phased out progressively in the service sector because of the potentially inflationary impact.[9] The emphasis has shifted to competition policy with the setting up of a Competition Commission, controlled by the Economics Ministry, and with extensive powers to prevent unfair competition.[10] Other policy decisions, *inter alia* the introduction of economic pricing in the nationalized industries and the removal of restrictions on capital investment overseas, can also be seen as indicative of the Government's faith in the Market. Moreover, industry has been told bluntly that it must become more competitive if it is to survive but should not expect the state to bear the cost of essential adjustment. In this new industrial strategy there is no place for lame ducks and 'companies are responsible for their own expansion',[11] — i.e. they should not look to the state for assistance. Similarly, the sectoral approach to industrial problems, which characterized the Industrial Redeployment strategy (and the 'Industrial Imperative' which preceded it)[12] was to be officially dropped. State action should be limited to creating the macroeconomic conditions favourable to development (primarily through the improvement of the financial situation of the corporate sector)[13] with 'exceptional' interventions supplementing (rather than replacing) market forces.

This is the Barre government's theoretical position. In practice, however, it has been forced to compromise on — if not progressively abandon — its liberal (i.e. free market) position.

A TEST CASE: THE STEEL CRISIS

The first test of the Government's new hardline attitude was the Steel Crisis. The French steel industry is technically in private ownership. In practice, however, the state has been closely involved in its investment plans and pricing policies as well as playing a critical role in the numerous restructuring operations which have taken place over the last twenty years. Indeed, it can be argued that it is this continuous and damaging intervention which, by impeding the industry's ability to adjust to the changing international situation, is largely responsible for its parlous condition today.[14]

The latest and most serious crisis to affect the industry emerged in 1978 when, over-manned and uncompetitive, it was on the verge of bankruptcy. The radical and long-overdue 'Steel Plan' finally proposed by the Government in September 1978[15] tackled the industry's lack of competitiveness by proposing a further rationalization of capacity and the shedding of more than 21,000 jobs by 1980 (in addition to the 16,000 jobs due to disappear under the previous (1977) rationalization plan). After initial resistance, in the shape of violent protest from the steel-workers in the areas most affected by the draconian redundancy proposals, and riots in Paris in the spring of 1979, the steelmaking unions have finally accepted the reorganization plan. The Government handled the affair so badly (typically, there was no consultation prior to the announcement of the plan) that agreement was only won as a result of a number of concessions. The price was generous redundancy payments and re-training schemes, with the promise of new jobs as an additional sop.[16] Additionally, one company has agreed to defer the redundancies.

The financial problem presented more difficulties. After considering various options, a formula was adopted which allows the Government to preserve the fiction of allowing industry to sort out its own problems. It has nevertheless assumed *de facto* control of the industry since about two-thirds of the equity is now owned by the state or the financial institutions it effectively controls. The industry, in other words, has been all but nominally nationalized.[17]

The steel crisis is only one example of the fact that the state's promised withdrawal from industrial affairs has not yet taken place. Despite the resolve to allow restructuring to be carried out by market forces, the Government has shown more than a passing interest in restructuring operations, especially those affecting the declining and labour-intensive industries. Despite the anti-interventionist rhetoric, in other words, it has approached the problem of industrial adjustment with a strategy which attempts to balance a hard-line attitude to commercial viability with a concern for the problem of unemployment and the health of the 'social fabric'. This ambivalence can be seen in its handling of the textile industry which has been particularly affected by competition from the low-wage newly industrializing countries. When the Boussac group was on the verge of bankruptcy, the Government refused to bail it out, contrary to all expectations, and in spite of the employment consequences of its closure. Yet, at the same time, it launched the so-called 'Vosges Plan', providing this region, the centre of the French textile industry, with funds for restructuring. More recently, it has demonstrated that if the threat to an industry goes beyond 'acceptable' limits, it is not averse to resorting to blatant protectionism, as the decision to issue 'technical visas' for imported Italian sweaters demonstrates.[18]

Nor has intervention been restricted to the sensitive declining industries. On the contrary, the Government has not hesitated to promote restructuring in the growth industries or to step in and block potential foreign takeovers which might constitute a threat to 'national independence'. In innumerable cases, from the Lucas-Ducellier imbroglio to RHM's attempt to buy into the mass-produced end of the French bakery industry (just to mention two examples involving British companies), the French government has intervened, prodding French companies into producing a 'French solution' rather than expose the national industry to competition from incoming foreign companies. Indeed, perhaps the best example of the French government's schizophrenia over foreign competition is its reaction to British Leyland's announcement of its planned technical co-operation with Honda; accusing the British of creating a 'Trojan horse' hardly squares with the official line of stimulating competition to increase the efficiency of French industry.[19]

Despite the non-interventionist rhetoric, then, the Barre government's industrial policy is broadly in line with that of previous regimes. Indeed, the 'new' industrial strategy currently being put together at the Ministry of Industry differs from earlier versions primarily in its shift of focus to the firm rather than the sector (although the firms selected to lead industrial recovery, and benefit from state assistance, are located in designated 'key' sectors).[20] Prima facie, the Barre government's new strategy is likely to be more interventionist (if more selective) than that of its predecessor. Significantly, at the institutional level, an attempt appears to be being made to introduce coherence (i.e. to plan) industrial policy decisions by gathering together at least some of the previously dispersed industrial policy functions and centralize them in the Ministry of Industry.[21] On past experience, however, this may be no more than a cosmetic change.

More important than the nature of the Government's interventions, (i.e. whether they are planned or *ad hoc*) is their frequency. There is no evidence, in this respect, that the scale of state intervention (measured by the number of *dossiers* handled, or the volume of public funding) has diminished under Barre.

Has the Government's policy demonstrably improved the health of French industry, and, more generally, that of the economy? This can to some extent to determined by examining its impact. One of the most direct and obvious consequences of Barre's policies in the context of the continuing recession is the radical, belated and therefore painful rationalization of the French industrial structure. During the last three years, the number of bankruptcies has increased from 1,000 per month to 1,300 per month (compared with less than 800 per month before the crisis), while the number of redundancies (for 'economic' reasons) has increased from 20,000 to 32,000 a month. French industry is therefore much slimmer and, presumably, more efficient. At the same time, the abolition of price controls and the various measures introduced to improve company liquidity have clearly improved the financial viability of those firms which have weathered the crisis,[22] generating a climate of confidence which is (temporarily) boosting industrial activity.[23]

If the Barre government's policies have finally provoked a response from French industry in the shape of rationalization and greater specialization, exposure to the icy blast of foreign competition has also galvanized an overdue adjustment, the key feature of which is the substitution of capital for labour. The three years of the Barre Plan have therefore been marked by a massive shake-out of labour while substantial increases in productivity (20 per cent over the three years, compared with 8 per cent between 1973 and 1976) have also swelled the ranks of the unemployed who currently number, in crude terms, in excess of 1.4 million.[24] It is small wonder, therefore, that the general public is critical of a 'redeployment' which makes industry more efficient at the cost of increasing unemployment, higher taxes and falling living standards.

Acknowledging that while the Government's policies cannot be held wholly responsible for all the bad economic indicators, they have exacerbated a worsening trend; Barre has been forced to demonstrate more

flexibility than his initial hardline position would suggest. Thus, despite
the initial refusal to repeat the error of his predecessor, allowing the
political aim of keeping down unemployment to distort his economic
judgement, he has been forced to take remedial action. A number of
job-creation schemes have therefore been introduced including a series
of 'Employment Pacts' designed to attack the problem of unemployment
among the young (and incidentially providing firms with subsidized
labour).[25] Similarly, in the face of mounting criticism and pessimistic
forecasts suggesting a deepening of the recession, the Government announced a series of measures at the end of August 1979 designed to
give a boost to the flagging economy and fulfil its commitment to protect
the living standards of the lower paid.[26] This was followed by the
announcement that the Budget for 1980, while not exactly reflationary,
would be a 'Budget de soutien', with a planned deficit of Fr. 31 billion.[27]

     If the proposals — or at least the timing of the announcement — were
designed to nip in the bud the campaign being mounted against Barre's
economic policies, the plan failed miserably. Nor was criticism limited
to the Opposition parties on the Left and the trade unions. Indeed, in
September, Michel Debré, the Gaullist ex-Prime Minister and self-styled
Cassandra of French politics, launched a full-scale attack on the Government for its departure from financial orthodoxy and announced that
he would refuse to vote for the Budget in the National Assembly. Furthermore, declaring that France was in 'a state of economic war', he proposed
a detailed alternative strategy to deal with the country's economic problems.[28] This spurred the RPR into action and its new economic spokesman,
Jean Méo, was given the task of devising the party's official alternative
strategy. How does it differ from the Government's actual policies?
And to what extent is it a viable alternative (i.e. an operational plan rather
than a political prescription dictated by electoral considerations)?

THE GAULLIST ALTERNATIVE

The official Gaullist strategy pays homage to the Debré Plan but is careful
to distinguish itself from the latter by the precision of its propositions
(which are costed and accompanied by proposals for raising the requisite
revenue) and the studious examination of the French problem in an
international context. Condemning the Barre government's policy of
'autostrangulation' which has launched France on the slippery slope
towards economic complacency, the Gaullists reject its strategy of moderate growth (la croissance 'douce') and call for a growth rate of 4 to 5 per

cent per annum (i.e. twice the current rate) to attack the problem of unemployment and supply the means for modernizing the industrial structure and improving living standards.[29] At the political level, such an objective presupposes 'the existence of a true national will and its translation into a Plan, which provides the only means of articulating clear choices in such a difficult period'. At the operational level, a higher growth rate can be achieved by stimulating investment, increasing exports, boosting the construction industry and streamlining agricultural production. Up to this point, there is no radical divergence from the Government's medium-term objectives, as spelt out in the Report on the Options for the Eighth National Plan (see Chapter 5). Similarly, on the sticky issue of import controls (which Debré claimed were imperative given the state of economic warfare), the Gaullists agree that such controls may be justified in certain cases, provided the degree of protectionism is 'neither more nor less than that operated by the Japanese, Germans, Italians or Americans' (i.e. their main competitors). They suggest it should be supplemented by a more 'offensive' approach to develop or maintain a French presence in certain 'strategic' sectors (such as steel, chemicals, shipbuilding, etc.), using selective sectoral assistance. The Gaullist strategy therefore offers little that is new or distinctive. Indeed, it is an 'alternative' only to the extent that it differs from the current economic policy of the Government in *scale*, calling for *more* growth, *more* intervention to guarantee national independence, the revival of (i.e. *more*) National Planning, and so on. Moreover, the timing of its presentation suggests that the formulation of this strategy was motivated not so much by the belief that it constitutes *per se* a more appropriate prescription for the country's economic ills as by the need of the Gaullist party to distinguish itself, in the eyes of the electorate, from its coalition partners. This view seems to be supported by the marshalling of traditional Gaullist symbols (growth, national independence and the National Plan) and the adoption of disruptive parliamentary tactics apparently dictated by electoral appeal rather than indicative of disagreement on points of principle. Thus, the defeat of the entire revenue section of the Budget for 1980 seems to have been motivated less by disagreement over the proposed tax regime (significantly, the Minister for the Budget is a Gaullist) than by the desire for a trial of strength with the Government. This would seem to be confirmed by the subsequent dispute about the level of public expenditure, in the shape of the Gaullists' insistence that the Government cut the central administration's budget by Fr. 2 billion. This has provided the Gaullists with the opportunity of presenting themselves as the defenders of the taxpayer against 'Government waste'. What they do not make explicit is that they are *not* opposed to public expenditure in principle. On the contrary, their own programme presupposes a not inconsiderable volume of expenditure. They are seeking not so much a reduction in the absolute volume of public expenditure as the *redeployment* of part of it into productive investment.

Is the Gaullists' alternative strategy viable? A Government spokesman dismissed it as 'not a really *serious* proposal'[30] on the grounds that it constitutes a statement of aims with which no-one would take issue, but which are unrealistic. They fail to take account of the severity and, indeed, the nature of the current crisis and totally ignore France's fundamental weaknesses (notably her dependency on imported oil which constrains her potential competitiveness and undermines the Government's strategy for inflation-free economic growth). Chirac stands by the Gaullist strategy, however, claiming that the current rate of growth is the result of a calculated economic choice which not only is indicative of the Government's overcaution but also betrays its faulty analysis. In other words, it is hiding behind 'l'excuse pétrolière'. Although he concedes that the international environment has had an adverse impact on French performance, putting upward pressure on the inflation rate and holding back economic growth, Chirac suggests that his argument is vindicated by other European countries (notably West Germany, the benchmark for French performance in the economic and industrial sphere), which have apparently negotiated the crisis more successfully than France. But, as was pointed out earlier, France was much slower than other industrialized nations to take advantage of the respite offered immediately after the 1973 crisis (when oil prices were relatively stable) to make essential adjustments. Moreover, it is quite clear that the slowness of response (which was partly due to faulty diagnosis) was in the period immediately after the 1973 crisis, i.e. during the 1974–76 Chirac regime.

The Gaullists are clearly determined 'to show public opinion that an alternative economic strategy is possible'. Whether they are prepared to follow this course to its logical conclusion – bringing down the Government in a vote of confidence over its economic policy in the Assembly – is a moot point. Prima facie, it seems more likely that the party will continue to use its muscle until it engineers the removal of Barre and an end to the politics of austerity he has come to represent.

BEYOND THE CRISIS?

If the antics of the Gaullist party and a series of 'scandals' are making life difficult for the Barre government, it can take some heart, as the end of 1979 approaches, from the fact that its policies appear to be beginning to work. Barre has always maintained that it would take a full three years before his prescription had any effect and there are indications that his refusal to be deflected from his chosen course will, in the longer term, pay off. Thus, despite the widening trade deficit which is now reflecting the most recent oil price rises,[31] exports continue to increase, suggesting that French companies are maintaining their competitiveness against overseas producers. In September, for example, total sales overseas were up by 25 per cent compared with 1978, with exports for the motor industry and the agro-food sector particularly strong.[32] Significantly, in a recent report, the Patronat (the French employers' association) suggested that this strength is partly due to the Government's policy of abolishing price controls and promoting competition by encouraging inward investment.[33]

There are other signs which suggest that the French economy is adjusting to the pressures of the latest oil price rises better than was expected in the summer. During the last two months, the rapid escalation of unemployment seems to have slowed down (an improvement which is officially attributed almost wholly to the latest job-creation schemes)[34] and consumer demand is buoyant, despite the fact that real incomes are not rising. Furthermore, public opinion has swung round in favour of Barre. Two recent opinion polls show that he has made a spectacular recovery in general popularity. In one of these, 41 per cent of those interviewed said they were satisfied with his record, compared with only 28 per cent a month previously.[35] Barre's position appears to have been further strengthened by the reassurance that his premiership is safe, at least for the next six months. This may, of course, be conditional; given the approach of the presidential elections, Giscard has to weigh his confidence in Barre as 'the best economist in France' and 'one of the best Prime Ministers' against the unpopularity generated by his restrictionist policies and his handling of the difficult times ahead. For, if the Government has ridden out the Boulin affair,[36] it still confronts a number of problems.

The most intractable difficulties are in the economic policy area, notably the continuing problems of inflation and unemployment and the related threat of industrial unrest. In this respect, the forecasts are far from propitious. According to the National Statistical Institute

(INSEE), inflation is unlikely to fall below between 9 and 10 per cent during 1980 and will still be in the region of 7 per cent per annum in 1985, assuming, of course, that there is no third energy crisis. Unemployment is expected to deteriorate in the medium term, too, despite the recent improvement, with more than 2 million expected to be unemployed by 1985.[37] Indeed, the Government interprets the recent outbreak of industrial action in both the public and private sectors as not simply the 'hot autumn' promised by the leader of the Communist party, Georges Marchais, but also a worrying sign of the progressive worsening of the labour situation and all that this implies.[38] The impact of inflation and unemployment has, to date, been cushioned by the conjunction of rising real incomes and generous 'economic benefits'. How long the French worker can be expected to grit his teeth and accept the austerity of the Barre Government's policies, especially when living standards start to fall, is highly questionable. For a Government attempting to steer a steady course between the Scylla of greater (and ideologically unacceptable) intervention and the Charybdis of its liberal intentions, the outlook is somewhat bleak.

At the political level, the most immediate problem is the uncertainty which surrounds the intentions of the RPR. On the one hand, there continues to be a threat of an unholy alliance between the Gaullists and the opposition parties to defeat the Government over its economic policies. In terms of planning, public expenditure, employment policy, economic growth, and the like, there are certain similarities to the alternative policies presented by both elements. However, differences not only in political temperament and ideology but also over the long-term objectives of public policy make such an alliance unlikely. The parties of the Left, which differ widely enough among themselves over economic policy, see their task as changing the underlying balance of advantage and disadvantage in society — involving a long-term redistribution of resources between social groups. Gaullist demand management is conservative, and aims at preserving and revitalizing the potential for economic growth which they see as the great achievement of postwar state capitalism. However, a more profound blockage exists on the electoral level. The RPR is generally perceived as being to the *right* of the UDF, despite Gaullist protests to the contrary. Its hierarchial organization and authoritarian populist style mark it more deeply than its interventionist policy. And from this position in the party spectrum, an alliance with the Left might undermine much of its popular support and seriously damage its electoral credibility.

Furthermore, many Gaullist leaders are profoundly divided about the Chirac–Debré strategy. Current and former RPR cabinet ministers in various

Barre governments, such as Olivier Guichard and Alain Peyrefitte, see their role much more as that of a ginger group, softening and modifying the official liberal, monetarist line on a day-to-day basis. As this chapter has shown, they have not been unsuccessful in the face of crises like that in the steel industry. They are committed to maintaining the present coalition and preventing Giscard from moving towards an alliance with the right-wing Socialists, as was foreshadowed in his book *Démocratie française* and in the cross-bench support which was achieved for his early social reforms on such issues as divorce, contraception and abortion. Futhermore, Giscard, in his foreign policy stances and initiatives in Africa, towards Europe, and *vis-à-vis* the Carter Administration's line on the Soviet invasion of Afghanistan and the question of the Olympic Games, has appealed to the image and tradition of General de Gaulle himself. The virtual disowning of RPR ministers during the European election campaign by Chirac, the *'affaire du perchoire'* in April 1978 (the election of Chaban-Delmas as President of the new National Assembly over Chirac's official RPR candidate), and the decline of Gaullist electoral support during 1979 all indicate that the RPR does not respond monolithically to Chirac's leadership. Thus Chirac's strategy will only be credible within the parameters of the coalition politics of the *majorité* so long as *either* it forces Barre to change tack (and here the proponents of a 'softly, softly' approach from within the Government may have the upper hand in the long run) *or* it provides a base for a credible bid by Chirac for the presidency in 1981.

And finally, within the majority coalition itself, support for more interventionist economic policies is not limited to the RPR. The Radical Party, too, has pretensions to be a ginger group, although the defeat of Jean-Jacques Servan-Schreiber in a parliamentary by-election, and the total failure of his strategy to present a separate Radical list in the European elections, has reduced the influence of the Radicals within the UDF. The centrist CDS, too, with its postwar Christian Democratic tradition, has often been unhappy with Barre's austerity programme. In this context, the often bitter internal opposition within the governing coalition over economic policy is not merely an excuse to defeat the Government and bring it down (with or without left-wing help), but in fact concerns various attempts — by force (Chirac) or by cajolery and negotiation — to convince Giscard to replace Barre with a 'moderate'. Chirac's confrontation tactics cannot fully succeed, because in so far as they are directed against Barre, they are indirectly aimed at Giscard himself. And the bitterness between the President and his former Prime Minister may not be such that private dinners will erase the legacy of conflict. At the same time, an alternative moderate protocoalition, formed perhaps around a personality like Chaban-Delmas, and coming to the fore should Giscard lose confidence in Barre, is an undeniable possibility. Thus far, however, there is no sign of that crucial loss of confidence; Barre's economic strategy is Giscard's too, and so long as Giscard is President, any party within the majority seeking to present an alternative economic programme will be bound to oscillate between a strategy of confrontation — like Chirac, but also like Servan-Schreiber in the 1979 elections from another direction — and one of negotiation. But disagreements over policy as such are not likely to go away, and may well get deeper.

Notes

1   Notably, Giscard's ill-fated 1963 Stabilization Plan. The initial Barre Plan was based on a three-month price freeze, backed up by restrictions on credit and a pay restraint policy which stipulated that wages should not increase faster than prices. Measures were introduced to increase energy saving and restrict oil imports and strict limits were imposed on public spending to eliminate the deficit which had reached Fr. 43 billion in 1975 (3 per cent of GDP).

2   See Chapter 5, 'The Budgetary Process and the Plan' (Diana Green).

3   The minimum wage is, in fact, inflation indexed.

4   Prime Minister Barre, interviewed in the *Rhône-Alpes* newspaper, 12 July 1979.

5   Landlords agreed to limit increases to 19 per cent. It is not, however, only the private sector landlords who have broken the guideline; public authorities like the *Ville de Paris* and the *Caisse des dépôts* are equally responsible for rent increases well in excess of the recommended limit.

6   Interview in *Le Matin*, 4 September 1979.

7   See Diana Green, 'Individualism versus Collectivism: Economic Choices in France', *West European Politics*, Vol. 1 No. 3 (October 1978), 81–96.

8   Ibid.

9   The price of manufactured goods has increased by more than 29 per cent since the abolition of controls. The introduction of economic pricing in the nationalized sector was deferred for six months for electoral reasons. In the last two quarters of 1978, these prices rose by 12 per cent and will have increased by about 15 per cent by the end of 1979.

10 The new Commission replaces the old Monoplies and Mergers Commission (Commission technique des ententes et des positions dominantes). It was set up in July 1977.

11 Report on the Adaptation of the Seventh Plan.

12 This was the label attached to the industrial approach of the 1960s which provided the motivating force for the Fifth and Sixth National Plans.

13 The strict monetary and credit controls imposed under the Barre Plan have to some extent been offset by a series of measures to improve company liquidity. The main reforms in this area were introduced in the so-called 'Loi Monory' of July 1978.

14 For greater detail see 'The French Steel Industry', one of the case studies carried out by the present author as part of the study of *French Policies to Promote Adjustment*, commissioned by the Department of Industry in 1979.

15 The crisis erupted in the run-up to the 1978 elections. Understandably, the decision on how to deal with it was deferred until after the elections. Indeed,

when a number of prominent bankers turned up at the Ministry of Finance to discuss their worries about the industry's insolvency, they were told to go away until after March 19th!

16 A new Fr. 3 billion Industrial Adaptation Fund was created, extending even further the battery of regional aids, designed to attract investment to the areas affected by the planned closures, mainly in the North and Lorraine.

17 The Left's proposal to nationalize the industry was dismissed as irrelevant to the industry's problems. More to the point, it was ideologically unacceptable to a right-wing regime.

18 This system, introduced in August 1979, is in theory a means of monitoring the quantities of sweaters involved and their countries of origin. In practice, it is an administrative device to limit trade with OECD countries (especially Italy), in order to protect the French clothing industry.

19 That is, exposing the French car industry to Japanese competition via the 'Trojan horse' of BL's distribution network in France.

20 Yet another new scheme has been devised, featuring another version of the quasi-contracts which have proliferated during the 1970s. 'Development contracts' are medium-term agreements to be drawn up between the state and selected firms (in a range of 'key' sectors from robots to the industrial application of microbiology) which specify precise targets (and sanctions for non-fulfillment) in return for reimbursable state aid.

21 A new committee is to be set up called the CRI (Comité de Renforcement Industriel), chaired by the Director General of the Ministry of Industry. It will report directly to the Council of Ministers. It will have an intervention budget (whose level is as yet undetermined) to provide venture capital for expanding companies.

22 Net profits are expected to have increased by 18 per cent by the end of 1979 according to a poll by the SAFE, reported in *L'Expansion* 9 November 1979.

23 INSEE, Index of Industrial Production, October, 1979.

24 The number of people looking for jobs has increased by 52 per cent over the last three years (+48,000), while job vacancies have fallen by 33 per cent (−43,000).

25 It is estimated that about 270,000 young people have been found jobs through these schemes.

26 Fr. 2.5 billion is to be made available in the form of Government credits to inject new life into the housing and public works sectors. A once-and-for-all special social security payment will put an additional Fr. 2 billion into the pockets of nearly 5 million low income families at the beginning of the school year. And the guaranteed minimum wage was increased by 2.2 per cent as from 1st September. (*Le Monde*, 30 August 1979).

27 See Chapter 5, above.

28 *Le Monde*, 25 and 29 August 1979.

29 The following section draws heavily on the report and Chirac's personal version of the official line as recorded in an interview in *L'Expansion*, 9/22 November 1979.

30 Interview with a member of Giscard's private office in November 1979.

31 According to the Ministry of Trade, France's oil bill has increased by 54 per cent during 1979.

32 Motor industry exports (cars and components) increased by 15 per cent in the first nine months of 1979. The agro-food sector produced a positive balance (Fr. 373 million) in the same period.

33 *Le Monde*, 15 November 1979.

34 The seasonally adjusted figures for October showed unemployment down by 1.1 per cent compared with September, to 1.34 million. The uncorrected figures show an increase, however, from 1.42 to 1.48 million.

35   *L'Express*, 24 November 1979.
36   The suicide of the Minister of Labour in the wake of a property scandal. Boulin was widely believed to be Giscard's first choice as a replacement for Barre.
37   *L'Expansion*, 9/22 November 1979.
38   The air traffic controllers started selective stoppages in November as a result of a pay dispute. In the private sector, similar disputes took place in the Alsthom-Atlantique engineering company, the Ducellier motor components company, Renault's industrial vehicles division and a division of the Rhone-Poulenc chemical company.

9 The Economic Analysis and Programme of the French Communist Party: Consistency Underlying Change*

Mark Kesselman

For a brief period during the 1970s, it appeared that a social, political and economic experiment was about to occur in France comparable to those of Chile and Portugal in the 1970s and the French Popular Front forty years earlier. The vehicle was to be an electoral coalition, the Union of the Left, negotiated by the *Parti Communiste Français* — PCF, and the *Parti Socialiste* — PS. Although the Common Program, in which the left parties enumerated their reform proposals, was rife with ambiguities and contradictions,[1] even its bitterest critics were fascinated by its progressive possibilities, as evidenced by their dismay over the rupture of the alliance that began in September 1977. Trotskyist Henri Weber, for example, criticized the Common Program on the grounds that it represented a cynical attempt by the large bureaucratized parties to 'recuperate' the militant surge of May 1968.[2] Yet this implied, no doubt correctly, that although the Left parties may have chosen to accept the May movement's qualitative demands for equality and local control only out of self-interest, in so doing they were forced to become more progressive.

For several years, the internal dynamics of the major Left parties brought them together, a convergence doubtless facilitated by the possibility of initiating extensive reforms during the heady period of economic expansion and social protest following May 1968. However, in the gloomy period which began in the middle 1970s, the two parties were driven apart by their divergent analyses of how to deal with the accelerating economic crisis. In order to understand the significance of the potential challenge posed by the mobilization of nearly half the electorate around a program that sharply challenged the economic policies of the regime, it is necessary to situate the French Left's economic analysis within a general theoretical framework. In the long-range strategy of the PCF, at

least, the congeries of reforms proposed in the Common Program was
intended to prepare for a basic transformation of the contours of capitalist
society.

THE POLITICAL ECONOMY OF CAPITALISM

Social theorists as divergent as Anthony Giddens and Nicos Poulantzas
have argued that a fundamental feature of capitalist societies is the bifurcation of the political and economic spheres.[3] In contrast to pre-
capitalist and postcapitalist societies, where control of the means of
production and political domination are fused, the two spheres are
structurally differentiated under capitalism. Control over the means
of material production and legal domination are separated within capitalism. The state can neither compel workers to work nor compel capitalists
to invest. Under capitalism, both the production and investment processes
are privately directed. Despite the enormous range of state economic
regulation, incentives, and prohibitions in the present era, the sphere of
production remains private.

This is not to say that the economy and polity do not intersect. The
state continually intervenes, but such intervention generally seeks to
assure private capital accumulation and private control of the economy,
thereby reproducing the separation of the political and economic spheres.
Claus Offe and Volker Ronge have suggested that the agenda of the state
is shaped by these structural arrangements. Although the government
does not control production directly, it is dependent on taxes appro-
priated from the surplus generated by successful capital accumulation.
Consequently, 'every occupant of state power is basically interested in
promoting those conditions most conducive to accumulation.'[4] The
bifurcation of economy and polity means that there is a dual determination of power within the liberal democratic state: 'By its institutional
form, access to political power is determined through the rules of
democracy and representative government; by its material *content*, the
use of political power is controlled by the course and the further requirements of accumulation.'[5]

Despite the fact that political power is hypothetically shared equally
by all citizens as a result of democratic rules, in practice capitalist regimes
have rarely been challenged by working-class and other subordinate
groups excluded from control. Nearly all social and political forces in
advanced capitalist societies have come to accept private control of production by a highly restricted group. So pervasive is capitalist hegemony

that capitalism appears the only alternative. Virtually no major political party in any capitalist nation in the past several generations has proposed such drastic extensions of public control of production as to signify the abolition of capitalism.

This is not to deny that political parties compete for votes and propose differing economic policies. As Otto Kirchheimer points out, however, the significance of competition is belied by the fact that each party claims it is best qualified to accomplish the same basic task of finetuning the economy that all agree should remain in private hands.[6] Douglas Hibbs has compared Left and Right political parties in advanced capitalist societies, in an attempt to discern contrasts between their economic policies. He found that the critical division concerns the relative priorities parties accord to combatting inflation versus employment. Left parties are more inclined to stress alleviating unemployment at the expense of controlling inflation whereas the converse is true for rightist parties. Both Left and Right, in Hibbs' analysis, accept the supposedly inexorable logic of the Phillips curve, which posits an inflation/employment tradeoff.[7]

Yet, it might be asked, is it not the case that in all industrialized capitalist societies save for the United States, a socialist labor party ranks among the largest parties? While this is of course the case, it does not preclude these parties supporting capitalism. Social democratic and other leftist parties have sponsored programs of transfer payments, collective consumption, and tax measures to redistribute income and benefits in a more egalitarian manner. Public welfare programs initiated by the Left have helped to lower the costs of food, medical care and shelter. Yet, as Anthony Giddens has pointed out, precisely because social democratic regimes alleviate the gravest problems created by capitalist production, while leaving control of production in private hands, they may represent a mature and stable form of capitalism rather than an alternative to it.[8]

During the 1970s, France appeared to present a sharp contrast to the typical pattern shown among the capitalist nations. Two of the four major parties and several small parties, with combined support exceeding half of the electorate, opposed private economic control and the separation of the economic and political spheres. The Union of the Left proposed to transcend capitalism through extending public control over the economy. However, the attempt was never made as the alliance dissolved prior to the 1978 elections. The divergent economic analyses of the two major Left parties played an important role in their inability to remain united.

THE FRENCH COMMUNIST PARTY'S ECONOMIC PROGRAM

Although both the Socialist and Communist parties warrant detailed study, the major focus here will be on the PCF. The evolution of the PS has been more transparent. In the 1970s, the party reversed its steady decline by appealing to new social forces and responding to the demands for participation and control (*autogestion*) generated by rapid industrialization. Additional opportunities were provided by the fact that a conservative regime from which the Left was excluded fostered rapid economic growth at the expense of social justice. Additional inequalities joined those already existing in a rigidly stratified society. On most measures of social equality and progress, France ranked near the bottom of the major capitalist nations.[9] After pent-up social grievances erupted in 1968, the PS manoeuvred creatively to develop rhetoric and proposals reflecting the qualitative demands of the May Movement. Its success was crowned by achieving a position as one of the largest parties in France.

The Common Program, signed in 1972, not only conferred added credibility on the PS as a potential governing party, but helped bring it closer to a victory it could never achieve alone. The party, however, was in an exposed position. It was essential for the PS to check its coalition partner: any electoral advantage the PS enjoyed by the mid-1970s was mitigated by the PCF's greater number of militants, superior party organization, and privileged relationship with the largest trade union (the Confédération Général du Travail — CGT). The PS needed to demonstrate to skeptical fringe voters that it would not be smothered by the PCF embrace. It needed to display a sense of 'realism' and 'economic sobriety' to counter the PCF's perceived 'radicalism'. For the PS, the Common Program was probably as far left as it could safely appear to go (even in 1972, it had resisted PCF proposals for more extensive reforms).

These considerations stiffened the resolve of the PS leadership when negotiations began in 1977 to revise the Common Program prior to the 1978 elections. The two parties soon clashed head-on. For reasons to be explored below, the PCF demanded a substantial increase in the number of parent companies and subsidiaries that would be nationalized by a Left government; a different method of compensating shareholders of firms to be nationalized; a steep increase in the minimum wage; severe reduction in income differentials; and an administrative reorganization which would have facilitated PCF direction of strengthened economic planning machinery. Although the conflicts between the two partners (and their small ally, the Left Radicals) did not appear insoluble during the spring and summer of 1977, an impasse soon developed and the five year Union of the Left shattered at the very moment when victory appeared near.

Most observers agree that the PS positions were less mysterious than the PCF. What explains the sudden shift in the Communist Party position in 1977, which caught even the party's own militants by surprise? The PCF's economic policy was part of its overall theory of state monopoly capitalism.[10] First developed during the 1960s, the theory attempted to account for the changes that had occurred in France and other capitalist nations since the end of the Second World War. The theory involved a shift from a focus exclusively on the privately controlled means of production to an emphasis on the intertwining of monopoly capital and the state, a development the PCF considered to represent a new stage in the evolution of capitalism. In this view, the state had emerged as an essential instrument for directing a wide range of critical functions in the service of monopoly capital: not only was it property-holder, producer, and consumer, but it performed overall regulatory functions of banking, credit, and investment. The growth of the state temporarily enabled monopoly capital to stave off crisis tendencies. As opposed to the earlier PCF approach, which stressed economic stagnation and working-class immiseration, state monopoly capitalism theory recognized the importance of the long wave of economic expansion beginning after the Second World War. These changes in capitalism rendered obsolete the earlier theory.

Since the character of capitalism had changed, revolutionary strategy needed to be adapted as well. In the PCF view, more emphasis needed to be placed on struggles to gain control of the state. Further, changes in class structure, to be identified in a moment, enlarged the constituency potentially receptive to a Left appeal and narrowed the ranks of the exploiters to a small (albeit powerful) fraction of the bourgeoisie (monopoly capital). Meanwhile, working-class struggles achieved democratic rights which potentially made possible a peaceful, democratic transition to socialism. The new strategy involved the use of the electoral arena by the Left to gain control of the state and then using it to sponsor a series of structural economic reforms. In this manner, the PCF intertwined its political and economic analysis and looked toward the day when it could begin to integrate the two spheres in the transition to a socialist society.

In the PCF view, emphasizing the crucial role of the state demystified the apparent separation of economy and polity under capitalism. For example, struggles over wages assumed a directly political character in an era when the state established the minimum wage. The theory also reached beyond the dynamics of the accumulation process to explain basic changes in social (class) structure. State-fostered changes, notably the concentration of capital, decimated traditional social groups (independent entrepreneurs and shopkeepers, artisans, peasants — even the proletariat) while creating new middle strata composed of intellectuals, state and service sector workers, and skilled salaried technicians and engineers.

Although these workers were not members of the proletariat, they were exploited by monopoly capital and collectively (if indirectly) contributed to the creation of surplus value in the new, more collective production processes. Hence, the social forces that could be knit into an anti-monopoly coalition stretched from the traditional working class through a diverse variety of groups to include even those from the ranks of small and medium-sized businesses.

Although the theory of state monopoly capitalism was devised to account for the economic boom of the 1950s and 1960s, the PCF began to adapt the same theory to explain what it argued were new crisis tendencies as economic stagnation developed in the 1970s. The PCF argued that the new crisis orginated in the fact that the state was overextended and, since monopoly capital had eliminated large sectors of small and medium business firms, fewer potential sources of profit remained to be exploited by monopoly capital. Further, the introduction of new technology both created unemployment and reduced the working-class base which was the ultimate source of profits.

During the late 1960s and early 1970s, the PCF began developing the strategic consequences of its altered social, political and economic analyses. In the social realm, the PCF began to broaden its ideological appeal to the middle strata by emphasizing democratic liberties and engaging in the alliance with the Socialists. The alliance was judged a useful way to strengthen the PCF's links to the middle strata while preserving its own primary base within the working class.

In the political realm, more emphasis was placed on the role of the state in transforming monopoly capitalism through a series of structural reforms. A parallel can be drawn between the PCF's changed view of the state (which it had bitterly dismissed earlier) and its dramatic about-face in 1976 on the issue of nuclear weaponry. The PCF dropped its opposition to nuclear armaments because, it argued, Fifth Republic governments had come to rely so heavily on them (to the detriment of conventional forces), that without nuclear arms French independence would be jeopardized. In a similar fashion, the PCF came to accept the importance of the state in an era of state monopoly capitalism. Rather than merely denigrating the state's role, the PCF henceforth accepted it both as a fact of life and a potent weapon. The party's strategic goal shifted to gaining control over the state and using its powers of economic intervention and regulation to hasten a socialist transition.

The PCF now believed that the Left could gain control of the state by democratic means, through mobilizing the enlarged social base that opposed monopoly capital. The long-term goal was to use the state in a democratic manner to fuse the economic and political spheres. The medium-term aim was to tip the balance away from state subordination to monopoly capital and toward public control over economic and political institutions. The PCF identified a first stage — the transition to the transition — which it termed advanced democracy.

In the economic sector, three inter-related mechanisms were to achieve the goal of public control: nationalization of production and finance, national planning, and democratic management. Nationalization was the key to the PCF strategy: everything hinged on expanding the public sector. Nationalization would permit coherent, rational planning in accordance with centrally determined goals. As a companion measure, democratic management would be instituted, with authority over the production process delegated to tripartite councils of state, worker and consumer representatives.

The break-up of the Left alliance cannot be explained without reference to the dominant role nationalization played in the PCF's overall strategy: in this interpretation, the PCF saw extensive nationalizations as crucial for achieving its diverse goals. PCF leaders and economists frequently stressed the fundamental differences between their version of nationalization and previous nationalizations.[11] In France and other capitalist nations, nationalization has meant bailing out ailing industries and useful but unproductive services for capitalism. The PCF proposals, by contrast, would serve the very different purpose of tipping the balance from private to public control of the economy. It was for precisely this reason that a minimum threshold of takeovers was essential: otherwise, 'monopoly capital domination over the ensemble of economic and social life will persist.'[12]

The general approach of the PCF toward nationalization was summarized well by Pierre-Yves Cossé:

Every nationalization is a step toward the final objective of the socialization of the overall means of production and exchange: it directly weakens state monopoly capitalism, the cause of the crisis; it provides a supplementary base of control by the party of the working class . . . The PS for its part proclaims itself selective; it wishes to establish collective power over a limited number of industrial groups while limiting the transfer of property to the minimum necessary. Nationalization is not a road automatically leading to socialism but merely one of the instruments necessary for the realization of economic and social transformation.[13]

Most importantly, nationalizations would give the Left control over the true political-economic powers in French society. The industrial firms slated for takeover were among the largest, strongest, and most technologically advanced in France. When these firms were added to existing nationalized industry, the public sector would employ 32 per cent of the industrial workforce and would absorb 45 per cent of all investments and 75 per cent of all R+D.[14] Further, through nationalizing the major private commercial banking and insurance institutions, the state would gain control over most of French finance capital. In conjunction with democratic management and national planning, control over finance capital would give a Left government the necessary tools to make the French economy the most rationally organized of any capitalist society.

Nationalizing the most powerful elements of monopoly capital would decisively weaken monopoly capital by taking away its economic power to compel government servitude. The state would no longer be forced to base economic policy on the interests of monopoly capital. This in turn would free the government to introduce progressive measures regarding wages, pensions, paid vacations, and working conditions (the public sector has traditionally played a vanguard role in regard to social welfare measures). An enlarged public sector would sponsor welfare gains that would be adopted by private industry and thus benefit the entire working class. These measures would presumably facilitate PCF recruitment as well. The major nationalized industries — the railroads, Renault, electricity and gas — are already PCF and CGT strongholds. The expansion of the public sector would also represent an expansion of the Left's social base in its struggle with capitalism.

Finally, the PCF's economic proposals provided a means to resolve the economic crisis afflicting France. In the PCF view, sluggish investment policies by monopoly capital and the state were responsible for sagging demand and unemployment. This pattern could be reversed if the PCF's economic program were implemented. Vigorous state investments, along with other progressive measures, could revitalize French industry, increase demand, reduce unemployment, and create new prosperity.

Since the PCF did not have an opportunity to apply its economic proposals, their validity cannot fully be determined (critics charged that the party's policies would prove highly inflationary and would quickly provoke economic chaos). What does seem clear is that the PCF's class and political analysis, which suggested that an alliance with the PS would suffice to attract large numbers of new recruits to the party from the middle strata, proved unduly optimistic. Although millions of recruits flocked to the two parties, most gravitated to the PS, the less radical of the two. Despite the PCF's 'new look' and many new members, it attracted few additional voters and steadily lost ground within the alliance as the PS grew. An additional worry beyond the absolute growth of the PS was the fact that the PS nearly drew even with the PCF in working-class support, a development unprecedented in the post-war period.

It has frequently been asserted that the PCF seized on the issue of nationalizations as a pretext to break the Left alliance whereas the real reason was the shift in the balance of power between the two parties. Political calculations concerning the respective power of the parties probably played a role in PCF planning, but the equation can as plausibly be reversed: it may have been precisely because the PS was recalcitrant regarding the PCF's economic demands that the relative power positions of the two parties assumed such importance for the PCF. If the PS had proved more tractable on the nationalizations issue, the growth of the PS might have deterred the PCF less. In this interpretation, national-ization and other economic proposals were not a mere pretext for breaking the alliance; they were the crucial issue for the PCF.[15]

If the PCF was weaker than the PS and came to power on an inadequate platform, how could it promote the decisive steps toward a socialized economy — or, worse, avoid being saddled with responsibility for an economic crisis and/or an austerity program resented by its working-class supporters? The PCF's refusal to 'administer the crisis' might have been strengthened by the example of the Italian Communist party following the 1976 legislative elections. As a result of its quest for the 'historic compromise', the PCI trapped itself in an awkward position by calling on Italian workers to practice 'revolutionary austerity', a plea which brought the party neither increased popular support nor state power. During the very moment when the PCF leaders must have been pondering the acceptable limits to compromise, the PCI exemplified the pitfalls if the limits were exceeded.

Although Louis Althusser and other party critics are correct that the PCF leadership changed its political line and broke the alliance in an arbitrary, secretive manner, the leadership's judgement rested on a solid base.[16] The alliance was bringing the party neither increased power (it was declining relative to its major coalition partner and failing to improve upon its own past electoral performance) nor the opportunity to achieve its ideological goals. Unless PCF leaders could reasonably estimate that the alliance would produce substantial benefits in the future, it was not worth the enormous risk it entailed. By 1977, this became increasingly problematic. PCF leaders have never been known for their audacity and, given the sombre outlook, a strategic retreat seemed the most prudent course. With several years hindsight, this decision appears far more rational than during 1977–78, when the turn appeared inexplicable.

The abrupt reversal probably saved the PCF from the potentially incalculable damage of finding itself elected to power in alliance with a much stronger and more conservative Socialist party. In this situation, PCF power would have consisted of the ability to disrupt but not to initiate its plans for structural reforms. The PCF's retreat to a defence of the interests of the working class and poor prior to the 1978 election had the desired effect of redressing the balance of power with the PS. The move partially re-established the party's vanguard and working-class credentials, demarcated it from the PS, and frightened off enough potential PS voters that the two parties emerged from the election with a roughly equal electoral following.

FROM 'UNION OF THE LEFT' TO 'UNION AT THE BASE'

As 1978 drew near, the PCF became increasingly isolated as a result of its own initiative as well as political and economic changes beyond its control. Its repeated criticism of the PS as veering to the Right was partially true, although one reason may be that through repetition it became a self-fulfilling prophecy. Following the election, the PCF discerned a broad coalition of forces, including the PS, responding favorably to President Valery Giscard d'Estaing's call for a new social consensus in France. In the PCF view, the appeal attempted to obscure a multi-pronged offensive consisting of: intensified austerity policies shifting the costs of the economic crisis to French workers; an industrial redeployment policy sacrificing entire sectors of the French economy to multinational corporations based in France, West Germany and the United States in particular; and political and economic integration within the Atlantic and European alliances, subordinating French national interests to multinational-dominated capitalist powers. Giscard's policies were described by Paul Boccara, a party economist who was a principal architect of state monopoly capital theory:

Some people talk of sacrifices necessary for the new 'economic war'. In reality, this means that the French and France are asked to accept damage to their individual and family life, the destruction of entire sectors of the economy, the curtailment of fundamental social and cultural activities, and the abdication of sovereign powers to directorates who are primarily foreign; in brief, the sacrifice of themselves, their children, their regions, and their country. All this to defend what? The selfish interests of several cosmopolite French-based firms . . . alongside more powerful multinational groups based in the United States and West Germany.[17]

As another PCF publication summarized, 'With M. Giscard d'Estaing's policy, the future of France is jeopardized as well as the future of the French nation as a coherent, sovereign collective ensemble.'[18]

The hardening of the PCF's position resulted in an abandonment of its former, more optimistic reformist perspective in which socialism could be achieved through a series of structural reforms. Party leaders ceased to speak of structural changes instituted at the top. Instead, they advocated 'union à la base', direct action at the grass roots to protest state and private assaults on workers' wages, jobs and living conditions. The PCF stressed its total opposition to all forms of capitalism and frequently linked social democratic parties (including the PS) to international and state monopoly capitalism (the suggestive links were strengthened by the fact that the Federal Republic of Germany was ruled by the Social Democratic Party).[19] PCF criticism of the PS thus took a more virulent turn during the period. Whereas between September 1977 and the 1978 legislative elections the PCF accused the PS of veering to the Right, in the period following the election the PS was treated as indistinguishable from the representatives of foreign capital that dominated the governing coalition in France. Overall, the PCF characterized itself as representing French national and working-class interests against the rest of organized forces in France.

In its attempts to defend the French nation against multinational and supranational onslaught, the PCF discerned one potential ally; its former bitter opponents, hard-line Gaullist nationalists. In an editorial in *Humanité* on December 15, 1978, René Andrieu noted the similarity between the Gaullists' and the PCF's opposition to what Andrieu termed Giscard's 'debasement of France'. He pointed out that Gaullist leader Chirac's anti-Giscard attacks contained:

Language familiar to us [Communists] . . . Should we be irritated by the convergence? Let's speak frankly: we rejoice that, in an area decisive for France, the policy of resignation of the Government is challenged by an increasing number in the majority coalition. And we have not forgotten that at certain important moments in our history — the Resistance and the struggle against the European army — Communists and Gaullists worked together to defend national independence.

By making overtures to the Gaullists, the PCF signified its abandonment of a Left alliance strategy. In its view, the struggle to defend French national interests had to take priority during this sombre period over the attempt to achieve broad-gauged social reforms. This did not signify an abandonment of grass-roots struggles — in an eclectic, pragmatic, and somewhat haphazard fashion, the party embraced any and all protests that occurred in France. But it represented a substantial retreat from the previous period, when the first priority was the attempt to seek structural reforms in an alliance with the PS.

CONCLUSION

What explains the PCF shift and the partial reversal of alliances that has occurred since 1977? One reason is conjunctural. Certainly any party fears an adverse shift of power within an alliance, and the substantial PS growth could not help but jar the PCF. In the medium term, the party was preparing for the 1981 Presidential elections. Since the party planned to run its own candidate, it needed to differentiate itself from the PS and neutralize its electoral competitor by driving away Socialist party sympathizers.

Perhaps more important is that PCF leaders apparently decided that the PS had become an untrustworthy ally. Although in fact the PS appears to have been quite constant in its political-economic analysis following the 1972 signing, it did become less circumspect about clashing with the PCF and supporting its own position as its power grew.

What brought these latent conflicts into the open, galvanizing the PCF offensive, was the deepening economic crisis and PCF calculations of what this meant for the party. During the Left union period of 1972–77, the PCF tried a conciliatory strategy of an alliance negotiated at the top. For years, the party and the CGT restrained working-class militancy on the grounds that immediate demands had to be subordinated to the election of a Left government. Undue militancy at the grass roots, it was felt, would prove counterproductive by frightening wavering voters.[20]

The muting of worker demands could not survive the continuing economic crisis, and the PCF's attempt to restrain working-class protest came under increasing stress. By late 1977 and mid-1978, the working class had achieved neither electoral victory nor the benefits that might have been obtained by social struggle. Following the break-up of the alliance, there was bitter popular disillusionment with a strategy that had produced no tangible rewards, a feeling exacerbated by the continuing post-election struggles within and between the Left parties.

Party militants were not alone in their disgust with electoral and alliance politics. The PCF leadership also developed a distrust of the strategy it had ardently sought. For the first time in its history, the PCF had failed to achieve substantial gains from an electoral alliance. Its modest successes in the 1978 elections derived from its ability to retain the support of its working-class constituency in the regions traditionally loyal to the party. Since the party's more flexible theoretical analysis and strategy did not appear to contribute to whatever successes the PCF achieved in 1978, the alliance, and possibly the theoretical analysis on which it rested, became expendable.

The early 1980s are a particularly unfavourable juncture for the PCF, compounded of a continuing French economic crisis, the betrayal of French national interests by the regime, and the failure of the PCF's attempt to achieve structural reforms through an alliance resting on diverse classes and political parties. The PCF has not yet found a new theory and strategy appropriate to the new situation. And, given the shift away from the immediate prospect of progressive change, the party defined its role as struggling to check the further advance of reactionary forces, not fostering a transition to socialism.

Notes

* I am grateful for suggestions from Martin Schain and Samuel Bickel on an earlier draft of this chapter.

1 For a good brief comparison of the two parties' positions on nationalization, see Diana Green, 'Individualism versus Collectivism: Economic Choices in France', *West European Politics*, Vol. 1, No. 1 (October 1978), pp. 81–96; and my 'Continuity and Change on the French Left: Revolutionary Transformation or Immobilism?', *Social Research* (forthcoming, March 1980).

2 Henri Weber, 'L'Union de la Gauche', in Denis Berger, Henri Weber, and Jean-Marie Vincent, *Le Ve République à bout de souffle* (Paris: Galilée, 1977), pp. 67–146.

3 Anthony Giddens, *The Class Structure of the Advanced Societies* (London: Hutchinson University Library, 1973), and Nicos Poulantzas, *State, Power, Socialism* (London: New Left Books, 1978).

4 Claus Offe and Volker Ronge, 'Theses on the Theory of the State', *New German Critique*, Vol. 6 (Fall 1975), p. 140.

5 Ibid.

6　Otto Kirchheimer, 'The Transformation of the Western European Party Systems', in Joseph LaPalombara and Myron Weiner, eds., *Political Parties and Political Development* (Princeton, N.J.: Princeton University Press, 1966), pp. 177–200.

7　Douglas Hibbs Jr., 'Political Parties and Macroeconomic Policy', *American Political Science Review*, Vol. 71 (December 1977), pp. 1467–88.

8　Giddens, *The Class Structure of the Advanced Societies*, Chap. 9.

9　See, for example, OECD, *Income Distribution in OECD Countries: Public Sector Budget Balances* (Paris: OECD, 1976).

10　PFC, *Traité marxiste d'économie politique: Le Capitalisme monopoliste d'Etat* (Paris: Editions Sociales, 1971). I have also benefited a great deal from Keitha Sapsin Fine's subtle *Theory and Practice in the French Communist Party: State Monopoly Capitalism and Class Struggle, 1958–1978* (London: Allen and Unwin, forthcoming).

11　See, for example, 'Nationalisations, Le Clé de Voute', *Economie et Politique*, Vol. 6 (November 1977), pp. 56–79 (as well as the many PCF publications on nationalization cited on p. 78).

12　Marc Bormann, 'La Gestion démocratique dans le secteur publique', *Cahiers du Communisme*, Vol. 54 (January 1978).

13　Pierre-Yves Cossé, 'Les Nationalisateurs', *Projet*, No. 122 (March 1978).

14　See Fine, *Theory and Practice in the French Communist Party*.

15　This interpretation of the weight of various factors influencing the PCF leaders' decision to shift position, like all interpretations of the shift, is based on pure conjecture. PCF leaders' public explanations are unconvincing and no confidential information regarding Political Bureau deliberations has been divulged. The present interpretation is substantially at odds with most others, which emphasize the importance that power considerations presumably had in PCF leadership thinking to the relative exclusion of ideological factors. However, the present interpretation suggests that the PCF leadership does not seek power for its own sake but for the purpose of achieving their vision of socialism.

16　Louis Althusser, *Ce qui ne peut plus durer dans le parti communiste* (Paris: François Maspero, 1978).

17　Paul Boccara, 'Deux stratégies fondamentales qui s'opposent dans les luttes', *Cahiers du Communisme*, Vol. 34 (November 1978), p. 21.

18　'La France et la Stratégie des Multinationales', *Economie et Politique*, Vol. 7 (November 1978), p. 73.

19　In *Economie et Politique*, November 1978, p. 68, a photograph of Helmut Schmidt and Giscard d'Estaing is juxtaposed to one of Schmidt and François Mitterrand.

20　This is not to say that the PCF's extensive organizational base at the grass roots, consisting of the party apparatus, its privileged ties to the CGT, and the network of organizations which it sponsored or influenced, did not always count heavily in the PCF strategy for social transformation. But the PCF probably attempted to limit protest before the elections in order to better utilize its organizational strength during the process of achieving structural reforms following a Left electoral victory.

10 Corporatism and Industrial Relations in France*

Martin A. Schain

Recent analyses of political stability in Western Europe have emphasized the importance of the relationship among major producer groups within 'neo-corporatist' structures as a basis for consensus building and conflict-management. Corporatism has been defined as a pattern of policy formation in which major producer organizations collaborate both with one another and with the state in the development of policy. In this process, major interests have (or are granted in various ways by the state) a virtual monopoly of representation within their respective categories, and collaboration is frequently characterized by an interpenetration between interest organizations and the state bureaucracies. Corporatism, however, is more than a model of policy-formulation; it is also a model of social control, and an implied explanation for a declining intensity of social and economic conflict in Western Europe. In exchange for integration into the policy-making process, major producer groups regulate and regularize mass action. Thus open conflict is channelled into limited bargaining.

The corporatist paradigm as understood to connote *a political structure within advanced capitalism which integrates organized socioeconomic producer groups through a system of representation and cooperative mutual interaction at the leadership level and of mobilization and social control at the mass level* can be a heuristic tool for appropriating the social reality of many western liberal democracies. As a working model in political analysis, it has manifest advantages over pluralist theory unencumbered as it is by the latter's unwieldy assumptions of extensive group multiplicity, passive stage behavior, and stability as a product of overlapping membership and the unseen hand of group competition.[1]

At the heart of this corporatist pattern is the relationship among trade unions, employer organizations and the state, a relationship that has developed around mutual advantages for all of the partners. For employers, participation in quasi-public decision-making institutions means the acceptance of state intervention in economic management, and a recognition of the role of organized labor in participating in certain kinds of management decisions. In exchange, employers gain considerable financial support from the state, as well as a process for the management of social and industrial order from the trade unions. For the trade unions, a commitment to social order is the price of organizational stability and incremental change. Organizational stability is supported by privileged access to public decision-making institutions as well as by the tools of institutionalized power, such as official recognition, checkoffs, closed shops, etc., all of which are useful for the maintenance of organizational power. For the state, the participation of organized producer interests is the price of influence over economic management in a capitalist economy.[2]

This regularized relationship among organized industrial interests promotes social and political stability in two related ways. First, the corporate bargaining process itself promotes integration of the representatives (and perhaps the interests) of the masses of industrial workers into a system of mutual accommodation. Second, many aspects of industrial relations can be 'institutionally isolated', thus separating industrial conflicts from influence over other spheres of society. 'Increasingly, the social relations of industry, including industrial conflict, do not dominate the whole of society but remain confined in their patterns and problems to the sphere of industry.'[3] DiPalma notes that

> If the load of issues on a set of decision-makers is light, they may find it easier to accommodate each single issue. For example, the practice of entrusting the solution of many social problems to corporate negotiations — common to many European countries — clearly alleviates parliamentary work, and improves the parliaments' decisional capacity. Incidently, one should also notice that when prenegotiated issues arrive in parliament, they are already partially aggregated, and thus easier to handle.[4]

However, a key assumption behind this stable pattern of industrial relations, indeed a condition for the establishment of the pattern, is the strong organization of groups engaged in collaboration, particularly the strong organization of the trade unions. Organization facilitates the establishment of regulatory norms and institutions, since such arrangements for bargaining can only begin to emerge once the security of the actors is assured.

> Organized groups stand in open, and therefore controlable conflict . . . Organized interest groups of subjected classes have means to enforce recognition of their interests at their disposal; moreover, they are in principle accessible for negotiations, i.e., regulated disputes. One cannot deal with unorganized, loosely connected rebels . . . Thus, the conclusion is suggested that the democratization of industrial conflict begins with the organization of industrial classes.[5]

Moreover, organizational control over mass action facilitates the autonomy of elites within the bargaining process, a key condition for mutual accommodation and for the enforcement of agreements that are reached.[6]

Thus, the key elements in the corporatist pattern of industrial relations are related to one another. While organization is a condition for the effective exercise of the representative function that makes bargaining possible, institutionalized bargaining strengthens the organizational position of elites by creating privileged access, by providing weapons of organizational control, and by lending legitimacy to recognized organizations.[7] Both organization and the institutionalized strength of elites are the basis for limiting conflict in the industrial relations system, since mass action is a controlled weapon in the bargaining process, and the bargaining process is defined and limited by elite understandings.

While this corporatist model of industrial relations has certain weaknesses when applied to various cases in the real world, among the advanced capitalist societies in Western Europe, it is probably least applicable to France.[8] This 'deviance' of France was seen by one otherwise optimistic study of French politics as the core problem in the development of political stability and economic growth in France.

> It must be noted here that one of the principal reasons for the apparent deviance of France . . . has been the relatively poor state of labor–management and labor–government relations . . . Clearly, and this is especially true for France, failure to stabilize these relationships in a mutually satisfactory way will be a continuing flaw in political and social consensus, as well as a threat to economic growth. We see here a striking example of the limitations which culture and other institutions can set upon the urge to regularity and stability inherent in modern economic organization.[9]

In general, this deviation from the pattern is attributed to the ideological rigidity of labor leaders, compounded by the fears of French businessmen and their preoccupation with any threat to their own authority. Under these circumstances, elite corporate bargaining has not been institutionalized, and has proceeded mostly in fits and starts.

Ideological rigidity is supported by the persistence of 'leftism' among French workers, and by the divisions within the French trade union movement.[10] By 'leftism' is usually meant the voting inclinations of French workers, and the radical programs presented by trade-union organizations. The divisions within the trade-union movement, it is argued, lead to irresponsibility in collective negotiations, and tend to generate a pattern of competitive bidding toward more radical objectives.[11]

The search for a 'solution' to the French problem, then, tends to focus upon the reduction of 'leftism' among French workers, as well as changing attitudes and approaches towards bargaining among trade-union and employer elites. Therefore Lipset sees hope in the fact that, while workers have remained loyal both to radical trade unions and to 'the parties of their class', their commitment appears to be more formal and less intense.[12] Other observers now seem far less sure about the reduction of the intensity of 'leftism', but some agree that there have been important changes in the attitudes and approaches of employers and trade unions. Here the measure has generally been the increase in the number of collective bargaining agreements in France, especially since 1955.

> While union patterns and loyalties remain fairly frozen, some change is apparent in French industrial relations practices. Here one senses more realism, reflecting perhaps the greater initiative of some employer groups, caught up in day-to-day problems.[13]

> The beginnings of mutual acceptance by management and workers, the more practical attitudes of both, and the shared desire for economic growth to be shared by all, have helped France to catch up with her neighbors, both economically and ideologically. In particular, collective bargaining agreements between management and labor have been much more prominent since 1955 . . .[14]

A 1975 government report emphasized that while employer associations have shown increased interest in collective negotiations in recent years, initiatives have come most frequently from the unions. Nevertheless, 'The ideological positions of the unions leads many employers not to accept [them], in practice, as valid representatives [*interlocuteurs privilégiés*].'[15]

Is the inability to develop stable patterns of corporate consultation in France due principally to the ideological rigidity of the employers and the unions? The argument in this paper is that an important factor is frequently forgotten in the analysis of the instability of industrial relations in France. The effectiveness of union bargaining is dependent upon the authority of union elites, which is related to the actual or presumed power of the unions within the industrial area. Union power is based upon their ability to mobilize workers and to prevent mobilization. Thus, the authority of unions over their mass constituency is an essential element of their power in bargaining. In France, the authority relationship between union elites and their mass constituency has been weak and conditional; this has been the essential condition of the bargaining relationship among the unions, the employers and the state. One aspect of this weakness can be seen in the inability of unions to recruit workers into their ranks; another is the conditional role union elites play in strike movements.

ORGANIZATION: DENSITY AND AMALGAMATION

As a percentage of those eligible (density), trade-union membership is small in France, far smaller than in any modern industrial country. While this fact is frequently cited, it is important to appreciate some of the details of this pattern. According to membership estimates secured from the three major trade union confederations, there is a significant difference between the public and private sectors in rates of union membership, as well as some interesting fluctuations over time.

The highest and most stable rates of union membership have been achieved among civil servants and industries in the public sector. Here 40 to 60 per cent of the workers appear to be union members. In the private sector, however, the rate of union membership varies between 5 and 25 per cent; the one exception is the printing industry, where 35–40 per cent of the work-force is probably unionized. Since the First World War, there have been wide variations in unionization in private manufacturing, with massive influxes of workers just after the First World War, during the Popular Front and just after the Second World War, and rapid declines soon afterward.[16] In the public sector, membership increases have been more gradual, and less pronounced.

Finally, although the level of union membership in individual enterprises varies considerably, few of the enterprises where trade unions have an established presence seem to have a rate of unionization higher than 15 per cent. At the Renault plant at Billancourt, for example, where both the CGT (the Communist-dominated General Confederation of Labor) and the CFDT (the French Democratic Confederation of Labor, non-Communist, but generally to the Left of CGT) are considered to be present in some force, only about 10 per cent of the workers were union members before 1958; the percentage is now about double that.[17] This is typical of large manufacturing plants. Some of the more technologically advanced plants are reported to have much higher rates of unionization, but the CFDT estimates that in all of the metals industries (which employ about 10 per cent of the entire labor force in France), the CFDT and the CGT together have organized about 20 per cent of the workers.[18]

There is some evidence that differences in union membership between the public and private sectors, and among enterprises, can be accounted for by the effectiveness of the union organizations in the daily life of the plant or industry. The highest membership exists where the unions exercise a coercive influence among workers, for example among teachers, where they have been able to establish some control over the promotion system. High membership also exists in other parts of the public sector where unions have been able to provide more extensive services. In the private sector, where unions have been generally excluded from any significant influence over the daily life of the plant, membership has remained low.[19]

Between 1968 and 1974, all of the trade-union confederations reported relatively large increases in membership, particularly in the private sector. Much of this new membership, however, was gained in plants that had not been organized before 1968, and therefore has increased union presence extensively. This was facilitated by new legislation that for the first time gave legal protection to plant unions in enterprises with more than fifty workers. By 1974, the number of plant unions had more than doubled, and the percentage of enterprises with at least one plant union had increased from about 21 per cent in 1969 to 43 per cent in 1974.[20] Thus, while union presence is more extensive, the density of union membership does not appear to be significantly greater.

Organizational amalgamation in France is a complex problem. Since 1966, there have been a series of agreements on joint action between the two largest national confederations, the CGT and the CFDT. These agreements have provided both national organizations with a basis for common action, despite periodic conflict between them at the national level, and frequent conflict between militants at the plant level.[21] The CGT-FO (Workers' Force, which split from the CGT in 1948, in response to Communist domination of the CGT) has refused to formally collaborate with CGT and the CFDT in any of the programs for common action. Nevertheless, both at the national and the plant levels, FO organizations have in fact joined in common or 'parallel' action.

There is some evidence that the divisions within the union movement have contributed to the low level of membership.[22] However, this is far from clear, since the evidence cited seems to indicate that workers who do not join unions are reacting to what they regard as the 'political' involvement of *all* of the union organizations. Probably the strongest net impact of divisions within the trade union movement is the uncertainty that this injects into the bargaining process. As the Sudreau report notes:

> The engagements undertaken in the name of the workers are inevitably precarious. The representative unions are not always signatories to an agreement. Each is free to participate or not in negotiations, to sign or not to sign the agreement, to associate itself ultimately [with the agreement] or to denounce it.[23]

Certainly, the low rate of unionization and the divisions among the trade-union organizations reduce the authority of union representatives in the bargaining process. Far more important, however, is the inability of the union organizations to control the strike weapon. Indeed, in France, there is a tendency to see the strike as a process with its own momentum and its own independent force, rather than to see it as an organizational weapon.

THE STRIKE PROCESS

Trade-union control over strike action is a variable rather than a constant that can be taken for granted. In general, unions have not been able to call strikes at strategically opportune moments, nor have they been able to prevent inopportune strikes from taking place and spreading. Every union initiative is, in effect, a test of its power to mobilize, which, in turn, becomes a key factor in subsequent negotiations with representatives of the employers or the state. Organizational control generally increases at the lowest levels, and is inversely proportional to the duration of the strike. Therefore, union initiatives are usually at the plant level, and for short duration; as often as not, a formal strike call will follow, rather than precede the outbreak of a strike.

In private enterprise, and in nationalized enterprises such as Renault, there are two kinds of strike orders: orders at the plant level, and orders at the regional or national level. Strike orders at the plant level will vary considerably, but they are almost always for a short duration, and they never seem to extend beyond the confines of a single plant of a company. If a strike spreads, it generally spreads throughout the industry of a region, rather than to other plants of the same company. While calls for unlimited strikes do occur from time to time, they are quite rare. When work in a factory is brought to a complete halt for a long period of time, it is usually because a limited strike has developed into a protracted conflict through mass support, because workers are locked out, or because a group of workers occupy key points of the production process within the factory. 'The idea of a strike, as accepted in Britain and the United States, as a dispute which once opened, continues until the exhaustion or surrender of one or another of the combatants is so unusual as to merit the special term *grève illimitée*, a strike without end.'[24]

The degree to which plant level strike orders are uncoordinated with any broader strategy is apparent in a survey that was taken of plant militants. When militants were asked whether they consult with their federations before and/or after engaging in strike action, they replied as shown in Table 10.1. In fact, it is only ten years ago that any of the major union organizations began to compile statistics on strikes being led by their militants.[25]

Table 10.1   Consultation between plant militants and union organizations*

	Percent Before	
	Chemicals	*Metals*
CGT	15	16
CFDT	31	14
FO	4	15
	Percent After	
	Chemicals	*Metals*
CGT	72	68
CFDT	41	39
FO	50	76

*J. B. Reynaud, P. Bernoux and L. Lavorel, 'Organisation Syndicale, idéologie et politique des salaires', *Sociologie du Travail*, Vol. 8, No. 4 (1966).

However, it is not clear that even plant-level militants are able to initiate or prevent strike action. The phenomenon of 'spontaneity at the base' has often been characterized as a new pattern;[26] but my analysis of the most important strikes before 1968 supports the contention that even at the plant level, the authority of union militants has been conditional, and that strike initiation has been a process of 'dialogue' between militants and workers. Union 'bosses', who can call men off the job under most circumstances, do not exist in France at any level. 'No one speaks of 'Dupont's union' or 'Durand's union'. Nor do workers get a vicarious satisfaction out of the display of power or wealth by their leaders. Government, whether of state or trade unions, still inspires distrust. Whatever their real power or way of living, union officials receive modest pay and need frequent mandates from their membership.'[27] The most frequent pattern is that union militants, sensing mounting dissatisfaction, will call for a limited action, usually a brief stoppage accompanied by a meeting and demonstration. At this point, the mass action will develop and expand in unplanned directions, and union organizations will be challenged to support a 'base-carried' movement.

The most important change in French strike patterns since 1968 has been the even more pronounced tendency towards the initiation of strike action that is not clearly controlled by union militants. In an analysis of twenty-five strikes during the two years after the 1968 events, Serge Mallet concluded that the most fundamental characteristic of all of these strikes was 'the active intervention of the base (unionized and non-unionized) which leads and controls the struggle itself.'[28] Even before the 'events' of 1968, workers had sometimes initiated strikes in opposition to local union militants by occupying factories, workshops or offices. This form of action has grown during the last ten years. In July 1975, the CGT reported that of the 180 enterprises on strike, forty-two were being occupied.[29] After considering strike patterns in France, the Sudreau Commission noted that 'To the effects of union pluralism, must be added the consequences of a certain spontaneity at the base. This has always existed in the French worker tradition, and for several years, notably with the rejuvenation of the active population, it has assumed greater vigor.'[30] Thus, the devolution of strike initiation to the militant at the plant level is a recognition by the trade union organizations of the conditional authority that they hold over the strike. The unions do issue strike calls, but they do not control the initiation of action as an organizational weapon.

Orders for brief stoppages at the national or regional levels are generally intended by the unions to be a show of strength at a particular moment, or a test of their ability to mobilize workers — usually for an hour or two — at a given point in time, or an attempt to show solidarity with 'struggles in progress'. For example, on 13 May 1976, the CGT and CFDT issued a joint declaration calling for brief work-stoppages for diverse demands, 'to give a greater impetus to current demands . . . and to strike at the intransigence of management and at the refusal for real negotiations.'[31]

Such national industrial or inter-industrial actions have always met with mixed success. Thus, in January 1966, the CGT and CFDT signed a national, interprofessional agreement on common strike action that also defined common objectives. The agreement was followed by a series of brief, national actions that culminated in an inter-industrial general strike on 17th May. The national strike calls were strongly supported, and there was a modest increase of strikes at the plant level as well. Nevertheless, a second national inter-industrial call on 14th June was followed only sporadically. After the summer holidays, the two confederations 'invited' their militants to pursue strike action, but the strike level declined.[32]

Hesitant, because of the 'non-combative social climate' during the autumn of 1966, in February 1967 the two confederations supported a one-day strike 'of national magnitude', leaving local organizations to choose what kind of action they would take and for how long. While there was considerable participation in the public sector, participation in the private sector was scattered and disappointing.[33] However, during the next two months, strike activity increased dramatically in the private sector, which led the confederations to claim that the February strike had been the spark that had set off this new series of strikes.

A close examination of the pattern of conflicts that developed in 1967, however, shows that each strike appeared to gain support from the other, but that there seemed to be no relationship to the national strike in February. The statement issued by the CGT and the CFDT, that events in March and April demonstrated that 'the discontent of the workers is becoming concrete with great force and with a higher level of combativity', certainly seemed to be true. This development, however, was generated by specific plant conditions, rather than by any national initiative by the union organizations.

For the unions, their ability to act is dependent upon the ever-present reality of *climat social* (social climate), the level of anger, frustration and rebellion felt by the workers at any given moment. A successful strike-call indicates an accurate reading of the rebellion-level; the failure of workers to follow a union initiative, or the explosion of a grass-roots rebellion that is unanticipated by the unions means that plant level militants have failed to do their job. Union organizations essentially react to the level of discontent, and often contend that the purpose of a strike is 'to permit them to measure the combativity and the discipline of the base'.[34] Because social climate varies from plant to plant (and even from workshop to workshop) most strike calls are issued at the plant level, and because union organizations can never be quite sure of their following, they are likely to call brief walkouts, when they have the choice, although survey research among French workers clearly shows a preference for, and an appreciation of the efficacy of long strikes at the regional and national levels.[35] (Nevertheless, figures from the Ministry of Labor indicate that perhaps 20 per cent of the strikes each year last more than a week.) Finally, because social climate varies from plant to plant, it is not possible to develop an intensive strike movement against all of the plants of one company across the country.

If we approach strikes from the perspective of social climate, we can understand that the act of striking in France implies a far more radical act than in most countries. Rather than an instrumental action for specific goals, the strike in France is often seen as 'a rupture of the social order. . . [that] incarnates radical and millenarian tendencies.'[36] As with many movements that are carried by strong mass feelings, strikes are rarely set off by a single cause, and often the objectives are formulated after the action has already begun.[37]

The style of strikes in France is often far closer to what we understand as a political demonstration: mass meetings, marches and frequent attempts to mobilize the support of the broader population. Indeed the style of the strike is to politicize, rather than to isolate industrial conflict. Nevertheless, the objectives of strike action are generally modest by any standard. 'Those who sequester executives, those who occupy the factories, those who resort to direct action are not necessarily committed to a fundamental transformation of society; they often share the illusion that some reforms will be sufficient to change their conditions.'[38] Thus, there is a notable gap between the radicalism of the form and the modesty of the objective.

THE IMPACT ON BARGAINING

The real authority of union elites in the bargaining process is linked to the level and the intensity of mass action. For all of the parties in industrial relations the social climate is the essential ingredient — in fact precondition — for the bargaining process. The representativeness of union negotiators at every level is always in question, and 'their power to mobilize supporters constitutes an essential criterion of their representativeness.'[39] This means that for purposes of bargaining, the unions must offer 'proof' that they speak for someone, and this 'demonstration', as we have seen, is often out of their control. Thus, although there is poor linkage between action and negotiations, there is a strong dependence of one upon the other.

Strike action, in France, is fundamentally different from similar action in most other industrialized countries. The strike level is not an index of the breakdown of bargaining, and is not a test of strength through which bargaining is continued through other means. It is a pre-condition for bargaining, and therefore precedes, rather than follows, any serious bargaining effort. This function of strikes in the system of industrial relations therefore supports and encourages a high level of strike action, even for modest demands.

Thus, with an eye on future collective negotiations, the CGT and CFDT generally issue a call to action each September – the *Rentrée Sociale*.

'Union action at the time of the *rentrée* is indispensable' affirmed M. Edmond Maire [National Secretary of the CFDT] . . . 'It is even more simple,' declared M. Georges Séguy [National Secretary of the CGT] . 'We do not decide that on such a day, at such an hour, in such a branch, that such a plant will go on strike. . . . We say that there is great discontent and great combativity. These are the two criteria that must be grasped in order to understand that the climate is for action.' After having once again demanded negotiations at all levels, M. Séguy indicated: 'If the demands cannot be settled [by negotiations] their solution must be seen in terms of action.'[40]

The year before, M. Séguy had encouraged CGT militants:

. . . to be everywhere the initiators of action, at the head of the workers' struggle . . . attentive to everything that goes on among the workers . . . [to take care] to create the best conditions for the expression and the concretization of the creative initiative of the masses.[41]

For the unions, a high level of strike activity is an opportunity from which advantages can be extracted at many levels. 'The unions seek, most often, to draw general advantages from each local conflict, while the employers naturally attempt to limit the effects.'[42] However, there is generally little direct connection between strike action and the regular contacts of collective negotiations. According to the estimates issued by the Ministry of Labor, less than one per cent of the strikes each year are directly related to collective agreements. Moreover, data from the Ministry of Labor and the CGT indicate that most action at the plant level fails to meet its objectives – see Table 10.2. Therefore there is a high level of action and even violence (if we consider the growing incidence of plant occupation) for relatively little payoff. Since most effective bargaining takes place beyond the plant level, that is at a different level from where strike action is centered, there is only a remote connection between the action that generates power for union negotiators, and the

Table 10.2   Strikes: percentage ending in settlement and failure*

	Settlements	Failures
1959–62	54	46
1963–65	43	57
1969–71†	45	55

*Ministère du Travail, *Statistiques du Travail et de la Sécurite Socialé 1960–66*; Centre Fédéral de Documentation d'Etude Economique et Sociale, Fédération des Travailleurs de la Métallurgie, CGT, *Bilan des Luttes et Succès*, 1969–71.

†These figures are for the metals industries only, and therefore are not strictly comparable to those for the other periods. However, during this period, strikes in these industries were widespread and intense.

bargaining itself. 'How can it be explained to workers that the sectors where combativity is greatest are not necessarily those where union action is the most effective, and that the results of negotiations are not proportional to the amplitude of the mobilization?'[43]

Since 1966, there has been what one group of authors call a 'rebirth of negotiation'. At the inter-industrial level, with the encouragement of the government, a series of 'inter-professional agreements' have been negotiated that have set up procedures for dealing with security of employment, job retraining, and the shifting of massive numbers of workers from hourly to monthly pay status.[44] Similarly, in major industrial branches, there has been the kind of intensive negotiation of some important innovations that has rarely taken place in French industry. Although the negotiations for some of these agreements began in 1966–67, it was only after the 'stimulus' of the events of 1968 that any substantial progress was made. This intensity of negotiations continued throughout the period when Chaban-Delmas was Premier (1969–72), encouraged by the Government as the core of its program to alleviate the social tensions of the events of 1968, the *'politique contractuelle'* (see below). While few of these agreements were direct reactions to a specific strike movement, they were negotiated in the context of the heightened social climate of those few years.[45]

The precariousness of such negotiations is obvious. For the unions, negotiating benefits is no problem. In fact, all of the major inter-professional agreements after 1968 were for benefits of various kinds. The employers and the state, however, can expect few benefits of social order from union organizations that have so little authority over strike action.[46] Indeed, at the very moment when union authority in the bargaining process was strongest, its authority in controlling action was being more strongly challenged than ever before.[47]

Nevertheless, the threat of social disorder sometimes has been effectively 'canalized and amplified' by the trade-union organizations. Their authority over strike action may be weak, but in fact there is no one else with whom to talk. For example, in September 1975 at the same time that a number of strikes involving plant occupations were in progress, the CGT and the CFDT announced a day-long series of demonstrations. 'The turnout was honorable, but the factories continued to function. At the Matignon [the residence of the Premier] they observed the day with interest. Coldly. It was not a great demonstration of force, but it was the best controlled by the CGT and the CFDT for a long time.'[48] Sensitive to the charge that the government did not have things under control, Premier Chirac decided to 'ease the atmosphere' by proposing to the unions and to the employers that negotiations be opened on lowering the retirement age and reducing the work-week.

Similarly, the government reacted to a high strike level in 1957 by legislating a third guaranteed week of vacation for all French workers. Two years earlier, the management of the state-owned Renault works responded to a strike wave that year, 'an explosion of anger', with a *contre feu*, a new kind of plant agreement that would establish salary levels, working conditions and numerous benefits with a negotiated agreement, rather than by *ad hoc* arrangements in the midst of a crisis. This novel approach has now spread to many of the largest plants in France, but it has not succeeded in significantly reducing the strike level in these plants.

What is surprising is that it has taken so long for norms and regulatory institutions to begin to develop at the plant level, since the plant has been the focus of conflict. However, until 1968, union organizations had neither legal existence nor protection within the plant gates. Given this weakness, the unions have been reluctant to focus their bargaining efforts where they had the least strength; the employers, for their part, preferred *ad hoc* settlements with weak bargaining agents to stable relations with an institutionalized union (see below). Although direct negotiations at the plant level have grown significantly since 1968, the problem of authority and power remains. For the unions that 'canalize and amplify' action, authority over strikes is still conditional; for the employers there is still a strong tendency to question the power of the union negotiators. Therefore, for both, action remains a testing ground and a precondition for effective bargaining. However, the usefulness of having someone with whom to negotiate was an important consideration in the government case for the legalization of plant unions in December 1968.[49]

The tacit assumption that social climate has a momentum of its own undermines the real power of the unions as bargaining agents. While trade unions are frequently effective in crisis management, and can even wield some authority in bargaining in anticipation of social crises, their day-to-day institutionalized power is small. This is apparent from their weak organization structures, and the lack of guarantees for their organization stability, growth, and representative function.

Trade unions in France function with small budgets, few personnel and meager resources. At the confederal level, the CGT is reported to have 154 paid personnel, the CFDT 122 and FO 54. About half the CGT budget of 4 million dollars is allocated directly in salaries; most of the remainder goes for propaganda and office expenses.[50] The industrial federations and the departmental and regional organizations in each of the confederations have budgets of their own, but they are also small and support few personnel. For their strength, the unions rely on the unpaid volunteers at the local and plant levels — the 'militants'. For about a quarter of their resources, they depend upon various forms of state payments. The work of the militants is supported by free hours, to which they are entitled by law, when they serve as shop stewards, on plant committees and (since 1968) as official union delegates. However, only in the larger plants are the unions able to dominate the plant committees and control the election of shop stewards. This means that at all levels, the unions have few personnel and resources for recruitment and strike organization and control. Although the CFDT and FO have small strike funds, they are not capable of supporting an intensive strike effort. The dependence upon unpaid militants further reduces organizational control.

A good part of this organizational weakness can be attributed to a lack of the institutional protection and guarantees that have become commonplace in other industrial societies. Except for some parts of the public sector, such guarantees have not been freely offered, nor have they been intensely sought by the union organizations themselves. The Sudreau Report made a remarkable plea for the strengthening of the trade union as an institution; remarkable because it had to be made at all:

Finally, the *politique contractuelle* in the country only exists with the representative confederations. The foundation of legitimacy of the union function is the scope of its activities: the union organizations synthesize and express the collective aspirations of the workers; . . . they contribute to the training of worker representatives; they offer a means of advancement for their militants; finally . . . they constitute a factor of social regulation by aggregating centrifugal forces which would otherwise be manifested in a dispersed way.[51]

Such institutional weapons as the dues checkoff, the closed or union shop and the recognition of a union monopoly over the negotiation process have never been established in France. Indeed, at the plant level, where strike action is most intense, union organizations are least institutionalized. Until 1968, union sections had no legal existence or protection within the factory gates, although some enterprises had recognized plant sections by agreement. Most employers could neither be convinced nor compelled to grant the union organizations this base, whatever benefits it would bring in easing strike settlements.

'Why should we give this gift to the unions?' one of the leaders of the employers' association declared to us. 'To recognize the plant section would be to give to the trade unionists space, time and the means to recruit adherents and to collect dues; this would be to practically incite the personnel to join. Where would our interest be?'[52]

Even after the plant sections were granted status by legislation in 1968, however, they were effectively established only in the largest plants. Nevertheless, the number of plant sections grew rapidly from about six thousand in 1969 to almost sixteen thousand in 1974. Thus, the minimal protection given by the new legislation was of considerable help in giving the union organizations a broader base of support.[53] The base, however, is precarious. The unions lack the resources and the authority to take full advantage of the sections, and the employers have avoided going beyond the immediate demands of the law.

The fact is, that despite the 'rebirth of bargaining', the stability of union authority at any level has improved very little. While unions are now present within the enterprise, so are plant committees, shop stewards and a variety of specialized commissions. Despite all of the bargaining in which they are engaged, unions have not gained control over the one issue that provokes the vast majority of strikes each year:

The determination of actual wages, both in principle and in fact, remains within the jurisdiction of the enterprise. In a certain number of cases, genuine wage agreements are negotiated in the enterprise, but they rarely, so far as we know, fix wages in francs. Generally, they limit themselves to guaranteeing percentage increases in wages. But even this practice is not general. For most wage earners the actual wage is not a subject of negotiations.[54]

ORGANIZATIONAL WEAKNESS AND THE
POLICY-MAKING PROCESS

Because of their inability to mobilize a mass base effectively, and because of their dependence on a shifting social climate, the unions have not been able to make their weight felt in the development of policy that has had an impact on them and on the workers for whom they claim to speak. Their advice and acquiescence generally has not been considered necessary by the state for the successful development and implementation of policy.

Ezra Suleiman's study of the French administrative process makes the point that French administrators carefully distinguish between 'professional associations' and 'interest groups or lobbies'. While professional associations are favorably regarded and are well-integrated into policy development and the decision-making process, interest groups are sometimes formally consulted, but presented with *faits accomplis*: 'We ask for their [interest groups'] advice only *after* we have a completely prepared text. And we do this just to make sure that we haven't made some colossal error.'[55] The basic consideration in deciding that a group is an interest group appears to be the criteria we used to analyze the organization strength of the trade unions: density and amalgamation.

> Directors often commented that the major problem with regard to the administration's relations with interest groups' relative unrepresentativity. 'It is hard to negotiate with a group when you don't know how many members it represents,' said one Director. It was frequently noted that the fragmentation of interest groups was a decisive factor in their unequal (or inferior) relationship to the administration.[56]

Trade unions are 'interest groups', of course. They possess very little with which to exchange for influence in policy-making, except during periods of social crisis, when they become the only available *interlocuteurs valables*. Professional associations 'render as much service to the agency as they receive from it.' Trade unions 'are seen purely as *demandeurs*, who seek to attain their goals by spectacular means.' Because they are 'poorly organized, fragmented, and unrepresentative, they can neither provide the administration with indispensable information, nor can they represent a particular administration in its battles with another administration.'[57]

This analysis, based upon interviews with administrators, is confirmed by case studies. Trade unions, for example, have been more or less isolated in the process of industrial and economic planning. There is widespread agreement that 'Labor's role is largely a matter of public relations. The real contact is between industry and the state, and these two effectively exclude the "third partner" from serious discussions.'[58] Given this process, it is hardly surprising that much of the most significant legislation that has dealt with the working class condition has been passed in spite of the vigorous opposition of the trade unions (see below).

The unions are quite aware of their general impotence in the process of policy-development and policy-making. However, they have remained in various consultative bodies because they have been able to gain information and establish some meaningful contacts with sympathetic administrators. Moreover, the unions sometimes attempt to use even unsuccessful negotiation and consultation as a tool for mobilization.[59] Beyond specific advantages, however, is the feeling that has been expressed among unionists that they must prove that they are serious 'that the *mouvement ouvrier* is capable of going beyond the stage of slogans, and expressing concrete propositions . . . This active and serious participation does not have the objective of consolidating the regime, but on the contrary must furnish us with the arms, the supplementary arguments for our action in favor of an economic policy oriented towards a priority of satisfaction of the needs for well-being and culture of the popular masses.'[60]

While governments have been able to virtually ignore the trade-union organizations in the development of socio-economic policy, they have also pursued policies through which they would be able to exercise at least minimal influence over social climate. One policy line has been an attempt to develop institutional alternatives to unions at the plant level 'to associate the worker more broadly with the life of the enterprise'.[61] Much of the discussion prior to 1968 about how to integrate workers into a socio-economic consensus focused on finding alternatives to the trade unions.[62] This strategy is best illustrated by the legislation on plant committees in 1965, and the ordinances dealing with profit-sharing in 1959 and 1967.

In July 1964 M. Mathevet, representative of the CFDT and rapporteur of the section on social activities, presented to the Economic and Social Council the case for the recognition of the plant union. His report was rejected. M. Aumonier, representative from the Christian employers group explained that he opposed the proposal because 'the enterprise cannot admit an outside element that will not rally to the common cause . . . union freedom must not be opposed to the freedom of the enterprise'.[63] As an alternative, he proposed a strengthening of the plant committee, and protection for a non-voting union representative within the committee. Aumonier's proposal had the support of the Minister of Labor. Both the minister and Aumonier were convinced that in this way union representatives would be placed in a position where they would be more likely to form co-operative relations with their employers, and would be more securely tied to the firm. In this way, and on this level, 'the union must finally be an instrument of co-operation'.[64]

Aumonier based his position largely on a 1963 study of the plant committees by Georges Montuclard.[65] Contrary to the conventional wisdom, Montuclard concluded that the plant committees were functioning and that participation in the committees he had studied had given the worker representatives a commitment to the enterprise. In answer to the question of whether the committees were *transformatrice* (transforming agents) or *absorbante*, he contended that they were the former. Perhaps most important, from the point of view of Aumonier, Montuclard concluded that the committees could not be considered a simple tool of the union organizations. 'In spite of the links with the union, the committee remains a "sociological entity" which has its own rhythms. If the union ideology tends to orient the committee, it remains true nevertheless that its existence [that of the committee] exerts a constant pressure on union orders.' Thus, while the committees had not spawned company unions, they had served to develop a counter-force to the unions within the enterprises.[66]

The government proposal passed the Assembly on 29 June 1965, overwhelmingly. Nevertheless, following the vote, the employers' association issued a statement, declaring that 'we shall never permit union penetration into the enterprise. It will be necessary to impose this upon us by force, which is not yet the case'.[67]

The legislation, however, did not satisfy the unions. When the opportunity arose to raise the issue once again, during the events of 1968, they did so. Part of the 'Grenelle Agreements', among the unions, the employers and the government, resulted in the legislation of December 1968 that granted legal recognition to the plant union. However, it was only under crisis conditions that the government consented to deviate from its path; that is, under conditions that sharply augmented the power of the unions.

Another, perhaps more obvious, attempt to promote the plant committees as alternative structures to the unions has been the set of profit-sharing schemes that have been packaged under the name of *intéressement*. In 1959, a government ordinance modified the collective bargaining legislation to permit the negotiation of a new form of plant agreement. Under the stipulations of the ordinance, workers could 'participate' in the enterprise in several different ways: either by sharing in the profits, by sharing in the stock, or by sharing in the fruits of increased productivity.

Like other accords, the agreements could be reached by management and union representatives. However, the ordinance also provided for a way of bypassing the unions, if the employer could gain the consent of two-thirds of the employees.[68] Despite the coolness of both the unions and employers, by 1966 there were 202 such contracts in force, involving about 104 thousand workers.[69]

A change in approach by the government to the questions of *intéressement* came in July 1965 when Louis Vallon, the left-wing Gaullist Chairman of the National Assembly Finance Committee wrote an amendment into the 1965 finance law requiring that an ordinance be issued 'defining the ways by which the rights of workers to the increase in value of assets of an enterprise due to self-financing be recognized'. After some delay, on 22 June 1967 the Assembly passed a second legislative act authorizing the government to issue an ordinance that would assure participation of the workers in the fruits of expansion of the enterprise. The report of the Assembly stated that the intention was to establish 'new relations between workers represented by their unions, and employers', as well as to open 'a wide range for negotiation between employers and workers'.[70]

The ordinance, issued on 17 August 1967 *required* most enterprises with more than 100 workers to establish a 'workers' profit sharing fund'. This fund could be used for investment in the company itself, or for investment outside of the company, but the benefits could not be drawn by the workers for five years.[71]

None of the unions favored the 1967 ordinance. They strongly suspected that this was a part of a Gaullist plan to undermine their meager authority. And indeed they had some reason for these fears. The ordinance contained a provision for the negotiation of agreements between the employers and the plant committee. Between 1967 and 1970 82 per cent of the accords were in fact negotiated with the committees, without any official approval from the union organizations.[72]

The practice of *intéressement* brings into question whether this program is at all relevant to encouraging bargaining relations between employers and unions since the unions have been largely bypassed in these 'new relations'. Moreover, the pattern of these efforts has been continued in other areas. Two of the major national agreements between employers and the major trade unions after 1968 dealing with employment security and with job retraining were to be implemented on the plant level. In both cases the plant committee, rather than the union sections, were chosen as the relevant institution. 'This was a crucial decision, since it gave preference to the consultative organism legally incapable of negotiating, to the detriment of the union and, of course, the formal agreement.'[73]

The employers preferred to deal with an institution that was not directly related to the bargaining system, thereby avoiding pressure for formal commitments within the enterprise. The unions, on the other hand, were reluctant to get involved in negotiating job reductions, and were uncertain about the role they could effectively assume in job retraining.

After 1968, however, the government was more reluctant to pursue this course and, with some hesitation, made an attempt to regularize corporate contacts and bargaining as a basis·for social stability. During the period between 1969 and 1973, the government gave priority to a *politique contractuelle*, in order 'to regularize conflicts, and to make the strike the ultimate arm of the workers'.[74] In the implementation of this policy, the government sought to isolate negotiable areas for bargaining in the public sector, and to deal most directly with the CFDT and FO. This would isolate the more hostile CGT, and would place pressure on employers in the private sector to bargain on issues (such as vocational training and employment security) that would otherwise be the subject of legislation. The real novelty was that for the first time the state consented to bargain with the unions on wages. Moreover, this process represented a serious attempt to begin to build a process of corporate consultation. It was flawed from the beginning, however, by the antagonism of the CGT, and was more seriously flawed after 1972, with the departure of Chaban-Delmas and the rapid slow-down of the economy.[75]

With the announcement of the Barre Plan in 1976, prepared without any consultation with the union organizations, the process of corporatist contacts completely broke down. The government refused to negotiate on wage increases in the public and nationalized sectors, and, in return, the CFDT joined the CGT in announcing that it would refuse to sign any new contracts. Government strategy for managing social unrest then shifted from bargaining and consultation to direct legislation. Three legislative measures, dubbed 'National Pacts on Unemployment' were passed in 1977, 1978 and 1979, which created incentives for training and hiring young people (where both unemployment and social unrest are concentrated). In addition, public money was channelled into public works projects, particularly in the Nord and Pas de Calais departments, and in Lorraine, where many jobs have been lost due to crises in shipbuilding and the steel industry.[76]

In reaction to a renewed strike wave in the fall of 1979, as well as a new agreement for joint action between the CGT and the CFDT, the Barre government once again moved towards corporate bargaining. President Giscard d'Estaing announced a new effort to develop a 'social consensus' through collective consultations, and once again the favored partner appeared to be the CFDT.[77] These new proposals are interesting as part of a government attempt to neutralize opposition and maintain social order, while it is pursuing a policy of austerity. Given the experience of the early seventies, however, it would be difficult to argue that the French government is convinced that it must begin to build a process of corporatist consultation as a basis of long-term social stability.

In fact, labor policy in France seems to be a series of *ad hoc* responses to specific situations, that incorporate minimal corporatist consultation, consultation with alternative institutions, as well as some direct benefits to workers. As long as union organizations remain highly dependent on social climate in order to assert their influence, it seems unlikely that corporatist processes will develop in France.

INDUSTRIAL RELATIONS IN FRANCE AND THE CORPORATIST MODEL

The essential aspect of industrial relations in France is the weakness of trade union organizations, combined with poor control over mass action. Organizational weakness means that in order to be effective in any process of bargaining, unions must constantly 'demonstrate' that they are representative, that they have a viable base of support. Therefore a tendency toward mobilization is built into the system.

Mobilization is also encouraged by the employers and the state, since for bargaining purposes, all of the 'social partners' have demonstrated a strong sensitivity to the fluctuating social climate and impending threats to social order. Given the independence of the social climate from union control, however, neither the employers nor the state has been willing to grant the union organizations the recognition of institutionalized power — access and consultation — nor have they willingly granted to the unions those tools with which they might enhance their organizational strength. In fact, they have sought to fragment that strength by creating institutional alternatives.

There is also a tendency to politicize industrial conflict. Politicization often attracts broader communal support for strike action, which is often the only way of sustaining a strike for any period of time in the absence of strike funds and well-financed organizations. The lack of institutionalized power for trade unions means that the limited industrial arena is less acceptable.

For all parties there is a tendency to wait for social crises in order to bring about important changes. The reason is not so much stalemate, but powerlessness. At times of social crisis, trade-union elites suddenly gain true 'representative' power, the state is most concerned with social order, and employers are under most pressure to make concessions: in fact, under these circumstances, the employers' organizations can most easily justify to their member associations any concessions that must be made.[78]

Of course bargaining relationships exist, and have even expanded, in non-crisis situations. Indeed, some important agreements have been reached. However, the dependence of this system on fluctuating social climate means that it is highly unstable and will probably remain so, as long as union organizations are unable to gain control over mass action.

The French case directs our attention to several problems that the corporatist model does not fully consider, principally the impact of the dynamic relationship between elites and masses in the trade union movement. In effect, the French case exposes the weak link in the system of industrial relations. The integration of union elites into the system depends upon *both* strength of organization and control over mass action. Where one or both of these conditions are absent, corporate bargaining is difficult to sustain.

There appears to be increasing awareness of this problem in the growing literature on industrial relations and industrial conflict. Several recent studies have carefully explored the thesis first elaborated by Ross and Hartman in 1960, that, because of improvement in the working-class condition, changes in employer attitudes and the institutionalization of industrial conflict, the strike is virtually 'withering away' in advanced industrial societies.[79] By 1970, it was obvious that the strike was not withering away, and that in fact there had been a resurgence of strike activity in advanced industrial societies.[80] This, in turn, raised questions about the variations in strike activity, the strength of organization of trade unions and the institutionalization of industrial conflict.

Cross-national studies of strike fluctuations have concluded that industrial conflict responds to variations in trade-union structure: the more decentralized the trade-union structure, the greater the degree of autonomy of subordinate structures, the higher the level of strike activity.[81] Strike activity has also been found to vary with the degree of institutionalization: 'the low level of institutionalization means that the commonplace and recurrent conflicts of capitalist society are difficult to resolve without frequent recourse to strike action'.[82] Therefore the French pattern of industrial conflict appears to be unique only in degree.

There is also work that indicates that elite autonomy declines with a high level of industrial conflict, and that the willingness (or the ability) of trade-union elites to accommodate to the bargaining process also declines as industrial conflict increases and is not well-controlled.[83] This is in accord with what we have discovered about the French case. It appears that organizations whose power is dependent upon mass action themselves become dependent on the conditions of that action. From the French case we know that control is weakest and dependence is greatest when the constituency upon which the organization relies is outside of its organizational network, but within its organizational framework.

Therefore, the variations in level and control of industrial conflict are related to the institutionalization of industrialized conflict. We know from the French case that decentralized industrial conflict supports a decentralized pattern of decision-making for strikes, and 'A structurally complex and fragmented trade union movement — especially when accompanied by a parallel structure of employers' associations — inhibits institutionalization.'[84] Poorly controlled industrial conflict has also been related to the challenge to the general understanding that has been behind corporatist bargaining in Europe:

> The direct threat to the order could come largely, if not solely, from the social-democratic, leftist, and trade-union leaders. As long as they came to terms with the existing elite by accepting the early post-war agreements avoiding fundamental challenges to power relationships, the establishment accepted them. Toward the end of the 1960s and in the 1970s, they moved to more aggressive positions, demanding substantial alterations.[85]

Finally, the French case lends support to the criticism that has been elaborated of the notion that prolonged and frequent conflict leads to the development of regulatory norms and institutions. This is least likely to occur when elite control over mass action is decentralized and highly conditional. Therefore, the containment of conflict implied by the notion of 'institutional isolation' is itself highly conditional. This is obvious, if we consider that one of the more important consequences of 'worker militancy' in Europe has been the increasing 'spillover' of industrial conflict into the political arena.[86]

Notes

*   Parts of this paper appear in *The Tocqueville Review*, (Winter 1980). I am grateful to Mark Kesselman for his comments on an earlier draft of this paper.
1   Leo Panitch, 'The Development of Corporatism in Liberal Democracies', *Comparative Political Studies*, (April 1977), p. 66.
2   Samuel Beer, *British Politics in the Collectivist Age* (New York: Alfred Knopf, 1966), p. 321.

3   Ralf Dahrendorf, *Class and Class Conflict in Industrial Society* (Stanford, Calif.: Stanford University Press, 1957), p. 268.

4   Giuseppi DiPalma, *The Study of Conflict in Western Society* (Morristown: General Learning Press, 1973), p. 18.

5   Dahrendorf, *Class and Class Conflict in Industrial Society*, p. 259.

6   Ibid., p. 258, and DiPalma, *The Study of Conflict in Western Society*, pp. 7–10.

7   For further elaboration of these relationships, see Beer, *British Politics in the Collectivist Age*, p. 331, Dahrendorf, *Class and Class Conflict in Industrial Society* pp. 257–61, and Theodore Lowi, *The End of Liberalism* (New York: W. W. Norton, 2nd edn. 1979), pp. 52–63.

8   Gerhard Lehmbruch, 'Liberal Corporatism and Party Government', *Comparative Political Studies*, (April 1977), pp. 96–115.

9   Harvey Waterman, *Political Change in Contemporary France* (Columbus, Ohio: Charles Merrill, 1969), p. 27.

10   Everett M. Kassalow, *Trade Unions and Industrial Relations* (New York: Random House, 1969), Chap. VI.

11   *Rapport du comité d'étude pour la réforme de l'enterprise*, présidé par Pierre Sundreau, 7 février 1975 (La Documentation Française, 1975), p. 25. Hereafter, this will be referred to as the *'Sudreau Report'*.

12   Seymour Martin Lipset, 'The Changing Class Structure and Contemporary European Politics', *Daedalus* (Winter 1964), p. 280.

13   Kassalow, *Trade Unions and Industrial Relations*, p. 123.

14   Waterman, *Political Change in Contemporary France*, p. 30.

15   *Sudreau Report*, p. 25.

16   For details on membership, see my forthcoming book, *The French Trade Union Movement: Mass Action, Organization and Politics* (Ithaca, N.Y.: Cornell Unversity Press, forthcoming).

17   See Walter Kendall, 'Labor Unions in France', *European Community*, No. 135 (June 1970).

18   These figures were made available to me by the Fédération des Travailleurs de la Métallurgie, CGT, and by the Fédération Générale des Métaux, CFDT (for 1973). Also see Serge Mallet, *La Nouvelle classe ouvrière* (Paris: Editions du Seuil, 1963), p. 60.

19   See Michel Crozier, 'White Collar Unions: The Case of France', in Adolf Sturmthal, ed., *White Collar Trade Unions* (Urbana: University of Illinois Press, 1966), p. 114; and James M. Clark, *Teachers and Politics in France* (Syracuse: Syracuse University Press, 1967), pp. 95–6.

20   Ministry of Labor figures.

21   At the national level, the confederations have openly disagreed about a variety of political issues, and have been in on-and-off dialogue since 1970. In general, the CFDT tends to be more in sympathy with groups of the far Left than the CGT has been. At plant level, the 'deterioration of relations' between militants of the two organizations that is constantly cited in the press seems to be related both to the competition between the two unions, as well as the more free-wheeling style often expressed by CFDT militants. See, for example, *Le Monde*, 6–7 April 1975, 25 June 1975, 2 October 1979, 6 October 1979, and *Humanité*, 29 September 1979.

22   See: Andrée Andrieux and Jean Lignon, *L'Ouvrier d'aujourd'hui* (Paris: Éditions Gonthier, 1966), pp. 174–7; Charles Micaud, *Communism and the French Left* (New York: Praeger, 1963), p. 141; and G. Adam, F. Bon, J. Capdevielle and R. Mouriaux, *L'Ouvrier français en 1970* (Paris: Armand Colin, 1970), p. 157.

23   *Sudreau Report*, p. 25.

24   Kendall, 'Labor Unions in France'.

25 Such figures are now made available irregularly by the CGT, Fédération des Travailleurs de la Métallurgie. See *Le Monde*, 24 July 1975.
26 See, for example, Serge Mallet, *Le Pouvoir ouvrier* (Paris: Éditions Anthropos, 1971), pp. 217–18.
27 Val Lorwin, *The French Labor Movement* (Cambridge, Mass.: Harvard University Press, 1954), p. 164.
28 Mallet, *Le Pouvoir ouvrier*, p. 195.
29 *Le Monde*, 24 July 1975.
30 *Sudreau Report*, p. 25.
31 *Le Monde*, 22 April 1976.
32 See *L'Année politique, economique, sociale et diplomatique en France*, 1966, pp. 199–200.
33 *L'Année politique*, 1967, p. 270.
34 *L'Express*, 17–23 March 1969, p. 5.
35 Adam *et al.*, *L'Ouvrier français* . . ., pp. 186–7.
36 Guy Caire, *Les Syndicats ouvriers* (Paris: P.U.F., 1971), p. 522.
37 On this point, see Jacques Juillard, 'La Grève', *Formation*, No. 69 (September–October 1966).
38 Capdevielle and Mouriaux, 'Les Organisations syndicales sont-elles dépassées?' *Le Monde Diplomatique*, June 1971.
39 Alfred Grosser, 'France: Nothing But Opposition', in Robert Dahl, ed., *Political Oppositions in Western Democracies* (New Haven, Conn.: Yale University Press, 1966), p. 187.
40 *Le Monde* 28 August 1974.
41 *Le Monde*, 8 September 1973.
42 *Sudreau Report*, p. 27.
43 G. Adam, J.D. Reynaud, and J-M. Verdier, *La Négociation collective en France* (Paris: Les Éditions Ouvrières, 1972), p. 37.
44 For a good summary, see ibid., Chap. 2.
45 See the analysis in Abreu and Jobert, *Practiques contractuelles et conflits du travail: le système français des rélations professionelles* (Paris: CREDOC, 1973).
46 This problem was posed by Bernard Brizay, in 'Le Pouvoir syndical grandit, mais les syndicats s'affaiblissent', *Entreprise*, 17 October 1970.
47 See Adam *et al.*, *La Négociation*, p. 29.
48 *Le Point*, No. 158, 29 September 1975.
49 See Abreu and Jobert, *Practiques contractuelles*, p. 31 and Adam *et al.*, *La Négociation*, p. 70.
50 Joanine Roy, 'Les Plus pauvres', *Le Monde*, 3 June 1975 and 'De Quoi vivent les syndicats?' *Entreprise*, 11 January 1974.
51 *Sudreau Report*, p. 59.
52 Marc Clairvois, 'Les Syndicats ouvriers face à leur sous-développement', *L'Expansion* (November 1967), p. 112.
53 Ministry of Labor surveys, 1970–75.
54 J. D. Reynaud, 'France: Elitist Society Inhibits Articulated Bargaining', in Solomon Barkin, ed., *Worker Militancy and its Consequences* (New York: Praeger, 1975), p. 291.
55 E. N. Suleiman, quoting a Director in the Ministry of Housing and Equipment, *Politics, Power and Bureaucracy in France* (Princeton, N.J.: Princeton University Press, 1974), p. 336.
56 Ibid., p. 341.
57 Ibid.
58 John McArthur and Bruce Scott, *Industrial Planning in France* (Boston, Mass.: Division of Research of the Graduate School of Business Administration, Harvard University, 1969), pp. 418–19; also see Reynaud, 'France: Elitist Society', pp. 311–12.

59 *Le Monde*, 8 March 1969.
60 *Formation* (February 1962).
61 Interview with M. Grandval, the Minister of Labor, in *Combat*, 29 June 1965.
62 Some left-wing intellectuals, such as Serge Mallet, also argued that the enter-
    prise was becoming a much more stable environment for union organization and
    union control: see *La Nouvelle classe ouvrière*.
63 *Le Monde*, 13 July 1964.
64 Grandval, in *Notre Republique*, 31 January 1964.
65 *Le Dynamique des comités d'entreprises* (Paris: CNRS, 1963).
66 Cited by André Gentil, 'Un regard neuf sur les comités d'entreprises', *Per-
    spectives Socialistes* (August 1964), p. 16.
67 *L'Année politique*, 1965, p. 181.
68 Christine Champel, 'Relance de l'intéressement', *Revue de l'Action Populaire*,
    No. 159 (June 1962).
69 See report by Pierre Costa-Noble, *Revue Politique des Idées et des Institutions*
    (December 1966), p. 484.
70 The report is cited in *Liaisons Sociales* (September 1968), p. 8.
71 See *French Affairs* (Nos. HS367 and M301, Ambassade de France, Service
    de presse et d'information).
72 Philippe Decharte, 'Des Comités d'entreprise a l'actionnariat', *La Vie Française*,
    24 April 1970.
73 Reynaud, 'France: Elitist Society', pp. 307–8.
74 Cited in Areu and Jobert, *Practiques Contractuelles*, p. 32.
75 See George Ross, 'Gaullism and Organized Labor' (paper presented at the
    Conference on Two Decades of Gaullism, Brockport, New York, June 1978).
76 See 'The Fight Against Unemployment: What is Being Done in France' (French
    Embassy, Press and Information Division, 1979).
77 *Le Monde*, 30 September–1 October 1979, p. 6.
78 See Michel Crozier, *The Bureaucratic Phenomenon* (Chicago: University of
    Chicago Press, 1963), pp. 244–51.
79 *Changing Patterns of Industrial Conflict* (New York: Wiley, 1960).
80 See Douglas Hibbs Jr., 'Industrial Conflict in Advanced Industrial Societies',
    American Political Science Review, (December 1976).
81 Myron Roomkin, 'Union Structure, Internal Control and Strike Activity',
    Industrial and Labor Relations Review (January 1976).
82 Geoffrey K. Ingham, *Strikes and Industrial Conflict: Britain and Scandinavia*
    (London: Macmillan, 1974), p. 84.
83 See George Strauss, 'Control by Membership in the Building Trades Unions',
    American Journal of Sociology, Vol. 61 (1956), pp. 527–37.
84 Ingham, *Strikes and Industrial Conflict*, p. 43.
85 Barkin, *Worker Militancy and its Consequences*, p. 37.
86 Ingham, *Strikes and Industrial Conflict*, p. 87.

11 Rural Change and Farming Politics:
A Terminal Peasantry

Sally Sokoloff

This chapter is concerned to investigate political change in the French peasantry under the Fifth Republic. An immediate problem of definition arises in so far as the author believes that in these years the French peasantry has ceased to exist, both as a social and economic entity and as a group which strongly influences political ideals and practices in contemporary France. A peasant society, which historically takes its place within societies at a halfway stage between feudalism and capitalism, has five main characteristics: the peasantry has relative autonomy in its economic life and in its general dealings with the national society, and empowers an elite of traditional notables to mediate politically between itself and the broader society; at the level of local peasant communities, internal relationships are more important than external ones, and the family is structurally fundamental to all aspects of peasant life. Though the peasantry co-exists with a partially industrialized society, to be a peasant is to be part of a peasant society.[1] Such a society no longer exists in France.

The term peasant as used in France in the 1970s carries a less and less social and economic meaning and conversely a more and more political meaning (although the political content of such a term varies). For the purposes of this chapter, the term 'peasant' will be eschewed and the more neutral and more accurate term 'farmer' will be used to describe the landowning or land-renting agricultural worker, and the term 'rural society' for the wider rural setting. Unlike the peasant, the farmer shares the values of the national society and engages in extensive market economic relations: he relates to society at large through a wide range of civic, syndical and specialist organizations; the locality and the family plays a less fundamental role in his activities. Furthermore, although constituting a separate world, the French peasantry had occupied a special place in the nation's political ideology. Ideologically, it was recognized as the social ground-work of the Third and Fourth Republics, and politically it enjoyed dis-proportionate electoral influence and state protection. Since 1958, the ideological rudiments of a land-owning Republic have been replaced rapidly by the new values of industrialization, productivity, technocracy and consumerism. Peasant society has been undermined by a potent double-binding change. Not only have the values of a peasant society been denigrated and thrown aside, but peasants have found it well-nigh im-possible to join the new value system, as they were urged to do, for economic reasons discussed later in this paper. The half-way house of 'family farming' has proved a hard path for many, and the promised integration has not been achieved. As one observer concludes about the recent fate of the European peasantry, 'by imposing on to the farmer the "ideology" of being and behaving like an "entrepreneur", of keeping him at the same time to the status of a "family farmer", has *isolated* him from general society.'[2] It is not only sociological or anthropological criteria which posit the demise of the peasantry but also rural France itself by the 1960s was highly conscious of the severity and character of the change. As Edgar Morin wrote of Plodémet in south-western Brittany, 'the peasant class is rapidly disappearing. Everyone, including the most active exponents of modernization and the most ardent union-ists, is aware of living through the last days of the peasantry.'[3]

This paper will be divided into four parts. In the first, the broad eco-nomic changes experienced by agriculture will be considered. In the second, the role of public policy is measured. The third part will ex-amine the place of farming co-operatives and syndical organizations: such bodies have a part to play both in affecting public policy and in articulating the aspirations and grievances of farmers in a period of spec-tacular economic change. In the fourth part, political change among farmers is scrutinized, with the aim of explaining changes in rural political commitment since 1958. Change in rural society at its broadest is ex-amined in the brief conclusion.

1. AGRICULTURAL CHANGE AND FAMILY FARMING

In the last two or three decades, the number of people working on the land in France has declined enormously, and agriculture's percentage contribution to GNP has also diminished. In 1960, 4.1 million people worked in agriculture, but by 1970 the figure was down to 2.8 million. A peak in the rate of decline was reached in the early years of the Fifth

Republic, with 115,000 farmers leaving every year between 1954 and 1962. The rate slowed down to 88,000 per annum between 1962 and 1968, but rose again in the mid 1970s when about 160,000 people were leaving agriculture each year. Between 1968 and 1974 alone, farmers and agricultural labourers counted together decreased as a percentage of the male workforce from 15 to 10 per cent. The disappearance of farmers and agricultural labourers consititutes a large part of the staggering fall in employment in primary occupations from 27.4 per cent of the active population in 1954 to 10.1 per cent in 1975 (to the benefit of the tertiary sector which employed just over half the active workforce by 1975).[4] The continued decline in the agricultural workforce in the last ten years has been partially concealed by the fact that rural depopulation no longer necessarily accompanies loss of agricultural employment: ex-farmers and ex-labourers can move into non-agricultural employment without uprooting their homes. The 1975 statistics showed that the population resident in rural communes was stabilizing after a long period of depopulation (although the category of a 'rural commune' is notoriously indiscriminate, meaning only a small commune with no village or bourg of over 2,000 people). Furthermore, French farmers are an ageing group: the most rural departments also have the most top-heavy age structures. Most projections concur that France will have about a million remaining farms by the mid-1980s, the large majority of them using only family labour.[5] It seems that there is an inexorable economic pace-setter for the elimination of small farms. Only the internal character of the French rural economy can set limits on the dwindling number of farms, and this point will be pursued in this part of the paper.

It has become apparent from the experience of agricultural transformation so far that the continued natural fall in the number of farms does not destroy the category of the small to medium-sized farm, although a certain adjustment to the idea of what constitutes a small farm does occur. The farms which have gone recently were mostly in the very small category, and they have been absorbed by the 'next smallest' category. There has been no wholesale cannibalization of many small farms into a few large ones. For all the social disruption of the exodus, the average size of farms has increased only marginally, from 14 hectares to 18 hectares in the 1960s, to 23 hectares in 1976 and probably still under 25 hectares now (a hectare is two and a half acres). In the 1960s, many experts and policy-makers acted on the supposition that the farm of over 100 hectares was the rational basis for agriculture's near future: the EEC Mansholt Report and the French Vedel Report of the late 1960s are the most notable examples of this 'giganticist' frame of mind.[6] Some agronomists continue to believe that extensive farming on units of about two or three hundred hectares, as currently practised in the Paris Basin wheat and beet zone, is the only rational path for French agriculture.[7] Nevertheless, the projection of one million farms by 1985 would be nowhere near this technical ideal.

'Small farms' are now defined as a unit of under 50 hectares capable of being run by a family with the aid of labour-saving machinery. Such farms will constitute the norm in the 1980s and onwards if current conditions continue. The rejection of giganticism, which was always an expectation rather than a reality, has had two important facets. On the one hand, government has taken a decision that it cannot face the presumedly adverse political costs of assuming responsibility for the complete recasting of agriculture along large-farm lines. Such a recasting would entail the uprooting of even more farmers, greater potential unemployment in the industrial labour market, and an increase in the financial and social costs of urbanization. On the other hand, there has been a theoretical re-evaluation of the function and capacity of small farms. Rural economists and sociologists (who, as Henri Mendras has pointed out, themselves increase inversely with the decrease of peasants!) now believe that the encroachment of industrial-style capitalism into agriculture is curtailed by certain factors specific to farming. Capitalism is steadily penetrating agriculture, but not by turning peasants into wage-labourers on large-scale farms with industrial methods. Rather, surplus-value can be best squeezed out of agriculture by allowing farmers to maintain their small market production, while imposing all the costs and none of the benefits of land and property on them. Farmers are persuaded that their farms can survive as units of family production by way of modernization, but the mechanisms and institutions by which they modernize (credit banks, preferential agreements with agribusiness interests, co-operatives, etc.) serve to bind them more closely into an integrated system of agriculture from which they will be more easily displaced in the future.

The small farm structure will persist on two conditions: first, that agricultural production is polycultural and intensive, thus giving the best returns to farmers who can give individual attention to the care of livestock; second, that farmers continue to consider land, a factor of production whose costs the capitalist regards with caution, as an instrument of production and also essential to their self-definition and social status. In other words, small farmers are induced to tend livestock and to pay the purchase price of land at levels at which any self-respecting capitalist would balk on the basis that money invested in land was 'dead' capital. The farmer's brave attempts to behave in a 'rational' economic fashion, as exhorted, cannot succeed in a system where private property in land (at high prices) continues. The present uneconomic cost of agriculture is what has prevented agribusiness interests, whose intervention in the poultry and pork markets evoked much attention in the 1960s, from pursuing the full vertical integration of agriculture which would have truly proletarianized the farmer. It is cheaper to allow small polycultural farms to bear the costs of land, the costs of a rapidly evolving technology, and the poor return on labour obtained in agriculture.[8]

Opinion on the future of the small farming system appears to be divided into two schools of thought. One school of thought optimistically sees current small-farm agriculture as the basis for a rural renaissance towards the end of the century as population grows, ecological considerations cause decentralization of population, and as Europe rejects the irrationality of an economy that denatures food and builds butter mountains.[9] Another regards the small-farm system as a temporarily finely-balanced system which could soon be swept away by the deeper penetration of capitalism into the countryside.[10]

2.   PUBLIC POLICY

Agricultural policy in the Fifth Republic appears a never-ending drama of conflict and rapprochement between governments and farmers, with many changes of Ministers and many shifts in the direction of policy. Through the morass of activity and change, two facts stand out. Firstly, the general orientation of policy has been constant throughout the Fifth Republic: the aim has been to encourage agriculture to become more productive and efficient, to employ fewer workers, while maintaining the most tenacious family farms and defusing the political discontent arising among the rural classes from economic change. These aims are obviously incompatible in their purest forms, but they remain constant in the mind of government. Balance between them and emphasis of policy may alter, but the same ingredients are always there. Secondly, the level and intensity of the formal relationship which has developed between government and farmers exceeds that of any other area of French economic or social activity. The character of the relationship is discussed in Part 3 of this chapter and it is important for our understanding of the general character of politics in the Fifth Republic: at this point it should be registered as equally important for public policy as for pressure group activities.

Beyond these two phenomena (constant policy aims and intense co-operation and consultation between government and farmers) stretches the compelling economic reality. The author holds, possibly controversially, that twists and turns in public policy have had little immediate impact on the immense agricultural changes since the 1950s, only functioning on the margins of the economic changes sketched in Part 1 of this chapter. For example, the pace of the population exodus from farming appears to have little relationship to the evolution of policy. Economic and social change had by itself stimulated a great burst of population outflow from the countryside in the mid and late 1950s, preceding the Gaullist state's embarkation on a full-blooded campaign for rural modernization in the early 1960s. When the government reached the peak of its enthusiasm for modernization in the mid-1960s, a relative slowdown in the decline of farms was observed. In the Pompidou presidency (1969-74), just as government appeared to be taking a more circumspect approach to agricultural change, a fresh wave of departures from farming commenced, assisted by the rise in land values in the early 1970s. The observer is faced in this instance with the paradox of an outstandingly close relationship between farming pressure groups and government, and much frenetic activity in policy-making: yet had policy been sparse and weak-kneed, one cannot say that the general lines of agricultural change would have been much different from what they were.

Nevertheless, it is worthwhile casting a glance over the course of public policy in the Fifth Republic, as some notable, though limited, forms of change have been affected by policy. This is to say that some government policies have influenced the internal contours of change: although the margins of change have not been touched, the character of change within the margins has been channelled and made orderly and less tumultuous by the effect of policy. Broadly speaking, French agriculture has been integrated into a swiftly modernizing capitalist France and Europe since the 1950s: the pace of integration has not been fundamentally affected by policy, although some of its character may have been.

Governments in the last years of the Fourth Republic had been presiding over a substantial rate of agricultural change, much of it self-generated from within the sector, which they underwrote in the two first Economic Plans (1952-54, 1954-57). The Third Plan which began in 1956 and theoretically ran on until 1961, required agriculture to increase its production by 20 per cent overall and anticipated the departure of 80,000 people every year from the sector. While endorsing this substantial and natural exodus, the last Fourth Republic governments also took steps to fulfil the perennial and pious promise of equalizing the income of farmers with that of workers in other sectors, by indexing agricultural prices to the prices of industrial products consumed by agriculture (as long as agricultural production did not exceed the limits laid down in the Third Plan). Indexation and price support policies reached their apogee in the Gaillard decrees of September 1957, and farmers believed they had at last achieved a measure of security and parity with the industrial sector.[11]

The reserved approval given to de Gaulle's interregnum between June and December 1958 and to his new Fifth Republic by the chief farming organizations was shattered by the abolition of indexation at the end of 1959, which testified to the government's determination to make agriculture, like the entire French economy, face up to its real weaknesses and its new prospects in the EEC. Between late 1959 and 1965, agricultural policy entered a confusing period in which governments' various attempts to harness the rural sector to nation-wide economic modernization was matched by its search for allies and mediators among the competing farming pressure groups and by de Gaulle's determination to take the lead for France in shaping the contours of the EEC with agriculture as one great pawn on the French side. The search for effective participatory allies among farmers led to the government giving a preferential ear to advice from the Young Farmers' CNJA (see Part 3), much of which was embodied in the new laws (*lois d'orientation*) passed in 1961 and 1962 providing the legal framework for desired forms of agricultural change. De Gaulle's political manoeuvres in the EEC led to an impasse in 1965 when farmers were reduced to fighting his stalling techniques which were holding them out from the ostensible benefits of the current terms of the Common Agricultural Policy. The EEC crisis passed, and the more staid and conservative FNSEA resumed its place as the chief mediator between farmers and the state. Despite another hiccup in government–farmer relations with the Vedel Report of 1969 (a French version of the EEC Mansholt Report which sketched the future of a totally mechanized and almost depopulated European agriculture), policy in the late 1960s and 1970s has been much less evangelistic than in the earlier 1960s and much more prepared to merely tinker with the terms of change generated from within the sector. Still, governments have faced the bitterness and reproaches of those farmers still subject to profound change, notably the viticulturalists, in the 1970s.

Looking beyond this broad and sketchy account of the political side of public policy, which policies can we distinguish as having an appreciable impact on French agriculture? The answer is threefold.[12] First, the levels of price support for different agricultural products offered either domestically by government or (increasingly) through the CAP have affected the position of different agricultural producers over the last twenty years. Cereal farmers were given substantial price support during the 1960s, and those farming large arable areas by 'industrial' methods still enjoy quite extraordinary rates of price support. Meat and dairy farmers who were dissatisfied and insecure in the 1960s and early 1970s have since then been reaping the benefits of considerable price support: small to medium-sized dairy farms now make up the backbone of the million farms which are likely to last well into the 1980s (see Part 1 for an explanation of the survival of the 'family farming' dairy and animal sector). Farmers specializing in vegetables, vegetable oils, fruit and vine cultivation have experienced great changes in market conditions in the last twenty years, largely due to their exposure to Common Market competition: it seems unlikely that government policy, by price support or market regulation, can provide more than a token or temporary prop against competition from other EEC countries.

Secondly, public policy has helped to make the exodus of small farmers from the sector more orderly and rather more fair and humane than it would have been otherwise. Through the IVD (*Indemnité viagère de départ*), ageing farmers surrendering their farms receive a modest but, to them, appreciable pension. The IVD helped to lower the average age of farmers, and to improve the conditions of land handover between fathers and sons. By the mid-1970s it had been taken up by half a million farmers, freed $8\frac{1}{2}$ million hectares, led to the formation of 95,000 new farms and added land to 280,000 others. Along with the slow but steady improvement in social benefits for farmers under the Fifth Republic so that they now qualify for family allowances, sickness benefit etc. on the same terms as other sorts of workers, IVD had a great impact on the living conditions of retiring farmers who otherwise would have clung on to inefficient farms: benefits and IVD pensions jointly provide an astounding 19 per cent of the total annual income of all French farmers. But the magnitude of these benefits in financial and humanitarian terms conceals the paucity of their contribution towards structural change in agriculture: as noted in Part 1, the disappearance of hundreds of thousands of small farms has led to a marginal increase in the average size of farms.

Thirdly, policy, through a whole battery of measures, has pushed farming co-operatives, improvement agencies, and credit organizations towards certain forms of modernization which governments have regarded favourably. For example, in an attempt to guide and rationalize land sales so as to increase average farm sizes to levels regarded as economically viable, government has empowered departmental SAFERs (*Sociétés d'Aménagement foncier et d'Etablissement Rural*) to intervene in land purchase and sales. By the mid-1970s, fifteen years after their inception, these semi-public land agencies had been annually involved in up to 15 per cent of the total market in land, but the SAFERs themselves were the first to point out that they needed a 20 per cent minimum share in the land market in order to have a real impact on farm structures. Furthermore, conservative legal interpretations in contested cases has tended to muzzle the powers of SAFERs, and the rights of property remain strong and resistant against modernizing trends which would logically lead to some sort of land socialization or nationalization: the CNJA had argued when SAFERs were instituted in 1962 that powers tantamount to socialization would be necessary to make the new agencies effective. Another policy-sponsored attempt to bypass the problem of small family farms in an even more radical way is through the GAECs or group farming co-operatives: these are discussed in Part 3, but it is worth noting here that they have had a much smaller impact on agriculture than the SAFERs.

Perhaps the semi-public agency which has the greatest potential influence over farming structures, markets, and technical conditions is the CAM (*Crédit Agricole Mutuel*). Apart from being a major banking and investment power in the French economy as a whole (20 per cent of France's savings were in the *Crédit Agricole* in the late 1960s), the CAM has vastly enlarged the scope of its intervention in the rural world during the Fifth Republic, now providing 80 per cent of the financial needs of farming. Its main impact on farmers is through financing land purchase and improvements and modernization by means of loans granted for up to thirty years. It also finances new food processing organizations and the commercialization of agricultural markets, working according to the criteria of the Ministry of Agriculture and the CAP. Generally speaking, it has been able to lay down the criteria of modernization to which farmers must conform in order to benefit from the plethora of benefits and subsidies proffered by the state and the EEC: it has responsibility for deciding which farms survive and which founder, bringing a degree more rationality into the sifting process than the operation of entirely free market conditions would have done. Nevertheless, its influence is confined to the internal workings of French agriculture rather than touching the general economic trends experienced over the last twenty-five years.

3. SYNDICALISM AND CO-OPERATION

Agricultural interests have closer and more direct links with the state than perhaps any interest group or class in the Fifth Republic. In one sense, the ousting of the ideological and political priority given to the peasantry by traditional Republicanism has given way to an equally fruitful network of relationships in the field of pressure-group activities. But simply to say that farmers operate singularly direct pressures on the French state would be an underestimate: qualitatively, the relations between state and farmers are becoming increasingly institutionalized so that they are closer to a full corporatism than to simply successful pressure group activities. The establishment of a special and exclusive world of relations between farmers and the state has occurred partly because the 'rural world' has vanished as an object of defence for farmers, leaving farmers in their own eyes 'alone' at the centre of the agricultural process, with only the state to look to. Ministers of Agriculture of the Fifth Republic have also been happy to promote closer professional relations with farmers, in an attempt to defuse farmers' protests and to by-pass the traditional political-parliamentary channels. Furthermore, the rise of closer collaboration between interest groups and state bodies has been a general trend in the Fifth Republic, although not to the extent reached in agriculture.

Whatever the reasons, relations between agricultural syndicalism and the state have become more direct, stable and confident in the last twenty years: participation by syndicalist representatives in the state apparatus has become general and hierarchized. For example, there are regular meetings between leaders of the professional organizations and the Ministry of Agriculture: since 1972 an annual meeting brings together top agricultural leaders and civil servants under the prime minister's chairmanship: similar collaboration is found all the way down the administrative ladder, especially at the departmental level, where the application of decisions is implemented: and there are a multitude of organisms, of varying status, where functionaries and professionals work together.[13] From department to department, there is a striking consistency and intensity of relations between the chief representatives of local syndicalism and civil servants concerned with farming: within this relationship, the power in the hands of the farmers' representatives is considerable, especially that of the President of the departmental Chamber of Agriculture and the President of the department FNSEA (sometimes one and the same person).[14]

The range of organizations of a syndicalist, professional, co-operative, or interest group character is bewilderingly large, as is the range of those bodies established by government initiative but counting on professional advice and participation. At the most immediately political end of the syndicalist spectrum are those groups which are not conceded government recognition as accredited advisors. The *Mouvement de Défense des Exploitants Familiaux* (MODEF), which continued to grow in the mid-1970s, reaching a membership of 200,000 and a 30 per cent vote from farmers and 40 per cent from retired farmers in the Chambers of Agriculture elections of 1970 and 1974 is the notable example, since its uncompromising opposition to the state's domestic and EC agriculture policies theoretically precludes any co-operation between itself and state bodies.[15] *Paysans Travailleurs*, a socialist offshoot of the CNJA (*Centre National des jeunes agriculteurs*) and nothing like the size of MODEF, is another of this ilk.[16] Even the most extreme Left groups, offshoots of May 1968, have ventured into small peasant organization in a handful of mostly barren exercises in reviving the class war among farmers in poor regions. They denounce both MODEF and *Paysans Travailleurs* as agencies of Communist reformism or of capitalist modernization.[17] Yet there are strong pressures on all syndicalist farmers' groups to seek firstly the benefits of unified action (admittedly usually on a protest basis) with the leviathan FNSEA (*Fédération Nationale des Syndicats d'Exploitants Agricoles*) and secondly to seek to pressurize the state by collaboration as well as by protest: MODEF has sought entry to national consultative status (unsuccessfully) and its activities in the departmental Chambers of Agriculture have sailed close to collaboration at times, although it has been careful to maintain the primacy of its role as a tribune for the despair of small farmers.

    Central to any consideration of government farming relations however, is the FNSEA which remains, along with its Young Farmers constituent part, the heart of a web of interlinkages between farmers and the state. Through the FNSEA and its departmental components, the FDSEAs, farmers have maintained an apparent unity of response to the government, despite the fact that the FNSEA has often had severe internal disagreements and has to perform a constant balancing act between the interests of big and small farmers.[18] In particular, the FNSEA has managed to reconcile leadership by big-farming interests with the incorporation of the CNJA movement of modernization: the Young Farmer hotheads of the early 1960s, encouraged by Gaullist Ministers of Agriculture, have rejuvenated the leadership of the FNSEA without endangering professional unity as the old leaders feared they would. The conservative Republicanism of the FNSEA has been turned into conservative Gaullism and latterly conservative 'regime-ism', if such a term can be excused. The net impact of the Young Farmers' movement has been assessed, depending on political standpoint, as either a sell-out whereby modernizing radicalism and idealism was neutralized by contact with power, or as a movement through which the younger generation of farmers clarified its view of the necessary transformation, secured its own survival, and forced its policies on the archaic FNSEA.[19]

Despite periodic claims that 'peasant unity' is broken up once and for all and that current economic trends are deepening a class struggle among farmers, the FNSEA has achieved the remarkable feat of maintaining a rough and ready professional unity, while presiding over the death-throes of the peasantry. Its privileged status with government is insufficient to explain its continued dominance: the hold of an ideology of unity over the minds of farmers must be recognized as both deep and rational. Indeed, the smaller the remnant group of farmers becomes, the more it is to their advantage to stick together to extract maximum concessions from government: all farmers, excepting a very small group of large farmers, are in a similar economic boat and have many common fears and insecurities.

In co-operatives, too, one finds evidence of the dual and sometimes contradictory character of farmers' organization similar to the balancing act performed by the more political FNSEA. Generally speaking, co-operatives simply aim to maximize certain benefits for farmers, for example, through joint purchase of raw materials and machinery (CUMA) and through joint processing and marketing acitivites (COPA). Sometimes co-operation extends to the pooling of labour resources (GAEC). Their activities are important politically, however, in that they have acted as ideological agencies for the discouragement and elimination of small farms. This despite the fact that co-operatives can vary enormously in the number of farmers they include in their territorial scope, and in their general purposes. A co-operative can be a temporary means by which small farmers stave off challenges to their traditional way of life for a decade or so.[20] But small co-operatives become compelled by the exigencies of market forces to move onto a wider scale, and as they extend to the cantonal, then the departmental, then the regional level, the sensitivity to the needs of small farmers becomes diluted. At the wider level, exclusive criteria or minimum standards begin to be applied to the farmer participants: for example, participating farms may have to be of a certain size, with a certain number of animals or of a given minimum yield. Increasingly, state benefits such as credit facilities are restricted to those in the co-operatives, and the norms laid down by the co-operatives exclude small farmers who are then doomed without co-operative support. Two well-documented examples of the process by which co-operation itself becomes the means of sorting out those who will modernize and perhaps survive from those who will founder are the history of the co-operative dairies in the Jura'[21] and of the right-wing syndicalist movement in Western Brittany where the Landerneau organization has exercised region-wide modernizing pressures on all farmers.[22]

Even the most idealistic and exemplary form of co-operation, the 'group-farming' co-operatives of GAECs (*Groupement Agricole d'Exploitation en Commun*) turn out to have a similar dual role for small farms. Group farming goes beyond co-operative buying, selling, and sharing of machinery: it attempts to use labour co-operatively over several farms grouped together. There are currently about 6,000 group-farming units, each of between two and ten 'family' farms, and on average each group is about 100 hectares in size. The aim of the GAECs is to achieve labour reform and co-operation while by-passing the thorny problem of land reform (individual ownership of land or rent relationships are untouched). It is true that slight gains in productivity and in the social benefits, notably holidays, to participants have been achieved, but the GAECs have always been patronized by medium-sized farmers already intent on modernization: they have been avoided by small farmers who cannot always meet the criteria laid down for norms and standards of production. Group farming is fast becoming a convenient means by which close relatives, fathers and sons, or brothers and brothers-in-law, obtain the maximum state benefits for their farms. Interestingly, group farms are territorially concentrated in the regions where Young Catholic social and political influence has been greatest (East and West France) and are rarely found in Communist rural areas. Like other sorts of co-operatives, they occupy an ambiguous position both economically and politically towards the small farmers they were intended to aid. As one observer puts it: 'They can be regarded as a rural institutional response to the development of a "grants economy" in French agriculture.'[23]

The growing diversity of professional organization in agricultural syndicates and co-operatives represents a growing participatory element in French farmers' experience of the Fifth Republic, although participation is scarcely voluntary when the farmer is faced with the integrative pressure of co-operation or of capitalist agribusiness or with the alternative of shutting up shop. Despite the increase in participation by farmers which does represent a step away from their classic isolation, professional unity under the FNSEA's aegis has ensured that big farming élites remain the most important influence over government policies. The élitist character of state-farming relations has been enhanced by the shift in the Fifth Republic to a 'productive' social coalition, to borrow Tarrow's terminology: 'Politically, Gaullism represents a shift from the Third and .

Fourth Republic policies which made the peasantry a ward of the state to a more selective alliance with "productive" groups on the periphery.'[24] As long as centrist or right-wing forces remain in the ascendant, influences could work on this professional relationship. The left-wing groups incur the problem of persuading farmers that they would gain from class struggle and from disunity rather than unity; they also have to persuade farmers that the government does little or worse on their behalf, despite the plethora of institutions of the 'grants economy'. Their case is not improved by the fact that their own reforms would also rest on a relationship of wardship and tutelage between the government and farmers. The corporatist professional relationship between farmers and state is very deeply rooted in the historic experience of peasantry and farming community and in the practices of the Fifth Republic.

4. POLITICAL CHANGE AMONG FARMERS: IDEOLOGY OR INSTRUMENTALISM?

The farming vote is less important proportionately than in the past simply because of the fall in the numbers of farmers and agricultural labourers. All political parties are somewhat less attentive to agricultural issues than in the past in the sense that other classes and issues have serious claims on their concern. Obviously, the farming vote remains important in the rural areas of western and southern France. Even here, however, both the degree of ruralism and the degree of farming workers within the rural population has fallen. For example, the four 'most rural departments' saw a fall in the percentage of people in rural communes between 1954 and 1968 (from 86 to 81 per cent in Creuse, 79 to 71 per cent in Cantal, 80 to 63 per cent in Côtes-du-Nord, 81 to 58 per cent in the Landes): it is also rare nowadays to find a rural commune where over half the working population is engaged directly in agriculture.[25] Nevertheless, all serious political parties appeal to farmers at election times, as to all substantial sectors of society. Also, the general view of agricultural policy as an important component of French EC policy tends to keep agricultural issues in the forefront of political concern. It has further been suggested, although not followed up by substantive analysis, that the farming vote can be electorally vital at the cantonal level because the farming vote is deviant from the local norm at this territorial level.[26] The smaller the margin becomes between Right and Left in France today, the more the electoral importance of small social groups such as farmers is enhanced.

The political orientation of the farming community has changed during the Fifth Republic. The peasantry has never been united politically (although the ideal of unit comes much closer to fulfilment in the professional syndicalist area) and has supported all major political movements and parties, giving support to both conservative and left-wing parties during the Third Republic, although more to the former than the latter. During the Popular Front period and between 1944 and the 1950s, left-wing parties gained substantially among the peasantry and in some regions, notably parts of southern France and the north-west corner of the Massif Central, Communist voting appeared to be the permanent result of a left-wing tradition among the peasantry. However, the political commitment of the peasantry was qualitatively partial, its perception of electoral and parliamentary politics always imperfect, and its relations with parties dogged by misunderstanding and distrust. Conversely, it has been posited that the development of an agricultural syndicalism shaped by the ideal of peasant unity and run by rural notables was a more real representation of the true political state of the peasantry.

Under the Fifth Republic, the farming community has taken a clear turn rightwards in its electoral commitment, moving to the Right within the framework of the general ironing out of regional political differences and the 'nationalization' of political commitment. Gaullism has been the principal instrument of this change, although the farming vote could now equally go to any strong group or party on the Centre-Right: at the 1978 legislatives, the Gaullist RPR and the Giscardian UDF were competing for an identical electorate.[27]

Gaullism made a belated appearance among farmers after 1958: relations which had been apathetic between de Gaulle and farmers became strained and bitter as his early Ministers of Agriculture spearheaded the modernization framework through the *lois d'orientation* of 1960 and 1962 and as they tried to renege on the level of price support which the farmers regarded as their rightful tribute from the Republican state. In 1958, farmers and agricultural labourers made up a fifth of the adult population but only 7 per cent of the Gaullist vote came from them. The most striking examples of domestic mass political defiance to the Fifth Republic in its early years were not working-class strikes or demonstrations but farmers' demonstrations, blockades, embargos, and violence directed against the government's agricultural policies. By the 1962 legislatives, however, farmers gave the Gaullist party 32 per cent of their votes (exactly the national average of Gaullist voting) and gave a favourable response to the referendum on direct presidential election. But in 1965, when de Gaulle and the chief agricultural syndical organization (the FNSEA) were at loggerheads over the Common Agricultural Policy, farmers voted against de Gaulle in the presidential election of that year and were held (statistically) responsible for de Gaulle suffering the indignity of a second ballot. This was only a temporary setback, however, (although instructive in that the FNSEA appeared to be able to exert direct political influence over its members), and the swing towards the Right begun in 1962 continued in 1967 and 1968. In the legislative elections of June 1968 farmers gave nearly half their votes (48 per cent) to the Gaullist party. And in the unsuccessful referendum on regional and Senate reform in 1969, farmers remedied their anti-Gaullism of 1965, being the one socio-professional group (apart from retired people) to say 'yes' to de Gaulle's inconsistent proposals. In the presidential election of 1969, Pompidou did better among farmers than de Gaulle had ever done. By 1969, the Gaullist party had mopped up all support for traditional right-wing parties among farmers.[28] The Gaullists largely maintained their support among farmers in the 1973 legislatives, when they were on the wane electorally: of the mere thirteen departments where the Gaullist vote increased in 1973, against the national trend, ten were rural departments of the Centre and South.[29] And in 1978 RPR voting was greater among farmers than in any other socio-professional group: 31 per cent of farmers voted RPR (and 27 per cent UDF).[30]

How can the growing right-wing orientation of farmers be explained given their coolness towards de Gaulle before 1962 and given the rupture of the early 1960s? A discussion of possible explanations throws much light on the political character and motivations of farmers in recent years. The first area of explanation concerns the linkages between class, religion and political commitment. Recent research has shown that the correlation between religious practice and voting is the chief constant which can explain French electoral choice over and above changes in parties, policies, and Republics. Farmers, with certain regional exceptions, have been bound up in locally religious and conservative communities. Class has been growing in importance as a correlative of vote, if not as an explanation. Farmers lack a clear recognition of their own class, and weak class consciousness goes hand in hand with apolitical, right-wing or conservative attitudes. For example, 44 per cent of a sample of farmers claimed to have no feeling of belonging to any social class. Even among the farmers who did feel they belonged to a class, consciousness was divided: 17 per cent (of the whole sample) believed they were 'peasants', 12 per cent working-class, and 9 per cent middle-class. Among the same farmers' wives, weak class consciousness was even more pronounced: 47 per cent believed they did not belong to any class, although 23 per cent felt they were 'peasants', 10 per cent middle-class, and 9 per cent working-class. The traditional difficulty experienced by Marxists and others in defining the class of peasants and farmers is reflected by the hesitancy of farmers themselves. Lack of class consciousness, which may grow among farmers as they come to no longer regard themselves as peasants, favours status quo and conservative attitudes to society in general and to politics.[31]

A second area of explanation concerns general opinion of the Fifth Republic among farmers. The hostility felt towards governmental policies has diminished since the mid-1960s: many of the farmers who engaged in violent protest in the early 1960s have now left the land, so the constituency for protest has simply melted away, although the survivors have not been adverse to the revival of occasional violent protest in the last few years. Non-agricultural aspects of the Fifth Republic have undoubtedly been attractive to farmers, notably the firm foreign policy stands taken by de Gaulle, the political stability, and the idea if not the reality of orderly social progress for which Gaullism stood. Farmers stood on the sidelines in May 1968, supported the government during the period of backlash, and have clearly (like the majority of people in France) been swayed by arguments that the ruling alliance is the only guarantee against disorder, chaos and poverty.[32] Furthermore, those farmers who are surviving the deluge have seen an overall increase in their net income, which is now on average equal to the income of industrial workers, although quite possibly substantially better (because of the better chances for tax avoidance and the burying of profits in the farm). Farmers still feel that they are insufficiently rewarded for their labour and commitment and that society undervalues their product (viz. the much quoted fact that a bottle of milk costs less than a bottle of mineral water), but there is a groundswell of grudging satisfaction with improvements in real living standards among farmers. Uncertainty about the future is more responsible for violent protest than is the current standard of living.

The third attempt at explaining right-wing trends among farmers argues that growing support for status quo politics in the Fifth Republic reflects a fundamental 'materialist' attitude to politics: farmers will vote for the party or alliance which promises them most in material gains and which carries out its promises in governmental policy practices. It can be argued that the nature of the bargain struck between the Third Republic and the peasantry was of this ilk, although it must be emphasized that if peasants provided the electoral and ideological bedrock of the Third Republic, they always stood on the sidelines as a real political force. The materialistic interpretation of farming politics has been stretched to cover the character of all Fifth Republican politics and is part of a general re-interpretation of modern France as a society dominated by pragmatic assessment of interest rather than by the clash of political principles and ideals. As a recent English observer puts it, 'there was mounting evidence to suggest that the French were divided less over a fine and idealistic sensitivity about the political requirement of the country than a crude and reassuring calculation of materialistic self-interest'.[33]

I have already argued that it is not possible to see a direct connection between government policies and the role of modernization of agriculture and of the elimination of the peasantry but that policy can affect the nature of the transformation in many detailed ways. Farmers believe, and government encourages the belief, that policy can make a great deal of difference not only to the terms of modernization but also to the rate of change. There is a connection between farmers' support for the majority coalition since the late 1960s and the policy change towards a less ruthless government pressure for modernization which began at about the same time. Farmers and government are partners in a new type of trade-off, even if the power of policy to affect basic socio-economic trends is exaggerated and misconceived. Crude assessment of self-interest and of the location of power has been observed at play in many rural constituencies in the Fifth Republic. It is worth quoting at length from a case study of the Corrèze, which in under fifteen years overturned its long left-wing tradition (a 40 per cent socialist vote in 1849) and went Gaullist (by 1968 two out of three seats in the National Assembly went to Gaullists).

At the beginning, the regime of the Fifth Republic was rejected; then . . . it was recognized that opposition no longer paid dividends because the centre of power was no longer in parliament. Once this had been realized one wondered whether it would not be more advantageous for defending local interests to move towards the party which had the ear of the executive branch — the source of all important future decisions? Certainly this was a rather vulgar sort of calculation. But who could blame those who lived in a region which had been left behind by progess and who knew that the only weapon at their disposal in the fight against being excluded from development was their very ballot paper? . . . . It is a clever hypothesis; . . . and is confirmed by the tactics of candidates who were later to benefit from voting shifts: far from traditional politics, from ideologies and from the empty rhetoric of the notables of bygone era, what these candidates promised was efficiency, growth, the stemming of the rural exodus, and the attention and concern of the political system. All that was neither of the Right nor of the Left: it was *gaullien*.[34]

There were some special reasons for the dramatic change in the Corrèze — the survival of a virulent anti-Communist minority which was prepared to vote Right in the new political environment of the Fifth Republic, the ageing generation of left-wing leaders, the deliberate strategy of Gaullists like Chirac who were parachuted into the department and cleverly played on the theme of their power in the executive. Despite this, however, some general factors emerge from the Corrèze case. It may be, for example, that the peasantry has always been a 'governmental class', reflecting its historic role as a special ward of the French state, but that this relationship has become even clearer than ever before because of the transfer of power from parliament to executive in the Fifth Republic. Instrumental politics simply become more obvious when they are channelled entirely through the executive rather than through the murky channels of parliamentary influence, and executive instrumentality links up in the case of farmers with the already highly developed professional corporate links between themselves and the executive.

The argument becomes extremely complex, however, when one attempts to draw links between attitudes to modernization and the growth of Gaullist and governing alliance voting among farmers. Much ink has been spilt in attempting to spell out exactly what modernization means for French politics as a whole, partly because interest arose out of the question whether France could serve as an example of an 'end-of-ideology' European case. The type of instrumental and pragmatic attitudes which it is argued farmers have shown since 1958 lent strength to the case that modernization leads away from left-wing voting towards moderate political parties. Unfortunately, the case does not hold good as soon as one descends to the micro-level, since rural despair over economic prospects appears to lead to governmental electoral commitment in some cases and to electoral commitment to left-wing parties performing a 'tribunitaire' function in other cases, to either Gaullism or to communism! The Corrèze case can be offset by the experience of similar departments in Limousin and the Centre which retain their 'backwoods communism'.[35] François Goguel points out that in departments traditionally of the Left, Gaullism encroached in the cantons eager for growth and modernization but remained weak in the most regressive cantons,[36] but this finding is contradicted by the Corrèze case where Gaullism triumphed not only in a modernizing constituency but also in a backward, depopulating, and previously left-wing constituency.[37] If the Centre region is excluded from analysis, however, a correlation does exist between rural areas embarking on modernization and pro-government voting.

If Gaullism carried farmers rightward, the PCF has diluted its concern for farmers as an electorally declining group. Between the 1930s and the 1950s, peasants made up the second largest group in the Communist clientele, second only in importance to the working-class, but now the new petty-bourgeoisie has taken its place. Much post-war solicitude for farmers by the PCF was a sensible manoeuvre to acquire influence over the very small peasantry before its inevitable proletarianization took place. This pool of support has been virtually mopped up, though the PCF still keeps a syndicalist finger in the farming politics pie through MODEF. The Common Programme of the Left in its original form devoted only two pages out of eighty to agricultural policy. There is a radical element in the Left's commitment to better social benefits for small farmers (some of which have already been conceded by the government), limitations on land speculation, fairer distribution of price subsidies, and more democratic bodies for organizing the market. But the means by which change is to be achieved remain vague and the aim of technical modernization remains similar to that of government. Indeed, in glibly promising to reconcile modernization with the maintenance of a prosperous small-farming sector, the tone of the Left's agricultural programme is very much like that of the Government, with the notable exception of the Left's hostility to big-farming interests.[38]

The Left's attitude to small farmers is a combination of residual and nostalgic attachment to a class which in the recent past has not done badly by the Left, of declining but still important electoral interest, and of demagogy. All the Left can properly promise to small farmers, in the context of its overall policy of social and economic transformation, is a degree more solicitude in the final stages of the demise of the peasantry than that met with under Gaullist and Giscardian rule. Whether the small peasantry, as the Communists persist in calling it, can be the basic element in the agricultural transition to socialism remains debatable. However, in relation to the point made earlier about the growth of instrumentalist attitudes among farmers, were the Left to come to power one might see the farming community again swinging in its political favour. A leftward turn by farmers would certainly be in line with the rationale of the instrumentalist explanation.

CONCLUSION: RURAL POLITICS AND CHANGE IN THE FIFTH REPUBLIC

There is another channel, apart from support for political parties and participation in syndicates and co-operatives, by which farmers can express their political views and policy preferences, albeit in a rather diluted form. This is at the level of the commune, often centred on the village, the centre of the local community. Three recent countervailing forces are at work which decide what degree of local political influence farmers can exert. First, the exodus of population from small villages has affected the artisan, small shop-keeper, and rural service tradesmen and intermediaries worse than it has affected farmers themselves: so in some cases, local farmers find that the old holders of local power, the *petite-bourgeoisie*, have left a vacuum which they can fill. The farmers find that they remain, while the 'rural world' which they previously shared has gone. A second and related aspect of the decline of rural and village life has been the departure of the traditional notables, both conservative and radical, who have also been drawn away from the villages into small and medium-sized towns, or who no longer regard local communal politics as their rightful sphere. These two factors would tend to give farmers greater political influence within the commune than before. But a third force, that of village renewal, intervenes to reduce the farming element in local politics: with the recent growth of second-homes, tourism, small dispersed industry, and ever wider flung suburbs, new people are entering the villages and farmers may find themselves in the minority as a communal group, although their status as long-standing inhabitants stands them in good stead in any local power struggle.

Nevertheless, the small scale of many rural communes (with 23,000 communes of under 500 population in 1975 despite pressure from the prefectoral administration to promote communal fusions in the early 1970s)[39] and the large number of municipal electoral offices to be filled (half a million people serve on municipal councils or as mayors, a high number for a country of 53 million people)[40] open local politics to potential farming influence. In the last twenty to thirty years there has been a broadening of the professional spectrum active in local politics, as landed gentry and industrialists disappear from local electoral office, and by the 1970s 14 per cent of mayors were farmers (the third largest category, after 26 per cent retired and 23 per cent teachers and professionals). Thus farmers are found more than proportionately in mayoral office.[41] Tarrow, in his comprehensive study of peripheral communities, argues that during the Fifth Republic people of lower class (including farmers) have entered local politics, replacing the old politics of personal acquaintance by a new politics of associational grouping and village-based and profession-based organization.[42] He also speculates that the recent spectacular development of associational activity in the small communes arises directly out of the commune's need to look to the state for aid in modernization.

Many other observers, in a spate of village micro-studies, have also paid testimony to the growth of associational activity in a rural France long since singled out for criticism of its social isolation, lack of voluntary interest groups, and political negativity. Rural sociologists have recently added their weight to the view of French villages as living organisms with freshly developing institutions of survival: they have asked what it is that causes some villages to survive while others founder. Surprisingly, political favouritism to right-wing communes by the state agencies does not appear to be important.[43] Rather, the sociologists point to the 'survivor-village' of the next few decades as having the following characteristics − a minimum of 500 inhabitants, good communications to the nearest bourg, the restructuring of local community around a dominant local system (economic institutions such as a co-operative, or a strong family and kinship network, or a collective village institution, more likely to be the local church than the school). Institutions and local relations must be numerous and lively, with specialized institutions linking the collectivity to the outside world. Intense sociability is vital, whether focused around the church, a local fête, or a dominant local professional organization such as a farmers' syndicat. The more the outside world penetrates a community, the more it requires some sort of regulatory and unitary ideology to hold it together. Recent studies suggest that these are not impossible requirements, and that farming institutions and the ideology of farmers' unity may well supply a vital ingredient.[44]

This conclusion on the nature of the local political community open to farming influence is in some ways in contradiction with other conclusions reached in this paper. Elitism, big-farming interests, and a technocratic ideology is obviously found in the economic, political and the syndicalist spheres of farming activity, and appears to be a likely outcome of the combination of ruthless dynamism and classic conservatism met with in the policy-making of the Fifth Republic. Yet the corporatist slant which it is argued has been reforged and reasserted in relations between farmers, politics, and the state since 1958 is capable of a different interpretation, opening up growing numbers and types of channels of communication between the rural community and the state and national community, and giving rise to potential pluralistic and consensus-seeking practices in policy-making. Schools of interpretation of very recent French history have tended to be polarized into those who seek to adopt the classic conflictual interpretation to modern circumstances and those who believe that consensual practices, relationships and institutions imply the achievement of a relatively open and pragmatic democracy in the form of the Fifth Republic. Perhaps it is time, in the context of contemporary France, to investigate the ways in which a consensual

240   *Sally Sokoloff*

society, in search of compromise rather than of protest, can co-exist with an elitist political and social reality and with a technocratic ideology. The case of farming politics appears to provide us with an example of such a combination.

Notes

1   H. Mendras, *Sociétés Paysannes: Eléments pour une théorie de la paysannerie* (Paris: Armand Colin, 1976), pp. 11–12.
2   A. J. Jansen, *Constructing Tomorrow's Agriculture, Report on a Cross-national Research into Alternative Futures for European Agriculture* (Wageningen, Netherlands: Agricultural University, 1975), pp. 14–15.
3   E. Morin, *The Red and the White — Report from a French Village* (New York: Random House, 1970), p. 94.
4   J. Beaujeu-Garnier, *La Population française après le recensement de 1975* (Paris: Armand Colin, 1976), pp. 128–35, 179–85.
5   M. Gervais, 'L'Economie agricole française 1955–1970', in Y. Tavernier, M. Gervais, C. Servolin, eds., *L'Univers politique des paysans dans la France contemporaine* (Paris: Armand Colin, 1972), pp. 16–17 (henceforth referred to as *L'Univers politique des paysans*).
6   For a résumé of the Mansholt Plan, see P. Le Roy, *L'Avenir du marché commun agricole* (Paris: Presses Universitaires de France, 1974), pp. 37–60. See also H. Délorme, 'Les Paysans et le Plan Mansholt', in *L'Univers politiques des paysans*, pp. 583–608.
7   J. Klatzmann, *Les Politiques agricoles — idées fausses et illusions* (Paris: Presses Universitaires de France, 1972), pp. 85–7.
8   C. Servolin, 'L'Absorption de l'agriculture dans le mode de production capitaliste', in *L'Univers politique des paysans*, pp. 54–75; C. Servolin, 'Crise de l'agriculture ou crise de l'économie rurale: l'avenir des petites exploitations', in P. Coulomb, M. Gervais, H. Nallet and C. Servolin, *L'Agriculture dans le système social* (Paris: Institut National de la Recherche Agronomique, 1974), pp. 5–15; M. Jollivet, 'Sociétés rurales et capitalisme', in M. Jollivet, ed., *Les Collectivités rurales françaises*, Vol. 2, *Sociétés paysannes ou lutte de classes au village?* (Paris: Armand Colin, 1974), pp. 230–45.
9   P. Hall, ed., *Europe 2000* (London: Duckworth, 1977), pp. 87–92; H. Mendras and M. Jollivet, eds., *Les Collectivités rurales françaises*, Vol 1 (Paris: Armand Colin, 1971), pp. 21–31 and 187–99.
10   Jollivet, 'Sociétés rurales et capitalisme'.
11   P. Houée, *Les Etapes du développement rural*, Vol. 2, *La Révolution contemporaine (1950–1970)* (Paris: Les Éditions Ouvrières, 1972), pp. 82–6.
12   Information on the agencies described in the remainder of this part are gleaned from Houée, *Les Etapes du développement rural*, pp. 170–95, and M. Gervais, H. Tavernier and M. Jollivet, 'La Politique agricole' in G. Duby and A. Wallon, eds., *Histoire de la France rurale*, Vol. 4 *La Fin de la France paysanne* (Paris: Seuil, 1978).
13   P. Coulomb and H. Nallet, 'Le Syndicalisme agricole', in Coulomb *et al.*, pp. 51–5. *L'Agriculture dans le système social*.
14   P. Grémion, *Le Pouvoir périphérique, bureaucrates et notables dans le système politique français* (Paris: Éditions du Seuil, 1977), pp. 225–7; see also C. Mora, 'Les Chambres d'agriculture et l'unité paysanne', in *L'Univers politique des paysans*, pp. 507–81.

15   Y. Tavernier, 'Le Mouvement de défense des exploitants familiaux', in *L'Univers politique des paysans*, pp. 467–95; and Gervais *et al.*, *Histoire de la France rurale*, Vol. 4, pp. 492–501..

16   For a partisan account of the history and character of the *Paysans-Travailleurs* group, see F. Prevost, *Mutation dans le syndicalisme agricole — le courant paysans-travailleurs* (Lyon: Chronique Sociale, 1976).

17   See, for example, an account of grass-roots activity by the UCFML (*Union des Communistes de France Marxiste-Léniniste*) *Le Livre des paysans pauvres* (Paris: Maspero, 1976).

18   P. Coulomb and H. Nallet, 'Les Organisations syndicales agricoles à l'épreuve de l'unité, in *L'Univers politique des paysans*, pp. 379–413.

19   M. Debatisse, 'Trente Ans de combat syndical 1946–1976' (Paris: Supplément Information Agricole 467, FNSEA, 1976); Y. Tavernier, *Le CNJA* (Paris: Fondation Nationale des Sciences Politiques, 1966); Y. Tavernier, *Le Syndicalisme Paysan* (Paris: Armand Colin 1969), pp. 135–98; B. Hervieu and A. Vial, 'L'Eglise catholique et les paysans', in *L'Univers Politique des Paysans*, pp. 291–315; Gervaise *et al.*, *Histoire de la France rurale*, pp. 466–92.

20   Soon Young Soon Yoon, 'Provençal Wine Cooperatives', in J. Boissevain and J. Friedl, *Beyond the Community: Social Process in Europe* (Department of Educational Science, the Netherlands, 1975), pp. 75–90.

21   M. Dion and M. Dion-Salitot, *La Crise d'une société villageoise — les survivanciers, les paysans du jura français (1800–1970)* (Paris: Éditions Anthropos, 1973).

22   S. Berger, *Peasants against Politics — Rural Organization in Brittany 1911–1967* (Cambridge, Mass.: Harvard University Press 1972) pp. 217–29; and Morin, *The Red and the White*, pp. 84–115.

23   P. Raup, 'French Experience with Group Farming: the GAEC', in P. Dorner, ed., *Cooperative and Commune, Group Farming in the Economic Development of Agriculture* (Madison: Wisconsin University Press, 1977), pp. 327–45. See also for a more leisurely analysis of the economic, social and political implications of GAECs, J. Murphy, *The Third Way — Group Farming in France* (unpublished Ph.D. dissertation, University of California, Santa Barbara, 1977).

24   S. Tarrow, *Between Center and Periphery, Grassroots Politicians in Italy and France* (London: Yale University Press, 1977), pp. 74–5.

25   Beaujeu-Garnier, *La Population française après le recensement de 1975*, p. 128.

26   D. Derivry, 'Analyse écologique du vote paysan', in *L'Univers politique des paysans*, pp. 131–62.

27   *Le Monde, Dossiers et Documents, Les Élections Législatives de Mars 1978*, pp. 53–62; D. Goldey and R. Johnson, 'The French General Election of March 1978: The Redistribution of Support within and between Right and Left', *Parliamentary Affairs*, Vol. 31, No. 3 (1978), 307–37.

28   P. Rémy 'Le Gaullisme et les paysans', in *L'Univers politique des paysans*, pp. 255–72.

29   H. Wells, *An Ecological Analysis of Communist Voting in France and Britain* (unpublished Ph.D. dissertation, Stanford University, California, 1975), p. 100.

30   V. Wright, *The Government and Politics of France* (London: Hutchinson, 1978), Appendix 11, 'Voting Behaviour in the March 1978 General Elections'.

31   G. Michelat and M. Simon, *Classe, religion et comportement politique* (Paris: Presses de la Fondation Nationale des Sciences Politiques 1977), pp. 215–19.

32   Rémy, 'Le Gaullisme et les paysans'.

33   V. Wright, *The Government and Politics of France*, p. 138.

34   J. M. Denquin, *Le Renversement de la majorité électorale dans le département de la Corrèze, 1958–1973* (Paris: Presses Universitaires de France, 1976), from the preface by G. Burdeau, pp. 6–7. See also J. Lord, A. J. Petrie and

L. Whitehead, 'Political Change in Rural France: The 1967 Election in a Communist Stronghold', *Political Studies* Vol. 16, No. 2 (1968), 153–76.

35   Wells, *An Ecological Analysis*, pp. 108–10.

36   F. Goguel, *Modernisation économique et comportement politique après un échantillon d'un trentième du corps électoral français* (Paris: Armand Colin, 1969), pp. 86–7.

37   Denquin, *La Renversement*, pp. 20–4.

38   *Programme Commun de Gouvernement; Parti Socialiste, Parti Communiste, Mouvement des Radicaux de Gauche* (Paris: Flammarion, 1973). See for more details on PCF agricultural policies, F. Clavaud, J. Flavien, A. Lajoinie and L. Perceval, *Quelle Agriculture pour la France?* (Paris: Editions Sociales, 1974).

39   J. C. Thoenig, 'Les Institutions de gouvernement local et l'évolution contemporaire de la société française' (unpublished paper, given at 1977 Bordeaux Conference on Local Government in Britain and France, pp. 15–18).

40   P. J. Froger, *Le Maire et son village* (Les Sables d'Olonne: Editions le Cercle d'Or, 1976), pp. 84–5.

41   Tarrow, *Between Center and Periphery*, pp. 113–14.

42   Ibid., pp. 131–2.

43   Ibid., pp. 95–107.

44   Mendras and Jollivet, *Les Collectivités rurales françaises*, Vol. 1, pp. 21–31 and 187–199; also N. Eizner, 'De la "communauté rurale" à la "collectivité local" ', in ibid., Vol. 2 pp. 129–54; also M. Bodiguel, *Les Paysans face au progrès* (Paris: Presses de la Fondation Nationale des Sciences Politiques, 1975), pp. 165–78.

12 Communist Control of Municipal Councils and Urban Political Change*

Martin Schain

INTRODUCTION: CONDITIONS OF LOCAL POWER AND COMMUNIST GOVERNMENT

During the past fifteen years, empirical research has helped us modify many of the assumptions about administrative centralization in France.[1] Not surprisingly, many important differences have been found between the formal controls that the centralized administration has over local governments, and the effective power that it can exercise. Central control is clearly conditional, and within the context of the administrative command structure, there is a political bargaining process. Moreover, compared with other centralized systems, France may be far less centralized than we have usually assumed. Douglas Ashford, for example, concludes that 'in functional terms, the dominance of the Whitehall cadre over local affairs (in Britain) may be much greater than that of the French Bureaucracy. In this respect, Britain is more centralized than France.'[2]

The process that is described in the recent literature suggests that there are key conditions that determine (or at least support) variations in the ability of local governments in France to resist the central state, to influence decisions made by the state, and to innovate and initiate policy. The most important of these conditions is access to the administrative structure. While under the formal *tutelle* of the state, local officials have developed their political power by exploiting mutual dependency with representatives of the state, and by modifying the structural isolation of local government.

The field representatives of the administration need the mayors to facilitate the acceptance of the state, and to provide the information without which they cannot operate effectively at the local level. They also need the co-operation of the mayors for initiating numerous projects that can only be recommended by the administration.[3] For the mayors, co-operation with the field services provides the possibility for acting as a privileged conduit between the commune and the state. Special access enables a mayor to accomplish the objectives of his government more easily, to protect his commune in the implementation of national policy, to deal more effectively with individual petitions of his constituents, and to solidify local support.[4] In a recent survey by Crozier and Thoenig, most mayors expressed the opinion that the administrative field services were allies *vis-à-vis* Paris, rather than the instrument of the central state.[5]

In larger cities, local access to the center is frequently reinforced by the French tradition of *cumul des mandats*, which permits one person to hold several political offices at different levels of government at the same time. In the National Assembly elected in 1978, 68 per cent of the members are either mayors or municipal councillors, 61 per cent are members of departmental general councils, while only 17 per cent hold no local office.[6] *Cumul des mandats* often enables mayors to bypass the field services entirely, and to gain access directly to central decision-makers.

Thus, either through mutual dependency with the field services of the administration, through direct access to decision-makers at the center, or both, local officials have developed the power to resist, to bargain and to initiate. With proper access, local governments can effectively modify and even veto decisions made by the central state. However, connections are most essential for attempts to innovate and initiate new projects. In this sense, local power varies with access.

However, it appears that the exercise of local power has been quite restricted, and that policy initiation has been generally avoided in just those localities where the conditions seem to be most favourable.[7] There is evidence that this cautious use of positive power is related to the feeling of local authorities that policy innovation could undermine their support by shattering the local consensus upon which it is built.[8] In general, local power has been used to resist the imposition of policy from the center, and to promote the interests of individual constituents.[9]

The problem with this analysis of local power in France is that it virtually ignores localities governed by Communists, which are frequently treated as exotic exceptions to the general pattern. If they are exotic, they are both interesting and unimportant. In so far as Communist local governments have been studied at all, it is through excellent, but limited, case studies, the data from which have never been integrated into more general theoretical considerations of French local politics.[10] Studies of French Communism have made frequent reference to the experience of local government, but their concern is generally with the party, rather than the government.[11] Thus, there is very little data on Communist government at the local level, and what data there is has not been used extensively.

This could be understood more easily if the Communist experience was indeed exotic and unique. However, especially among the large towns in France, there is extensive Communist presence, and this presence has been growing at a steady rate. Communists now participate in the governments of 64 per cent of the medium and large cities in France (cities with over 30,000 population), and are mayors in 33 per cent of these cities.

The extensive Communist participation in local government raises many questions about the foregoing analysis of the conditions for local power in France. Although Communist local officials have had poor access to the political and administrative decision-making processes (especially under the Fifth Republic), they have been comparatively successful in initiating and developing projects in just those areas in which state co-operation and good connections would seem most important. If the conditions for local power elaborated above cannot explain the achievements of Communist local governments, then are there other ways of explaining them? Are there other ways of generating local power? I will first analyze, and then attempt to explain, the policy outputs of Communist local governments (those local governments with a Communist mayor).

The analysis in this article is based upon existing published and unpublished studies, as well as interviews, budget data and written material gathered in a sample of municipalities that elected Communist mayors in 1977. All of these municipalities have a population of over 30,000, and all of them are *union-de-gauche* cities — that is cities with a Socialist group on the municipal council. Cities with 30,000 or more people (with a few exceptions) elect their governments through an electoral system that gives all of the seats on the municipal council to the victorious list.[12]

1. THE INITIATION OF POLICY IN COMMUNIST-GOVERNED CITIES

Communist-governed cities certainly have expressed a will and desire to develop a distinctive kind of local government both in terms of policies and processes. In their public statements, Communist officials on the national and local levels constantly stress the importance of local government for what it can and should do, as well as its importance as a microcosm of the way that policy can and should be made by Communists. The second national contract, published in anticipation of the 1977 municipal elections, emphasized the quantity and the quality of collective services at the local level.

In the municipal council, Communist officials fight for the construction of schools . . . sports and cultural facilities in sufficient amounts . . . [as well as] day-care centers. They consider canteens, vacations, the most diverse social services as public services. They adapt fees to family resources. The elderly, the handicapped, the unemployed, women alone, families in need always find comprehensive, generous and effective aid with Communist officials . . . The Communists favor the diffusion of culture, organize quality activities for all ages, encourage freedom of creation, creative participation and expression of each and every person.[13]

The national contract makes a commitment to maintain and create employment opportunities, to fight for more low-cost housing, and to integrate this housing into 'balanced development and planned urbanism'. Indeed, the contract resembles a campaign statement for an election in the City of New York before the fall, rather than a campaign statement for the election of municipal councils in centralized France.

The will to develop distinctive programs and services, however, must be tested by patterns of policy outputs, and one measure of policy outputs is the pattern of priorities of local budgets. Communist governments can be differentiated from others by the way that they spend money, the way that they raise money and by the way that they finance their projects. Although Communist-governed cities generally spend somewhat more money per capita than cities governed by others, the difference in spending levels is modest, and indeed is not statistically significant, if we control for demographic variables.[14] What does differentiate the budgets of Communist-governed cities from others more clearly is the way that they choose to spend their money.

For example, a large percentage of their operating budgets has been consistently devoted to school programs and to social services for school children. Local governments in France have no control over the school curriculum, and teachers are paid and controlled by the Ministry of Education. Nevertheless, education in general, and primary education in particular, weighs heavily upon the budget of every city. Communes retain the entire responsibility for the construction of primary schools, as well as the responsibility for the care of the buildings and facilities. They are also obliged to pay a share of the expenses for the maintenance of secondary schools. Larger cities spent an average of 30 per cent of their operating budgets on such expenses in 1973.[15] However, beyond these obligations, communes can also choose to enrich and supplement the educational curriculum, particularly in such areas as music, sports and nature appreciation. In addition, communes can choose to provide such social services to school children and their families as canteens, day-care centers, gymnasiums and swimming pools.[16]

Communist municipalities have given priority to this kind of spending. Although, over the years, the initiatives of Communist municipalities in this area have spread to other 'modern' communes, innovation in educational programs has become an identifiable characteristic of Communist government at the local level. A study of municipal budgets (completed in 1975, but using data from 1968) concluded that there was a strong positive relationship between spending priorities in this area and the Left-political orientation of the local government. On the other hand, the author found a negative relationship for such maintenance functions as road repair, lighting, street cleaning and parking garages. He found that Communist local government spends 36 per cent more than non-Communist Left governments, and 49 per cent more than moderate Right governments per capita for education and educational support, while they spend 34 per cent less than non-Communist Left and 36 per cent less than moderate-Right governments for maintenance.[17]

The most dramatic budget shifts from 1976 to 1978 among my own sample of Communist municipalities elected in 1977 were also in reductions in spending on maintenance functions and increases in social and educational expenses. In addition, I found a universal concern with developing new programs and facilities for social and educational services, as well as a commitment to new programs in culture.

Thus, Communist local governments have chosen to spend a large proportion of their operating budget on the development and the financing of social and educational programs. They have also chosen to pay for these programs largely out of tax money collected locally. Taxes paid in Communist-governed municipalities are higher than those paid in other communes. Korbielski calculated that while the operational budgets of the Communist communes were 13 per cent higher than those of other communes, they collected 26 per cent more in taxes than the others.[18] This money has been spent on financing municipal operations and services. Non-Communist municipalities have tended to pay out of tax revenues for a high proportion of the operating expenses of those municipal functions that they favor, financing a proportion of the expenses of other functions with higher fees for service.

Communist municipalities, on the other hand, have tended to support both favored and less-preferred functions with tax revenues, rather than fees for service.[19]

Both the willingness of Communist municipalities to collect higher taxes, and their propensity to use that money to support municipal operations has sometimes been explained as a function of their tax base. While the level of direct taxes collected by localities is decided locally, the proportion of direct taxes paid by business is fixed by the state according to a complex formula, and depends upon the extent and earnings of business and industry in a town. Thus, it is argued, since so many Communist-governed cities are heavily industrialized, the proportion of direct taxes paid by business is very high. This permits these cities to raise more tax money with fewer political consequences, and with a greater redistributive impact.[20]

However, in analyzing figures recently released by the Ministry of the Interior, I found that for cities over 30,000 population in 1976, the mean percentage of direct taxes covered by the business tax was 53 per cent, while the percentage of business taxes in Communist-governed cities was 55 per cent. In fact, I discovered only a small variation among the groups of cities governed by the different parties (52 per cent for both the non-Communist Left and the moderate-Right).[21] We have also found that the variation of the percentages of business taxes within the Communist and non-Communist groups of cities is also roughly similar, indicating that the options with regard to taxation are generally similar.

Thus, Communist-governed cities are distinctive in terms of the priority of the services they supply, and the way they choose to pay for those services. By choosing to raise and use local resources in the way they have, they have stretched many of the restrictions of the centralized education and education-support programs. However, in other ways they have not pursued policies that would maximize their autonomy from either central decision-making or central control. For example, compared to non-Communist municipalities, they have not sought to pay for their investment projects through self-financing. Jerome Milch found that while Montpellier (then governed by a moderate coalition) financed more than a third of its investment with savings drawn from its operating budget, Nîmes (Communist) financed only about 20 per cent of its investment this way, relying heavily upon government loans for the rest.[22] Montpellier, by spending more of its direct revenue on investment, kept its debt low and reduced its reliance on the state. Its population paid for this in other ways, however, because this mode of financing reduced the amount of money available for operating functions, and because users of services paid more in fees. Jean Montaldo, using a 1974 government survey of middle-size cities in three provincial regions, found that relative to taxes collected, self-financing was three times higher in Montpellier than in Nîmes. In general, self-financing for non-Communist cities was about two-thirds higher than for Communist-governed cities.[23]

In a sample of cities that I surveyed, where Communist mayors had been elected in 1977, I found a drop in self-financing relative to taxes collected in the budgets submitted for 1978 in three out of five cities. This drop is quite significant because it was effected so quickly. The sample presented below includes one provincial city (Reims), two industrial towns in the Paris region (Sevran and Poissy), and two bedroom suburbs of Paris (Chelles and Athis-Mons). With the exception of Poissy, the investment programs in these cities have either been maintained at high levels or (in the case of Athis-Mons), have been vastly increased. Thus, in order to increase and/or develop new services, Communist-governed municipalities have increased their dependency on the central state for investment. (See Table 12.1.)

Table 12.1   Percentage of revenue devoted to self-financing of investment in five French cities: 1976 and 1978

	1976 (Non-Communist)	1978 (Communist)
Reims	7.9	5.0
Poissy	18.4	7.0
Sevran	None	5.7
Athis-Mons	9.7	2.4
Chelles	None	None

Note: The formula for self-financing is from the *Guide des Ratios des communes de plus de 10,000 habitants*, an annual publication of the Ministry of the Interior, Direction Générale des Collectivités Locales.

One kind of project in which Communist-governed municipalities have taken a particularly strong interest has been housing, particularly subsidized, low income public housing. Here differences between the policies of Communist and non-Communist cities are more difficult to assess through budget analysis. Public housing is not constructed directly by local authorities in France. In general the responsibility for such housing is in the hands of an independent *Office d'habitations à loyer modérés* (OHLM). These offices are established at the local or departmental level, and their members are responsible to and appointed by the prefect. Nevertheless, local officials can influence the make-up of the HLM councils, can lower the ultimate rental costs of HLM-built housing, and can sponsor additional housing by supporting housing construction by non-commercial groups.

The little evidence that we have indicates that localities in general, and Communist-governed cities in particular, have little difficulty influencing appointments to the administrative councils of the HLM offices.[24] In general, HLM offices have come to reflect the broad housing policies of the localities within their jurisdiction. The ultimate rents in subsidized housing are a reflection of the costs of constructing the housing units, and there is evidence that Communist-controlled offices have attempted to finance construction in ways that will keep costs down and that will minimize the expense to the municipalities. Thus an annual government report stressed in 1976 that certain Communist-controlled offices relied most heavily for financing on long-term loans from the Ministry of Construction and Housing.[25] Milch stresses that in contrast to Montpellier, Nîmes was willing to reduce the cost of public housing by providing the HLM office with cheap land (priced below the market value) and cheap services such as roads, sewage and street-lighting.[26] In addition, Nîmes, in contrast to Montpellier, has a relatively liberal policy towards underwriting housing construction by private companies. 'The primary concern of local authorities in Nîmes . . . has been the "social utility" of the proposed construction. If the project seems worthwhile, they have been willing to provide a guarantee regardless of financial considerations.'[27] This kind of policy has been followed frequently, by other Communist-governed municipalities and, as a result, they have sometimes been forced to pay lending institutions when private groups have defaulted.[28]

The evidence that we have indicates that Communist-governed cities have been committed to the construction of public housing, but we cannot demonstrate that this policy systematically differentiates Communist from non-Communist governed cities. Nevertheless, the differences that we have found among cities with regard to housing policy, indicates some of the important choices made at the local level. Moreover, these choices can be seen even more clearly if housing is considered in the context of urban planning and urban development. It is in this area that some of the differences between Communist and non-Communist local governments can be assessed more easily since urban planning priorities were a major issue in a number of cities where Communist lists were successful in the 1977 elections. We will focus on changes made by several governments within newly elected Communist mayors during the first year and a half after the 1977 local elections.

Housing and urban planning decisions of the previous governments were among the most sharply criticized by many of the Communist–socialist lists that were victorious in 1977. The general concern was with urban sprawl and poorly planned, 'inhuman' housing. Of the sample of eight Communist-governed municipalities in which I interviewed intensively a year after they came to power in 1977, housing and urban planning had been a major issue in the election campaigns of four, and a significant issue in three others. Clearly, housing was important in all of these cases, and the former governments were sharply criticized for planning the development of housing in such a way that access for low-income renters would be quite difficult. However, there were other considerations that were at least as important.

In two cities (Athis-Mons and Antony) in the Paris region, plans had already been approved for the destruction or major renovation of an older center-city area. Prior to the election of 1977, in Athis-Mons, Communist and Socialist militants had blocked the bulldozers that were about to begin renovation. The very first day that the new municipal council met (on 25 March 1977), they suspended application of the construction plans in the development zone. Within a year, the city government was able to renegotiate the development plans. In Antony, the development plan had been far more broadly conceived, and was integrated into the general zoning plan (the POS) that had already been approved by the prefect. During their first year in office, the new local government undertook a major revision of the POS, while continuing negotiations with the field services of the Ministry of Equipment for permission to implement the changes. While the expansion of low income housing (and facilities to serve that housing) were under consideration, the major revisions were concerned with the preservation of the older center-city area.

In Sevran, also in the Paris region, massive reconstruction of the center-city was already in progress, and bitterly opposed by the incoming Communist–Socialist coalition. Here, the new government pledged to modify what it could to save what was left of the core of the center-city and to preserve and improve the older one- and two-family homes. Their plans did not call for the expansion of low-income housing. During the first year in office, the modification of the urban plan was still under consideration. A major concern of the new government in Sevran was the size of the buildings being constructed, as well as the lack of provision for green space and communal institutions in the existing plans. These were also the principal concerns that motivated changes in zoning and construction plans in two other cities — Houilles and Villeneuve-St.-Georges.

In Houilles, I attended a meeting of the city council, where the balance of green space to low income housing was discussed (but not settled), and the Mayor of Villeneuve bluntly told me that his government had changed its POS to prevent the development of 'another Vitry' (a Communist-governed suburb of Paris with massive low-income housing developments).

Certainly, Communist mayors appear to have some conflict over the emphasis on balanced development. The former mayor of Vitry reminded me that there was far more pressure to expand low-income housing during the sixties than there is now, especially in Communist-governed cities, since 'bourgeois' cities were not willing to accept and support such housing (a point confirmed by a regional administrator in the Ministry of Housing and Equipment, the ministry responsible for public housing starts). Even now, the mayor of Chelles — a bedroom suburb some distance from Paris — mused that, while it would not be desirable to build more low-income housing in Chelles, five or six hundred units would have to be built during the next five years to cover a thousand requests. Nevertheless, in general, Communist local officials appear to be far more committed to balanced urban development than either their non-Communist predecessors or, for that matter, than their party colleagues had been in the past.

In this foregoing analysis, I have attempted to demonstrate some of the ways that policy choices in Communist-governed municipalities in France can be differentiated from choices made by other municipalities. I should add that it is easier to generalize about policy choices in Communist-governed cities as a group than about choices made by cities governed by other parties. Korbielski demonstrates that the variation among Communist-governed cities with regard to budget priorities is considerably less than among other party groups. Deviation from the pattern among Communist-governed cities tends to occur among smaller towns, outside of the Paris region, where the Mayor is probably less integrated into the party structure; while for cities of the non-Communist Left and the center, those that deviate most from the mean of their group tend to be centers of large agglomerations, where the Mayor is most likely to be an important notable, not easily influenced by party considerations.[29]

If we can identify and differentiate similar policy choices in cities governed by Communist Mayors, it is reasonable to assume that these choices reflect local, rather than national, priorities, unless of course these cities are sufficiently similar that our findings simply reflect the central-government distribution of resources and benefits to a particular kind of locality. This, however, does not seem to be the case. Changes in housing and urban planning policy were, in many cases, changes in previous policy that had already been approved and even encouraged by the central authorities. Moreover, it is no longer true that Communist-governed cities are industrialized suburbs of large urban centers, with large working-class populations and special needs that are sharply differentiated from those of other French cities.

For some time, two trends have been rapidly changing this stereotype. The first is the relative decline in the blue-collar work-force. In all of the older Communist-governed cities, the percentage of the working-class population has been declining during the past ten years. Ten years ago, of cities of over 30,000 with Communist Mayors, 74 per cent had a working-class population that was higher than the national mean of 41 per cent. Among these *same cities* today, only 55 per cent now have a working-class population higher than the national mean of 39 per cent (see Table 12.2).

Table 12.2   Distribution of cities over 30,000 population by percentage of working-class population*

	Percentage of Cities			
% of Working-Class Population	1968 Comm.	Non-Comm.	1978 Comm.	Non Comm.
60% +	5	1	0	1
50–59%	31	8	14	7
40–49%	45	30	38	17
30–39%	19	50	43	54
20–29%	0	11	6	21
	100	100	100	100
Mean % Working-Class Population	46%	39%	41%	36%

*These figures, and those given in the text above, are derived from the French census of 1968 and 1978; (a) INSEE, *Recensement de la population, 1975*, résultats du sondage au 1/5, communes de plus de 5000 habitants (Paris 1976), Tableaux P1, P3, P11, P24; (b) INSEE, *Recensement de la population, 1968*, résultats du sondage au 1/4, fascicules départementaux (Paris, 1971), Tableaux A3, A7, A13.

Accentuating this trend is the large increase in the number of Communist governments that has been elected, through *union-de-gauche* agreements, in more middle-class towns, during the past ten years. In 1978, only half of the Communist-governed cities had working-class populations above the national mean. In fact, I found that the distribution of Communist cities with different levels of working-class populations was not dramatically different from that of non-Communist cities. Finally, in 1958, only three of the larger cities governed by Communists were outside of the Paris region, but today, thirty of the seventy-two are in the provinces.

Thus, similarities in policy priorities among Communist-governed cities, particularly in policies that necessitate considerable support from the central authorities, such as investment strategy, housing and urban development, are a good measure of the ability of localities to make autonomous choices and mobilize resources from the center. This ability depends upon their access to and relations with central authorities. However, it also depends upon their own resources for developing policy initiatives. School services, social services for children, public housing and choices in urban development are not generally imposed from the center in France; they depend upon local initiative, and then are weighed against national criteria by the central authorities for funding. Both in the pattern of access with the center, and the process of developing policy initiative in Communist-governed cities, I have found important differences compared to cities governed by other parties.

2.   ACCESS TO THE CENTER

It is usually assumed that Communist local officials have poor access to centers of administrative and political decision-making. However, the problem seems to be somewhat more complicated. Communist officials frequently complain that they lack the advantages of informal relations with government officials and administrative field services. 'The Prefect must always appear non-partisan', stressed the new Communist Mayor of Houilles (an industrial suburb of Paris), 'but municipal governments of the majority have an old-boy system unavailable to us.' Another Communist Mayor (the Mayor of Sevran) felt that while he experienced no overt prejudice, there was a tendency of the administration to favor and encourage the governments of the center-Right, while the mayor of Villeneuve-St.-George was quick to cite numerous slights and acts of discriminatory behavior.

On the other hand, Communist Mayors did not generally argue that the administration discriminates against their policy proposals and against their requests for aid. Those Mayors who are or who have been Deputies or Senators, and have some experience in Paris (such as the Mayors of Antony, Poissy, Chelles and Reims), claim to have made easy and useful contacts. Furthermore, several of these Mayors argued that, while there have been instances of political discrimination, the acceptance of their proposals is generally related to the quality of the dossiers that they submit, as well as to the priorities of the government and/or the ministry. The Mayor of Reims, for example, stressed that while political considerations may determine industrial investments, they do not determine investment requests for public projects.

If a project conforms to existing legislation, if it meets needs, if the financial plan holds up, there is no reason to turn it down . . . Political decisions are those concerning industrial investment, not those concerning public works projects. Tell me, are the cities of the Right better equipped than those of the Left in France? No — not at all!

Providing that proposals for aid are 'solid, well prepared, straight and clear', he claimed, there is no systematic discrimination against Reims because its Mayor is a Communist.

Several directors of ministerial field services interviewed in the Paris region all agreed that their relations with Communist Mayors were 'highly political', and a technical advisor to the sub-prefect of Corbeil-Essonne noted that technical reasons were sometimes given to cover essentially political decisions on urban projects.

However, much of the prejudice against Communist Mayors appears to be expressed in lack of access for individual favors and personal requests. A former chief advisor to the Prefect of the Essonne department confided with some exasperation that in many ways his dealings with the Communist-governed municipalities were easier than with those of the center-Right. While the former presented formal requests for subventions and loans for specific projects, the latter inundated his office with special requests for individual favors, special letters and appointments. It is possible, however, that poorer (or more formal) access for state aid is compensated by the activist orientation of the Communist-governed cities.

One study contends that Communist Mayors have been highly effective in manipulating the administration — sometimes by infiltrating the field services (one suspects not too often), but more frequently by exploiting the same interdependence between Prefect (and administrative field services) and local elected officials exploited by other Mayors, but perhaps with more determination and for different policy objectives.

As for non-political administrators, the PC uses its power to influence them: it shimmers before them career advantages ('certain administrators see in us the means to release their aptitudes'); it impresses them with its incessant applications. The activism of the PC can be explained by its will to convince those who are hesitant and those who are *attentistes*, if not by the cogency of its ideas then at least by its force.[30]

Montaldo cites the example of Arles, where the Communist local government subcontracted a great deal of its construction work to a company associated with the *Caisse des dépôts et consignations*, the principal source of loans for local governments, which in turn approved a large loan for the city.[31] Thus, Montaldo argues, the city was able to play one part of the administration against the other. An internal report given to me by the former (Communist) Mayor of Vitry indicates that Vitry also attempted to negotiate this kind of trade-off for a large urban renewal project in the early sixties. In this case, however, the city was not able to reach agreement with the company. Negotiations apparently broke down over the small number of low-income apartments proposed by the general contractor but a compromise agreement was worked out with the Ministry of Equipment a year later.[32] In the case of Vitry, the city got the housing it wanted, but it sacrificed what it regarded as a more desirable urban plan. However, both of these cases illustrate the complex bargaining process that goes on between Communist-governed cities and the central administration.

In this sense, it is difficult to assess whether Communist-governed cities get more or less than other cities in the process of center–periphery relations, since many initial requests are subject to revision in the bargaining process. Tarrow presents evidence that Communist-governed cities have succeeded in getting as much (or as little) in investment loans and grants per capita as other cities.[33] Communist local officials frequently confirmed my contention that other municipal governments demanded less and therefore got less. For example, a Socialist Assistant Mayor of Antony, who is also an important official of the urban planning institute for the Paris region, emphasized that proposals from Communist-governed towns were perhaps better received by administrative decision-makers, because their governments are better organized and are more reliable. None of the Communist Mayors interviewed felt that the difficulties of formal access were a major factor hampering the achievement of their policy objectives. Instead, they expressed objections to the burdens placed on all communes by the present system of center–local relations.

Numerous studies of French local government make the point that local power, while considerable in center–periphery relations, has been used most frequently to resist change rather than to innovate. Clearly Communist-governed cities do not fit into this pattern (as a group). Their relations with the central authorities are in a number of ways different from those of other cities, and these differences are related to the goals that they are seeking. Relations are based less upon the personal network of contacts of the Mayor, and more upon the skill of the local government in bureaucratic bargaining and maneuver. Far more depends upon 'the quality of the dossiers', than on 'the network of contacts'. However, what most clearly differentiates these cities from those analyzed in much of the literature is not so much their pattern of access and their relations with the center, but the objectives that they seek, and their objectives are related to the way that they develop policy initiatives at the local level.

3. POLICY DEVELOPMENT AT THE LOCAL LEVEL

The most basic element that differentiates Communist-governed cities from most others is the way that they justify holding power. Except to alleviate urgent and pressing problems, innovation and change has generally been viewed as dangerous by most conservative Mayors because it endangers the political harmony of the commune. Harmony is built on *apolitisme*, the idea that local government is not political, and on a mayoral coalition based on service, personal favors, and on the privileged access accorded to the Mayor by the administration. Initiatives for change tend to endanger harmony by raising divisive issues, and by undermining some traditional notions of good management (low taxes and low debts).[34] While a different pattern has been pursued by certain reform Mayors (Grenoble and Rennes are the most frequently cited examples), Communist-governed cities are different as a group.

Communist local officials have openly staked their claim to local power on their ability to get things done. The second national contract, published in 1977, stresses that Communists should be judged by what they do and what they intend to do, an echo of the criteria by which the national party judges its local victories:

[Electoral success] is a tribute to the quality of administration favorable to the people, a tribute to the Communist officials in the municipalities. But we should declare above all that the time is over when the reverse is true: that the Communist ideal rallies more votes than its men, because they have not yet demonstrated their administrative capabilities. This argument is now out of date, and the Communists are properly considered those who get things done, despite the obstacles imposed by the government.[35]

The typical local contracts proposed by Communist-led lists of candidates mention specific proposals for change and development, in addition to general criticisms of national government policies. While most of the local contracts (or manifestos) have been a product of negotiations with the Socialists, the political importance of these documents is the same. They publicly tie Communist local government to policy commitments, rather than to personality or patronage networks. Moreover, the need to elaborate a program appears to create an impulsion towards active government. In response to questions about the objectives of their governments, the Communist Mayors interviewed by the author consistently referred to the priorities of the municipal contracts.

In addition to policies themselves, the Communists link the success of their governments to an open process of policy development.[36] A high level of popular involvement is necessary, they argue, to support claims for state support. Although privately Communist local officials have sometimes questioned the efficacy of public demonstrations of support, the long-standing emphasis upon public mobilization generally distinguishes Communist local governments from others. In effect, Communists argue that the legitimacy of their presence at the local level should be based on their ability to deliver procedural and substantive justice.

Tarrow's data on Communist Mayors indicates that they tend to justify their policies in terms of collective benefits more frequently than Mayors from other parties. Sixty-four per cent of his Communist sub-sample relate their projects to the maximization of collective interests, compared to 47 per cent of the Socialists, and 41 per cent of the others.[37] There is also some survey evidence that this view of the role of local government is shared by those who vote for Communist-led lists.[38]

A second element distinguishing Communist local officials from others, and supporting initiatives and innovation, is the party structure within which they operate. The Communist party, I have found, has not provided an important link or conduit for accomplishing policy objectives in the daily routine of governing. Similarly, Tarrow reports that most of the contacts of Communist Mayors, as those of other Mayors, is with administrative officials.[39]

Nevertheless, the party structure has been an increasingly important factor in stimulating, defining and ordering local policy-planning and policy-making. Through the party structure, a link has been established between national priorities and local politics, through a national network of direct contacts among Communist Mayors that has slowly developed. The party structure at the federation level for some time has provided an arena within which Communist local officials have made contact, discussed problems and compared accomplishments. Jean-Pierre Hoss, in his study of Argenteuil and Bezons (during the mid-sixties) — two Communist towns in the Paris suburbs — observed that these kinds of contacts between the two Mayors were frequently marked by a kind of policy competition. 'The objective of these contacts is to confront the problems of the two cities, to study possible solutions, but above all, to harmonize municipal policies . . . so that one commune is not further ahead — or behind — the other with regard to accomplishments. Whatever is undertaken in Bezons must be [undertaken] in Argenteuil, and vice-versa . . .'[40]

In the early 1970s, with the expansion of its presence at the local level, the Communist party began to modify and reinforce the structure through which it co-ordinated and influenced policy at the local level. Rather than rely upon the regular party organization, the central committee began to establish direct contact and co-ordination among Mayors and municipal councillors.

During the spring of 1972, the central committee organized a general meeting of Communist Mayors and other elected officials for the first time.[41] A year later, the effort was formalized when the party refurbished an existing quarterly journal with a new format (*Bulletin de L'Élu communiste*): 'not only as a source of information and a bulletin where party *responsables* write, but also a place for the exchange of experience and points of view of Communist elected officials.'[42] At the same time, the secretariat of the central committee established a special *Commission Centrale de Politique Municipale* to co-ordinate policy.

In February 1978 in anticipation of the legislative elections, the quarterly (which had been renamed *Communes et Départments d'Ajourd-'hui* in 1975) was transformed into a monthly to serve as the official publication of the *Association Nationale des Élus Communistes et Républicains*, that had been launched nine months earlier. Both the new publication and the association, which had been gradually organized in each department, represented a considerable effort to encourage direct contact among Communist Mayors and municipal councillors, and to train and socialize a large influx of new elected officials, whose numbers had doubled as a result of the 1977 municipal elections. 'Thousands of new municipal councillors, confronted from one day to the next with complex problems of administration, needed information and exchanges of experience in quantity, quality and with rapidity.'[43]

This structure of direct contacts is enhanced by the network of service organizations for localities that the Communist party has been developing for some time. From summer camp services to studies for housing and urban development to computer services, firms associated directly and indirectly with the party can provide these services. While the provision of these services by party-related organizations is not unique to the Communists (other parties also seem to have their networks), the extent of the network is probably larger than that of other parties. This reduces the dependency of Communist-governed municipalities on the parallel services offered by the prefecture, which is particularly important for smaller cities and towns.[44]

The principal impact of the national party connections appears to be similar ways of thinking about policy and policy alternatives at the local level. While all of the Mayors I interviewed strenuously denied that the local party section had any supervisory role in policy-making, they readily admitted the connection between national and local priorities, at least in a general way. With the development of a national contract in 1971 and 1977, the national line on general objectives and priorities became clearer, and — seemingly — a more powerful stimulus.

On the other hand, there are certainly differences in substance, style and process among Communist-governed cities, differences that are sometimes related to demography and tax structure. Thus, Antony and Athis-Mons, with relatively small working-class populations, have placed more emphasis on balanced urban development (with a smaller number of housing units) than have Vitry and Chelles, which have a large number of demands for housing. Chelles and Antony, which have a small industrial base and therefore rely heavily on regressive local property taxes for their income, depend more heavily than other Communist-governed cities on fees for service, rather than tax revenues, to finance their municipal operations. After the 1977 election, the new municipal council in Chelles decided to reorganize the city bus service, and to charge (sliding scale) fees. Until 1977, the service had been free. A number of Communist and Socialist local officials that I interviewed also insisted that there was an important difference in style and process between the older Communist 'bastions' and the cities with newly-elected Communist and *union-de-gauche* governments. The newer governments, they insisted, were more open, more pragmatic, less bureaucratic, and better organized than the older ones.

The Communist party link has also stimulated policy innovation in an indirect way, through the unity of the Left agreement with the Socialist party. Indeed, the unity-of-the-Left strategy has been more effective in restructuring political life at the local level than in achieving national power. The first local alliances between the Communist and Socialist parties were concluded during the 1959 municipal elections. By 1971, the new Socialist party actively encouraged such unity-of-the-Left coalitions, and directly intervened in several cases to prevent the formation of 'third-force' (centrist) coalitions (as a result of a resolution passed by the Issy-les-Moulineaux Congress, which specifically rejected such alliances).[45] In 1977, in all but a few of the 221 towns with more than 30,000, the Communists and Socialists presented united lists, in fulfilment of a national agreement.

As a result, the structure of politics has been altered in the 141 towns (of over 30,000) where the Communists and Socialists govern together. Both parties provide the basis for a co-operative-competitive relationship that defines the politics of these municipalities. Where the balance of forces is close, as it is in many of the union-of-Left governments elected in 1977, the competition is particularly intense.

For most of the seventy-two municipalities with Communist Mayors, co-operation between the two groups is defined by a local municipal contract negotiated during the preparation for the 1977 municipal election. There remain, however, many areas of competition that center on disagreements on the details of the programs, disagreements on the hiring of municipal personnel, and innumerable disagreements on process and consultation. To varying degrees, government in these municipalities is competitive party government, with each of the parties attempting to outbid the other in order to build support. Almost all of the documented disagreements in these towns can be understood from this perspective.[46] The decision-making process tends to be one of bargaining between group leaders in the municipal bureau. The emerging competition has resulted in a complex system of bargaining between party group leaders in the municipal bureau, on one hand, and between the local government and the administration on the other. Thus in Antony and Athis-Mons, both party groups agreed that the existing urban development plan was unsatisfactory, and joined in pressuring the administration for revision; however, they intensely disagreed on an acceptable alternative plan for over a year. Competition and opposition are not generally found in French local governments.[47]

Another aspect of the political process in Communist-led municipalities relevant for policy activism is the mobilization of local associations for political objectives. My interviews and observations confirm Hoss's analysis that in fact there has been a conscious attempt to integrate these associations into the development of policy, and to use this mobilization to generate support from the state.[48] In addition to mobilizing existing associations around specific projects, Communist-led governments have also attempted to organize new groups, such as neighborhood committees,

for the same purpose. 'We want the creche that you need', the Mayor of
Antony told the author he explained to a neighborhood committee.
'Help us to secure the credits from the state.'[49] However, the mobilized
associations may not simply serve to support the objectives of the municipal government. The head of the Socialist group in Antony noted with
some pride that he had forced changes in the local urban plan by leaking
details of a report to some of the local associations. While there is little
information on the role of local associations in local politics, there is
therefore some evidence that the active associations can become an instrument in center–periphery relations, and part of the competitive process in local politics. However, I found no evidence of associations initiating policy or effectivly opposing local government proposals.

Finally, pressure for municipal innovation is stimulated by the general
politicization of local policy-making. In large towns governed by the
center-Right, policy-making tends to be a collaborative effort between
the Mayor and the (civil-service) heads of the municipal services, while
the elected members of the municipal council tend to play a more peripheral role.[50] In Communist-governed municipalities, the work of the
municipal services is subordinated to that of the committees of the
municipal council (the *commissions municipales*), which play an active
and continuous role in the development of policy. The importance of this
process of politicization of policy-making was alluded to frequently by
both elected officials and civil servants in cities that elected Communist
Mayors for the first time in 1977. The most important consequence of
this process, particularly in cities in which there is a *union-de-gauche*
coalition, has been continuous stimulation for policy initiative. Even
in the absence of party competition, however, where Communists have
governed alone, active council committees have served as a point of
access for local associations and as a source of new ideas and projects.

The will and commitment of Communist-governed municipalities to
make policy development the main focus of their activity is based upon
the judgement that their support is enhanced in this way, a judgement
that is not shared by many municipal governments committed to
'apolitical' consensus government. Will and commitment are also supported by the dynamics of the party structure, and by the process through
which policy is developed at the local level. Communist local government
is obviously conditioned by party connection far more than by the privileged access of a powerful mayor.[51] For the power of developing policy,
these factors may be more important than access to centers of administrative and political decision-making.

CONCLUSION

In terms of the scope of their objectives, and the structure and process through which these objectives are developed and achieved, Communist-governed municipalities are different as a group from those governed by other parties. Unlike other municipalities, the Communists treat local government as a party effort, both locally and nationally. Their efforts emphasize the expansion of such services as education and educational services, the development of housing aid, and, more recently, the development of balanced urban planning. Most of all, unlike other municipalities, the Communists tend to view local government as an arena for policy innovation and change. This emphasis is consistent with their view of legitimacy at the local level, as well as with their strategy for building support.

For the more 'apolitical' communes of the center-Right, policy innovation tends to be limited by fears of undermining the local harmony upon which support and legitimacy are built. Even where access to the center is good, it is frequently used to protect the commune against incursions from the center, to mold policy initiatives from the center to local needs, and to promote individual petitions.

The policy emphasis of Communist-governed cities demonstrates the considerable variation in the French system of center–periphery relations, variations that are given scant consideration in the existing literature. What most clearly differentiates Communist-led municipalities as a group from the others is not the determined will of one or several Mayors to achieve certain objectives, but a political structure and process that stimulates and supports policy innovation. The support system (in this case provided by the Communist party) both strengthens initiative and weakens the dependency relationship between the municipality and the field services of the administration. While this pattern is most characteristic of Communist-governed municipalities, other cities share at least some of these characteristics.[52] The Communist experience illustrates well the ability of local governments in France to initiate and mold policy priorities. This activist pattern (though not the same pattern of priorities) may become more characteristic of local government in France if the national parties develop greater coherence and greater control over local elites.[53]

Notes

*   Earlier versions of this chapter were presented at several professional meetings, and a somewhat different version was published in *Studies in Comparative Communism* (Winter 1980). I would like to thank Philip Cerny, Jack Hayward, John Frears and Mark Kesselman for their comments and suggestions.

1   For a summary of this literature, see Mark Kesselman, 'Research Perspectives in Comparative Local Politics: Pitfalls, Prospects and Notes on the French Case', in Terry Clark, ed., *Comparative Community Politics* (Beverly Hills, Calif.: Sage, 1974), pp. 364–7; and Sidney Tarrow, *Between Center and Periphery: Grassroots Politicians in Italy and France* (New Haven, Conn.: Yale University Press, 1977), Chap. 1; also see Pierre Grémion, *Le Pouvoir périphérique* (Paris: Seuil, 1976); Michel Crozier and Erhard Friedberg, *L'Acteur et le système: les contraintes de l'action collective* (Paris: Seuil, 1977); and Jerome Milch, 'Influence as Power: French Local Government Reconsidered', *British Journal of Political Science*, Vol. 4 (1974), pp. 139–62.

2   Douglas Ashford, 'Are Britain and France Unitary?' *Comparative Politics*, (July 1977), p. 489.

3   See Mark Kesselman, *The Ambiguous Consensus* (New York: Knopf, 1967), pp. 62–3; Jean-Pierre Worms, 'Le Préfet et ses notables', *Sociologie du Travail* (July 1966), p. 250; Grémion, *Le Pouvoir périphérique*, p. 303.

4   Crozier and Freidberg, *L'Acteur et le système*, p. 223.

5   Michel Crozier and Jean-Claude Thoenig, 'La Régulation des systèmes organisés complexes', *Revue Française de Sociologie* (January, 1975), p. 1.

6   *Le Monde*, 22 March 1978, and Alain Guede and Gilles Fabre-Rosane, 'Portrait robot du député 1978', *Le Matin de Paris*, 19 April 1978.

7   Grémion and Worms, 'La Concertation régionale: innovation ou tradition?' in Institut d'Etudes Politiques de Grenoble, *Aménagement du territoire et développement régionale* (Paris: La Documentation Française, 1968), p. 59; and Jeanne Becquart-Leclerq, *Paradoxes du pouvoir local* (Paris: Presses de la FNSP, 1967), p. 205.

8   Jack Hayward, *The One and Indivisible French Republic* (New York: W. W. Norton, 1973), p. 32.

9   Crozier and Friedberg, *L'Acteur et le système*, pp. 233–4.

10   In fact there are only two studies known to the author in which any attempt has been made to integrate data from Communist municipalities into a more general treatment of French local politics and center-periphery relations: Tarrow, *Between Center and Periphery*; and Milch, 'Influence as Power'. Also see François Platone, 'L'Implantation municipale du parti communiste français dans la Seine et sa conception de l'administration communale' (Mémoire, Diplome supérieure d'études et de recherche politiques, Paris, FNSP, 1967); Jean-Pierre Hoss, *Communes en banlieu: Argenteuil et Bezons* (Paris: Armand Colin, 1969); Paul Thibault, 'Le Communisme municipal', *Esprit*, (October 1967) and Jean-Claude Ducros, 'Politique et finances locales', *Analyses et Prévisions*, II (1966).

11   See the essays by Tarrow, Milch, Lacorne and Lavau in Donald Blackmer and Sidney Tarrow, eds., *Communism in Italy and France* (Princeton, N.J.: Princeton University Press, 1977).

12   There are now 221 cities in France with a population of greater than 30,000. Of these, seventy-two have Communist mayors. The present electoral law stipulates that in cities of this size (with several exceptions) the winning list takes all of the seats on the municipal council, which elects the mayor. However, as a result of an agreement between the Communist and Socialist parties, almost all of the seventy-two cities with Communist mayors are *union-de-gauche* coalitions of Communists and Socialists.

13 Marcel Rosette, *La Gestion communale dans l'action* (Paris: Editions sociales, 1977), pp. 361–2.
14 See José Korbielski, 'Tendence politique des municipalités et comportements financiers locaux' (paper presented at the conference on Politics, Policy and the Quality of Urban Life, Bellagio, Italy, June 1975), p. 6.
15 Guy Herzlich, 'Les communes et l'école: 3600 ministères de l'éducation', *Le Monde de l'Education*, March 1977, p. 7.
16 Ibid., pp. 7–14.
17 Korbielski, 'Tendence politique', p. 9. Also see the author's doctoral dissertation, 'L'Influence de la structure de communes urbains sur leurs dépenses de fonctionnement' (thèse pour le doctorat des sciences économiques, Université de Rennes, 1975), pp. 310–12.
18 Korbielski, 'Tendence politique', p. 22.
19 Ibid., p. 24.
20 Montaldo, *Les Finances du P.C.F.* (Paris: Albin Michel, 1977), pp. 14–18.
21 These figures are derived from *Evolution de la fiscalité directe locale*, 1976 (Paris: Ministère de l'Intérieur, Direction Générale des Collectivités Locales, 1977).
22 Milch, 'Influence as Power', pp. 143–5.
23 Montaldo, *La France communiste* (Paris: Albin Michel, 1978), pp. 140–1.
24 Montaldo, *La France communiste* pp. 165–75; and Milch, 'Influence as Power', pp. 148–52.
25 Cour des Comptes, *Rapport au Président de la République, 1976*, cited in Montaldo, *La France communiste*, p. 174. The report did not allude specifically to Communist-run offices; however, all of the offices it mentioned were in fact Communist-run.
26 Milch, 'Influence as Power', p. 150.
27 Ibid.
28 However, this has not been a problem only for Communist-governed cities. See Cour des Comptes, *Rapport . . . 1978*, pp. 56–9.
29 Korbielski, 'L'Influence de la structure', pp. 310–12.
30 Montaldo, *La France communiste*, p. 159.
31 Ibid., pp. 159–60.
32 This internal report (1974), entitled *Le Grand ensemble*, attempts to explain the origins of the urban renewal project and the compromise with the Ministry of Equipment reached in 1963. Tall apartment towers were constructed to reduce the charges per apartment, but the social consequences were disastrous. 'This was the unfavourable aspect of the compromise, the aspect that we question most strongly today, but necessary at the time if we wanted to construct "social housing" in spite of the financial disengagement of the state' (p. 3).
33 Tarrow, *Between Center and Periphery*, pp. 104–6, and 167–72.
34 Hayward, *The One and Indivisible French Republic*, p. 32; Becquart-Leclercq, *Paradoxes du pouvoir local*, pp. 201–3; also see Suzanne Berger, Peter Gourevitch, Patrice Higonnet and Karl Kaiser, 'The Problem of Reform in France: The Political Ideas of Local Elites', *Political Science Quarterly* (September 1969), 436–60.
35 Jean Gacon, 'Géographie et sociologie électorale du P.C.F.,' *Cahiers de l'Institut Maurice Thorez* (January–February, 1973), p. 23.
36 Rosette, *La Gestion communale dans l'action*, pp. 9–10.
37 Cited by Jerome Milch, 'The P.C.F. and Local Government', in Blackmer and Tarrow, *Communism in Italy and France*, p. 353.
38 Jack Hayward and Vincent Wright, 'The 37708 Microcosms of the Indivisible Republic: The French Local Elections of 1971', *Parliamentary Affairs* (Autumn 1971), p. 234.

39   Tarrow, *Between Center and Periphery*, p. 167 and Tarrow in Blackmer and Tarrow, *Communism in Italy and France*, pp. 162–72.
40   Jean-Pierre Hoss, *Communes en banlieu: Argenteuil et Bezons* (Paris: Armand Colin, 1969), p. 120.
41   *Le Monde*, 7 May 1972.
42   *Bulletin de l'Élu communiste*, 1/2 ème trimestre, 1973, p. 10.
43   Marcel Rosette, *L'Élu d'Aujourd'hui*, February, 1978, p. 3.
44   The various support services provided by the party are critically elaborated by Montaldo, *Les Finances du P.C.F.*, pp. 137–68.
45   See Lacorne, in Blackmer and Tarrow, *Communism in Italy and France*.
46   Nevertheless, these disagreements have been well-controlled (in general), and the intensity of the conflict between the national parties has not been reflected at the local level.
47   See Becquart-Leclerq, *Paradoxes du pouvoir local*, Chap. III.
48   See Hoss, *Communes en banlieu*, p. 123.
49   The *Grand ensemble* report for Vitry puts heavy emphasis on popular mobilization to pressure the state into paying for a reorganization of the urban development and housing project.
50   Hayward, *The One and Indivisible French Republic*, p. 34.
51   However, there are Communist Mayors who are reputed to be 'red notables'. The Mayor of Chelles was frequently referred to in these terms. See Denis Lacorne, *Les Notables rouges: la construction municipale de l'union de la gauche (1971–77)* (Paris: Presses de la F.N.S.P., forthcoming), Chap. III.
52   See Becquart-Leclerq, *Paradoxes du pouvoir local*, pp. 205–6; Hayward, *The One and Indivisible French Republic*, pp. 34–5; Chrisophe Warngy, *Louviers: sur la route de l'autogestion* (Paris: Éditions Syros, 1976), esp. pp. 70–89.
53   See Frank Wilson, 'The Revitalization of French Parties', *Comparative Political Studies* (April 1979).

13 Independence and Economic Interest: The Ambiguities of French Foreign Policy*

William Wallace

The legacy of General de Gaulle still shapes the context, and permeates the rhetoric, of French foreign policy. A decade after his death, the international environment has altered markedly. The special relationship with the Soviet Union which he cultivated now exists only through limited commerical benefits and occasional political exchanges. The quarrel with the United States which he pursued has been reduced to a relationship of wary understanding. His attitudes towards Germany, Britain, the Middle East and Africa have been subtly altered, under the pressure of external circumstances and the redefinition of national interests. French defence policy has edged cautiously back towards a balance between strategic and conventional forces, and towards co-operation with NATO. French industry, both public and private, has pursued selective co-operation with American companies, in preference to integration with other European firms. Yet the presidency of Giscard d'Estaing still emphasizes the continuity between his foreign policy and that of his Fifth Republic predecessors, even as Giscard's distinctive priorities, France's limited resources and the expectations and demands of its foreign partners bring out considerable and cumulative changes in emphasis.

This chapter can address itself only to a few themes drawn out of the complicated network of France's active and 'globalist' foreign policy. The most fundamental issue, for a volume concerned with the economic aspects of public policy, is the balance between ideological objectives and economic interests in the formulation of French foreign policy. A related theme is how far French foreign policy reflects a coherent and strategic approach, balancing the impulse to maintain independence against the necessities of interdependence – as its admirers claim – or rather a set of well-executed tactical responses disguising the essential incoherence of Giscardian foreign policy — as its critics maintain. Two further themes relate to the institutions through which policy is made and managed, and the domestic context within which it is framed. How far does France now have a personal foreign policy, controlled and directed from the Élysée, rather than a government policy emerging from the conflicts and compromises of a bureaucratic machine? Does public acceptance of the centralized and secretive character of foreign policy-making leave French governments largely free of domestic constraints, or do the problems of coalition politics and the competition for public approval through incessant electioneering set close limits to governments' freedom of action even in the heart of the *domaine réservé*?

These issues are at the centre of the academic debate about French foreign policy.[1] In order to examine them it is necessary, first, to discuss its traditional language, style and objectives, and the relevance of the *étatiste* tradition for foreign policy; then to outline the institutional structure and domestic context within which policy is made; then to consider some of the different dimensions of French foreign policy — defence, foreign trade, international finance, policy towards the United States, Africa, the Soviet Union and the Middle East. The final section will then examine the central paradox of French foreign policy — the relationship between the high aspirations embodied in the aims of policy and the limitations inherent in the means at France's disposal.

GRANDEUR AND TRADE

Two traditions intertwine in French foreign policy: the identification of state and nation, the concern to maintain national independence, to protect international status, and to promote French culture; and the consciousness of economic vulnerability, with the consequent commitment to promote economic strength through state efforts both at home and abroad. Both have their origins in French history and experience — and geography — stretching back well before the Fourth Republic, even before the Revolution of 1789. Both were reinforced and reinterpreted by President de Gaulle. De Gaulle laid greater emphasis on national status and independence, on a foreign policy of 'grandeur', with economic diplomacy as a means to that end. His two successors have in practice, if not in public rhetoric, reversed this balance: pursuing economic objectives through all the instruments available to a centralized state, and using traditional diplomacy and international initiatives to gain economic advantage abroad and to maintain political support at home. But in the

Gaullist conception of foreign policy, the two dimensions are inseparable. An insistence on status, an active foreign policy, were necessary to supply influence in the pursuit of national interests — and above all economic interests — beyond what France's limited resources could provide; while economic strength — a sound economy with a strong currency and adequate resources for defence and foreign policy — was vital to the maintenance of independence and of international standing.

De Gaulle's concept of foreign policy owed much to his experience of the Second World War, when intransigence and an insistence on status were necessary to compensate for his weak position as the exiled resistance leader of a divided and occupied country. 'Our grandeur and our force,' he wrote in a dispatch from the Middle East to Free French Headquarters in 1941, 'consists uniquely in the intransigence we show in defending the rights of France . . . Mr Churchill will understand without doubt that he can only lean on something that offers resistance.'[2] But the essentials of his approach were shaped before the war, reflecting on the interaction of domestic divisions and uncertainty in foreign policy, and harking back to the humiliations of the Franco-Prussian War of 1870–71 and the painfully-won conclusion of the Great War of 1914–18. The distinction which Gaullist ideology draws between the interests of France and the interests of Frenchmen carries echoes of Rousseau and of the conflict between proponents of a strong state and supporters of popular republicanism during and after the French Revolution. But de Gaulle added his particular emphasis to this distinction, seeing in a concentration on France's prestige and status a means of persuading Frenchmen to rise above their deep-seated domestic divisions. His often quoted conclusion to the first paragraph of his War Memoirs, that 'la France ne peut être la France sans la grandeur' is prefaced by the remark that 'seules de vastes entreprises sont susceptibles de compenser les ferments de dispersion que son peuple porte en lui-même' - that foreign policy has a vital domestic role to play, offering a means of uniting the nation and distracting the French from their destructive domestic quarrels.

Straightforward nationalism, a strong sense of national interest, a conservative approach to international relations, and a sense of the narrow line between success and failure — or strength and weakness — in foreign policy, were drawn together in this overall perspective. The same classic declaration of Gaullist faith, with its assertion that 'la France n'est réellement elle-même qu'au premier rang', notes that 'notre pays, tel qu'il est, parmi les autres, tels qu'ils sont, doit, sous peine de danger mortel, viser haut et se tenir droit' — must press its interests directly at the centre of global diplomacy if it is to avoid defeat and failure. The political implications of the Gaullist perspective followed from this, reflecting and restating older strands of French foreign policy: the insistent challenge to the United States, as the dominant power and thus the greatest threat to French independence; the search for a balance in Europe, at once coming closer to Germany (as the major threat to that balance) and attempting to contain it through the European Community, and through the traditional *entente* with Russia; the assertion wherever possible of an independent French role, deliberately out of step with its allies, struggling to maintain its privileged position in Africa and later to build up a special relationship with the Arab oil-producing countries of the Middle East, emphasising the distinctiveness of French culture and the links which tied *la Francophonie* to France; the symbolic importance of defence as the guarantor of national independence; and the concern with state action to promote economic interests.

The economic dimension of foreign policy was thus part and parcel of de Gaulle's perspective. After the devastation of the Second World War, he wrote,

> it was incumbent upon the state to create the national power, which henceforth would depend on the economy. The latter must therefore be directed, particularly since it was deficient, since it must be renovated, and since it would not be renovated unless the state determined to do so . . . But this conception of a government armed to act powerfully in the economic domain was directly linked to my conception of the state itself.[3]

This conception, it should be noted, was also not entirely novel to de Gaulle. The state which Henry IV created and Louis XIV expanded regarded a strong domestic economy as a necessary aspect of statecraft and state power. Interventionism in the French economy, and the protection and promotion of economic interests through foreign policy, were familiar strands in the French political tradition, even if restated and redefined in the aftermath of the Second World War.

De Gaulle returned to government in 1958 just as domestic recovery had reached the point where full exposure to international competition, through membership of the European Economic Community, had been accepted, while parallel negotiations under American leadership were lowering the barriers to international trade and easing international transfers of capital. He thus found himself presiding over the opening of the French economy to the challenge of European and American industry. His image of France as a backward economy in need of rapid and repeated renovation to meet the challenges of foreign competition and technological change, which was shared by almost all of the French political and techno-cratic elite, led him to characterize the problem in terms of economic war, in which little less than the survival of the nation-state was at risk. At his press conference of 5 February 1962, he called for 'a vast regeneration both within ourselves and in our relations with others' to meet the economic and technological challenges which faced France. In his New Year's Message for 1965 he warned, more sombrely, of the danger of Europe being 'colonized by foreign participations, inventions and capabilities'.[4] His fears of 'scientific slavery' were, indeed, echoed from the centre and the Left; Jean-Jacques Servan-Schreiber's *Le Défi Américain* provided a detailed and popular version of the same refrain, and Gaston Defferre talked of 'the economic invasion by the United States [as] a clear and present danger . . . the beginning of the colonization of our economy'.[5]

Resistance to American investment in France was therefore accom-panied by a determined drive to build up high technology in France, if possible independently, if not through limited collaboration with Britain and Germany: joining with Britain in developing Concorde, sponsoring 'national champions' in electronics and in oil, balancing its participation in Euratom with an increasingly independent nuclear programme. Mone-tary policy was also a symbol of national power and an instrument of foreign policy: the maintenance of the franc's parity a major factor in French economic policy from 1959 to 1968, the battle against the dollar and the American-imposed rules of the international monetary system a prime concern in foreign economic policy. Unhappy with many aspects of the European Economic Community, de Gaulle nevertheless used it to advantage to strengthen France's position as an agricultural exporter — establishing through the CAP guaranteed prices and export subsidies, thus helping to offset increasing dependence on external supplies of energy and raw materials and to overcome the problems of an economy still dependent on a very narrow base of industrial exports. For de Gaulle himself, the drive to modernize and revitalize the economy was above all a means to the end of maintaining national independence and inter-national standing. The nuclear and electronics programmes, for example, were heavily influenced by the demands of the *force de frappe* and by American attempts to block the transfer of technology to this symbol of French military standing. But he did not hesitate to involve himself and his prestige in the details of economic and industrial negotiations, lecturing the British Prime Minister on the irrationalities of the American proposals for international monetary reform and personally intervening in the Italian Government's choice between competing American and Franco-Russian systems of colour television transmission.

Ten years of presidential office, reinforcing and reinterpreting old themes of French foreign policy, successfully carrying France back on to the centre of the global stage, would have done much to establish de Gaulle's perspective as accepted doctrine on foreign policy — even if he had not left behind him a Gaullist party which regarded loyalty to his principles of foreign policy as the test of orthodoxy, and a Communist party which had proved adept at echoing Gaullist slogans in its repeated attacks on the political centre. But the strains of striving so high with such limited resources had been acute — leading to a progressive deterioration in France's conventional forces, diverting resources from consumption and social expenditure to public investment without significant economic return, and thus contributing towards the explosion of May 1968. The foreign policy which Georges Pompidou inherited on assuming the presidency in 1969, in the wake of substantial wage increases and in the expectation of forthcoming devaluation, was therefore yet more sharply constrained by consciousness of economic weakness. For some commentators 'the social and economic crisis of 1968' exposed 'the illusion of independence and autonomy', 'a general foreign-policy failure' which forced de Gaulle's successors to recognize the realities of economic interdependence.[6]

Certainly Pompidou as President inverted de Gaulle's priorities. 'For Pompidou, it was industrialization and the economy that became his supreme concerns; the goal of foreign policy was to support economic development rather than be supported by it.'[7] He did not break faith with the 'deux legs essentiels du gaullisme: la force de frappe et la non-participation officielle aux organismes militaires de l'OTAN', nor question 'les thèmes de l'indépendance et du refus de l'atlantisme'.[8] But on other issues he compromised, or shifted ground to a more easily defensible position: accepting British entry to the European Community, as a potential counterbalance to the growing economic and political weight of Germany, accepting a greater degree of co-operation in international economic issues through international institutions. For Pompidou as a civilian, who had come to Gaullism only after the liberation, defence and political prestige were less central than economic growth and industrial competitiveness. His presidency was characterized more by the vigour with which it pursued industrial exports, civil and military, than by the staunchness with which it defended France's honour; though his second foreign minister, Michel Jobert, a civil servant by background, became a vocal champion of Gaullist orthodoxy. The crisis in Franco-American relations which marked the end of Pompidou's presidency, with its personal and political antagonism between Jobert and Kissinger, recalled many of the central themes of de Gaulle's conception: independence, resistance to American hegemony, insistence on French initiatives. But it was also a conflict in which French policy-makers saw fundamental economic interests at stake: their dependence on Middle East oil, threatened by American's links with Israel and its efforts to confront the producers with a united front of industrial consumers; and their attempts to build up their exports to the Middle East through cultivating political relations with the oil-producing states.

Giscard d'Estaing, the first non-Gaullist President of the Fifth Republic, was at a yet greater distance from de Gaulle's experience and preconceptions. An administrator by training, his long experience as a member of de Gaulle's government had been as Minister of Finance, responsible for economic management and domestic and international financial policy. Fluent in English, he did not share the Gaullists' passionate resistance to Anglo-Saxon influences and the Atlantic connection; a technician as much as a politician, he attached more importance to efficiency than to prestige. Immediately on taking office, he moved to patch up M. Jobert's quarrel with the American Administration, signing the Ottawa Declaration which ended the bitter saga of the 'Year of Europe' and travelling to Martinique — French soil, but on the American side of the Atlantic — for a bilateral meeting with President Ford. Accepting the failure of French attempts to maintain an independent computer industry and the technological and political disadvantages of subordination to German or British control, he encouraged the merger of CII with Honeywell-Bull, as the strongest competitor to IBM.[9] The French nuclear power industry, for similar reasons of economic advantage and efficiency, was allowed to abandon its independent designs in favour of a licence from Westinghouse, and conversations on co-operation were opened with American civil aircraft firms. The rhetoric of Gaullism continued to be used when it suited the pursuit of economic advantage, as in the battle to win 'the arms sale of the century' in 1975 or in the pursuit of privileged economic ties with the oil-producers and the state-trading countries. But what remained — as critics have suggested — is a state pursuing its commercial, industrial and economic interests by all the means at its disposal.

Certainly, Giscard's presidency has been marked by tensions between 'the logic of interdependence' and 'the phraseology of independence'.[10] There is an element of deliberate illusion in Giscardian foreign policy: using activity and repeated initiatives to disguise retreats from Gaullism from a suspicious domestic public and to maintain the image of 'globalism' on the international stage. Economically, it has so far been extremely successful, maintaining France's position as one of the world's leading agricultural exporters through a stubborn defence of the Community's Common Agricultural Policy, rapidly expanding French exports to the Middle East and the Gulf in the wake of the oil-price increases of 1973–74 and after, holding on to French access to raw materials through active diplomacy and military involvement in Africa, attracting American investment and itself successfully invading the American market. Yet it would be too simple, and too cynical, to reduce French foreign policy to the single-minded pursuit of national economic interest. Even for a man without marked ideological commitments, the presidency carries an aura of prestige and a sense of France's proper standing on the international stage. The bureaucratic support for presidential policy is provided by a machine steeped in the *étatiste* tradition and deeply influenced by the experience of de Gaulle's presidency. And policy evolves within the context of a parliamentary coalition in which, until the 1978 elections, the Gaullists constituted the dominant component, and in which, as the party with the most seats, they remain an indispensable element, and of a domestic public which is accustomed to hear its political leaders talk of national independence and is unprepared to listen to a different tune.

INSTITUTIONS AND THE POLITICAL PROCESS

The presidency is the key institution in the formulation and direction of French foreign policy. The constitution of the Fifth Republic deliberately placed matters of foreign and defence policy within the responsibilities of the President, as 'le garant de l'indépendance nationale, de l'intégrite du territoire, du respect des accords de Communauté et des traités' (Article 5).[11] The concept of a presidential '*domaine réservé*', not explicitly outlined in the constitution, was set out by M. Chaban-Delmas in 1959: including within the reserved sector foreign affairs and defence, Algeria and the French Community in West and Central Africa. The distinction thus drawn between high foreign policy and commercial and economic policies corresponded, according to one expert commentator, to 'the ontological one between the interests of France and the concerns of Frenchmen'.[12] But almost from the outset de Gaulle included international monetary issues within the scope of his active concerns, as well as other industrial and economic matters whenever French prestige (or vital economic interests) were seen to be at stake. The Élysée thus gradually developed a pattern – and a concept – of selective intervention in issues of external relations, eschewing any attempt at full co-ordination, in any event impossible without a considerable expansion of its staff, in favour of direct control of those particular issues on which the President currently chooses to focus.

The 'presidentialization' of French government, generally remarked across the whole range of public policy, has been most marked in the external field. De Gaulle's original conception made for the deliberate removal of foreign policy from the normal processes of governmental deliberation, and the partial insulation of defence policy as well. He appointed non-political ministers to the Quai d'Orsay and to defence — Couve de Murville and Messmer — distinguished during his presidency by their low political visibility and their long tenure of office. (African affairs, yet more removed from domestic debate and scrutiny, were handled from the Élysée by Jacques Foccart, a civil servant with a long commitment to Gaullism who held his post until Pompidou's death in 1974.) Alone among senior ministers, the Foreign Minister was admitted to a weekly private meeting with the President, without even the Prime Minister being present: a practice faithfully continued by both Pompidou and Giscard. The Cabinet rarely, if ever, discussed questions of foreign policy; the Quai d'Orsay communicated for the most part directly with the Élysée. With foreign policy as a source of domestic prestige as well as international standing, it is hardly surprising that de Gaulle's successors have taken over and reinforced this personal direction of foreign policy. It is almost as if, one French diplomat remarked, 'only the head of state has the right to think'; 'French foreign policy', a Socialist Deputy has concluded, 'has become much more that of a man rather than that of the nation as a whole.'[13]

The institutional backing which the Élysée provides is skeletal by comparison with the British Cabinet Office and the Bundeskanzleramt (which of course cover the whole field, divided in Paris between the Élysée and the Matignon). De Gaulle's Élysée was divided into three sections, each representing part of the '*domaine réservé*' of the Fifth Republic's early years: the '*maison civile*', a small group of officials concerned with foreign policy and with those aspects of economic and social policy with which the President wished to be involved, headed by a Secretary-General; the '*maison militaire*', the President's personal military staff, headed by his '*chef d'état-major particulier*'; and the 'Secrétariat-Général pour la Communauté et les affaires africaines et malagaches'. headed by Foccart. This third section, which originally included nine administrative-grade officials who travelled extensively in Africa and whose responsibilities also included security and intelligence activities, was downgraded under Pompidou, and abolished by Giscard; though Giscard retained a '*conseiller*' with extensive African experience and close personal relations with francophone African leaders who played a not dissimilar role. The *maison civile* — the core of the Élysée, extending its interests and activities as Presidents have extended their political and administrative reach — has throughout the Fifth Republic been headed by a Secretary-General with extensive international experience, most often from the Quai d'Orsay. Giscard's Élysée includes, under the Secretary-General, a *'conseiller diplomatique'* and a more junior assistant to prepare presidential dossiers and to advise on foreign policy issues; in addition, two of the three *'conseillers techniques'* responsible for economic issues cover aspects of external policy, one following external economic questions, the other such key industrial sectors as the nuclear industry and computers.[14] This tiny staff has been able to maintain strategic control of French foreign policy only through exploiting the prestige and authority of the presidency and the network of personal ties which holds the French administration together.

The Prime Minister's larger staff at the Matignon also includes two officials specifically concerned with following the telegrams and advising the Premier on foreign policy, as well as a number of others whose responsibilities overlap external concerns. But in principle theirs was an ancillary role, working to a Prime Minister who was not directly involved in the central issues of foreign policy. Depending on their particular interests and their relations with the President, different Prime Ministers have played limited roles in the formulation of policy. Messmer, as a non-political Premier who even allowed the President to appoint his personal staff at the Matignon, had little active influence. Chirac, as a politician concerned to hold together the Assembly majority to support the President, intervened when in his opinion considerations of domestic politics were at stake — as after the European Council of December 1975, when his arguments are said to have been influential in persuading Giscard to stall his newly-delivered commitment to direct elections. Barre came to the premiership from a short spell as Minister for External Trade, and with a long experience and an established reputation in economic policy, including a period as a Commissioner of the European Communities; it was therefore natural that he should take an active interest in European Community matters and issues of international economic policy.

Throughout the Fifth Republic, with the single exception of Maurice Schumann's tenure between 1969 and 1973, the Foreign Minister has been a technician, whose first loyalty was to the President. Under Giscard the close, direct and subordinate character of the relationship has been particularly marked. When M. de Guiringaud, a career diplomat who had gained the President's approval for his adroit management of the opening stages of the 'North–South Dialogue', was asked on television on taking office in August 1976 how he defined his task as minister he replied, simply: 'to carry out the instructions of the President of the Republic'. The Quai d'Orsay, in de Gaulle's presidency, had however an assured bureaucratic role in the preparation of dossiers for submission to the Élysée and the execution of presidential decisions, even if its political role had been reduced from that which it played under the Fourth Republic. Under Pompidou, who did not share de Gaulle's reverence for traditional diplomacy, it lost standing and influence, while Jobert as Secretary-General at the Élysée, and later during his brief tenure of the ministry in 1973–74, bypassed its formal structure and treated its traditions with contempt. A further deterioration in its standing and morale in the first years of the Giscard presidency led to a substantial reform of its internal organization – till then little altered from the pattern established at the Liberation – and a commitment to expand its staff and budget, crowned by the appointment of Giscard's Secretary-General at the Élysée as its new minister in November 1978. The rigidity of the divisions between its political, economic and cultural directorates, which had corresponded to de Gaulle's conception of the division between high politics and external relations, was no longer appropriate to the more flexible and economically-oriented approach of his successors, and was to be moderated by a progressive *'geographisation'* of the organizational structure.[15]

Other ministries play central or peripheral roles in aspects of French foreign policy, as in all other advanced industrial countries. The Ministry of Defence, a massive structure subject to the strains of bureaucratic competition and civil-military relations familiar to all students of defence policy, is to some extent a world apart, though collaborating with the Quai d'Orsay on international security policy and disarmament. *'Finances'* is also an administrative empire, competing and collaborating with the Quai's powerful economic directorate on matters of international financial and economic policy. Its semi-autonomous Direction des Relations Économiques Extérieures (DREE), with its own Minister for External Trade, owes its anomalous position to the historic rivalry between *Finances* and the Quai d'Orsay for predominance in this sphere, and on many issues reports to both. On European matters the Secrétariat-Général du Comité Interministérielle pour les Questions de la Coopération Économique Europiénne (SGCI), housed in the DREE though formally part of the Prime Minister's office, mediates between *Finances* and the Quai and co-ordinates the activities of other ministries as they relate to Brussels. Given the importance of agricultural exports, the Ministry of Agriculture has a significant international dimension, both within the European Community and without. The Ministry of Industry is responsible for such matters as foreign investment and access to raw materials, both highly political on occasion. The Ministry of Co-operation has a specific role — and a circumscribed geographical coverage — in relations with the francophone African countries, in which it operates alongside (and on occasion independently of) the Quai d'Orsay, under the direction of the Élysée.

The strategic direction of the entire administrative apparatus is assured — in principle and in constitutional doctrine — by the Élysée. In this it is considerably assisted by the informal network provided by the ministerial cabinets and their contacts with the Matignon and the Élysée, and by the personal links which follow from the common training of the higher civil service and their membership of the *'grands corps'*. A further dimension of homogeneity in background and approach derived from the increasing *'technicalisation'* of ministerial office-bearers, which reached its apogee when Giscard d'Estaing, an *Inspecteur des Finances* and a former student at ENA, attained the presidency. A majority of the members of Giscard's personal staff, in turn, have passed through ENA to early responsibility in different parts of the state administration, as have a considerable proportion of their colleagues in the Matignon and in other ministerial cabinets. Graduates of ENA flow into the Quai d'Orsay — where their economic and mathematical training considerably assists the foreign ministry in its perpetual struggles with *Finances* — as into the other central ministries; and flow out again, with other members of the foreign service, on detachment to the Élysée, the Matignon, and other ministerial cabinets. De Gaulle's and Pompidou's presidential staffs indeed included more diplomats on detachment than any other group, though their number was reduced under Giscard, who brought with him a larger group of personal associates from his long experience as Minister of Finance.[16]

This structure, with its intense personalization of policy-making and centralization of authority, allows for great flexibility in the management of selected issues, for rapid initiatives taken with the President's authority and under his personal control. It is less a matter of bypassing the bureaucracy, as Presidents are forced to do in Washington when they are determined on initiatives, than of overriding a bureaucracy which accepts the ultimate authority of the Élysée. But the complex character of contemporary diplomacy, bringing together domestic and foreign economic and industrial interests in intricate bilateral and multilateral packages, necessarily limits the possibilities for personal control and central direction. More complicated patterns of policy-making are necessary to reconcile divergent bureaucratic perspectives and domestic interests. On occasion the Élysée and the responsible ministries find themselves at cross-purposes; some areas of policy operate for periods almost autonomously, beyond the effective reach of the thinly-staffed mechanisms for central co-ordination. Bureaucratic resistance to presidential wishes has not been unknown — the unavoidable differences between the various sections of a vast administrative machine being reinforced by the extraordinary secrecy which covers so much of French policy. Co-ordinating mechanisms extend from the Élysée and the Matignon, from the Council of Ministers and its associated *conseils restreints* through such formal structures as the Secrétariat-Général pour la Défense Nationale and the SGCI to informal interdepartmental working parties. The bureaucratic conflicts which characterize the management of any advanced industrial state are evident with the French administrative structure, even formalized in hybrid agencies or *'délégations'* which, as an official remarked of the Délégation pour l'Energie, 'reflect and represent the contradictions which led to [their] creation'.

From one perspective, the French government is extraodinarily free from domestic constraints in conducting its foreign policy. Within certain limits it is free of parliamentary control and accountability. It operates within a strong tradition of secrecy, accepted by a generally docile press. Its public is largely uninterested in foreign policy, and content to judge the government's performance according to its domestic policies. Even scandals such as the *Affaire Dassault* in 1976 or the circumstances surrounding the removal of Emperor Bokassa in 1979 appear to have made little impression on the French electorate. The *Canard Enchaîné's* image of the presidency as a monarchy with courtiers intriguing for power and personal advantage within an atmosphere of secrecy appears to be accepted by the mass of the French public as a characteristic feature of the Fifth Republic's constitutional order.

The National Assembly's capacities to influence the shape or the management of foreign policy were deliberately reduced by the Fifth Republic constitution, and have been reduced further by developments since then. Plenary debates on foreign policy issues, held once a year, are sparsely attended. The Foreign Affairs Committee, one of the most prestigious committees of the Fourth Republic Assembly, is given little information and attracts little publicity. Its president — for some years now Couve de Murville, de Gaulle's Foreign Minister and steadfast defender of the Gaullist faith — has access to confidential information, and travels abroad on occasion on governmental business; but the frustrations of the remainder of its sixty members are alleviated only by the opportunities for foreign travel which membership provides. The Foreign Minister attends the committee to answer questions once a month; but in a system in which he is only the executor of the President's foreign policy this is not of enormous assistance to the committee. Officials in the Quai d'Orsay are thus far less preoccupied with parliamentary business than their opposite numbers in Washington, Bonn or London. With an official as minister and only one other political appointee in his subordinate Secretary of State, the Quai d'Orsay indeed almost lacks political expression.[17]

There exists in France, as in other constitutional democracies, a number of lobbies concerned partly or primarily with aspects of foreign policy. In the defence sphere the usual associations of retired officers co-exist with the representatives of defence industries and the proponents of national security, all critical in different ways of the details of French defence policy, but rarely challenging its foundations. No Minister of Agriculture or of Foreign Affairs — or Prime Minister, or President — could fail to recognize the electoral strength and political determination of the agricultural lobby, even as they accept and share that lobby's objective of a prosperous agricultural economy with public support for its exports. There remains a significant pro-Israel lobby within France, cavalierly ignored by President de Gaulle in his reversal of French Middle East policy in 1967, and able since then only to influence the tone and nuances of that policy. There exist also lobbies for overseas economic development and human rights, largely based upon the churches, but far less numerous in their supporters and vigorous in their activities than their counterparts in Britain or the United States. It would thus be hard to argue that any domestic lobbies significantly constrain the government's freedom of action in foreign policy — although the close link between government and business sets the context for much French foreign economic policy. Over Algeria, indeed, de Gaulle overrode not only the objections of a number of powerful groups but also the clear sentiments of the majority of public opinion: deliberately pursuing the interests of France, against the expressed wishes of Frenchmen.

Yet the domestic context of French foreign policy is intensely political. Its intensity derives from the weight of the Gaullist inheritance, accepted as doctrine by the mass of the French public and reinforced and fought over by the political parties in their unceasing political struggle. Some UDR leaders see an appeal to the principles of national independence and intransigence as an attractive means of asserting their distinctiveness within the governing tradition; others, the old Gaullists who still carry some influence within the party, are simply concerned to defend the faith. Their competitors on the Left, the Parti Communiste Français, have adopted the mantle and rhetoric of Gaullism in the pursuit of electoral support and of their aims to loosen links with NATO and the United States and to retain a special relationship with the Soviet Union. The parties of the centre-Left and the centre-Right which dominated the Fourth Republic, heirs to the internationalist traditions of French foreign policy, have found themselves squeezed by these competing appeals to nationalism – gradually adopting their language for themselves, and modifying their stance under the pressures of coalition politics and electoral expectations. The combination of 'the great emotive power of the idea of national independence' with 'the ideological and political division of France into two camps of equal force', each of which is in turn divided over fundamental issues of foreign policy, has the result that 'no question of foreign policy . . . can be isolated from the internal political struggle'.[18] The advantages in this domestic struggle over the symbolic and ideological aspects of foreign policy lie, in most circumstances, with those who argue the case for national independence. Theirs, after all, is the simpler message, with the added attractions of patriotism to boot. Their opponents are forced to argue for compromise, to set out the complicated case for accepting the implications of economic and political interdependence to a country which has managed through adroit and vigorous diplomacy successfully to resist those implications. It is hardly surprising that they hesitate to try.

FOREIGN POLICY IN PRACTICE

Consistency and inconsistency, coherence and incoherence, are more easily examined in detail than in outline. French foreign policy in the complicated and uncertain international system of the late 1970s could not hope to retain the clear strategy, determined initiative and limited scope which was de Gaulle's initial conception – even if one accepts that de Gaulle's initial conception had a certain plausibility, not immediately lost in the mingling of other concerns and the pursuit of tactical advantage which came to mark de Gaulle's foreign policy. Giscard's foreign policy has been marked, it is true, by a commitment to international initiatives and a conceptualization of its strategic aims; but his initiatives have been scattered across a wide field, and its strategy has often seemed more rhetorical than real.

The strains of maintaining a coherent foreign policy have perhaps been

most evident in defence, where the progressive retreat from the Gaullist
vision has left French governments in an ambiguous relationship with
the integrated structure of NATO and stretched French forces between
their divergent roles. Pressure from the military for a more realistic interpretation of the conditions of war within the European theatre has led
Giscard to redefine the framework of defence in broader terms. The
limitations to national procurement imposed by rising costs and technological sophistication even on France's highly successful arms industry
were demonstrated in the aftermath of the 'arms sale of the century'
in 1975, when the French air force felt compelled to reconsider its ambitious designs for the next generation of fighter aircraft – leading to
France's acceptance of a degree of reintegration into the framework of
European and Atlantic defence co-operation through its membership of
the 'Independent' European Programme Group. There were several central
ambiguities in French defence policy at the end of the 1970s: about
relations with NATO, the status of French forces in Germany, the target-
ting of the strategic nuclear force and the nature of the European war
which its forces might have to fight. But these ambiguities did not carry
great penalties with them, nor was the budgetary burden impossible to
bear. The illusion of great power status and independent defence was to
a considerable extent maintained – and in diplomacy successful illusions
are arguably real gains.[19]

France's defence programme was also successfully bent to economic
objectives, through the active pursuit of military exports. Under Pompidou,
and to a lesser extent under Giscard, this has been almost an autonomous
part of foreign policy, with the Délégation Ministérielle de l'Armement
of the Ministry of Defence, and in particular its Directorat des Affaires
Internationales operating in 'a vacuum below the level of national presidential and legislative politics that is filled by the civilian and military
managers and technicians who preside over and direct the daily operations of the system'.[20] French arms sales spearheaded the export drive
to the oil-producing countries which was the determined response to the
rise in oil prices – while they also served to underpin and emphasize
France's independent diplomacy, providing a source of military supply
independent of the two global power blocs and with fewer political
conditions attached.

Giscard's policy towards France's European and North American
partners has been a compound of tactical retreats covered by rhetorical
reaffirmations, of initiatives repeatedly taken to cover French weakness
or to insist on French leadership, of intransigence and co-operation. In
this, as the central part of the Gaullist inheritance, the President has had

to pay careful attention to domestic reactions. He has operated through a bureaucracy which had to a considerable extent absorbed the commitment to national independence, and firmly believed in the pursuit of economic strength — an ethos, which he himself by and large shared. He and his advisers have sought to pursue political prestige and economic advantage: to promote international statesmanship and to protect the particular interests of France. French initiatives led to the series of Atlantic economic summits, as they had earlier to the institutionalization of European Councils of heads of state and government; while at the same time insisting on a 'European' alternative — on French terms — to American domination of alliance weapons procurement, resisting American proposals for international monetary reform, and remaining outside the Atlantic framework of the International Energy Agency. The re-establishment of good political relations with the American administration in 1974–75 was accompanied by a reaffirmation of 'the will to independence'. The acceptance of Atlantic co-operation both in economic and in security matters, through the Atlantic summits, was accompanied by a determination to dictate the pace and timing of co-operation. The insistence on being a little out of step, of deliberately differentiating French foreign policy from that of its allies, was a play directed partly at a domestic audience and partly at those with whom it had to bargain. French co-operation and goodwill, as President, ministers and officials united in demonstrating, could never be taken for granted, had always to be earned — thus aiming to compensate for their limited resources of finance and military presence by doing their best to establish the best bargaining position.

On European policy, the Giscardian presidency has similarly fought to dictate the terms of interdependence, and defend *à l'outrance* its economic interests. At the outset of his presidency Giscard was far more ready to accept the positive aspects of European co-operation than his expert officials, who had served Gaullist presidents for long enough to absorb their prejudices, or than his domestic public. After five years all parties have shifted some ground: Giscard successfully carrying the commitment to direct elections to the European Parliament through the National Assembly, while agreeing with the Gaullists a severe limitation on its powers, accepting a lessening of the formal barriers which separated the high politics of European Political Co-operation from the economic politics of the European Community, and, at the same time, insisting on the technical status of the Commission and resisting its participation in Atlantic summitry. The personalized character of French diplomacy was well suited to European Councils, and to the cultivation of the central relationship with Germany through Giscard's close and regular contacts with Chancellor Schmidt. The personal style and the personal conception of diplomacy was evident too in the immediate and political commitment to Greek entry, deriving some of its warmth from the friendship between Giscard and Karamanlis which had developed during the latter's exile. The pitfalls of personal diplomacy were illustrated in the wake of the parallel political commitment to Spanish entry, taken as a political initiative to gain French prestige and credit. The Ministry of Agriculture was not consulted by the Élysée before this commitment was made; but the domestic problems which it would have represented blew up in the approach to the 1978 elections, enthusiastically fanned by Gaullist and Communist candidates. Nevertheless, the elections past, the President overrode the agricultural lobby, reaffirmed the political commitment, and argued for the economic advantages France would gain.

Policy towards the Third World has been one of the most active areas of Giscardian foreign policy. The initiative of 1975 for a Conference on International Economic Co-operation brought a new international gathering to Paris, but without achieving many concrete results. The Euro-Arab Dialogue, established between the European Community and the Arab League (after some collusion between the French and Arab governments) in 1974, petered out in the aftermath of the 1978 Camp David Agreements; undaunted, the French first proposed a 'Gulf Dialogue' with the oil-producing states, and then a 'Trialogue' between Europe, the Middle East, and the African countries. If policy in the Middle East was focused on diplomatic initiatives, ministerial visits, and the continual search for exports, policy towards French Africa developed a harder side. Responding to the demands of francophone presidents to maintain the stability of the region, French forces were engaged in limited numbers in Mauritania and Chad, in 1978 in Zaïre, and in 1979 in effecting the removal of Bokassa. As always, the motives and the rationales were mixed: an insistence that France was acting on behalf of the general European interest, or that of the West as a whole; a willingness to demonstrate its international standing in a region where the United States hesitated to intervene; an active concern for security of supplies of raw materials, and for the economic rent which might accrue from controlling those materials; and a commitment to the defence of French culture and 'francophonie'. The concentration of decision-making in the Élysée for these limited military operations, as well as for the extensive consultations (and summit meetings) with French African leaders, is again remarkable. The constraints of domestic politics, evident in Gaullist and Communist charges that Giscard was pursuing an anti-Soviet policy and acting on behalf of the United States as 'the gendarme of the West', affected the presentation more than the substance of policy. The sharpest limitations on the substance arose from France's very limited military resources — exhausting its reserves of the all-professional *'forces d'intervention'* with the despatch of paratroops to Zaïre in 1978, and transporting them to their destination in American military aircraft for lack of suitable French machines.

CONCLUSIONS

The idea of an active foreign policy — the identification of State with Nation through a policy of national independence — was part of the ideological underpinning of the Fifth Republic, helping to shape the institution of the presidency empowered to act in the international domain and equipped to protect the national interest. The institutions and the ideology therefore complement one another. The French President is at once authorized and expected to act in foreign policy, the prestige of his office interacting with the prestige of France. Similarly, ideology and economic interest complement each other — or can complement each other in the hands of skilful diplomats and politicians. The ideological framework provides a rationale — not merely a cloak — for the pursuit of economic advantage through government-to-government relations on the basis of mutual interest and independence. The drive for economic advantage is in turn justified, and dignified, by the link with the preservation of national autonomy and international standing. The cynical image of French foreign policy, set out even in some parts of the French press in the wake of the Bokassa 'diamonds' scandal of 1979, is of the relentless pursuit of economic gain by an established political elite, sometimes on behalf of France, sometimes for personal benefit, limited only by the weak constraints of domestic politics. But this is too simple: it ignores the ethos and training of the political and administrative elite — the socialization of Presidents and ministers into the roles designed for them in the structure of the Fifth Republic. To some extent political leaders feel constrained to repeat the Gaullist litany to their domestic hearers, to refer to 'notre tempérament national' with its 'volonté arrêtée d'être réellement indépendante'.[21] But constant repetition brings a degree of belief: the successful assertion of a policy of independence in an interdependent world carries its own conviction.

'The basic traditional dilemma of France's defence policy — high objectives and limited means' is, indeed, the fundamental dilemma of French foreign policy as a whole.[22] The objectives which Giscard's presidency pursues are more economic in character than those of de Gaulle — and, paradoxically, the means which it lacks, especially in its extra-European policy, are more often military. But the basic dilemma, the gap between ambitious plans for economic growth and international competitiveness and the limited resources of raw materials, financial and diplomatic support, remains. In its consciousness of economic vulnerability, and its consequent determination to pursue economic security, the modern French state is not unlike Japan, though its parallel consciousness of *political* vulnerability, within a continent potentially dominated by Germany and an alliance actually dominated by the United States, adds an additional dimension to the French perception.

The means which French governments have in recent years called into play to supply this gap between aspirations and resources have been diverse. One consistent weapon, taken over from de Gaulle's presidency but wielded to effect by Giscard, is the insistence on prestige, and the use of prestige to win bargaining advantages, to wrong-foot France's partners and opponents, and to gain privileged access. French ministers, Prime Ministers, and Presidents have been very active international travellers, making state visits, holding intergovernmental conversations, and in their turn inviting a steady flow of foreign visitors to the glamour of Paris and the pomp of the French state. The 'mystery' of the French presidency, so beloved of General de Gaulle, and the concentration of negotiating power in the president's hands, are particularly suited to summitry — an international activity which Giscard has actively promoted. French ministers, officials and commentators have few scruples about vigorously attacking other governments, and as vigorously protesting if attacked in their turn. When M. François-Poncet visited Washington in the autumn of 1979, the shortness of his interview with President Carter was a matter for diplomatic representations and outraged comment in the French press as an insult to the dignity of France — though Mr Vance's visit to Paris some weeks thereafter passed both without an invitation to the Élysée and without a protest. French negotiators are rarely embarrassed at holding out in untenable positions, or setting out terms for negotiations which their partners find outrageous. Not only does it strengthen the image of national independence at home; it leaves them after a diplomatic retreat still often in a more advantageous position than what they would have achieved without such a '*preuve d'intransigeance*'.[23]

A second means to provide additional resources is to appropriate those of others to French objectives. In a sense, for instance, the basis of General de Gaulle's defiance of the Americans in the early 1960s was his calculation that the American commitment to the defence of Europe could be taken for granted and thus ignored, leaving France free to pursue her own aims alongside this. The concept of France as a 'free rider' on the international system has been applied both in the security and the economic sphere, as a country prepared to try the patience and exploit the resources of others in the confidence that other countries would ensure the continuing stability of the system.[24] An aspect of the close French relationship with Germany, from the 1950s on, was the attempt to harness German economic resources to support French foreign policy aims. The Yaoundé Conventions, negotiated through the European Community framework with francophone Africa, successfully achieved this in one major area of French concern. The negotiation of the Common Agricultural Policy achieved it in another. President Giscard placed more emphasis than his predecessors on sharing the burden of international responsibilities and on shouldering the defence of European interests in Africa. But he also claimed that in doing so France was speaking and acting for Europe, to the irritation of his unconsulted Community colleagues at the time of the intervention in Zaïre.

A third means of supplying at least the illusion of additional resources was the pursuit of an active foreign policy in itself: the presentation of repeated initiatives, plans and proposals, in the name of France, to which other governments are then invited to respond. Giscard's presidency has proliferated proposals for conferences and summits, dialogues and *démarches* — some of which have led to real achievements, others to early failure. Part of the rationale for these is domestic, providing the image of a government acting independently on the world stage to distract attention from the necessary compromises of multilateral co-operation. But more important was the image these were seen as creating for France abroad, not only in the Third World but also in the superpowers, as a state with which one had to deal, as a privileged *interlocuteur* commanding world attention without accepting a position subordinate to the established blocs. France on repeated occasions has irritated its Community partners by presenting positions agreed among the Nine as independent French initiatives, often a matter of days before the Nine had agreed to act in concert — in the recognition of Angola in 1976, for example, or in edging towards recognition of the Palestine Liberation Organization in 1979–80. France gained not only prestige, attention, the aura of authority from these activities; in a world in which government-to-government relations controlled so many aspects of economic life, it might also hope to trade image and prestige for material advantage.

It matters little whether one stresses the coherence of the overall approach which is implied in this attitude to foreign policy, or the flexibility — and frequent contradictions — of the tactics which serve it. French ministers and officials are well aware of the contradictions in their foreign relations, contradictions which flow from the basic incompatibility between the determination to preserve the autonomy of the nation state and the recognition of the logic of interdependence. The coherence of their approach lies in their determination to strike a balance as favourable to the preservation of autonomy as possible, and their willingness to use all means at their disposal to do so. In this they are assisted by the structure of the French state, concentrating power in the institution of the presidency and the person of the President. But the strength of the French presidency lies partly in the values and attitudes a stable regime shares with its bureaucracy, an administrative machine divided like others by the different perspectives of particular ministries and directorates but unified by its acceptance of central control and the ethos of the strong state. The public consensus which regime stability has created, stabilized further by the political stalemate between and within the opposing party coalitions, sets limits to the degree to which, and the speed at which, the presidency can move in new directions in foreign policy.

The established ethos of the administration, as well as the strength of the public consensus, would place tight constraints on any new presidency which sought to depart in any radical way from the pattern of Fifth Republic policy. But it is unlikely that a new presidency, even from the Left, would now wish to make such a radical departure. It is not only that the Socialist leadership has itself gradually adopted much of the language and outlook of Gaullist tradition, nor that coalition politics would constrain its freedom of manoeuvre. It is also that there is little incentive to change the outlines of a policy that has contributed to France's economic growth, has strengthened its access to resources of fuel and minerals, and has given France both greater self-confidence at home and greater prestige abroad.

Notes

*   I am grateful to the Thyssen Foundation for funding the research on which this chapter is based.

1   There are remarkably few interpretative volumes on Fifth Republic French foreign policy, and not many more articles. See, for example, Edward A. Kolodziej, *French International Policy under de Gaulle and Pompidou: The Politics of Grandeur* (Ithaca, N.Y.: Cornell University Press, 1974); Edward L. Morse, *Foreign Policy and Interdependence in Gaullist France* (Princeton, N.J.: Princeton University Press, 1973). Two very useful recent articles are Marie-Claude Smouts, 'Du gaullisme au néo-atlantisme: les incertitudes françaises' in Alfred Grosser, *Les Politiques extérieures européenes dans la crise* (Paris: Presses de la Fondation Nationale des Sciences Politiques, 1976), and

Marie-Claude Smouts, 'French Foreign Policy: The Domestic Debate', *International Affairs* Vol. 53, No. 1 (January 1977), pp. 36–50.

2 Quoted in John Newhouse, *De Gaulle and the Anglo-Saxons* (London: Deutsch, 1970), p. 31.

3 *War Memoirs* (English translation by Jonathan Griffin and Richard Howard) (New York: Simon and Schuster, 1964), p. 779.

4 The theme of 'scientific research and national independence' – the title of a French Government report of 1964 – is examined in Chap. 1 of Robert Gilpin, *France in the Age of the Scientific State*, (Princeton, N.J.: Princeton University Press, 1968).

5 'De Gaulle and After', *Foreign Affairs*, Vol. 44, No. 3 (April 1966), pp. 440–1.

6 Morse, *Foreign Policy and Interdependence in Gaullist France*, pp. 21–2.

7 Elijah B. Kaminsky, 'The French Chief Executive and Foreign Policy', *Sage International Yearbook of Foreign Policy Studies*, Vol. III (Beverly Hills, Calif.: Sage 1975), p. 54.

8 Smouts, 'Du gaullisme au néo-atlantisme', p. 82.

9 The history of the 'Plan Calcul' is outlined in John Zysman, *Political Strategies for Industrial Order: State, Market and Industry in France* (Berkeley and Los Angeles: University of California Press, 1977), Chaps. 3 and 5.

10 Smouts, 'French Foreign Policy', pp. 39, 42.

11 The Community which the French President is here commanded to protect is the *French* Community, then evolving from an empire into a commonwealth, not the EEC.

12 Pierre Avril, *Le Régime politique de la Cinquième République*, (Paris: Presses Universitaires de France, 1967), p. 205; Jean Massot, *La Présidence de la République en France*, (Paris: La Documentation Française, 1977), Chap. 4, provides a useful survey of the debate on the *domaine réservée* and the powers of the President.

13 Pierre Cot, 'Les Institutions', in Leo Harmon, ed., *L'Elaboration de la politique étrangère* (Paris: Presses Universitaires de France, 1969), p. 123.

14 *Le Point* (23 February 1976), provides a detailed description of the operation and personalities of Giscard's staff.

15 There has been no full-length study of the Quai d'Orsay since that produced by Jean Baillour and Pierre Pelletier *Les Affaires étrangères* (Paris: Presses Universitaires de France), 1962. The information here is taken from *Le Monde* and from interviews with French officials between 1976 and 1978.

16 Bertrand Badie and Pierre Birnbaum, 'L'autonomie des institutions politico-administratives', *Revue Française de Science Politique*, Vol. 26, No. 2 (April 1976), pp. 292–3. See also Ezra N. Suleiman, *Politics, Power and Bureaucracy in France* (Princeton, N.J.: Princeton University Press, 1974).

17 Very little has recently been written on the role of the National Assembly in foreign policy; much of the information here is based on interviews with members and officials. See also Smouts, 'French foreign policy' and D. Lavroff, 'Les Commissions de l'Assemblée Nationale sous la Vᵉ République', *Revue du Droit Publique* (November–December 1971), pp. 1429–65.

18 Smouts, 'French Foreign Policy', p. 37.

19 On defence, see Lothar Ruehl, *La Politique militaire de la Vᵉ République* (Paris: Fondation Nationale des Sciences Politiques, 1976).

20 Edward A. Kolodziej, 'France and the Arms Trade', *International Affairs*, Vol. 56, No. 1 (January 1980), p. 71.

21 Jean François-Poncet, 'Diplomatie française: quel cadre conceptuel?', *Politique Internationale* No. 6 (Winter 1979–80), pp. 9–10.

22 Pierre Lellouche and Dominique Moïsi, 'French Policy in Africa: A Lonely Battle against Destablization', *International Security* Vol. 3, No. 4 (Spring 1979). p. 128.

23   The quotation is from a UDF deputy in the Assembly debate on the Quai d'Orsay budget, 7 November 1979, attacking his own government for being too willing to compromise French interests in the European Community, *Le Monde* (9 November 1979).

24   See, for instance, Andrew Shonfield, *International Economic Relations of the Western World 1959-1971* (Oxford: Oxford University Press, 1976), Vol. 1, p. 104.

LIST OF CONTRIBUTORS

PHILIP CERNY is Lecturer in Politics in the University of York. He is the author of *The Politics of Grandeur: Ideological Aspects of de Gaulle's Foreign Policy* (Cambridge University Press, 1980).

DIANA GREEN is Lecturer in Political Studies at the City of London Polytechnic.

STANLEY HOFFMANN is Professor of Government and Director of the Center for European Studies at Harvard University. He is the author of many essays and books on French politics and international relations; the best known are *In Search of France* (with others) (Harvard, 1963), *Gulliver's Troubles: or, the setting of American Foreign Policy* (McGraw–Hill, 1968), *Decline or Renewal: France since the 1930s* (Viking, 1974) and *Primacy or World Order: American Foreign Policy since the Cold War* (McGraw–Hill, 1978).

MARK KESSELMAN is Professor of Political Science at Columbia University. He is the author of *The Ambiguous Consensus: A Study of Local Government in France* (Knopf, 1967).

HOWARD MACHIN is Lecturer in Political Science in the London School of Economics and Political Science. He is the author of *The Prefect in French Public Administration* (Croom Helm, 1977).

JANE MARCEAU is Project Director at the Centre for Educational Research and Innovation (CERI) of the Organization for Economic Co-operation and Development (Paris). She is the author of *Class and Status in France: Economic Change and Social Immobility, 1945–1975* (Oxford University Press, 1977).

KRISTEN R. MONROE is Assistant Professor of Politics at New York University. She is the author of the forthcoming study, *Presidential Popularity and the Economy*.

MARTIN SCHAIN is Associate Professor of Politics at New York University. He is the author of *French Communism in Power: Urban Politics and Political Change* (Frances Pinter Ltd. and St Martin's Press, 1981).

SALLY SOKOLOFF is Lecturer in Politics and Contemporary History in the University of Salford.

ANNE STEVENS is Lecturer in Contemporary European Studies in the University of Sussex.

292 List of Contributors

WILLIAM WALLACE is Deputy Director and Director of Studies at the Royal Institute of International Affairs, Chatham House. He is the author of *Foreign Policy and the Political Process* (Macmillan, 1971) and *The Foreign Policy Process in Britain* (Allen and Unwin, 1977), co-editor of *Policy-Making in the European Communities* (Wiley, 1977), and editor of *Britain in Europe* (Heinemann, 1980).

Index

Access to formal office, 27–8, 35
  democratization, 54
  limited by social origins, 62
  co-ordination, 279
Agricultural policy, 222–6
Agriculture
  absorption of unemployed, 5
  change of influence, 15
  decline in political power, 231
  decrease in number employed, 219–20
  effects of EEC entry, 224–5
  improvement in living standards, 234
  investment organization, 226
  modernization programme, 223
  political orientation of farmers, 233
  relationship with state, 227, 228
  retirement of very small farmers, 225
  size of farms, 220–1
  survival of small farm structure, 221
Agriculture Ministry, 277–8
Albert, Michel, 87
Algerian independence, 9, 12, 280
  referenda, 10
Aristocracy, conflict with bourgeoisie, 2
Auriol, Vincent, 62

Balance of payments, 160
Bankruptcies, 167
Bargaining, see Industrial bargaining
Barre, Raymond, 20, 42, 44, 94, 276
  consideration of replacements, 173–4
  improved popularity, 171
Barre Plan (1976), 112, 113–15, 160–3
  assessment, 162
  effect on trade unions, 211
  signs of success, 171
Bedel Report (1969), 224

Benefits, negotiations for, 203
Blum, Leon, 97
Bretton Woods agreement, 8
Budget
  aim of programme budgets, 106, 119
  balanced, 160
  deficits: 1969–80, 114
    during Barre Plan period, 162
    planned, 168; for 1980, 114
  emphases in Communist areas, 246–7
  short-term nature, 104
  see also Rationalisation des Choix
    Budgétaires (RCB)
Budgetary procedures
  conflict with National Plan, 104–5
  importance of balanced budget, 113
Bureaucracy, as guardian of state interests, 3
Business
  close links with politics, 67–8
  effect of inter-linking, 68
  owners as leaders, 51
  power in, 48–53
    of big groupings, 69
  recruitment practices, 68
  related to higher civil service, 85–8

Cabinet ministers
  business interests, 68
  wielding government power, 61
Cabinets ministériels, 53
  in tension with divisions, 91
Cadres supérieurs, 48–52, 66
  origins, 49
Capital
  isolated from international market forces, 5
  role of marriage in optimizing, 70–1

Capitalism
  advances following World War II, 6
  political economy, 178–9
Capitalist class, alliance of various
  elements, 4
Censure motions, 33
Central Planning Council, 111
Centralization of administration, 243
  historical basis, 126
Centralization of policy, 125
Cerny, Philip, 1–47, 159–76
Chaban–Delmas, Jacques, 16, 40, 44, 95,
  173–4, 203, 274
Chirac, Jacques, 16, 18, 20, 41, 44, 95,
  170, 276
Civil service, higher
  breadth of experience, 91
  claim to economic expertise, 82
  contacts of deputies, 62
  effect of recruitment policies, 83
  little recruitment of 'outsiders', 86–7
  origins of members, 85
  power possessed by, 53–7
  providing electoral candidates, 62
  providing local services, 129
  recruitment, 54
  related to big business, 85–8
  relationship between *corps*, 89
  role in economy, 79
  social origins, 55
  working- and middle-class representa-
    tion, 56
  see also Grands corps; *Pantouflage*
Closed shop, 206
Coalitions
  importance to party systems, 28
  in electoral strategy, 37
    considerations, 30
Colbert, Jean Baptiste, 81
Cold War
  effect on Communists, 9
  wish for independent role by France,
    10
Common Agricultural Policy (CAP),
  225, 274
Common Programme (1972–7), 5, 13,
  17, 40, 177, 180, 237
Communes
  administration, 127
  as channel for agricultural views,
    237–8
  co-operative projects, 133
  election of Municipal Councils, 130
  leadership by dominant *commune*,
    136

mayors as Senators, 64
mergers encouraged, 135
numbers, 128
population in rural areas, 238
Communist-controlled cities
  access to central administration,
    254–7
  decline in working-class population,
    253
  differences from non-Communist
    areas, 263
  emphasis on local services, 246–8
  local power as exception to rule, 244
  policy initiation in local govern-
    ment, 245–54
Communists
  appeal broadens, 182
  coalition with Socialists, 177, 260–1
  economic programme, 180–6
  effect of Cold War, 9
  emergence in mid-1930s, 5
  hardening of position to 1978,
    186–7
  influence in agriculture, 236–7
  network of service organizations,
    259–60
  support for invasion of Afghanistan,
    20
  working class candidates, 61
Confidence votes, 33, 35
Conseillers généraux, stability, 64
Contacts
  importance to power, 72
  informal, 91
Co-operation, Ministry of, 278
Co-operatives, agricultural, 229–30
Corporatism, 191
Coty, René, 62
Counter-inflation measures, 160
Coutrot, Jean, 82
Couve de Murville, (Jacques) Maurice,
  275, 279
Currency, stability of, 160

Debré, Michel, 20, 44, 94, 168
Decision-making process
  access related to social class, 65
  blocking strategy, 34
  importance to party system, 26–7
Defence Ministry, 277
Defence policy, 282
  on American and European alliances,
    282–3
Defferre, Gaston, 13, 271
De Gaulle, Charles

influence of war on foreign policy attitudes, 269
influence on foreign policy, 267, 268
involvement in economic policy, 94
oversight of domestic policy, 14
President of Fifth Republic, 9
regional proposals, 138
resignation (1946), 8; (1969), 15
support from farmers, 232-3
type of presidency, 31-2
de Guiringaud, Louis, 276
Départements
boundaries largely unchanged, 128
election of General Councils, 130
Depression, 5
Deputies
accumulation of power, 61-2
influence on local administration, 129
social origins, 59-60
election success dependent on, 61
of those with ministerial rank, 62
study of political origin and careers, 62-3
de Wendel family, 67
Diplomatic service, 278
Districts, functions of, 135
Dowries, 71

École Nationale d'Administration (ENA), 54-6
concentration on economic expertise, 82-3
cultural examination of candidates, 74
destinations of graduates, 86, 278
emphasis on articulate style, 92
graduates going into politics, 92
social origins of students, 54-5
École Polytechnique, 86
Economic policies
Communist mechanisms, 183
disagreement of Left parties, 177
influencing political decision-making, 159
interaction with foreign policy, 267
international aspects, 284
of Communists, 180-6
pre-election stimuli, 150-1
threat to government, 172
trade unions not consulted, 207
see also Agricultural policy
Economy
difficulties of early 1970s, 160
effects of international uncertainty

on planning, 115
international, 159
policy-making process, 88-97
at political levels, 93-6
role of higher civil service, 79
tradition of state intervention, 80-1
Education
expenditure on, 246-7
related to position in business, 49
rural, 132
Efficiency concept, introduced into budgetary procedures, 107-8
Elected representatives, gradual introduction of, 129
Elections, 12
1973, 17
1978, division of vote, 18-19
affecting political business cycle, 142, 145
effect of coalitions, 41
influence on economic stimuli, 150-1
Electoral procedure
strategies, 35-8
two-ballot system, 35
European Assembly elections (1979), 20
European Economic Community (EEC)
French policy on, 283
timing of France's entry, 270
Executive posts in business, 51

Faure, Edgar, 62
Fauvet, Jacques, 19
Fifth Republic
institutional topography, 31-8
significance, 9
special origins of elected representatives, 63
Finance Ministers, involvement in economic policy, 94-5
Finance Ministry
division into two parts, 96-7
planning role, 103
Finance of urban areas, 136
Foccart, Jacques, 275
Foreign Affairs Committee, 279-80
Foreign Ministers
attendance at Foreign Affairs Committee meetings, 280
function, 276
Foreign policy
basic traditions, 268
constraints in later 1960s, 272
few constraints, 279
Giscard's characteristics of, 285-6
influence of de Gaulle, 267

Foreign policy *cont.*
  institutions, 275–81
  lobbies, 280
  practical application, 281–5
  succession of initiatives, 287
Fourth Republic
  collapse, 9
  little change among deputies, 59
  parliamentary system, 8
François-Poncet, André, 286

Gaillard decrees, 224
Gaullists, 8–9
  alternative economic strategy, 168–70
  coalitions, 9–10
  deprived of control of presidency, 16
  restructured, 17
  seen to have similarities to Communists, 187–8
  try to recapture presidency, 43
General Agreement on Tariff and Trade (GATT), 8
General Council
  elections, 130
  members' sphere of influence, 131
Giscard d'Estaing, Valéry, 11, 12–13, 15–6, 44, 63
  'anti-planner', 103
  as Finance Minister, 94, 95
  candidate in 1981 election, 20–1
  conflict with Chirac, 16
  election to presidency, 40
  foreign policy, 273
    towards Europe and N. America, 282–3
  involvement in economic policy, 94
Government
  expenditure related to political business cycle, 148
  maintenance of power, 159
Grands corps
  elitism, 83
  membership from top ENA graduates, 89–90
  self-image, 84
  social origins, 55
  see also Civil service, higher
Grands fonctionnaires, 54
  links with banking groups, 69
Green, Diana, 101–24, 159–76
'Grenelle Agreements', 209
Group-farming units, 230
Guichard, Olivier, 173

Herzog, Philippe, 92
Housing policy, 249–50
  low-income, 252

Indemnité viagère de départ (IVD), 225
Industrial action, *see* Strikes
Industrial bargaining
  impact of unions, 201–6
  not solely union responsibility, 206
  problems of union organization and control, 213
'Industrial Redeployment' strategy, 163
Industrial relations
  importance of organization, 193
  poor state in France, 193
  reorganization since 1966, 203
  stable patterns, 192
Industry
  competitiveness encouraged, 113, 164
  foreign takeovers blocked, 166
  Giscard's policy, 273
  greater competitiveness achieved, 161
  interventionism, 166
  origins of leaders, 52
  policy under Barre, 164–5
  policy under Gaullists, 163–4
  profit sharing, 210
  providing electoral candidates, 61
  relationship between trade unions and employers, 192
  see also Pantouflage
Industry Ministry, 278
Inflation
  differing views of Left and Right, 179
  popular view of, 161
  unoptimistic forecasts, 172
Inspecteurs de Finance, 54
  basis of solidarity, 66
  moving to industry, 66
  social origins, 56–7
Inspection des Finances, 56–7
  greater political importance, 56
  places offered to top ENA students, 55, 56
Institut d'Études Politiques, 54
Institutional learning, 28
  in French party system, 39–44
Institutional power, access to, 48
Institutional structures, 28
  of Fifth Republic, 31–8
International environment, changing political structures, 8

Interventionism, 166
  French tradition of, 270
  frequency of cases, 167
  in capitalist economy, 178
Investment, self-financing, 249

Jacobins, strengthening of centraliza-
    tion, 127
Jobert, Michel, 272, 277

Kesselman, Mark, 177–90
Keynesian theory, 15

Land agencies, 225–6
Lecanuet, Jean, 32, 40
Left parties
  alliance broken by Communists, 185
  disagreement of economic policy,
    177
  practising stable form of capitalism,
    179
  strategy to achieve socialist society,
    181
Legislature, source of power of, 33
Local government
  alliances of Socialists and Com-
    munists, 261
  attempts to merge communes, 134
  development of political power, 242
  incidence of self-financing of invest-
    ment, 249
  largely unchanged since 1800, 128–9
  no reforms yet undertaken, 126
  nonpolitical characteristics, 257
  policy development, 257–62
  strengths of system, 131
Local policy consultation, 125

Machin, Howard, 125–41
Marceau, Jane, 48–78
Marchais, Georges, 18, 172
Marchal, Jean, 82
Marriage
  geographical study, 70
  importance in recruiting to top
    positions, 70
  reinforcing social contacts, 66
  within own social class, 70
Marshall Plan, 8, 96
  financing First National Plan, 102
Massé, Pierre, 82
Massé (fifth) Plan, 102
Mayors
  access to central decision-makers,
    244

co-operation needed by field admini-
    strators, 243–4
  frequently farmers in rural areas, 238
  in administration chain, 127–8
  of Communist-controlled cities,
    254–5
  power in *communes*, 136
  sphere of influence, 131
  traditional responsibilities, 129
Mendès-France, Pierre, 62, 68, 82, 97
Méo, Jean, 168
Mequillet-Noblot family, 67
Messmer, Pierre, 275
Metallurgical industry
  qualifications of leaders, 49–50
  trade union membership, 196
Ministries
  little intercommunication, 88
  use of programme budgets, 110
Mitterand, François, 13, 16, 20, 40
  support from Communists, 17
Monetary policy, 271
Money supply
  growth, 160
    during Barre Plan period, 162
    during Fifth Republic, 152, 153,
      154
    related to political business cycle,
      148
Monnet (First) Plan, 102
Monory, René, 97
Monroe, Kristen R., 142–58
Mouvement Réformateur, 16
Mouvement Républicain Populaire, 7
Municipal Council elections, 130–1

Napoleon, effect on administrative frame-
    work, 127
National Assembly
  ENA graduate members, 92
  little influence on foreign policy, 279
  relationship with presidency, 32, 33
National Economy, Ministry of, 97
National Plan *see* Plan
Nationalism, in foreign policy, 269
Nationalization, 17
  Communist demands, 180
  key communist strategy, 183–5
  of steel industry, 165
New Towns, 135
Nuclear weapons, 182–3

Office, hierarchy of, 29
Oil price rises, 14
  Chirac government's response, 163

298   *Index*

Oil price rises *Cont.*
  dislocation of economy, 159
Organization for European Economic
    Co-operation (OEEC), 8
Ortoli, François Xavier, 11

Pantouflage, 8, 53, 66–7
  effect on top echelons, 87
  one-way characteristic, 86
Parti Social Français, 5–6
  see also Socialists
Party structure
  basic unit, 29
  effects of bipolarization, 13
  factors tending to stabilization
    (1960s), 10
  need for credible presidential candi-
    date, 32
  of Fifth Republic, 9
  pattern of conflict for 1980s, 10–21
  rise of quadripolar system, 13
  transformation in 1960s, 39
  two-tier, 44
Peasant society
  characteristics, 218
  disappearance in France, 218
  in 19th century, 2–3
  political standing, 219
  reduction in importance, 15
  undermined by capitalist alliance, 4
Périer brothers, 67
Pétain, Marshal, 6
Peyrefitte, Alain, 173
Pierret, Christian, 92
Pinay, Antoine, 12
Plan
  conflict with budget, 104–5
  long-term nature, 104
  priority objectives, 111
  use of RCB, 111–13
  1st, 102
  5th, 102
  7th, 101
    impact of Barre Plan, 112, 113–15
  8th, 101, 115, 118–20
    attempt to harmonize with budget
      procedures, 118
Planning, characteristics of, 102–3
Planning Commission, 96, 103
Plant committees, 208–9
Poher, Alain, 15–16, 40
Poincaré, Raymond, 67
Policy-making
  links with *corps* power maintenance,
    90

long-term goals, 159
role of civil servants, 53
Political business cycle
  evidence for, 145–8
  need for study of, 143
  theory, 142, 144
Political class
  out of balance with administrative
    class, 5
  role in state mechanics, 3–4
Political parties
  changes following World War II, 7
  demonstrating credibility, 39
  19th century structural development,
    2
  role in society, 26
  see also Party structure
Political power, 57–65
Pompidou, Georges, 11, 13, 16, 40, 44
  foreign policy, 272
  in Rothschild's bank, 67
  involvement in economic policy, 94
  oversight of domestic policy, 14
  support from farmers, 232–3
Popular Front (1936), 5
  dissolution, 6
Poujadism, 58
Power, 48
  balance in capitalist economy, 178
  fields of power, 71–3
  'social surface' related to, 72
Prefects
  local influences on, 131
  policy implementation, 127–8
  traditional responsibilities, 129
Presidential elections
  1981, 20–1
  coalitions in both ballots, 41
  no bipolarizing effect, 40
Presidency
  credibility of candidates, 32
  de Gaulle's wish to strengthen, 31
  effect on policy of forthcoming
    elections, 14
  importance in foreign policy, 274–5,
    285
  involvement in economic policy, 93–
    4
  political control of, 11–12
  power balance with Prime Minister,
    42
  role of 'presidential majority' ques-
    tioned, 42
  source of power, 32–3
Price controls, abolition of, 167

Prime Minister
  involvement in economic policy, 94
  nomination by President, 33
Priority action programmes (PAPs), 101
  function, 112
    in relation to National Plans, 119
  link with RCB, 112
  rate of implementation, 116–17, 118
Profit sharing, 208, 210
Proportional representation, 29
Protectionism, 166
  Gaullist view, 169
Provisional Government (1944–46), 5
Public Establishments, 139
Public sector
  as employer, 80
  extent of interests, 80
  size, 79–80

Radical party
  changing affiliations, 5
  decline after World War II, 7
  integration into political balance, 4
Rassemblement du Peuple Français, 58, 68
Rassemblement pour la République, 17
Rationalization of Budgetary Choices (RCB), 101
  has not fulfilled expectations, 106, 107
  justification, 105–10
  successful aspects, 110
  use with National Plan, 111–13
Redundancies, 167
Referenda, 40
  election by proxy of de Gaulle, 44
Regional Councils, 139
Regional planning, 96
Regional policies, 125–6, 138–40
  criticisms, 139
  new structures (1972), 138
Regional Prefects, 138
  functions, 139
Regions, rise of political movements in, 133
Religious factors, 7
Républicains Indépendants, 63
Republican party, 18
Reynaud, Paul, 62
Rocard, Michel, 92
Rothschild family, 67
Rueff, Jacques, 82
Rural communities
  characteristics of 'survivor-villages', 239

decline in number of notables, 238
demands on local services, 126, 132
demography, 220
depopulation, 132
increasing political importance, 134–5

Schain, Martin, 191–217, 243–66
Schumann, Robert, 62, 67
Second homes, 132
Senate
  social origins of members, 64–5
  stability, 64
Servan-Schreiber, Jean-Jacques, 18, 173, 271
Simple-majority voting systems, 29
Social climate, influence of, on labour relations, 204–5
Socialists
  accused by Communists of Right tendencies, 187
  alliance with Communists, 177, 260–1
  clashes with Communists, 180
  growing support for, 185
  renascence, 40
  trends in restructuring, 17
Socio-economic structure
  effect on party development, 2
  state not in position to lead, 6
Sokoloff, Sally, 218–42
Stabilization Plan, *see* Barre Plan
State intervention
  legitimacy, 82–5
  tradition of, 80–1
Steel industry crisis, 165–8
Stevens, Anne, 79–100
Strikes, 197–201
  as political demonstrations, 201
  factors influencing, 200
  function in bargaining process, 202
  general (1966), 200
  government reaction to, 204
  initiation at plant level, 199
  lack of trade union control, 197
  percentage of settlements and failures, 203
  politicization, 212
Sub-Prefects, functions in administration chain, 127–8
Syndicalism in agriculture, 227–31

Taxation in Communist-governed areas, 247–8
Third Republic
  not suited to advanced capitalism, 4

Third Republic *cont.*
  slow change of deputies, 58
Third World policies, 284
Thorez, Maurice, 13
Tourism, affecting demand for rural services, 132–3
Trade, international, 270–1
  during Pompidou's presidency, 272
  improvement following Barre Plan, 171
Trade unions
  amalgamations, 196
  dependent on militants, 205
  lack of strike control, 197
  leftist influences, 194
  no legality before 1968, 204
  not always accepted by employers, 194
  not consulted on policy, 207
  powers of leaders, 198–9
  relationships with employers and state, 192
  small membership, 195–6
  small staff and budgets, 205
  weakness of organization, 207
  see also Syndicalism in agriculture

Unemployment, 113
differing views of Right and Left, 179
  factor in political business cycle, 144
  increase in redundancies, 167
  measures to tackle, 168
  slow-down in growth rate, 171
Union pour la Démocratie Française, 18
United States of America, relations with, 283

Urban Communities
  function, 135
  planning decisions, 251
Urban politics, 135–8
  power of leaders, 137
  variations in policy, 137–8
Urbanization, 125, 132
  population concentration, 135

Vallon, Louis, 210
Veil, Simone, 20, 53
Vichy regime, 6
Vosges Plan, 166
Voting
  importance of party system, 26–7
  links with social and religious factors, 58
  little change in alignments, 58
  simple-majority *v.* PR systems, 29

Wage restraint, 160, 161
Wages
  determination, 206
  levels, 17
  maintenance of purchasing power, 161
  of farmers compared with other workers, 223–4
Wallace, William, 267–90
Worker participation, 18
Working class, divisions of, 15
World War I, 4
World War II, 6

Yaoundé Conventions, 287